북한 핵 문제

미국 동향

북한 핵 문제

미국 동향

| 머리말

    1985년 북한은 소련의 요구로 핵확산금지조약(NPT)에 가입한다. 그러나 그로부터 4년 뒤, 60년대 소련이 영변에 조성한 북한의 비밀 핵 연구단지 사진이 공개된다. 냉전이 종속되어 가던 당시 북한은 이로 인한 여러 국제사회의 경고 및 외교 압력을 받았으며, 1990년 국제원자력기구(IAEA)는 북핵 문제에 대해 강력한 사찰을 추진한다. 북한은 영변 핵시설의 사찰 조건으로 남한 내 미군기지 사찰을 요구하는 등 여러 이유를 댔으나 결국 3차에 걸친 남북 핵협상과 남북핵통제공동위원회 합의 등을 통해 이를 수용하였고, 결국 1992년 안전조치협정에도 서명하겠다고 발표한다. 그러나 그로부터 1년 뒤 북한은 한미 합동훈련의 재개에 반대하며 IAEA의 특별사찰을 거부하고 NPT를 탈퇴한다. 이에 UN 안보리는 대북 제재를 실행하면서 1994년 제네바 합의 전까지 남북 관계는 극도로 경직되게 된다.

    본 총서는 외교부에서 작성하여 최근 공개한 1991~1992년 북한 핵 문제 관련 자료를 담고 있다. 북한의 핵안전조치협정의 체결 과정과 북한 핵시설 사찰 과정, 그와 관련된 미국의 동향과 일본, 러시아, 중국 등 우방국 협조와 관련한 자료까지 총 14권으로 구성되었다. 전체 분량은 약 7천여 쪽에 이른다.

2024년 3월
한국학술정보(주)

| 일러두기

· 본 총서에 실린 자료는 2022년 4월과 2023년 4월에 각각 공개한 외교문서 4,827권, 76만여 쪽 가운데 일부를 발췌한 것이다.

· 각 권의 제목과 순서는 공개된 원본을 최대한 반영하였으나, 주제에 따라 일부는 적절히 변경하였다.

· 원본 자료는 A4 판형에 맞게 축소하거나 원본 비율을 유지한 채 A4 페이지 안에 삽입하였다. 또한 현재 시점에선 공개되지 않아 '공란'이란 표기만 있는 페이지 역시 그대로 실었다.

· 외교부가 공개한 문서 각 권의 첫 페이지에는 '정리 보존 문서 목록'이란 이름으로 기록물 종류, 일자, 명칭, 간단한 내용 등의 정보가 수록되어 있으며, 이를 기준으로 0001번부터 번호가 매겨져 있다. 이는 삭제하지 않고 총서에 그대로 수록하였다.

· 보고서 내용에 관한 더 자세한 정보가 필요하다면, 외교부가 온라인상에 제공하는 『대한민국 외교사료요약집』 1991년과 1992년 자료를 참조할 수 있다.

| 차례

정 리 보 존 문 서 목 록					
기록물종류	일반공문서철	등록번호	2012050028	등록일자	2012-05-24
분류번호	726.64	국가코드		보존기간	영구
명 칭	미국의 한반도 문제 해결을 위한 6자포럼 제안, 1991				
생 산 과	북미1과	생산년도	1991~1991	담당그룹	
내용목차	* 11.6 Baker 미국 국무장관, 11.8자 Foreign Affair에서 6자회담 구성 제시 * 6자포럼 (남.북한, 미국, 일본, 중국, 소련 : 2+4)				

0001

외   무   부

관리번호 : [stamp]

종 별 :

번 호 : USW-5212

일 시 : 91 1023 1835

수 신 : 장 관(정안,미안,아일,기정) 사본:국방부장관

발 신 : 주 미국 대사

제 목 : 한국 안보관계 세미나

[stamp: 1992. 6. 30에 의거 예고문에 일반문서로 재분류됨]

연: USW-5186

1. 세종연구소와 당지 FLETCHER 대학 부설 IFPA(INSTITUTE FOR FOREIGN POLICY ANALYSIS)가 공동으로 주관한 "SECURITY DYNAMICS ON THE KOREAN PENINSULA" 제하의 세미나가 당지에서 10.21-22 간 개최됨.

2. 금번 세미나는 아국에서 세종연구소 정일영 소장, 합참 박종권 전략기획부장, 본부 조규형 안보정책과장등, 일본에서는 OTA 외무성 과학기술 국장등이, 그리고 미측에서는 LEHMAN 군축처장, SOLARZ 하원의원, LILLEY 전주한대사, MCDEVITT 국방부 동아태 담당국장등이 참석한 이외에 주재국 국방부, 합참, ACDA, 국무부, NSC 등의 실무자들이 다수 참가한 가운데 비공개 회의로 진행되었음.(당관에서는 본직및 국방무관, 안호영 서기관등 참석)

3. 금번 회의 토의 요지를 하기 보고함.

가. 북한 핵개발 문제

- SOLARZ 의원: 연호(USW-5186) 참조

- LEHMAN 군축처장

. 북한의 핵기술은 이락과는 달리 자체 개발한 기술이 많으므로 그만큼 더 강력한 검증이 필요할 것임.

- OTA 국장

. IAEA 는 핵개발을 방지하는데 필요조건이기는 하나 충분조건은 되지 못함.

- IAEA 는 이를 개선하기 위해 특별 사찰제, 유엔 안보리와의 협력 방안등을 강구하고 있음.

. 북한은 핵개발 국가로서는 IAEA 핵 안전협정에 가입하지 않은 유일한 국가임.

다. 한. 미 안보협력

외정실	장관	차관	1차보	2차보	아주국	미주국	분석관	청와대
안기부	국방부							

PAGE 1

91.10.24   09:23

외신 2과 통제관 BS

0002

- RONALD LEHMAN 군축처장

. 주한 미군감축은 북한의 핵개발등 안보상황을 고려하여 이루어져야 하는바, 미국으로서는 현재 30,000 명 정도까지의 감축은 별문제가 없을 것으로 보고있음.

. 미국은 동맹국들에게 GPALS(GLOBAL PROTECTION AGAINST LIMITED STRIKES)를 제공할 용의가 있음.

- MICHAEL MCDEVITT 국방부 동.아태 담당 국장

- EASI 제 2 단계는 전략적 환경을 고려하여 이루어질 것이며, 주한 미군 감축은 일정수준에 가면 평형(PLATEAU)을 유지하게 될 것임.

- STANLEY ROTH 하원 외교위 전문위원

- EASI 의 주한 미군감축은 주로 예산상 고려에서 이루어지고 있는 것으로 보는바, 주한 미군감축은 1 단계에서 하였으니까 2 단계에서도 하여야 한다는 식의 타성적 태도(BUREAUCRATIC INERTIA)로 임할 문제가 아님.

. 한반도 안보환경이 개선되지 않으면 주한 미군감축은 중단되어야 함.

- CHARLES KARTMAN 국무부 한국과장

. 남북한을 위요한 국제관계를 개관하면 일.중이 북한에 큰 영향력을 행사할수 있고, 소련은 나름대로 영향력을 유지하고 있으나, 미국이 북한에 미칠 수 있는 영향력은 극히 미미한 것으로 판단됨(극한 상황에 처한 북한의 예측 곤란한행동 가능성에 우려를 표명)

- 반면, 미국이 북한과의 관계를 급진전 시키는 것은 불필요한 오해의 소지가 있으므로 "동북아 평화협의 회의" 형태의 다자회의 소집도 유용할 것으로 판단됨.

나. 북한 군사력 평가

- GUY ARRIGONI(DIA, 북한 담당관)

. 북한 군사력은 아래와 같은 요인으로 큰 어려움에 직면하고 있음.

(1) 국제환경 변화

(2) 경제악화

(3) 병역적령 인구 감소

(4) 기술부족으로 방공망등 유지에 애로 발생

. 북한이 이러한 애로에서 벗어나기 위해서는 군인수를 줄이면서 효율을 제고시켜야 하는바, 아직 그런 조짐은 보이지 않고 있음.

. 북한 핵개발은 이러한 배경에서 출발할 수 있음.

PAGE 2

0003

라. 일본의 정치.군사적 역할제고

　- YAMAGUCHI 대령(일본 자위대)

　. 일본이 POWER PROJECTION 능력을 갖게 되면 역내 군사. 정치 균형에 심각한 충격이 초래될 것임.

　. 또한 일본은 세계에서 제일 인구밀도가 높은 국가의 하나로서 결코 핵무기를 보유하지 않을 것임.

　- OTA 국장

　. 일본은 평화헌법등을 이유로 아. 태지역내 집단안보에 적극적으로 참여하기가 어려울 것으로 봄.

　. (1) 북한과의 경제협력은 경제적 측면보다는 정치적 측면을 고려하여야 하고, (2) 이러한 사유로 서방제국이 북한과의 경제협력을 본격화하기 전에 한국과의 사전협의가 필요하다는 한국측 지적에 동감이며, 북한과의 경제협려과 관련하여 한국이 운전석에 앉는 것이 당연함.

　마. 군축. CBM

　- MICHAEL MOODIE(ACDA 부처장)

　. 효과적인 군축을 위해서는 MTCR, NPT, 호주그룹등 공급측면에서의 감축 노력도 중요하지만, 각 국가들에게 군축이 자신의 이익에 부합된다는 것을 확인시키는 수요측면의 노력도 필요함.

　. 한반도에서의 CBM 과 관련한 제안

　1) CBM 은 긴장완화에 필요조건이나 충분조건은 아님. 가령, 남. 북한 군사력의 비대칭성은 CBM 으로 해결될 수 없음.

　2) 한국은 지형상 종심이 짧으므로(SHALLOW LINEAR) 선제공격(UGLY EARLY ATTACK)이 유용할 수 있고, 따라서 투명성 제고를 위한 CBM 들이 특히 필요함.

　3) CBM 으로서 군배치 제한 구역설치(DEPLOYMENT LIMITATION)의 방법이 있으나, 이는 경우에 따라서는 침략자에게 유용할 수 있고, 특히 서울이 휴전선에 가까운 상황에서느 재고가 필요할 것임.

　4. 기타사항

　- 세종연구소와 IFPA 는 제 2 차 회의를 92 년 가을 서울에서 개최하기로 합의함.

　- 조규형 과장은 상기 회의 참석후 UN 제 1 위 참석을 위하여 10.23. 뉴욕 향발하였음. 끝.

PAGE 3

0004

(대사 현홍주-국장)
예고: 92.6.30. 까지

공　　　란

공　　　란

공   란

공 란

공   란

공　　　란

공   란

東北亞 平和協議會議 提議 關聯 推進 現況

〈참고자료〉

검토필 (1992.6.30.)

1991.10.28.

예고문에 의거 재분류(1992.12.31.)
직위   성명

재분류 : 1992.12.31.

外 交 政 策 企 劃 室

0013

I. 提議內容

1. 提議要旨

○ 盧 大統領은 88.10.18. 유엔 연설에서 "東北亞에 持續的인 平和와 繁榮의 確固한 바탕을 構築하기 위해 美國, 蘇聯, 中國, 日本과 南.北韓이 參加하는 東北亞 平和協議會議를 열 것을 提議"함.

2. 提議說明

○ 南.北韓間의 問題는 우리 민족의 自主的 力量에 依해 解決해 가되, 韓半島의 恒久的 平和는 東北亞 地域 대결 構造로 인하여 周邊 國家들과의 關係를 떠나 생각할수 없는 것이 現實임.

○ 關係國이 한 자리에 모이는 데에는 理念, 體制, 立場 차이 때문에 어려움이 있을지 모르나 이 地域의 平和와 安定, 發展과 繁榮을 위한 모든 問題를 폭넓게 다루어 나갈 수 있을 것으로 確信함.

○ 이 構想이 실현되면 韓半島의 平和와 統一을 위해 유익한 國際 環境을 造成할 것임.

II. 提議背景, 目的 및 意義

1. 提議背景

○ 2次 大戰후 40여년간 韓半島를 中心으로 한 東北亞 地域에는 南.北韓 및 4個 關係當事國間에 冷戰的 對決構造가 계속되어 온바, 이 對決構造를 새로운 平和 共存構造로 轉換시킴으로써 韓半島 問題 解決의 國際的 與件을 能動的으로 造成할 現實的 必要性 擡頭

○ 中.蘇의 改革政策과 現實主義的 外交路線은 이러한 韓半島 및 東北亞 對決構造의 平和 共存構造로의 轉換을 가능케하는 與件 造成

- 1 -

0014

o 이러한 現實的 必要性과 情勢變化를 背景으로 6共和國이 새로운 對
   北韓 關係를 追求하기 위해 推進한 7.7. 宣言 및 北方政策의 연장선상
   에서 東北亞 關係國間 協議의 틀의 必要性을 構想

2. 目的 및 意義

o 同 提議는 南.北韓 當事者間의 和解와 合意를 促進시킬수 있는 國際的
   與件 造成을 위하여 南.北韓 및 周邊 當事國들간의 理解와 協力의 틀
   을 마련하는 것을 주요 목적으로 함.

o 同 提議는 韓半島 問題解決과 東北亞의 恒久的 平和間의 不可分의
   關係를 浮刻시키고, 東北亞에서 冷戰的 構造를 終熄시키고 새로운
   平和秩序를 追求하기 위한 協議와 協力의 틀의 必要性을 처음으로
   提示했다는데 그 意義가 있음.

Ⅲ. 關係國 反應

1. 關係 各國의 反應

o 美國

   - 충분한 사전 協議가 없었던 狀況에서 당초부터 留保的 反應 表示

   - 특히 韓美, 美日 兩者的 安保協力 關係를 對 東北亞 安保政策의
     基底로 삼아온 미국으로서는 기본적으로 多者的 安保協議를 追求
     하는 움직임에 反對하는 立場

   - 다만 작년 후반부터 國務部 一角 (Solomon 次官補등)에서 韓半島에
     유럽형의 信賴構築과 軍備縮少 接近方式의 適用 可能性에 관하여
     조심스럽게 問題 提起

- 2 -

0015

o 日本

- 韓半島 및 東北亞 問題 解決에 직접 利害關係를 갖고 있는 日本으로서는 同構想을 원칙적으로 支持하고 가능한 寄與 用意 表明

o 蘇聯

- 블라디보스톡 宣言(1986) 및 크라스노야르스크 聲明(1988)에 나타난 蘇聯의 새로운 亞.太 政策과 1989년 中.蘇 北京會談時의 All Asia Process 提議 등과의 관련에서 同構想을 肯定的으로 評價

o 北韓

- 東北亞 平和協議會議 提議는 과거 "두개의 朝鮮造作"을 위한 6자 會談論의 再版에 불과하며 이는 韓半島를 영구 분열시키고 北方 政策 實現을 위한 凶計라며 단호히 거부
- 특히 日本 參與에 대한 反對 立場 表明

o 中國

- 北韓의 同構想 反對 立場에 同調하고 北韓이 主張하는 美國 參加下의 南.北韓 協商을 支持

o 기타 국가

- 濠州, 카나다, 몽골등은 1990년 이래 각각 CSCE 형의 亞.太地域 多者 對話 構想, 北太平洋(7개국) 協力 安保 對話 構想, 亞.太 8개국 協力體 構想등을 提起
- 금년들어 아세안 국가들은 東南亞地域 安保를 위한 多者協力體 必要性을 提起

2. 反應 評價

o 상기 關係國 態度에서 볼수있는 바와 같이 日本만이 肯定的 反應을 보였을 뿐 여타국은 微溫的 내지 反對 反應을 보였음.

- 3 -

0016

o 따라서 東北亞 平和協議會議 構想의 촉진을 위하여는 먼저 美國의
  理解와 協調를 確保하는것이 先行되어야 하며, 美·日의 支持를 基礎로
  北韓을 설득하여 南·北韓間의 合意를 도출함으로써 그 實現을 위한
  基本 與件을 造成해야 할것임.

o 다만 작년 이래 유럽 CSCE의 영향을 받아 亞·太地域 安保를 위한 多者
  的 協力과 對話의 必要性에 관한 각종 提議와 論議가 활발해 지고
  美國 行政府 一角에서도 韓半島 問題 관련 多者 協力 可能性 問題가
  提起되고 있음.

o 따라서 앞으로 어떤 형태로든 亞·太地域 安保를 위한 多者 協力과
  對話 推進에 유리한 雰圍氣가 造成되고, 美國도 보다 肯定的인 대응
  方案을 모색할 것으로 豫想되고 있음.

Ⅳ. 推進 現況

1. 東北亞 平和協議會議 推進委員會 設置

   o 組織

     - 委員長 : 外務部 長官(委員長 不在時 外務部 次官이 代行)
     - 委 員 : 청와대 安保補佐官, 政策補佐官, 安企部 2次長
                外務部, 國防部, 統一院, 文公部 次官

   o 機能

     - 東北亞 平和協議會議 實現을 위한 政策方向 및 推進方案 樹立
     - 關係 當事國과 交涉에 관한 事項 檢討 및 조정
     - 關係 當事國에 대한 反應과 對處方案 樹立
     - 同 會議 實現을 위한 實務對策 檢討

- 4 -

0017

- 學者 및 專門家 意見 수렴

- 弘報 方向 樹立

(※ 同 委員會는 1988.12.19. 1회 開催된후 召集되지 않았음.)

2. 東北亞 平和協議會議 推進 委員會 實務對策班 運營

   o 기존의 "太平洋 頂上會談 特別班"을 改編하여 外交政策 推進 特別班
     을 外務部內 設置

   o 同 實務 對策班은 委員會에 부의할 政策(案)을 豫備 審議하며 本 會議
     委任사항을 처리

3. 外交安保 研究院에 特別 研究班 설치

4. 중점 推進 公館 지정

   o 5개 公館(駐美, 駐日, 駐헝가리 大使館, 駐유엔 代表部, 駐홍콩 총영
     사관)을 지정

5. 東北亞 平和協議會議 推進에 대한 각계의견 수렴

   o 89. 2.11. 外務部 政策 諮問委員會 會議

   o 90. 3.25. 政策 諮問委員會 所屬 學者招請 간담회

   o 89. 6. 9. "東北亞 安保와 平和에 관한 學術會議" 개최, 東北亞
     平和協議會議 推進方案 논의

   o 89. 8. 4. 東北亞 平和協議會議 推進方案에 대한 外交安保研究院
     세미나 開催

   o 90.10.10-11. 한반도 군축문제에 관한 국제세미나 개최 (외교안보연구원)

   o 91.11.26-27. 아.태지역 안보에 관한 국제세미나 주최예정 (외교안보
     연구원)

- 5 -

0018

6. 國際 學術會議 參加

同 提議 實現에 유리한 雰圍氣 조성 및 同 會議 提議 目的 및 취지에 대한
有關國의 理解增進이 必要함으로 北韓포함 東北亞 關係國이 參加하는 國際
學術會議에 積極的으로 參加

- o 89.2.23-26. 하와이대 주관으로 호놀룰루에서 열린 "Peace and Security in the Asia Pacific Region"會議 참석

- o 89. 5.25-27. 조지 워싱톤대와 요미우리 신문 공동 主催로 東京에서
  開催된 "東北아시아 關係 專門家 會議" 참석 (북한 참석)

- o 89. 6.10-19. 말레이지아 戰略 및 國際 問題研究所(ISIS)주관으로
  쿠알라 룸프르에서 開催된 "Asia-Pacific Roundtable" 참석

- o 89. 7. 4.- 6. 韓國 國際 問題 研究所 주관으로 서울에서 열린
  "New Order in the Asia-Pacific Region" 회의 참석

- o 89.11.20-25. 연대 동서문제 연구소 주관으로 서울에서 개최된 "東
  北亞 平和와 협력을 위한 國際 學術會議" 참석

- o 90. 6.17-20. 쿠알라룸푸르에서 개최된 제4차 "亞.太地域 軍備統制에
  관한 Roundtable 회의" 參席 (북한대표 참석)

- o 90. 9. 4- 6. 블라디보스톡에서 개최된 제2차 "亞.太地域 對話, 平和
  및 協力會議" 參席 (북한대표참석)

- o 91.4.6.-9. 北太平洋 安保協力 學術會議 參席 (카나다 빅토리아)
  (북한대표 참석)

- o 91.5.27-30. 교또에서 개최된 유엔 주관 軍縮 세미나 參席 (북한대표
  참석)

- o 91.6.5-7. 마닐라에서 개최된 "90년대 ASEAN 및 亞.太地域 安保展望
  會議" 참석

- 6 -

0019

○ 91.6.10-14. 쿠알라룸푸르에서 개최된 제 5차 "亞.太 Roundtable"
參席

V. 推進 方向

1. 基本的 考慮事項

  ○ 同 提議는 南.北韓 關係 개선 및 北方政策의 진전을 염두에 둔 中長
    期的 構想에 바탕을 둔것이므로 南.北韓 對話 및 北方外交의 進陟과
    밀접한 관련하에 伸縮성있게 推進할 필요

  ○ 同 提議 推進에 있어 美國등 전통 友邦國의 理解와 協調가 불가결
    하다는 認識下에 이들과 긴밀히 協議하여 推進
    - 특히 美國과는 충분한 事前 政策 協議를 통하여 韓半島 問題는
      基本的으로 南.北韓 當事者間 合意가 先行된후 國際的 協力으로
      보완시키는 基本 接近 方法에 관한 共同 認識 强化 필요
    - 日本의 韓半島 問題에 관한 發言權 부여의 정도와 시기에 관하여는
      신중한 檢討 필요

2. 推進 方向

  ○ 南.北韓 對話의 進陟과 關聯하여 對北提起 檢討
    - 北韓의 參與가 同 提議 實現의 必須 要件
    - 따라서 南.北 總理會談을 통한 포괄적 合意 도달, 政治軍事 分科
      委의 進展등을 보아가며 本件을 北韓側에 提起하는 問題 檢討

  ○ 美國과의 協議 强化
    - 韓.美 兩國間 高位 政策 協議時 同 構想 關聯 긴밀히 協議

- 7 -

0020

- 특히 北韓의 核開發試圖, 美國의 戰術核 撤收 宣言, 南.北韓間 유엔 加入등 변화된 韓半島 狀況을 고려에 넣은 긴밀한 정책조율 및 共同步調 追求

- 특히 美國이 對北韓 核關聯 外交的 壓力 强化와 美.北韓 關係改善 의 側面에서 南.北韓 및 東北亞 關係國間 多者 協議의 기회를 모색 하려는 최근 움직임 관련 긴밀한 韓.美 協議와 신중한 對處 必要

끝.

- 8 -

0021

공   란

북한 핵문제 미국 동향

공　　　　란

공　　　　란

공   란

공　　　란

공　　　란

공   란

공　　　　란

공　　　란

공　　　란

공 란

공   란

공   란

　북한 핵문제 미국 동향

공 란

공 란

공   란

공　　　란

관리 번호	91- 2210

외 무 부

종 별 :

번 호 : USW-5357

일 시 : 91 1031 1148

수 신 : 장 관 (미일, 해외, 해신, 문홍)

발 신 : 주 미국 대사

제 목 : JAMES BAKER 장관의 잡기 기고 내용

1. JAMES BAKER 미국무장관의 ROREIGN AFFAIRS 기고관련 당관이 파악한 내용을 아래 보고함.

2. 동 잡지는 91.11 말경 시판되며 11 월 초순에 원고를 미국무부에서 사전배포할 것으로 보임. (게재될 원고는 18 페이지임)

3. 주요 내용

- BUSH 대통령의 아시아 순방에 맞춰 일종의 분위기 조성을 위한 동 기사는 한국을 미국의 아시아 안보정책상의 하나의 SPOKE (바퀴의 회전을 뒷받침하는 살)로 비유 대아시아 안보정책의 POSITIVE 한 측면을 기술

- 미국의 대아시아 관계가 폭넓게 지지를 받고 있음을 지적, 앞으로 아시아에서의 안전보장 관련 미국의 역할은 변화하지 않을 것이나 점차 MULTILATERAL 한 형태를 취할 것으로 예견하면서(구체적인 언급은 없음) 앞으로도 POSITIVE 한 발전 가능성을 제시.

- 한. 미 관계관련 한국을 미국의 아시아정책의 '하나의 기둥(PILLAR)'으로 묘사 한국의 경제발전, 북방정책의 성공등 DYNAMIC 하고 긍정적인 측면을 예시, 한국과 미국의 관계가 더욱 더 동등한 관계로 변화하고 있다고 밝힘.

- 핵확산 위협과 관련 BAKER 장관은 북한의 핵개발에 어떻게 대처하야 할 것인지 우려를 나타내고, '서울과 평양이 무기를 제조할 수 있는 핵물질을 생산및 획득하지 않는다는 확실한 보장을 하는 것'이라고 언급, 우리로서는 신경을 쓸 표현을 하고 있음. 아울러 BUSH 대통령의 핵무기 감축정책과 군비통제에 관해서도 언급

- 남북한 관계 관련 '6 개국 회담의 가능성을 미국은 탐색(EXPLORE)할 것'이나 이같은 FORUM 은 어디까지나 남북한간의 합의내용과 긴장완화를 보장하기 위한 목적임을 분명히 했음.

미주국 공보처	장관 공보처	차관	1차보	문협국	외정실	분석관	청와대	안기부

PAGE 1

- 한반도 장래와 관련 군사대결을 지양 한국인 모두가 받아들일수 있는 통일 한국의 모습을 제시하면서 아시아에서 주요 이슈인 한반도 군사대결, 일본의 북방도서 문제, 캄보디아 문제가 해결되면 '아시아 역사의 한페이지'를 넘기게 된다고 첨언

- 동 기고문의 서두에서 BAKER 는 이제 아시에서 전쟁이 아닌 방식으로 국제질서의 변화를 가져올수 있는 상황이 전개[5해변화를 가져올수 있는 상황이 전개되고 있다고 서술했음. 끝.

(공보공사-국장)

예고: 91.12.31. 까지

외 무 부

종 별 :

번 호 : USW-5371   일 시 : 91 1031 1751

수 신 : 장 관(미일,해외,해신,문홍)

발 신 : 주 미국 대사

제 목 : BAKER 장관의 잡지 기고 내용

연: USW-5357

연호를 당관에 제보해온 CFR 의 ROMBERG 는 BAKER 장관의 기고내용이 연호에 공개될때 까지는 동 내용에 대해 각별히 보안에 유념하여 줄것을 요청하여 왔으니 참고바람. 끝.

(공사 김봉규-국장)

예고: 91.12.31. 까지

미주국   문협국   공보처   공보처

91.11.01 09:07
외신 2과 통제관 BS

0041

공   란

공   란

공 란

공   란

공   란

공   란

공　　란

공 란

공 란

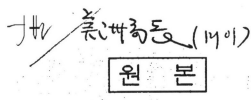

외 무 부

종   별 :

번   호 : USW-5404   일   시 : 91 1101 1855

수   신 : 장 관 (친전)

발   신 : 주 미국 대사

제   목 : 국무부 정무차관 면담

본직은 11.1(금) 국무부 ANOLD KANTER 신임 정무차관을 오찬에 초청(관저), BUSH 대통령 방한, 전술 핵철수 배경, 북한의 핵개발 저지, 동북아 6 자 협의회등 상호 관심사에 관해 의견 교환을 갖은바, 요지 다음과 같음.

1. 한.미 관계와 BUSH 아시아 순방

가. 동 차관은 먼저 한.미 관계는 단순한 이해관계의 차원을 넘어 우정으로 맺어진(EMOTIONAL) 특수한 관계라고 하면서 한해에 양국 대통령이 3 회에 걸쳐 만난다는 것은 이러한 사실을 증명하는 것이라고 평가하고 아시아 순방관련 다음 언급함.

- 금번 BUSH 의 아시아 순방은 언론의 비판적인 견해도 있으나 이를 변경하는 것은 스스로 잘못을 인정하는 것이므로 예정대로 추진할 것임.

- 미국은 아시아에서 계속적인 역할을 수행해야 할 것이며 이러한 정책 천명을 할 것임.

나. 동 차관은 또한 정상간의 대화가 잘 되고 있어 한미간의 우호협력 분위기가 잘 성숙되어 있다고 하면서 실무선에서도 계속 더욱 긴밀히 협조해 나갈 것을 다짐함.

장관,

0051

공 란

5. 미.소 핵무기 감축 협상

   - 동 차관보는 본직이 BUSH 의 새로운 핵 이니시어티브에 대한 고르바쵸프의 반응(10.5)과 관련 진전사항을 문의한데 대해 다음 설명함.

. 금번 중동 평화회의 참석시 마드리드에서의 미.소 정상회담에서는 이에대한 구체적 협의는 없음.

. 미측은 9.27. 기표명한 입장에서 보다 더 양보할 입장은 아니며, <u>핵물질 생산규제</u>, NO-FIRST-STRIKE 선언, 핵실험 금지등 소련측 제안은 받아들수 없다는 <u>입장임</u>. 일방적으로 추진이 가능한 것은 추진상황등 계속 소련측에 통보하면서 소련의 대응조치를 관망하고 있음.

6. 참고사항

- KANTER 정무차관은 10월초 부임하여 아직 현안문제에 대한 업무를 파악중이라는 점을 고려하여 금번 접촉시에는 세부적 현안보다는 동인의 한국에 대한 관심과 이해를 촉구하기 위해 양측 모두 배석자 없이 폭넓은 의견 교환을 갖었음.

- 본직은 또한 11.4(월) 오전 국무부 ZOELLICK 경제차관과 면담 예정임.끝.

(대사 현홍주-장관)

예고: 91.12.31. 일반

관리	91-1234
번호	

외 무 부

종 별 : 지 급

번 호 : CPW-3308

일 시 : 91 1104 1700

수 신 : 장관(아이,아일,미이,국기,정특,기정)사본:주홍콩총영사-중계필

발 신 : 주 북경 대표

제 목 : 외교부 국제문제 연구소 TAO BING WEI 접촉

검토필 (1992. 6.30.)

PNIO: 91-076

당관 윤해중 참사관은 10.31(목) 외교부 국제문제 연구소 TAO BINGWEI 학술위원과 만찬을 가진바 동인 주요 언급 요지 및 당관 평가 다음 보고함.

(정상기 서기관, SHI YONG MING 연구원 동석)

1. 한. 중 외교관 접촉

0 한국측은 수교와는 상관없이 우선 양국 외교관 접촉(중국 외교부 -한국 무역대표부간)을 주장하지만 양국 외교부 관원간 직접 접촉은 지난해 대표부 설립에 버금가는 수준의 관계 진전을 의미하기 때문에 중국측은 신중하게 결정하지않을 수 없음.

0 금번 APEC 회의시 한. 중 외상회담이 이루어질 경우 지난 10 월 뉴욕에서의 한. 중 외상 접촉시 전부장이 언급한 양국 외무성 직원간의 접촉이 상금 이루어지지 않고 있다는 것을 한국측이 제기해 봄직함.

0 (언제쯤 접촉이 완전 이루어질 것인가의 질문에 관해)

자신이 굳이 전망을 하자면 명년 상반기 까지는 상호 외교관 접촉이 이루어질 것으로 생각함.

2. 한. 중 수교 이전의 중간 단계

가. 자신이 보기에는 남북대화 및 일.북한 수교협상등 경과로 볼때 향후 한.중 수교에는 상당한 시일이 필요할 것으로 보이는바, 우선은 이에 따르는 중간단계를 설정하는 것이 필요할 것으로 보임.

나. 현재 양국 관계가 대한무역진흥공사-국제상회간의 합의에 의한 대표부 관계라 볼때 향후 중간단계는 양국 정부간의 합의에 의한 통상 대표부 단계를 가정 할 수 있음.

아주국 분석관	장관 청와대	차관 안기부	1차보 중계	2차보	아주국	미주국	국기국	외정실

PAGE 1

91.11.04   19:14

외신 2과 통제관 BW

0055

다. 여사한 봉상대표부 관계는 형식적으로는 영사관계 보다는 낮은 수준이나 실제로는 영사관계 보다는 훨씬 포괄적인 업무를 담당하는 수준의관계를 의미함.

라. 상기 한.중 외교관 접촉 및 중간단계 설정등 문제는 전기침 외교부장의 방한후 귀국 보고에 포함시킬 수 있도록 금번 양국 외상간 접촉에서 논의되는것이(한국측이 제기하는 것이) 바람직스럽다고 생각함.

3. 북한 핵무기 개발건

0 미국이 북한의 핵무기개발 의도나 능력이없다는 것을 잘 알면서도 대북한강경입장을 견지하는 진정한 이유는 한.일 양국의 핵무기 개발 의욕을 억제하는데 있음.

0 이것은 자신이 금년에 중국을 방문한바 있는 미국의 책임있는 정부관원 및 유명 학자들로 부터 직접 들은 내용임.(TAO 는 동 정부관원이 누구인지에 관해서는 언급 회피)

4. 미.북한 관계 및 주한 미군에 대한 중국측 견해

가. 미.북한 관계는 가까운 시일내에 크게 개선될 가능성은 없다고 봄.

나. 그 이유는 미국으로서는 세계 전략상 계속 미군의 한국 주둔이 필요하나 북한으로서는 과거 주장해온 주한미군 철수를 철회할 수 없기 때문임.

5. 일본의 재무장과 동북아 평화 협의회

0 남.북한간의 신뢰회복 조치가 이루어진다면 그 이후에는 노대통령이 제안한 동북아 수뇌회의 개최 추진이 용이해질 것임.

0 동북아평화협의회의 개최시 동북아 군축 문제가 주요 의제의 하나가 될 수 있으며 일본의 재무장 저지를 위해 여사한 협의회가 활용될 수 있을 것임.

6. 당관 평가

가. TAO 는 한.중 관계에 대해 신중론자의 입장을 취해온바, 양국 외교관 접촉의 명년 상반기 실현전망, 중간단계로 봉상대표부 상정등 언급은 향후 중국의 대한 구상의 일면일 수도 있음.

나. 북한 핵무기 개발에 대한 미국의 책임있는 정부관원의 언급이 사실이라면 지금까지 알려진 미국의 공식입장과 상이함.

다. 중국은 한반도 및 동북아 평화유지를 위해 장기적으로 동북아 평화협의회 개최가 필요하다는 생각을 갖고 있는 것으로 나타남.

예고: 92.12.31. 일반

PAGE 2

0056

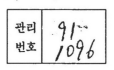

외 무 부

관리번호 91/1096

종 별 :

번 호 : USW-5451

수 신 : 장관 (미일,미이,기정)

발 신 : 주 미국 대사

제 목 : 미주국장 방미활동 (솔로몬 차관보 면담)

일 시 : 91 1105 1843

1. 금 11.5(화) 오전 미주국장은 PAAL NSC 선임보좌관과의 접촉에 이어 SOLOMON 동아.태 차관보와 면담을 가졌는바, 동 면담시 SOLOMON 차관보는 현재 미국은 대아시아 정책의 추진과 관련, 경제와 안보 양대문제에 초점을 맞추고 있으며, BAKER 장관과 BUSH 대통령 공히 한국방문시 이러한 기본인식에 입각, 아측과 협의에 임하게 될 것이라고 말함.(동 면담에는 미측에서 ANDERSON 부차관보, KARTMAN 한국과장, SCHMIEL 한국과 부과장이 배석하였으며, 아측에서 유명환 참사관, 김영목 서기관이 배석)

2. 경제문제와 관련, SOLOMON 차관보는 APEC 의 발전과 UR 의 성공은 같은 맥락에서 추진되어야 된다는 점이 강조될 것이라고 하고, 이러한 메카니즘에서의 협력외에 제반 양자문제의 해결을 위한 한국측의 협조를 촉구하게 될 것이라고 강조하였음.

3. 또한 동 차관보는 안보문제와 관련, 북한의 핵개발 저지가 시급히 해결되어야 할 현안이라고 하면서, 한. 미 양국이 현재 동원 가능한 모든 방안및 채널의 활용문제를 집중 협의하기를 희망한다고 하면서, 6 자 회의에 대한 미측 구상을 장시간 상세히 설명함.

가. 한.미간 고위협의의 기본 방향

- SOLOMON 차관보는 현재 국무부로서는 BAKER 장관과 BUSH 대통령의 아시아 순방, 방한을 종합적으로 한 맥락에서 추진하기 위한 내부 계획을 수립중이라고 하면서 한국이 UR 의 성공과 양자간 제반 현안의 진전을 위해 각별한 노력과 공헌을 해줄것을 요청할 예정이라고 말함.

- 특히, BAKER 장관이 헤이그 미-EC 정상회담에 참석후 서울에 오게되는 만큼, UR 과 APEC 등 국제무역 메카니즘의 성공적 발전문제에 초점이 자연스럽게 맞추어 질

미주국   장관   차관   미주국   청와대   안기부

것이라고 하면서, 아측의 전진적인 입장을 요망하였음.

  - 또한 솔로먼 차관보는, BAKER 장관이 APEC 에 큰 중요성을 부여하고, 아.태지역 국가들이 단합된 경제체제로 발전되기를 희망하고 있다고 전제하고, 말레이시아의 EAEG 제안은 정치적으로 APEC 역내 국가를 분열시킬 위험이 있다는 견지에서 미국도 이를 강력히 반대하고 있음을 강조하였음.

  - 이에대해 미주국장은, 아측으로서도 제반문제에 대한 미측의 입장과 희망을 잘알고 있으며, APEC 의 주도국가로서 아. 태 경제 공동체의 발전을 위해 미국과의 공동보조를 모색하게 될 것이라고 답변함.

PAGE 2

0058

라. 미.북한 접촉문제

- SOLOMON 차관이 현재보다 약간 격상된 미.북한 접촉 가능성을 검토하고 있다는 설명에 대해, 미주국장은 아측은 미.북한간의 격상된 접촉은 남북대화를 저해할 소지가 있으나, 북한측에 대한 분명한 메시지 전달 목적으로 1 회에 한하여 접촉하는 방안은 유연하게 검토코자 한다고 하고, 다만 아측과 충분한 시간을 두고 미측이 북측에 전하고자 하는 메세지 내용에 관해 사전에 협의할 필요가 있음을 분명히 강조함.

- 동 차관보는 이러한 아측 입장 표명을 평가한다고 하고, 미측은 남북대화가 모든 문제 해결의 원칙이며, 남북 관계상 한국의 입장을 훼손하지 않는다는 원칙과 전략을 견지해 오고 있다고 강조하면서, 만약 북한 핵문제만 아니라면, 그러한 격상된 접촉은 구상도 하지 않았을 것이라고 말함. 끝.

(대사 현홍주-장관)

예고: 91.12.31. 일반

PAGE 3

공   란

공 란

외 무 부

종　별 : 긴 급

번　호 : USW-5486

일　시 : 91 1106 2111

수　신 : 장 관(미일, 해외, 해신, 문홍)

발　신 : 주 미국 대사

제　목 : 베이커 장관 기고문

연 USW-5357

1. 당관은 금 11.6 FOREIGN AFFAIRS 지 겨울호에 게재 예정인 베이커 국무부 장관의 "AMERICA IN ASIA EMERGING ARCHITECTURE FOR A PACIFIC AOMMUNITY" 제하의 기고문을 입수한바, 주요 내용을 하기 보고함.

(동 기고문은 당지 시각 11.8 1800 까지 대외비로 되어 있으니 각별히 유의바람)

2. 요지

가. 아시아는 구주나 미주에 못지 않게 미국의 국익에 중요한 지역인바, 금번 부쉬 대통령의 아주 순방은 21 세기를 향하는 현시점에서 미국의 동 아시아 정책의 새로운 장(CHAPTER)을 여는 계기가 될것임.

나. 아시아는 눈부신 경제, 정치적 발전을 거듭하였으며 희망에 찬 미래를 갖고 있으나, 동시에 역사의 잔유물로 아직도 긴장이 존재하는 이중성을 가진 지역이며, 이 이중성의 극복이 우리앞에 가로 놓인 도전임.

이러한 도전은 3 대 지주 (PILLARS)를 바탕으로 극복되어야할것인바, 그 3 대 지주는 1)자유무역을 촉진하는 경제적 통합의 틀(FRAMEWORK), 2)정치적 자유화 3)아. 태 안보 유지를 위한 새로운(RENEWED)안보 구조 정착등임.

다. 미국과 아시아는 경제, 이민, 안보등으로 밀접하게 발전되어 왔음. 미국이 일본, 한국, ASEAN, 호주등과 맺고 있는 양자적 안보 협력이 아시아 안보의 주축을 이루어왔는바, 사안에 따라서는 다자방식에 의한 해결도 이루어 지고 있음(캄푸치아 문제, 남지나해 영토 분쟁, 한반도 문제도 가능지역)

라. APEC 은 미국이 아시아의 일원임을 상징(HALLMARK)하며, 서울총회에서 중국, 홍콩, 대만이 APEC 에 가입하게됨으로서 APEC 은 명실공히 범태평양적 (TRANS-PACIFIC) 협의체가 되었음. 아시아의 경제적 성장은 정치적 민주화로 연결되고

미주국	장관	차관	1차보	2차보	문협국	외정실	분석관	정와대
안기부	공보처	공보처						

91.11.07　12:16
외심 2과 통제관 BS
0062

있는바, 천안문 사태는 양자의 불균형이 빚어낸 산물(REFLECTION)이며, 중국,월남, 북한등 소위 "유교 문명권 공산주의" (CONFUCIAN-LENINIST)국가도 경제적발전과 정치적 개혁의 상승 작용(INTERPLAY)에 직면하게 될것임.

마. 미국과 아시아 주요 국가와의 양자 관계를 살펴봄.

1) 한.미 관계

0 미국의 아시아 개입(ENGAGEMENT)의 또다른 축은 한. 미 우방 관계임.

0 한국의 역동적 발전은 한. 미관계를 종전의 군사 동맹관계에서 정치적, 군사적, 경제적으로 대등한 동반자관계로 변화시키고 있음.

0 한국의 성공은 북한과의 끊임없는 정치적, 군사적 대치속에서 이루어졌다는데에 더욱 의의가 있으며, 한반도 내 핵확산 위험은 아시아, 태평양 전체 안정의 제일 큰 위협이 되고 있음.

0 북한의 IAEA 핵 사찰 거부는 그들의 진정한 의도를 의심케하며, 부쉬 대통령의 전략 무기 철수 계획 발표는 북한의 소위 전제 조건을 허울좋은 구실로 만드는 것임.

0 이락의 경우에서 보듯이 IAEA 안전 협정 체결도 무모한 정권의 핵무기 개발을 막을수는 없으므로, 한반도내 핵 비확산을 보장하는 유일한 장치는 남북한이 핵 물질 생산및 반입을 금지하는 데 합의(CREDABLE AGREEMENT)하는것임.

0 한반도내 긴장완화의 요체는 활발한 남북 대화에 있으며, 노대통령의 3 통 협정 제의와 같은 쌍방간의 신뢰 구축 분위기 조성이 필요함. 미국으로서는 북한이 세계 시민(GLOBAL CITIZEN)으로서 책무를 다할때 북한과의 접촉 수준을 격상할 용의가 있음.

0 휴전선을 중심으로 쌍방간에 막대한 병력이 대치하고 있는 한국은 동아시아에서 군비 통제의 이니시어티브가 필요한곳이며, 유럽식 신뢰 구축 조치및 궁극적으로 유럽식 재래식 무기 감축 조치가 가능함.

0 한반도의 화해 및 궁극적인 통일 과정은 한국의 이니시어티브에 의해 주도되어야할것이나, 미.소.중.일 4 대국도 한반도에 지대한 이해가 걸려있는 만큼 미국은 남북 대화 진전에 맞추어 긴장완화 및 남북간 협상 결과 이행을 보장하기 위한 남북한및 동북아 4 대 강국간의 회의(FORUM)창설 가능성도 모색할 것임. (WILL EXPLORE THE POSSIBILITY).

이하 USW-5487 로 계속됨.

PAGE 2

관리 번호	91- 2258

외 무 부

종 별 :

번 호 : USW-5487

일 시 : 91 1106 2114

수 신 : 장 관 (미일,해외,해신,문홍)

발 신 : 주 미국 대사

제 목 : USW-5486 호의 계속분

(2) 미.일 관계

- 미.일 관계는 아태지역의 번영과 안보, 그리고 탈냉전체제의 효과적 운영에 핵심적임.

- 미.일 양국은 점차 대등한 입장으로 발전해 왔으며, 양국관계의 형식과 실제(FORM AND SUBSTANCE)도 이를 반영하도록 하는 조정이 필요함.

- 상기 조정은 안보협력면에서 미.일간의 역할분담및 국방관련 기술 교류의증대, 경제적으로 SII 등 마찰해소, 제 3 세계 외채문제등 국제문제에 대한 협력강화(GLOBAL PARTNERSHIP)및 미.일 양국민의 상호 문화 이해증진으로 이루어져야 함.

(3) 미-아세안 관계

- 동남아시아는 공산주의 위협하에서도 발전을 거듭, 발전 모델의 귀감이 되고 있음.

- 아세안 국가에 대해서는 UR 의 성공적 체결을 위해 협력을 기대하고 있으며, 캄보디아 문제해결에서 있었던 협조를 바탕으로 인도지나 3 국을 포함한 동남아시아의 새로운 시대의 창출을 기대함.

- 필리핀내 미군기지 철수와는 관계없이 미국의 대동남아 지역에 대한 안보공약은 확고함.

(4) 미-호주관계

- 호주는 동남아시아와 남태평양 도서국가를 연결시켜주는 중요한 국가로서 전세계적 문제뿐만 아니라 지역문제에 있어서도 활발한 역할을 하고 있음.

- BUSH 대통령의 전반적 핵무기 감축 정책 발표이후 호주, 뉴질랜드와의 ANZUS 동맹의 활성화(REACTIVATION)을 촉구하고 있음.

(5) 미-중관계

미주국 안기부	장관 공보처	차관 공보처	1차보	2차보	문협국	외정실	분석관	청와대

PAGE 1

91.11.07 12:29

91.11.31 외신 2과 통제관 BS

0064

- 천안문 사건이후 미.중 관계는 상호 합의점을 상실한채 갈등상태에 있음.

- 그러나 단순히 중국에 등을 돌림으로써 문제가 해결되지 않으며, 오히려 중국과의 관계를 유지하면서 중국내 인권, 무기수출, 공정무역 문제등을 계속 촉구하여야함.

- 이러한 맥락에서 BUSH 대통령은 중국에 MFN 지위를 계속 부여하는등 대중국 개입정책(POLICY OF ACTIVE ENGAGEMENT)을 견지해 왔음.

- 또한 중국의 국제적 역할은 미국의 이익에 직접 영향을 주고 있으며, 캄보디아 문제 해결 및 한반도 긴장완화등에 있어 중국의 협조가 유익하였음.

(6) 아시아내 소련의 역할

- 아태지역내에서 소련의 역할은 계속 증대되어 오고 있으며, 캄보디아 문제, 걸프전에서의 미.소 협력및 한국과의 수교이후 동 지역내에서 미소 협력의 가능성은 증대되고 있음.

- 그러나 소련은 막강한 군사력을 유지하고 있고, 상금 시장경제 개혁을 완료치 않은 상태임.

- 미국으로서는 소련, 아시아지역과 태평양 연안국이 경제관계를 강화시켜 나가는 것을 환영하고 있음.

바. BUSH 대통령의 동아시아 방문은 아시아의 미래에 대한 희망을 반영(HIGHLIGHT)하는 것임. 그러나 아. 태지역 역사에 있어 새로운 페이지를 넘기기 위해서는 냉전의 유물이 청산되어야함. 휴전협정은 보다 항구적인 평화로 대체되어야 하며, 북방도서 문제가 해결되어야함. 다음 1 천년이 태평양 시대가 되기 위해서는 공영과 공동의 가치에 기초한 든든한 공동체 의식(STRONG SENSE OF COMMUNITY)이 다져져야함. 끝.

(대사 현홍주-국장)

예고: 91.12.31. 일반

3. 美國의 對아시아政策에 관한 國務長官 寄稿

ㅇ 베이커 美 國務長官은 外交關係에 관한 美國 최고의 권위
  季刊誌인 '外交問題'(Foreign Affairs) 최신호 (금년 11월
  市販예정)에 美國의 對아시아政策에 관한 寄稿文을 게재
  예정인 바, 그중 韓半島 관련 요지는 아래와 같음.

  - 韓國은 美國의 對아시아政策의 支柱로서 韓國의 經濟發展,
    北方政策 성공등으로 韓.美 關係가 더욱 同等한 關係로
    변화하고 있음.
  - 北韓의 核開發 沮止 對策으로서 南.北韓이 核武器를 製造할
    수 있는 核物質의 生産 및 獲得을 하지 않는다는 확실한
    保障을 하는 方案이 있음.
  - 韓半島 問題 관련 6者 會談 가능성을 모색할 것이나, 그러한
    會談은 어디까지나 南北韓間 合意內容과 緊張緩和를 保障
    하기 위한 목적임.   (駐美大使 報告)

0066'

공   란

공　　　란

공 란

공   란

공 란

공   란

공 란

공 란

공   란

공　　　　　란

공 란

공　　　란

공   란

공 란

공　　　란

공   란

북한 핵문제 미국 동향

공   란

공 란

공   란

공   란

공 란

공　　　란

공   란

공　　　란

공 란

공   란

공　　　란

공 란

공 　 란

공   란

공 란

공 란

공　　　　　란

공　　　란

공 란

공 란

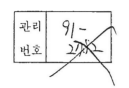

분류번호	보존기간

발 신 전 보

번 호 : WJA-5146   911111 2254 FL 종별 : 지급

WSV -3642 WCP -2064

수 신 : 주 수신처 참조 대사. 총영사

발 신 : 장 관 (미일)

제 목 : 미국의 6자포럼 구상

1. Baker 미 국무부장관은 11.8일자 Foreign Affairs지에서 아래 요지로 한반도문제 관련 6자회담 구상을 밝힌 바 있고, 11.11. 동경 국제문제 연구소에서의 연설에서도 유사한 구상을 제시한 바 있음.

   ㅇ 한반도의 화해와 통일과정은 남.북한의 주도하에 이루어질 필요가 있음.

   ㅇ 미.일.중.소등 4강국은 이해관계국이므로 미국은 남북대화의 진전을 보아 가면서 6자회담의 가능성을 모색(explore)할 것임.

   ㅇ 동 회담은 한반도에서 남북대화와 긴장완화를 지원하고, 관계국 공동의 안보 관심사항 논의를 촉진하며, 남.북한간 합의 도달시 이를 보장하는 장치를 마련할 것임.

2. Baker 장관의 상기 구상에 대한 주재국 정부의 입장을 지급 보고 바람.   끝.

(미주국장   반기문)

예 고 : 91.12.31. 일반

수신처 : 주일 대사 , 주소 대사 , 주북경 대표

보 안 통 제	

앙 고 재	91년 11월 1일	북미과	기안자 성명 문승현	과 장	심의관	국 장	차 관	장 관	0103	외신과통제

공   란

공 란

공 란

공   란

美國의 6者 포럼 構想에 대한 우리의 立場

1991. 11. 12.

外 務 部

1. 基本 立場

o 韓半島問題는 基本的으로 直接 當事者인 南.北韓間의
  對話에 의해 解決되어야 한다는 原則을 堅持함.

o 韓半島問題 解決을 위한 6者 포럼開催 問題는 派生될
  諸般 問題點들을 감안하여 신중하게 對處함.

o 다만, 趣旨는 다르지만 大統領 閣下께서 88.10. 東北亞
  平和協議會를 提議하셨음을 감안, 正面反對立場 表明
  보다는 北韓의 核問題에 局限된 6者포럼 내지 共同對應
  方案을 檢討함.

o 아울러 現在로서는 大統領 閣下의 11.8字 "韓半島 非核化
  및 平和 構築에 관한 宣言"을 바탕으로 IAEA와 UN次元,
  그리고 個別國家들에 의한 外交的 壓力을 가일층 强化함.

0108

2. 對美 言及要旨

    가. 北韓의 核武器 開發計劃은 韓半島는 물론 東北亞의
        安定과 平和에 대한 심각한 威脅이 되므로 韓.美兩國은
        北韓의 核開發 沮止를 위해 最優先的인 努力을 경주
        하여야함. 따라서 보다 效果的이고 强力한 對北韓
        説得과 壓力手段이 必要하다는데에는 韓.美 兩國이
        認識을 같이하고 있다고 생각함.

    나. 美國이 構想하고 있는 6者포럼은 北韓 核問題뿐만 아니라
        韓半島에서의 緊張緩和와 信賴構築을 포함하여 韓半島와
        관련한 諸般事項을 協議함을 目的으로 하고 있는 것으로
        알고 있음. 基本的으로 韓國政府는 韓半島問題는 直接
        當事者인 南.北韓間 對話에 의해 解決되어야 한다는
        原則을 堅持하고 있음.

    다. 다만, 北韓의 核開發을 沮止시키기 위한 全體的인 努力
        의 일환으로서 美國이 6者포럼 開催가 반드시 必要하다고
        생각하고, 核問題만으로 국한해서 論議될 수 있다고 判斷
        된다면 이에대해 신중히 檢討하겠음.   끝 .

〈必要時 追加 言及〉

- 議題가 우리의 基本立場에 반해서 韓半島 전반에 걸친 問題로 擴大될 可能性이 있음. 이 경우 北韓은 韓半島 非核地帶化, 駐韓 美軍의 전면 撤收等 우리로서는 受諾하기 어려운 問題를 주장함으로써 問題 解決을 長期化하고 複雜化시킬 것임.

- 우리로서는 休戰協定體制를 平和協定體制로 代替하는 問題의 경우, 南.北韓이 우선 合意에 도달한 후 美國과 中國이 參與 하는 「2+2」 會談形式을 考慮할 수 있으나, 韓半島問題 論議에 日本과 蘇聯을 끌어들여 6者 포럼의 形式을 취하는 것은 國民의 輿論에 비추어 볼때 바람직스럽지 않다고 봄.   끝.

0110

공   란

공   란

공　　　란

공　　　란

공 란

공　　　란

공　　　란

외 무 부

종 별 : 긴 급

번 호 : USW-5594
일 시 : 91 1112 2030

수 신 : 장 관 (미일,미안,해신)

발 신 : 주 미 대 사

제 목 : BUSH 대통령 ASIA SOCIETY 연설

1. BUSH 대통령이 금 11.12 저녁 ASIA SOCIETY 연례만찬에서 행할 예정인 연설문 주요 내용을 하기 보고함.(백악관에서 당관에 요약 발췌문 봉보)

2. 주요 요지

가. 서론

- 본인이 아시아 순방을 연기한 이유는 의회가 회기를 연장할 가능성이 많으며, 의회 개원중 해외여행을 하는 것은 안심이 되지 않기(DON'T FEEL COMFORTABLE) 때문임.

- 국내정치와 국제정치를 분리시킬수 있다는 것은 고립주의적 환상에서 나온 것이며, 고립주의는 전쟁과 공황만을 야기하였다는 점이 역사적 경험임.

- 미국의 아시아에 대한 주요 관심은 안보, 민주주의와 교역임.

나. 안보

- 미국이 아시아 각국과 갖고 있는 독특한(CUSTOM-MADE) 안보체제를 통해 아시아 안보가 유지되어 나갈 것임.

- 캄보디아 문제가 해결되고 있는바, 미국은 라오스와의 관계를 격상시킬 것임을 이자리를 빌어 발표함.

- 한국은 북한과의 관계를 개선하는 한편, 북에게 핵무기의 위협을 포기하도록 요구(CHALLENGE)하고 있음.

- 미.일.중.소및 한국은 북한 핵개발을 통제하기 위해 조직적인 노력(ORGANIZED EFFORTS)을 경주하고 있음.

- 주한 미군은 한국국민이 원하는한 계속 존속될 것임.

- 미.일은 대외원조, 일.소관계, 주일 미군, '페'만 사태등에서 보듯 긴밀히 협조하고 있음.

미주국 안기부	장관 공보처	차관	1차보	2차보	미주국	분석관	정와대	총리실

PAGE 1

91.11.13   12:10

외신 2과 통제관 CA

0119

다. 민주주의

- 미국은 민주주의의 확산을 지원하며, 결국에는 민주주의 개혁을 거부하는소수의 국가들도 동참하게 될 것임.

라. 경제

- 미국은 일본과 한국이 무역장벽을 제거하고, 제조업, 서비스, 농업등 재분야를 자유화할 것을 촉구함.

- 한편, 경제협력의 활성화를 위해서는 미국 국내조치도 필요한 바, (1) 미국의 자본소득세는 독일, 일본과 비교하여 너무 높으며, (2) 국제 경쟁력 제고를위해서는 금융업의 현대화가 요구됨.

마. 결어

- 미국은 아. 태지역의 항구적 평화를 위해서는 6 개의 주요정책(SIX KEYS)을 추진해야 할 것으로 봄.

(1) 무역자유화, 2) 안보협력, 3) 민주주의와 인권, 4) 교육과 과학의 개혁, 5) 환경보호및 6) 고유한 문화의 존중)

- 본인은 이러한 중요한 원칙의 신장을 위해 조만간 아시아를 방문할 수 있기를 기대하는 바, 아시아 각국과의 관계(TIES) 증진은 미국의 안보와 경제적 이익(PEACE AND JOBS)에도 도움이 될 것임.

3. 평가

- BUSH 대통령은 외교에 치중하여 국내정치를 등한히 한다는 여론을 의식 (1) 국내정치와 국제정치를 분리할 수 없으며, (2) 고립주의가 위험하고, (3) 본인의 아시아 방문이 미국민의 안녕과 경제적 이익(PEACE AND JOBS)에도 도움이 됨을 누차 강조한 것으로 사료됨.

- 또한 (1) 의회에 대한 불신감 표시, (2) 자본소득세및 금융 현대화 필요성 역설등으로 기본적으로 국제관계에 관한 금일 연설을 통해서도 국내문제에 대한 자신의 입장을 밝히는 기회로 활용한 것이 특이함.

- 한편, BAKER 장관의 FOREIGN AFFAIRS 기고문, BAKER 장관의 11.11. 일본 국제연구소 연설에 이어 BUSH 대통령도 아시아에 대한 미국의 이익을 (1) 안보, (2) 민주주의, (3) 교역의 세가지로 강조한 것이 금후 BUSH 대통령의 아시아 순방, 나아가서는 BUSH 행정부의 냉전후 대아시아 정책의 방향을 제시하는 것으로 평가됨.

- 아국과 관련해서는 특별히 새로운 점은 없으나, 아국의 비핵정책 선언을

평가하고 북한의 핵위협및 이의 해결을 위한 미.일.중.소및 아국의 '조직적 노력'을
강조한 점이 주목됨. 끝.
     (대사 현홍주-국장)
     예고: 91.12.31. 일반

외   무   부

종   별 : 긴 급

번   호 : USW-5596   일   시 : 91 1112 2255

수   신 : 장 관(미일,미이,기정) 사본: 청와대 외교안보좌관

발   신 : 주 미국 대사

제   목 : BUSH 대통령 ASIA SOCIETY 연설

    본직은 금 11.12(화) 뉴욕 ASIA SOCIETY 가 주최한 BUSH 대통령 초청 만찬 연설회에 참석하는 기회에, SUNUNU 비서실장, SCOWCROFT 안보보좌관 및 ANDERSON 국무부 동.아태 부차관보와 만나, BUSH 대통령의 아시아 순방일정및 금일 연설 배경에 대해 의견 교환을 갖은바, 다음 요지 보고함.

    1. 먼저 SUNUNU 비서실장은 BUSH 대통령의 아시아 순방 일정 재조정(RESCHEDULING) 방안을 오늘 연설이전에 결정하여 발표하려고 생각하였으나 관계국과 협의를 해야하기 때문에 일단 미루게 되었다고 말함.

    2. 또한 SCOWCROFT 보좌관은, BUSH 대통령의 아시아 순방일정을 조속히 다시 잡게 된것에 대해(RESCHEDULE) 반갑게 생각한다고 하면서, 행정부의 어느 누구도 아시아를 소홀히 생각하는 사람은 없으며, 금일 BUSH 대통령 자신도 이러한 점을 연설을 통해서 밝힌 것이라고 강조함.

    3. ███████████████████████████████

    또한 동 차관보는 11.8 아국정부의 비핵정책 선언과 관련 노대통령의 과감하고 훌륭한 지도력을 높이 평가하는 내용을 금일 연설에 반영하도록 노력한바 있다고 언급함. 끝.

    (대사 현홍주-장관)

    예고: 1992.12.31. 일반

| 미주국 | 장관 | 차관 | 1차보 | 2차보 | 미주국 | 외정실 | 분석관 | 청와대 |
| 총리실 | 안기부 | | | | | | | |

PAGE 1   91.11.13   13:25
외신 2과 통제관 BS

0122

128 북한 핵문제 미국 동향

EMBASSY OF THE REPUBLIC OF KOREA
WASHINGTON, D. C.

"긴급"

FAX COVER SHEET

USW(F)-4915

DATE: Nov 12, 1991

TO: 장관 (미안, 미심)   (총 7매)
   FAX: (   )   -
   TEL: (   )   -

FROM: 주미대사관
   FAX: (202) 797 - 0595
   TEL: (202) 939 -

NUMBER OF PAGES(INCLUDING THIS COVER SHEET) Seven

COMMENTS: 연 : USW(F) - 4907

· Bush 대통령이 Asia Society에서 행하는 연설문 transmit 합니다.

· 요구 및 개인적으로 관심하는 연설과 같은 내용을 청취합니다. ─

   4907-1

0123

REMARKS BY: PRESIDENT GEORGE BUSH
AT ASIA SOCIETY DINNER
WALDORF-ASTORIA HOTEL, NEW YORK CITY, NEW YORK
ZW-2-1 page# 1 TUESDAY, NOVEMBER 12, 1991

dest=swh,mwh,asia,fns11182,fns13126,fns12475,fns13497,usag
data

PRESIDENT BUSH: I'm just delighted to be here with all of
you -- (audio break) -- to see Asia Society President Robert Oxham
(ph) and then Vice Chairman Peter Erin (ph), and to you and to the
distinguished men and women in this audience, greetings and my
thanks for this opportunity to speak with you on topics of great
concern to us all. And I heard you were having broccoli, so I asked
to speak before the dinner -- (laughter) -- and I hope this hasn't
really fouled things up. But I feel strongly about that.

(Laughter) -- and -- no, but seriously, we do have to go
back. And I'm very pleased for this accommodation. And I hope you
all understand. But as you know, I have just returned from Rome --
that NATO meeting -- and The Hague for an EC meeting. And there I
worked with other western leaders to help build a post-cold-war
world that's characterized by mutual security, democracy, individual
liberty, free enterprise, and unfettered international trade. And I
want to talk tonight about those topics, but with the accent on
Asia.

But first, for audiences here and in Asia, I think it's
important to discuss once again why I will not travel to the region
later this month. As President, I must serve the entire nation in
the domestic and foreign arenas. And sometimes those obligations
clash. And when we planned our trip a couple of months ago --
worked out the schedule -- Congress had planned to adjourn early in
this month -- I believe it was November 2nd, possibly November 4th.
And now the members say that they will wrap up by November 22nd, but
who knows. We will reschedule the trip. But I will not leave while
Congress is wrapping up a session. It can commit too much mischief
in times like that. (Laughter.) And I saw Home Alone, that movie
-- (laughter) -- and I just don't feel comfortable leaving Congress
home alone.

But, make no mistake, however, I will not turn my back on my
responsibility to do the nation's business here and abroad. And in
times of economic pain, I certainly will not give up an opportunity
to work with our allies to create new markets, new jobs, and new
opportunities for American workers in agriculture, in manufacturing,
and in service industries. And I certainly will not permit us to
retreat into a kind of "Fortress America" which will doom us to
irrelevance and poverty. The notion that we can separate domestic
and foreign policy rests upon a stubborn fantasy that we can live as
an isolated island surrounded by a changing and developing world.

We tried isolationism, and we ended up fighting two bloody
world wars. And we tried economic isolationism, protectionism, and
we helped set off a world-wide depression. And I remain deeply
committed to building closer ties with the Asia-Pacific region.

4P07-2

①.

0124

Although much of our nation's heritage comes from Europe, our future points equally importantly toward Asia. Asia's transformed itself in the space of a generation into the most rapidly growing region on the face of the earth.

Asia-Pacific nations enjoyed staggering, real economic growth in the decade of the '80s. The **Australian** economy grew by 41 percent, **Japan's** nearly 52 percent, **Malaysia** almost 60 percent, **Hong Kong** -- there are many here from **Hong Kong** tonight --- 89 percent, **Singapore** 98 percent, **Taiwan** 116 percent, and **South Korea** 150 percent.

The Asia-Pacific region has become our largest and fastest growing **trading partner.** We conduct more than $300 billion worth of two-way trade annually. And together, we generate nearly half --- listen to this one -- together, we generate nearly half of the world's gross national product. American firms have invested more than $61 billion in the region and that figure will grow. Asians have invested more than $95 billion in the United States.

In everything from automobiles to microchips, from baseball to Australian rules football, we grow closer each day. A few years ago, it was fashionable to refer to the 20th century as the American century and the 21st as the Pacific century, as if we were engaged in some long-term competition with our Asian allies. I don't see it that way.

The United States will remain large and powerful, but in years to come we will deepen our partnership with our Asian friends in building democracy and freedom.

We'd be here forever if I tried to tick off our interests and activities country by country. So, forgive me, but instead, I will address three central issues in our relationships with the nations of the region: security, democracy, and trade.

In the area of security, Asia's variety has spawned a diverse pattern of political and strategic cooperation. Our custom-made agreements and relationships provide a strong foundation for future security.

Let me give you a few examples of how we seek to build the peace. The conflict in **Indochina** has preoccupied this nation for years. And finally, we've entered into a period of healing and constructive cooperation. We will work step by step to resolve the painful issues left by that war.

4807-3

0125

The Asian nations, Japan, Australia, and the UN Security
Council's permanent members, recently forged a Cambodian peace
process that promises free elections in a nation previously rent by
tyranny and genocide. Just yesterday, for the first time in 16
years, we sent an accredited diplomat to Cambodia to participate in
the peace-making arrangements.

We envision normal relations with Vietnam as the logical
conclusion to a step-by-step process that begins by resolving the
problems in Cambodia and by addressing thoroughly, openly and
conclusively the status of American POWs/MIAs.

And today, I am announcing that we will upgrade our relations
with Laos and that we soon will place an ambassador in Vientiane.

The Republic of Korea has moved to build better ties with
North Korea while boldly challenging the North to abandoning its
menacing nuclear weapons program, which is the greatest threat to
regional peace.

We welcome recently organized efforts involving us, the
Japanese, the Soviets, Chinese and Koreans to bring North Korea's
nuclear program under international supervision. And meanwhile, we
will maintain our military presence in the South as long as the
people want and need us.

In laying the foundation for peace through our global
partnership, we have worked closely with Japan in the area of
foreign aid. We are the world's two foremost providers of such aid.
And we also cooperate on development assistance. More and more on
environmental protection, trade, arms control, refugees and regional
peace.

We've urged the Soviet Union to take a progressive attitude
toward the northern territories in its discussions with Japan. The
Japanese have joined us in trying to lead the Soviet Union and
Eastern Europe toward free enterprise. They support more than
45,000 US military forces in Japan with $2 billion in annual host
nation contributions.

4P07-4

③

0126

WALDUKI ...

ZW-2-3-E   page# 1   TUESDAY, NOVEMBER 12, 1991

    dest=swh,mwh,asia,fns11182,fns13126,fns12475,fns13497,usag
    dest+=japan,austral,skor,prc,protrd,defic,humrt
    dest+=burma,nkor,bus,germany
    data

    Japan contributed nearly $13 billion to the multinational forces for the Gulf War, $10 billion of which went to the United States. This required new taxes, a very tough thing for any politician to ask of working people, but Japan deserves praise for choosing the right course.

    To the South, Australia casts a presence far larger than its relatively small population would suggest. It takes justifiable pride in its long tradition of defending democracy and its economic, political and cultural presence helps unite the Asia-Pacific region with the rest of the world.

    We can help ensure future peace in the region and defend our interests through a range of military arrangements. Bilateral alliances, access agreements, and structures such as the five power defense arrangement give us the flexibility we need.

    While we must adjust our force structure to reflect post-Cold War realities, we also must protect our interests and allies. And in this light, we cannot afford to ignore the important sources of instability in North Korea, in Burma, where socialist despotism holds sway, despite, I might say -- might add -- despite the heroic efforts
    Let me mention just a few words regarding China. China is vitally important. It is our policy to remain engaged. We believe this is the way to effective -- to affect positive change in the world's most populous nation. And that's exactly what Secretary of State Jim Baker is doing there this week.

    Fortunately, the key to future stability in the region lies not with arms but with balance. Democracy has swept across Asia with some notable exceptions, such as Burma and China and North Korea and Vietnam. And yet we remain engaged in the region and especially in China.

    If we retreat from the challenge of building democracy, we will have failed many who have worked hard, even died, for the cause.

    The United States will support democracy wherever it can, understanding that nations adopt political freedom in their own ways, in manners consistent with their histories and cultures.

4P07-5

0127

ZW-2-3-E page# 2   TUESDAY, NOVEMBER 12, 1991
        After decades of uncertainty, the future really does seem
full of hope. And even the intransigent few seem likely to join the
rest of the world in building a commonwealth of freedom.

        And ten
or afford to. And yes, we disagree on some important trade issues.
But we also recognize a more important fact: our faiths and values
have become linked forever. Contrary to the opinions of American
protectionists, free trade requires efforts by all parties involved
and too often trade disputes bring out the worst in people.

        Japan-bashing -- you've heard that expression -- Japan-
bashing has become a minor sport in some places in the United
States, and then some in Japan have become equally scornful of the
United States. And both our nations must reject those who would
rather seek out scapegoats than tackle their own problems.

        We made a good start. The Asia-Pacific Economic Cooperation
Group encourage growth in trade. The Uruguay Round of GATT talks
remains the single most important vehicle for advancing the cause of
free trade and sending off the scourge of protectionism.

        And we call upon Japan and Korea to work with us in breaking
down old barriers to trade, opening up markets in manufacturing,
services, and agriculture.

        Our Structural Impediments Initiative, those talks have
helped lower barriers to trade and investment. But we need to give
those talks new life -- give them a kick -- and create a better
climate in Japan for US businesses.

        The fact is that Japan, which nearly half a century ago
became a focal point of American hatred, has become one of our
closest and most treasured allies. And I enjoyed a warm and
constructive relationship working with Prime Minister Toshiki Kaifu.
And I look forward to spending time with my old friend Prime
Minister Kiiychi Miazawa (sp), significantly a man steeped in
Western and Eastern culture and superbly equipped to build bridges
of culture and trade between our two great nations.

        Together we can build an even more prosperous and spectacular
future, but only if we take up the tough rewarding task of promoting
worldwide economic liberty. We seek a vibrant international
economic system that unites markets on every continent. We in the
United States also must strengthen our economy. We level an
unacceptably high effective tax rate on capital gains.

        Germany -- no capital gains tax. The complicated Japanese
tax averages about 1 percent. This puts our own business people --
our own entrepreneurs and venture capitalists at a huge and shameful

4P07-b

0128

ZW-2-3-E page# 3   TUESDAY, NOVEMBER 12, 1991
    disadvantage compared to our Asian trading partners.

    We run an enormous and growing budget **deficit** which inflames
political divisions within our own country. We must take powerful
action to reduce that deficit while nourishing economic growth. To
compete internationally, we must modernize our banking industry and
make our industrial base more competitive. We must work with our
allies to build a stable and sound monetary regime.

    Perhaps most important, we must build human capital. We have
an obligation to prepare future generations for life in the 21st
century. The integrated global economy will demand more of us than
ever before, and our schools f liberation technology and no technology
does more for the cause of freedom than the means of mass
communication. No wall is high enough and no government
sufficiently despotic to shut off what some call a revolution o approach t
relations
with Asia. Our administration sees six keys to promoting lasting
peace in the Asia-Pacific region:

    Progressive trade liberalization; security cooperation; a
shared commitment to democracy and human rights; educational and
scientific innovation; respect for the environment; and an
appreciation of our distinct cultural heritages.

    Americans have always looked to the horizons for their
destiny, even from our earliest days. And we've grown great because
we've welcomed people from every continent, in every country and
we've tried to make use of their distinct talents when they come
here while c I look forward to traveling soon to Asia to advance these
important principles and to expand market opportunities for tens of
thousands of American workers and businesses. And as President, I
will continue building ties with our allies because those ties mean
peace at home and jobs for American men and women.

    And I want to thank the Asia Society for its vital
contribution to the cause of peace, prosperity, and understanding.

And I look forward to your help as I seek to build closer bonds of
affection and interest with the peoples of the vast, marvelous,
varied Asia-Pacific region.

    Thank you all and may God bless our Asia and Pacific friends
and the United States of America. Thank you very, very much.
(Applause.)

                              END

                         4P07-7

                                                        0129

공   란

공   란

관리번호 91-2814

외 무 부

종 별 : 지급

번 호 : JAW-6485

일 시 : 91 1114 2344

수 신 : 장관(미일,아일)

발 신 : 주 일 대사(일정)

제 목 : 미국의 6자 포럼 구상

대:WJA-5146

연:JAW-6431

1. 대호, 표제관련 일 와타나베 외상은 연호 보고와 같이 11.11(월) 오전 미.일 외상회담시 베이커 장관이 동 구상에 대한 의견을 문의한데 대해 "생각해 보겠다"는 신중한 반응을 보인바 있음.

2. 한편, 와타나베 외상은 11.11(월) 저녁 당지 KBS 특파원과의 인터뷰시 6자회담 구상에 대한 의견을 물은데 대해 "형태에 구애받지 않음. 원칙적으로는 당사국간 대화에 의한 문제해결이 바람직하지만, 주변국들인 미.일.중.쏘와 협의하는 것이 유익하다고 한다면 반대할 이유가 없다"고 밝혔음.(인터뷰를 행한 KBS 특파원에게 확인한 내용임)

3. 상기 관련, 당관 김영소 정무과장은 금 11.14(목) 일 외무성 무또 북동아 과장을 면담(11.12-15 간 국장방한중, 심의관은 국장대리로 국회출석중) 상기 "2"항 외상 언급내용을 확인한바, 동 과장은 일측입장은 상기 와타나베 외상이 언급바와 같다하고 아래와 같이 부연 설명함.

"기본정로는 남.북한 문제는 남.북 당사자간에 해결되어야 한다고 생각하며, 일본으로서도 공헌할수 있는 방법이 있다면 노력하겠음. 6_자라든지하는 형태나 숫자가 중요한 것이 아니고 형식에 관계없이 공동의 목적을 위해 할수 있는것이 있다면 노력해야 한다고 생각함."끝.

(대사 오재희-국장)

예고:92.6.30. 일반

예고문에의거일반문서로 재분류 92.1.30

미주국 안기부	장관	차관	1차보	2차보	아주국	외정실	분석관	청와대

PAGE 1

91.11.15   00:26

외신 2과 통제관 FM

0132

공　　　란

공   란

공   란

공   란

한반도문제 「2+2」 회담 제의 보도
====================================
당국자 논평
==========

91.11.15.

o 11.15자 일부 언론은 우리 정부가 한반도문제 관련 남.북한과 미국 및 중국이
  참여하는 「2+2」 회담을 미국 및 중국측에 제의했다고 보도한 바, 우리 정부는
  그러한 제안을 한바 없음을 밝히는 바임.

o 우리 정부는 한반도문제 해결은 직접 당사자인 남.북한간의 합의에 의해 추진
  되어야 한다는 확고한 원칙을 견지하고 있으며, 한.미 외무장관 회담(11.13),
  한.중 외무장관 회담(11.14)에서 이와같은 우리의 입장을 분명히 전달하였으며,
  미국과 중국도 이에대해 전적으로 동의한 바 있음.   끝.

0137

공   란

공   란

공   란

북한 핵문제 미국 동향

공   란

공　　　란

공 란

공   란

공   란

공　　　란

공　　　란

공   란

공   란

공   란

공 란

공   란

공   란

공   란

공　　　란

공   란

공   란

공   란

공   란

공   란

공 란

공   란

공 란

공   란

공 란

공   란

공		란

공　　　　　란

질 문 : 베이커 미 국무장관은 미국 시사 계간지 Foreign Affairs지의 겨울호에서
한반도에서의 긴장완화와 남북대화를 지원하고, 남·북한간 협상결과를
보장하기 위한 「6자 포럼」 개최 가능성을 모색할 수 있을 것이라고
밝혔는 데, 이에 대한 우리정부의 입장은 무엇입니까 ?

답 변 : 잘 아시다시피 우리정부는, 한반도문제는 직접 당사자인 남·북한간의
직접대화에 의해 해결되어야 하며, 다자협의의 대상이 될수 없다는 입장을
견지하고 있읍니다.

최근 독일통일 및 캄보디아문제 등 해결 과정에서 적용된 「2+4」회담
또는 다자회의 형식을 한반도에도 적용할 수 있을 것이라고 보는 견해도
있으나, 정치적 상황과 역사적 배경 그리고 국제법적 차원에 비추어 볼때
한반도문제는 다른 지역문제와는 근본적으로 다름을 고려해야 할 것입니다.

다만 남·북한간 대화를 통해 한반도문제 해결의 기본적인 틀이 마련되면,
이해관계가 있는 국가들이 적절한 단계에 가서 부차적이고 지원적인
역할을 하는 방안은 검토해 볼 수 있을 것입니다.

0169

질 문 : 그렇다면 한반도 휴전체제를 평화체제로 전환시키는 데 있어 남.북한과
미국 및 중국이 참여하는 소위 「2+2」형식의 회담은 가능하다고
보십니까 ?

답 변 : 다시말해 휴전체제의 전환을 포함한 한반도문제는 남.북한간에 먼저 협의
하고 합의되어야 하는 사항입니다.

그러나 UN군 사령관과 중국 인민의용군 사령관도 휴전협정에 서명했다는
법적 측면에 비추어 남.북한간 협의가 진전되는 과정에 맞추어 적절한
단계에서 미국과 중국의 참여는 고려될 수 있을 것입니다.

질 문 : 북한의 핵무기개발 저지가 무엇보다 시급한 사항임을 감안하여, 북한
핵문제에만 국한된 다자회의 개최는 검토해 볼수 있지 않겠습니까 ?

답 변 : 북한의 핵개발저지를 위해 우리는 미국을 위시한 주요 국가들과 협력하여
가능한 모든 외교적 노력을 경주하고 있읍니다.

0170

아울러 노태우 대통령께서 11.8. 천명하신 「한반도 비핵화 및 평화구축 선언」은 우리의 획기적인 정책선언임을 고려할 때, 이제 북한은 더이상 국제 핵사찰 수용을 지연시킬 구실이 없는 만큼, 우리는 주요 개별 국가들의 대북한 설득 및 압력과 IAEA 및 UN등 국제기구 차원의 노력을 더욱 강화해 나갈 것입니다.

다만 북한 핵문제 해결을 위한 6자회담 또는 다자회담 개최방안은, 이 회담이 만약 북한 핵문제만을 다루고 그외의 한반도문제 논의로 전개되지 않는다는 확실한 장치가 마련된다면 신중하게 검토해 볼수 있을 것이나, 그러한 장치마련이 될 것으로 낙관하기는 어렵다고 봅니다.

질 문 : 최근 미국 죠지 워싱턴 대학이 주최한 학술회의에 참석중인 북한측 인사 (최우진 북한 군축 및 평화연구소 부소장)은 북한이 6자회담 구상을 일응 긍정적으로 받아들이고 있는 듯한 발언을 한 것으로 전해지고 있는 데, 북한의 태도를 어떻게 생각하고 계시는지 ?

0171

답 변 : 동인은 미국이 구상하고 있는 6자회담에 대해 굳이 반대하지 않을 수도

있다고 하면서, 동시에 북한을 궁지에 몰아넣는 회담은 반대한다고 말한

것으로 듣고 있습니다.

이러한 발언이 북한의 공식적 입장을 어느정도 대변하고 있는지는 알 수

없지만, 동인이 일응 유보적이면서도 다소 유연한 태도를 보인 것은

실질적인 문제보다는 미국과의 관계개선을 위해 미국의 관심을 끌어보려는

생각에서 나온 것으로 보입니다.

0172

질문 : 남.북 회담 진전등 한반도에 화해 분위기가 확산되고 있는 현
       상황에 비추어 WHNS 협정이 과연 필요한가 하는 의문이 있는데,
       어떻게 생각하시는지요 ?

o 지난 5월 북한의 UN 가입 결정, 남.북 고위급 회담의 진전등에도
   불구하고 북한의 대남관계 정책이 근본적으로 변화하였다고 보기에는
   아직 시기 상조임. 즉, 적화통일노선 포기, 비무장지대 배치
   군사력 철수, 공격형 군사력 배치의 완화, 국방비 지출 비율
   감소등 구체적 긴장완화 조치를 취하지 않는 이상, 북한의
   대남전략에 근본적 변화가 왔다고 판단할 수는 없습니다.

o 또한, 북한은 우리의 계속적인 촉구와 세계적인 반대 여론에도
   불구하고, 핵무기 개발 계획 추진을 포기하지 않고 있습니다.

o 세계적으로 볼때에도 화해와 협력의 추세에도 불구, 지역 분쟁의
   발생 가능성이 상존하고 있으며 자신의 안보는 자신이 일차적으로
   책임져야 한다는 현실을 우리는 걸프전쟁, 동구등의 민족 분규를
   통하여 보아 왔습니다.

0173

o 한편 한반도 안보의 근간이 되었던 한.미 안보협력 관계는 커다란
   변화를 겪고 있읍니다. 즉 미국은 내부 경제적 어려움등으로 대외
   군사전략을 축소적 방향으로 재검토하고 있으며, 이러한 추세는
   주한미군이 단계적 감축 계획으로 나타나고 있읍니다.

o 이러한 제반 상황을 고려할때 화해와 협조의 분위기가 확산되고
   있는 가운데에서도 유비무환의 지혜를 잃지 말아야 된다는 관점에서
   정부는 한.미간 WHNS 협정 체결을 신중히 추진하게 된 것임을
   이해해야 합니다.

o 한.미간 WHNS 협정체결은 주한미군 감축과, 균형적 안보 부담이라는
   시대적 변화에 적응하면서, 만약의 북한의 남침사태에 대비하여
   둠으로서 안보적 불안을 해소하고 보다 안정된 남북관계 추진을
   뒷받침 하게 될 것이라 생각합니다.

0174

질문 : WHNS협정이 유사시 미국의 증원군 파견 규모를 규정하지 않고 있다는
비판이 있는데, 어떻게 보시는지요 ?

o 서독을 포함한 NATO 국가와 미국간의 안보조약은 그 체제와 내용에
있어 한.미간 안보조약과 다르다고 할 수 있읍니다. 즉 미국은
NATO 협약에서 NATO 국가에 대한 외부침략시 전투개입과 증원군 파견의
의무, 즉 미군의 전투개입을 자동적으로 하도록 되어 있는 반면,
한.미 상호방위 조약상에는 한국에 대한 외부침략시 미국의 개입은
한.미간 사전협의와 미헌법 절차에 따르도록 되어 있읍니다.

o 한.미 안보협력 관계의 모범이라 할수있는 한.미 상호방위 조약에
근거하여 한국에 유사사태 발발등 긴급 상황시에 미국이 증원군
파견을 즉시 이행할수 있도록 미증원군 파견 계획을 WHNS 협정상에
명기토록 하였으며 또한 그것이 아측의 지원계획과 균형을 이루도록
하므로써 한.미 상호방위조약상 추상적인 증원군 파견 가능성을
구체적으로 규정하게 된 것은 커다란 의의가 있읍니다.

0175

o 한가지 특기 사항으로 금번 교섭에 있어서 우리가 중점을 두었던
   것은 증원군 파견의 의무화보다는 유사시 미국의 증원군 파견을
   위한 결정을 용이하게 하는 현실적 규정을 둔 것임. 즉, WHNS
   협정 체결을 통하여 유사시 증원군 파견에 대비한 접수국의 군수
   지원 계획을 수립·유지해 둠으로써 미국의 신속한 증원군 파견을
   용이하게 할수 있게 된 것입니다.

0176

질문 : 한.미간 체결되는 WHNS협정이 예견하지 못한 지원을 제공토록
       하고 있을 뿐만 아니라, 협정 체결로 인하여 한국측에게 과도한
       부담이 생기게 되어, 불평등한 협정이라는 비판이 있는데 어떻게
       보십니까 ?

   o 「예견하지 못한 지원」(unforeseen WHNS)은 한반도 유사시
     미증원군이 도착하면서, 사전에 계획을 세워둔 사항 이외에
     예기치못한 불가피한 지원 소요가 발생 하였을 때, 증원군을
     받아들이는 한국측이 당시의 가용한 자산의 범위내에서 제공하게
     되는 지원을 말합니다.

   o 이와같은 지원은, 전시 자체가 유동적이고 그 상황변화를
     예견하지 못하는 것임을 감안할 때 군사적인 측면에서 그
     필요성이 충분히 인정되는 것입니다.

0177

o 또한 한국측의 부담 문제와 관련하여서는, 한.미간의 WHNS 협정
  자체가 전시대비 계획의 확충이나 군비증강을 수반하는 것이
  아니라, 양측간에 기합의된 지원사항의 체계적 재정비를 주목적으로
  한 일종의 정책 선언적 성격을 가지는 것이며 기본원칙만을 규정하기
  때문에 이 협정 체결 자체로 인하여 자동적으로 직접적인 비용의
  부담이 발생하지 않는다는 것을 정확히 인식할 필요가 있습니다.

o 동 협정 제8조에서 기술된 비용 책임 규정을 보면,
  - 본 포괄협정 체결로 인하여 기존 협정, 협약에 포함된 비용
    책임은 전혀 영향을 받지 않으며,
  - 추가로 체결되는 협정, 협약에서의 비용은 매 사안별로
    양측이 판단하여 적절히 분담 (Share)토록 되어 있듯이 분담의
    원칙만을 규정하고 있음을 간과해서는 안될것입니다.

o 또한, 제4조에서는 양측이 추가로 지원 협정을 체결하게 될 경우,
  각각의 국내법 절차를 거치도록 하고 있으므로 금번 포괄 협정
  체결로 인하여 임의적이거나 자의적으로 우리의 지원 비용부담이
  증가하는 경우는 발생하지 않는다는 것을 정확히 이해해야
  할 것입니다.

0178

질문 : 지금은 정부에서 「전시 지원 협정」이라는 명칭을 사용하고 있읍니다만 당초 전시접수국 지원 협정이라는 명칭을 사용하였을때, 이 「접수국」 이라는 말을 유사시 미국이 한국을 접수하여 전쟁을 수행하는 것으로 비판한 적이 있었읍니다. 물론 오해에서 비롯된 것으로 생각합니다만, 어떻게 보시는지요 ?

o 접수라는 말이 한자로는 두가지 뜻이 있다는 것을 말씀드립니다. 즉, 무엇을 받아 들인다는 뜻의 접수(接受)가 있고, 어떤 곳을 점령 또는 점거한다는 뜻의 접수(接收)가 있는데 본래 우리가 사용한 접수국(接受國)이라는 말은 미국의 증원군을 받아드리는 나라라는 뜻으로 쓴 것입니다. 그러나 한글 표기에 있어서는 그러한 구별이 안되므로 일부에서 이를 후자의 뜻을 갖는것으로 왜곡한 비롯된 것이라고 생각합니다.

0179

o 또한, Host Nation의 번역인 접수국(接受國)이라는 말은 외교사절을
   파견, 접수하는 경우등에서 지난 수십년간 국제법 또는 조약 규정에
   있어서 사용해 온 말인데 (예컨대 "외교관계에 관한 비엔나 협약등),
   전문적인 용어라는 점에서 한글로 표기할 경우에는 일반 국민이
   오해할 소지는 있을 수 있다고 보아 정부는 그러한 용어 자체를
   삭제하기로 결정하였읍니다.

o 문제는 그러한 용어의 뜻을 잘 알면서도 일부 운동권이 국민을
   현혹 또는 선동하려는 목적에서 악용하고 있다는 사실을 지적
   하고자 합니다.

0180

외 무 부

종   별 :

번   호 : USW-5777   일   시 : 91 1122 1738

수   신 : 장관 (미일,미안,정특,해기,기정) 사본:국방부장관,주미대사

발   신 : 주 미국 대사대리

제   목 : 한.미 관계 해리티지 재단 세미나

1991.12.31.에 예고문에 의거 일반문서로 재분류됨

1. 금 11.22. 당지 헤리티지 재단 주관으로 'KOREAN-AMERICAN RELATIONS: THE CHALLENGES OF MATURITY' 제하의 한.미 관계 세미나가 개최된바, 주요 연사로는 국무부 SOLOMON 차관보, USTR ADAMS 부대표보, 국방부 안보지원국 MCDEVITT제독, 헤리티지 재단 PLUNK 연구원, 당관 구본영 공사가 참석함.

2. 동 세미나는 발언내용의 비공개(OFF-THE-RECORD) 조건하에 1 부에서 경제문제, 2 부에서 안보문제를 토의한 바, 안보관계 토의 요지를 하기 보고함.(1 부 토의는 별전 보고)

3. 세미나 요지

가. SOLOMON 차관보 기조연설

- 노태우 대통령은 올림픽 개최, UN 가입, 북방정책, 남.북한 관계, 핵문제등에 있어 뛰어난 지도력(VERY IMPRESSIVE LEADERSHIP RECORD)를 발휘하였으며, 내년에 대통령 선거가 있게 되는바, 그 후임 대통령은 이에 상응한 지도록 발휘에 큰 노력이 필요할 것임.(DIFFICULTY IN COMPETING WITH PRESIDENT ROH)

- 북한의 핵개발등 한반도에 긴장이 계속되고 있으며, 금번 SCM 에서 주한 미군의 추가 철수가 동결된 것은 이러한 배경에 따른 것임.

- 북한은 미국과의 직접대화 채널을 구축한다는 전략(GAME PLAN)을 고수하고 있으나, 한반도 문제는 우선 남. 북한간에 해결되어야함.

미국이 핵문제등에 관해 미국의 분명한 입장을 전달하기 위하여 미.북한 접촉 수준을 격상하여야 한다는 의견도 있으나, 구체적인 정책결정이 이루어진 바는 없음.

- 최근 BAKER 장관의 FOREIGN AFFAIRS 의 기고문등과 관련, 미국이 한반도에 대하여 독일방식의 2 PLUS 4 회의를 추진한다는 인상을 주었으나, 중국, 한국등이 이에대해 문제점(FIND IT CONSTRAINING)을 가지고 있으므로 미국으로서는 2PLUS 4

미주국	장관	차관	1차보	2차보	미주국	미주국	외정실	분석관
청와대	안기부	국방부	공보처					

PAGE 1

방식보다는 좀더 느슨한(LOOSE) 형태로 이를 추진해야 한다고 봄.

- 한국과 미국은 한반도에 핵무기를 배치하여서는 안된다(THE GOAL OF A DENUCLEARIZED PENINSULA)는데 인식을 같이하고 있음.

- 북한 핵시설에 대한 군사공격설이 언론에 보도되고 있으나 (1) 북한 핵시설은 지하에 건설되는등 포착(LOCATION)이 어렵고, (2) 한반도에서의 전쟁위협등으로 현실적인 대안이 될수 없음.

- 북한은 핵개발로 말미암아 엄청난 정치적 댓가를 지불한다는 것을 이해해야 하는바, 가령 BIDEN 과 같이 진보적인(LIBERAL, AND ANTI-MILITARY) 의원 조차도 북한의 핵개발에 대해 매우 강경한 의견을 가지고 있음.

- 중국은 UN 가입 문제등에서 보듯이 북한에 대해 상당한 경제적, 외교적 영향력을 행사하고 있음.

나. MCDEVITT 제독

- 한반도 안보와 관련 핵문제만이 부각되고 있으나, 한.미 안보관계의 주요 현안은 1) 핵문제 이외에, 2) 한반도 방위의 주된 책임을 한국에 이양하는 문제, 3) 변화하는 전략환경하에서 군사적 억지력을 유지하는 문제, 4) 통일후 주한 미군의 계속 주둔문제 등임.

- 냉전시대의 주한 미군의 역할은 주로 북한의 도발방지였으나, 한반도 통일후에는 탈이념적 분쟁요인(한국에 대한 일본의 위협, 일본에 대한 통일 한국의위협등)을 억제하기 위해 축소된 규모에서 주한 미군의 계속적 주둔이 필요할 것임.

(이에대해 당관 안호영 서기관은 미국의 고위 관리들이 통일후에도 한반도에 미군이 계속 주둔하여야 한다고 공개적으로 발언하는 것은 한국내의 운동권이한.미 관계를 비난하는데 악용할 소지가 있다는 점도 고려되어야 할 것임을 지적함)

다. PLUNK 연구원

- 북한의 핵개발을 방지하는 효과적인 방법은 남한내의 핵무기가 철수된 후에 북한에 대해 상호 핵사찰을 제의하는 것임.

- 이제 미.북한간의 접촉을 격상할 시기가 도래한 것으로 보이는 바, 이는 북한의 고립감을 완화시키는 이외에 미국의 메시지를 북한에 분명히 전달할 수 있는 채널을 제공할 것임.

4. 평가

가. SOLOMON 차관보는 기조연설도중 3 회 이상에 걸쳐 특히 외교문제에 대한

PAGE 2

노대통령의 지도력을 높이 평가한다는 발언을 하였는바, 당관 안서기관이 접촉한 세미나 참석자들은 이점이 인상적이었다고 평가하였으며, 특히 USTR ADAMS 부대표보는 외교문제 이외에 민주화, 사회간접자본 확충문제등에 대한 지도력도 평가할 수 있었으리라고 덧붙였음.

　　나. SOLOMON 차관보는 또한 6 자회의 제의와 관련, 미국으로서는 북한의 핵개발 방지에 대해 역내국가들간에 공동인식이 형성되고 있고, 이를 효과적으로 이용하는 방법으로서 6 자 회의도 가능하다고 보았으나, 중국, 한국등이 이를 적절한 방식으로 보지 않았으므로 보다 느슨한 형태의 협력방안을 모색하고 있다고 함으로써 베이커 장관 동아시아 방문이후의 6 자 회의에 대한 미행정부의 입장을 소상히 밝혔음.

　　다. MCDEVITT 제독은 봉일후에도 주한미군의 계속적 필요성을 강조한바, 이는 11.7. 당지에서 개최된 제 6 차 한. 미 안보연구협의회에서 국방부 안보지원국 CARL FORD 부차관보의 발언과 동일한 것으로서 미국의 책임있는 관리들이 이 문제를 계속 강조하는 것은 주한 미군 문제에 대한 국내운동권의 민감한 반응등을 고려, 한.미간의 다각적 협의가 필요한 사안으로 사료됨. 끝.

　　(대사대리 김봉규-국장)

　　예고: 91.12.31. 일반

PAGE 3

0183

공   란

공   란

9

蘇, '2+4회담,반대입장 시사

外務部 情報狀況室
受信日時 91.12.5. 11:30

(서울=聯合) 소련은 제임스 베이커 美국무장관이 지난달 8일 발간된 미국의 외교전문계간지 '포린 어페어즈' 겨울호에 기고한 글에서 韓半島 통일을 위한 南北韓 美·日·中·蘇 등이 참여하는 이른바 2+4회담을 제의한 것에 대해 기본적으로 반대입장인 것으로 내외통신이 5일 전했다.

이와관련 前소련외무차관이며 現과학원동방학연구소장인 마하일 카피차는 최근 니혼게이자이(日本經濟)신문과의 회견에서 베이커의 구상이 한반도 정세를 올바르게 이해하지 못하고 있는데서 출발한 것이라고 지적하고 이에 반대한다는 뜻을 밝혔다고 북한의 중앙통신이 3일 모스크바발로 보도했다.

카피차는 이어 한반도문제는 독일의 경우와 여러가지 면에서 차이가 있으며 때문에 2+4 방법에 의한 해결은 불가능하다고 강조한 것으로 이 통신은 전했다.(끝)

북한 核개발하면 한국두 핵무장 가능성
日외무성관리, 北 진짜 핵시설 숨길수두

(東京=聯合)吳俊東특파원=일본 외무성의 한 고위 관리는 4일 하우 "여러가지 증거로 볼 때 북한이 원자폭탄을 개발하고 있는 것은 틀림없는 사실"이라고 주장하고 "북한이 원자폭탄을 개발하면 한국두 이에 대항하기 위해 원폭 개발에 착수, 쌍방의 핵무장을 가속화 시킬 공산이 크다"고 말했다.

이 고위관리는 5일부터 빈에서 열리는 국제원자력기구(IAEA)이사회에서 논의될 북한의 핵개발 문제등에 언급하는 가운데 이같이 말하고 특히 "북한은 IAEA의 핵사찰을 받아 들인다 하더라두 이라크처럼 진짜 핵 시설은 숨겨놓고 가짜 핵시설만 사찰시키도록 속이려 들지 모른다"고 강조했다.

그는 또 "미국은 북한이 원자폭탄을 개발한 다음 행동을 억제시키는 것과 개발 전에 그만 두두록 하는 것 중 어느 쪽이 비용등 여러가지 면에서 부담이 큰가를 신중이 검토하고 있다"고 말해 상황 여하에 따라서는 미국이 북한의 핵관련 시설 폭격에 착수할 가능성이 있음을 시사했다.

이 고위 관리는 특히 "미국은 일본 정부에 북한의 핵관련 시설이 존재하고 있음을 부여 주는 두면을 넘겨 줬다"고 밝히고 "미국은 일본이 생각하는 이상으루 북한의 핵개발에 신경을 곤두 세우고 있으며 갖고 있는 정부두 매우 정확하다"고 덧붙였다.(끝)

0186

정 리 보 존 문 서 목 록

기록물종류	일반공문서철	등록번호	2020010125	등록일자	2020-01-21
분류번호	726.64	국가코드	US	보존기간	준영구
명 칭	북한 핵문제 : 미국 의회 동향, 1992. 전3권				
생 산 과	북미1과/북미2과	생산년도	1992~1992	담당그룹	
권 차 명	V.1 1-2월				
내용목차	* 1.14 상원 외교위원회 동아태소위원회, 북한의 핵개발 관련 청문회 개최 2.6 상원 외교위원회 동아태소위원회, 북한의 핵확산과 미국의 정책 청문회 개최 2.26 하원 정보위원회, 북한 핵무기에 관한 비공개 청문회				

0001

원 본

외 무 부

종 별 : 지 급

번 호 : USW-0212

일 시 : 92 0114 1938

수 신 : 장관(미이)미일,정안,정특,기정)사본;국방장관

발 신 : 주 미 대사

제 목 : 상원 외교위 북한 핵확산 관련 청문회

1. 상원 외교위 아태 소위(위원장; ALAN CRANSTON)는 금 1.14(화) 북한의 핵 개발 위협을 중심으로 핵확산에 관한 청문회를 개최, SIG HARRISON 카네기 재단 선임 연구원, WILLIAM TAYLOR CSIS 부소장, PAUL LEVENTHAL 핵통제 연구소(NUCLEAR CONTROL INSTITUTE)소장, WILLIAM HIGINBOTHAM 핵물질 관련 컨설턴트, LAWRENCE SCHEINMAN CORNELL 대학 교수등 학계 인사들로 부터 증언을 청취한바 증언요지 아래 보고함(당관 박흥신 서기관 참석)

가. HARRISON 연구원

- 12.13 남북 불가침 선언및 12.31 남북 비핵화 합의에 따라 북한 핵문제의해결 전망이 밝아졌으나 서면 합의를 실천에 옮기는 것은 쉽지 않을것인바, 북한이 핵 개발을 포기토록 하기 위해서 한. 미 양국은 다음과같이 대북한정책을 전환해 나가야함.

1) 미.북한 외상 회담 제의

검토필(1992. 6. 30.)명

0 미국은 핵문제가 북한과의 관계 정상화 문제와 불가분의 관계에 있음을 인정해야함. 이제 베이커 국무장관이 김영남과 고위급 회담을 갖고 핵문제와 더불어 경제. 정치적 정상화, 재래식 군비 감축, 미군 철수 문제등을 함께 협의할 시기가 도래했다고 보며, 초기 탐색 단계에서는 북한 김용순을 상대로한 차관급 회담도 무방할것임.

0 이러한 미.북한 회담을 통해 북한이 핵 개발 포기시 얻게될 정치.경제적 이득을 확실히 밝혀둘수 있을것이며 이는 남. 북한간의 상호 핵사찰 합의 이행을촉진하게될것임.

2)한국의 독일식 흡수 통일 방식 지양

0 한국이 독일식 흡수 통일 방식을 추구할 의사가 없음을 북한측에 안심시키지

미주국	장관	차관	1차보	2차보	미주국	외정실	외정실	분석관
정와대	총리실	안기부	국방부					

않는한, 북한은 체제 유지를 위한 마지막 보루로서 핵 개발에 대한 유혹을 버리지 못할것임.

0 북한을 안심시키는데 가장 설득력이 있는 방법은 재래식 병력의 상호 감축에 있음. 이는 남한에 비해 재래식 병력의 유지에 훨씬 경제적 부담을 안고 있는 북한의 입장에서 볼때 남한의 높은 수준의 국방비를 유지하는것은 북한에게 이에 상응한 국방비 지출을 강요함으로서 경제 파탄및 체제불안을 초래하기 위한것으로 볼수 있기 때문임.

0 통일 방식에 있어서 남한이 한민족 공동체 대신 두체제의 무기한 공존을 기초로 하는 느슨한 형태의 CONFEDERATION 제도를 추구하는것도 북한의 우려를 던다는 차원에서 생각해 볼수 있을것임.

3)핵우산 제거

0 북한이 핵 개발을 포기토록 하기 위해서는 한국 방위의 기초로서 핵 억지개념을 포기해야하며, 한. 미 양국은 조만간 핵 우산 제거에 합의해야할것임.

0 미국이 한국에서 핵무기 선제 사용 전략을 포기한다 하더라도, 북한의 은밀한 핵개발 및 사용 시도시 미국은 핵무기에 의한 대응 공격(SECOND STRIKE) 능력을 유보하고 있는것임.

나.TAYLOR CSIS 부소장

0 최근 북한이 갑자기 태도변화를 보이고 있는것은 국내 경제 사정의 악화와 무력통일의 비현실성에 대한 지도층의 자각에 그 원인이 있다고 봄. 김일성은고립과 개방이라는 두가지 선택의 기로에서 후자를 택한것으로 보임.

개방을 통해 김일성은 일본과의 경제 협력, 남한기업과의 합작 투자, 대미 직접 교섭및 수교등을 기대하고 있을것임.

0 그러나 북한 지도층은 변화를 추구함에 있어 아래와같은 딜레마에 빠져 있음을 한. 미 양국의 정책 결정자들이 유의해야 할것임.

-북한이 추구하는 근대화에 필수적인 해외 자본과 기술, 경영 방식의 도입이 각종 사회 부패 현상을 초래할것이라는점

-국내 경제 악화로 군사비의 대폭 감축이 불가피한 상황이나 북한은 남한의군사 공격 위협에 대해 병적일만큼 심각한 우려를 갖고 있다는점.

-이러한 우려 때문에 대남 억지력 증강을 위해 핵무기 개발을 추진하였으나, 오히려 이로인해 정치.경제적으로 더큰 고립에 빠지게 되었다는 점.

PAGE 2

0 따라서, 한. 미 양국은 대북한 정책에 있어 아래 요소를 고려할 필요가 있음.

-북한의 고립이나 붕괴를 기도하는것은 위험하며 이보다는 북한의 체제 변화를 유도하되, 국방력과 대화 유지라는 TWO-TRACK 전략이 바람직함. 노 대통령의 북방정책은 이러한 측면에서 성공적이었음. 동구의 경험에서 보듯이 개혁 정책은 일단 시작되면 그자체의 생명력을 갖게되는것임.

-북한은 대외 개방을 통해 현재의 딜레마에서 빠져 나오면서 동시에 이를 통해 개혁을 유보하고자 할지도 모르므로 대북 관계 개선은 신중을 기해야함. 미국과 일본의 대북한 경제 원조는 북한의 IAEA 핵 사찰, 인권 문제등과 단계적으로 연계하여 치밀한 계산하에 추진되어야함.

-남북대화에서 남한이 추구해야할 당면 목표는 북한의 체제 변화를 유도하면서 군사적 긴장완화와 군축을 추진하는것임. 보다 장기적으로는 북한의 기습 공격 가능성을 줄일수 있도록 양측사이에 제한적 배치 지역(LIMITED DEPLOYMENT ZONE)설치를 협상하는것이며, 상설 군사위 설치, 영공 개방 협정등도 검토할 가치가 있음.

다양한 군축 조치는 특히 남한의 이익에 부합됨. 남한측이 일단 군축 문제를 남북 대화의 최우선 목표로 설정하기만 한다면 선택적으로 합의할수 있는 분야는 많다고봄.군축 문제에서 대북한 협상 전략은 구체성(SPECIFICITY), 조건부(CONDITIONALITY), 단계적 추진(PHASING)이라는 3 대 원칙이 기초가 되어야하며,북한도 나름대로 정당한 안보 우려를 갖고 있다는점을 인정해야함. 북한의 타협적 태도를 기대한다면 남한도 타협할 준비가 되어 있어야함. 북한에 진정한 안보 우려가 있다는 사실은 양측이 보다 솔직하게 협상에 임할수 있는 중요한 동기를 제공한다고 봄.

-미국은 대북한 관계 개선의 전제 조건으로 북한의 IAEA 핵 사찰과 국가 테러 포기를 내세우고 있으나, 과거 북한의 테러 행위에 대한 시비는 가리지 말고,일단 두가지 조건이 충족되며, 한. 일 양국과 협의하에 대북한 수교를 추진해야한다고 봄.

다.LEVENTHAL 소장

0 일본의 핵 잠재력은 미국의 한반도 비핵 지대화 노력에 가장 큰 위협 요소가 되고 있음. 일본은 향후 20 년간 100 톤의 플루토늄을 생산 계획으로 있으며 이는 미국의 전체 핵 보유량과 거의 맞먹는 분량임.

0 남북한의 비핵화 합의에도 불구 양측은 공히 선택의 여지를 남겨두고 있는바,

PAGE 3

일본이 핵물질을 계속 축적하고 있는한, 남북한이 무한정 플루토늄 생산을포기할것으로 기대하기는 어려움. 따라서 한반도의 안정을 위해 일본으로 하여금 플루토늄 생산 계획을 중단토록 설득해야할것임.

0 미국은 현재의 차별적인 플루토늄 사용 정책을 종식하고 핵물질에 대한 범세계적 금지 정책으로 전환해야할것임.

라. SCHEINMAN 교수

0 이락의 예를 통해 IAEA 사찰 제도의 헛점이 드러났듯이 동 사찰 제도의 한계를 인정하고 동 한계를 극복하기 위한 추가적 조치를 취해 나가는것이 중요함(IAEA 에 의한 특별 사찰 제도 철저 이행, IAEA 에 핵 시설에 관한 조기 보고제도 채택, 각국의 핵관련 활동에 관한 모든 정보의 IAEA 보고등)

0 미국은 핵 비확산 검증 제도의 강화및 지속성 유지에 지도적 역할을 수행해야하며, IAEA 체제의 강화를 위해 정치적, 정신적 지원은 물론 재정적, 인적 지원및 필요시 정보 지원을 제공해야함. 또한 IAEA 안전 제도의 이행을 돕기 위해 유엔 역활을 강화해야함.

0 브라질-알젠틴의 경우 IAEA 안전제도와 더불어 지역적인 상호 비확산 보장 합의가 효과를 거두었는바, 한반도의 경우에도 남북한간의 CBM 및 상호 사찰등을 포함 핵 비확산 합의를 권장해 나갈 필요가 있음.

2. 질의 응답 요지(CRANSTON 위원장 단독 질의)

0 (북한의 플루토늄 재처리 시설이 식별키 어려울만큼 낮은 수준으로 가동될 가능성에 대해)

처리 시설이 은밀하게 위치하고 핵물질(FEED SOURCES)이 외부로부터 반입되지 않을경우 식별되지 않을 가능성이 있으나, 핵물질이 외부로부터 반입될 경우에는 쉽게 식별이 가능함(HIGINGOTHAM)

0 (북한이 안전 협정 서명후 비밀리에 핵물질을 수출할 가능성에 대해)

안전 협정 서명국은 핵물질 이전시 IAEA 에 보고토록 되어 있으나 핵 물질의 INVENTORY 를 숨길경우 이를 식별하기 어려움(HIGINBOTHAM)

0 (남북한간의 핵 관련 합의가 북한의 핵 개발 포기를 의미하는지에 대해)

북한이 최근 IAEA 의 사찰에 응하였으나, IAEA 사찰팀과 함께, 한. 미 합동사찰팀의 사찰을 허용할지는 분명치 않으며, 기존 시설의 해체를 약속하지도 않았음(SCHEINMAN)

PAGE 4

O (북한 경제 상황)

- 북한은 현재 식량 부족 및 분배 체재의 취약등으로 80 년대 중반 소련이 겪은것과 유사한 어려움을 겪고 있음(TAYLOR)

-북한은 주 공급원이던 소련의 원조를 더이상 받지 못하고 있으며, 소련의 붕괴로 인해 교훈을 얻고 있음(HARRISON)

O (북한의 생화학 무기 능력 관련)

TAYLOR 는 북한이 생화학 무기를 보유하고 있다는 증거가 있으며, 동 무기를 단거리 미사일에 장착할수 있는 능력을 조만간 갖추게 될것이라는 보도가 있음.

3. 관찰밀 평가

O 미 의회가 휴회중임에도 불구, 금번 청문회가 개최된것은 북한의 핵개발 위협에 관한 미 의회의 깊은 우려와 관심을 반영함.

O 증언자들은 최근 남북한간의 불가침 교류 협력합의 및 핵관련 합의에 대해 일반적으로 긍정적으로 평가하면서도 북한의 핵 개발 포기 여부에 대해서는 회의적인 시각을 보였는바, HARISON 카네기 재단 연구원이 북한의 핵 개발 포기를 보장하기 위해 미.북한 외상 회담 및 핵 우산 제거를 제의한것은 여하한 경우에도 북한의 핵 개발을 방지해야한다는 일부 미측의 우려를 대변하고 있는것으로보임.

O KESSLER 상원 외교위 전문위원에 의하면 상원 아태 소위는 미.북한 고위급 회담 이후 행정부 인사를 초치한 가운데 북한 핵관련 청문회를 재개 예정이라는바, 동 청문회 개최시 추보 예정임.

(대사 현홍주-국장)

첨부; USW(F)-0239

92.12.31 까지

주 미 대 사 관

USW(F) : 0239   년월일 : 920114   시간 : 19:05

수 신 : 장 관 (미이.미일.정안.정특.기정)

발 신 : 주미대사

제 목 : 첨부 (상원외교 청문회 증언문 1매) 출처 : (   )

보 안 통 제

(0239 - 51 - 1)

외신 1과
동 제

0007

NORTH KOREA AND NUCLEAR WEAPONS:

NEXT STEPS IN AMERICAN POLICY

Selig S. Harrison

Senior Associate
Carnegie Endowment for International Peace

**Testimony Prepared for a Hearing of the Subcommittee on East Asian
and Pacific Affairs, Committee on Foreign Relations, U.S. Senate,
January 14, 1992.**

0239 — 51 ~ 2

0008

2

Mr. Chairman, thank you for the invitation to testify here today.

My testimony is based on study of North and South Korea dating back to 1968, including visits to the North in May, 1972, and October, 1987; intensive coverage of the South during my tenure as Northeast Asia Bureau Chief of The Washington Post from 1968 to 1972, and frequent visits to the South thereafter as a Senior Associate of the Carnegie Endowment for International Peace since 1974.

I have analyzed U.S. policy in Korea in my books The Widening Gulf: Asian Nationalism and American Policy (The Free Press, 1978) and Dialogue With North Korea (Carnegie Endowment, 1990); in five books to which I have contributed, The Security of Korea (Westview, 1980); United States-Japan Relations and the Security of East Asia (Westview, 1978); Korea 1991: The Road to Peace (Westview, 1991); Korean Challenges and American Policy (forth coming, Paragon, 1992) and the Korean-American Alliance (forthcoming, Cato, 1992); two Foreign Policy articles, "One Korea?" (1975) and "Dateline Korea: A Seoul Divided" (1987); and a recent article in World Policy Journal, "A Chance for Detente in Korea" (Fall, 1991).

The opportunity for the reduction of tensions in Korea and the resolution of the nuclear controversy with the North is more promising than ever before in the wake of the North-South non-aggression declaration signed on December 13 in Seoul and the December 31 North-South nuclear free zone agreement. But

0239 —5/-3

0009

3

translating this progress on paper into concrete progress will not
be easy. Pyongyang can be persuaded to give up its nuclear option,
in my view, but only if the United States and South Korea make
three basic changes in their policies toward the North.

First, the United States should recognize that the nuclear
issue is inseparable from the broader problem of normalizing its
relations with the Kim Il Sung regime. The time has come for a
high-level dialogue between Secretary of State James Baker and
North Korean Foreign Minister Kim Yong Nam in which this issue is
discussed side by side with economic and political normalization,
conventional arms control and the withdrawal of U.S. forces.

While exploratory talks could appropriately be held at the
level of the Undersecretary for Political Affairs and a North
Korean of comparable stature, such as Kim Yong Sun, Secretary of
the Central Committee of the Workers Party in charge of its
International Department, definitive agreements would require the
participation of Kim Yong Nam, who is a member of the Workers Party
Politburo.

Such a multi-track dialogue would enable Washington to spell
out clearly the economic and political benefits that the North
could expect if it agrees to abandon its nuclear weapons program
once and for all. It would also provide an opportunity to reinforce
the North-South dialogue on nuclear inspections with a bilateral
exchange on this issue. In the absence of such a direct exchange
with the United States concerning the inspection of U.S. bases in
the South, it is unlikely that a North-South inspection agreement

0239 —51-4

0010

4

will be consummated.

The nuclear-free zone agreement initiated on December 31
stipulates that a Joint Nuclear Control Committee is to hold its
first meeting within 30 days after the agreement is formally signed
on February 19. When the Nuclear Control Committee meets on or
before March 19, the South will seek acceptance of its December 14
proposal for mutual "pilot" inspections that would include the
North's suspected reprocessing plant and U.S. bases where nuclear
weapons have been stored. So far, the North has not replied to this
proposal.

Second, the South should recognize that the nuclear issue is
not likely to be definitively settled in the absence of meaningful
and continuing steps to reassure Pyongyang that it is not seeking
a German-style unification-by-absorption. The nuclear option is
attractive to the ruling elite in the North above all as a "last
card" to guarantee the survival of the regime.

The most convincing form of reassurance would be provided by
serious movement toward the mutual reduction of conventional
forces. Why is this so? Because the North spends five times more of
its GNP on defense than the South does and is thus unable to
develop its consumer industries. In Pyongyang's perspective, Seoul
hopes to destabilize the Communist system by sustaining high levels
of defense spending that the North can only continue to match at
the cost of further undermining its economy.

In its unification posture, the South could also do much to
allay the North's anxieties by seeking a loose confederation based

0239-51-5

0011

5

explicitly on the indefinite co-existence of two separate systems,
in place of scenarios such as President Roh's "Korean Commonwealth"
that accept co-existence in the opening stages but envisage
eventual elections in which the South would dominate by virtue of
its larger population.

Third, both Washington and Seoul should recognize that equity
is the key to settling the nuclear issue. If they expect the North
to surrender its nuclear option, they must be prepared to give up
the concept of nuclear deterrence as the basis for the South's
defense. In this concept, the U.S. threatens the first use of
nuclear weapons if the North attacks the South with its
conventional forces.

At present, while removing its nuclear weapons from the South,
the U.S. continues to deploy nuclear missiles in its Pacific
submarine fleet and has not ruled out their use in any new Korean
conflict. For this reason, Pyongyang has repeatedly called not only
for the removal of U.S. nuclear weapons from the peninsula but also
for lifting the U.S. nuclear umbrella as part of a multilateral
agreement on a nuclear-free zone.

The U.S. is saying to the North, in effect, "you give up your
nuclear option, but we will keep ours in order to make our security
commitment to the South credible." In my view, it will be difficult
to obtain airtight and durable inspection access to the North
unless the U.S. gives up its nuclear first use strategy in Korea.
This would still leave the U.S. with a nuclear second-strike
capability that could be used against the North if it develops

0239 - 51 - 6

0012

6

nuclear weapons secretly and seeks to use them.

The Nuclear Umbrella

It is not correct, as some observers argue, that the North
would be escalating its demands if it should renew its demands for
removal of the nuclear umbrella. In its formal presentation at the
review conference on the Nuclear Non-Proliferation Treaty in
August, 1990, Pyongyang made its acceptance of International Atomic
Energy Agency inspections conditional on an "agreement to assure
the Democratic People's Republic of Korea against the use or threat
of use of nuclear weapons" as well as on the removal of U.S.
nuclear weapons from the peninsula. More recently, last July,
reaffirming its proposal for a North-South nuclear free zone
agreement, it stipulated that such an agreement would have to be
guaranteed by the United States, the Soviet Union and China in
order to be effective.

The United States and South Korea have so far ignored the
demand for lifting the nuclear umbrella. They argue that the North
should give up its nuclear option in return for the removal of U.S.
nuclear weapons from Korean territory. Until recently, Washington
and Seoul focused on getting the North to sign an agreement
permitting I.A.E.A. inspections, which it is legally obliged to do
as a signatory to the N.P.T. Even if the North were to sign and
implement an I.A.E.A. inspection agreement, however, fears of its
nuclear ambitions would persist. This is because I.A.E.A.
safeguards would permit continued stockpiling of weapons-grade

0239 -51-7

7

plutonium so long as the material remained open to inspection. Precisely for this reason, the proposal for mutual inspections put forward by the South on December 14 with American encouragement and guidance was designed to get access to the North's suspected reprocessing plant in addition to the Yongbyon reactor as the quid pro quo for permitting the North to inspect the Kunsan Air Base and other U.S. bases in the South where nuclear weapons have been stored.

Hopefully, the North will make a conciliatory response to the South's December 14 proposal for "pilot" inspections when the Joint Nuclear Control Committee meets in March. But a definitive response is not likely. In order to get the North to give up its nuclear option completely and accept an airtight inspection system, Washington and Seoul would sooner or later have to agree to the removal of the nuclear umbrella. This would require negotiating some form of comprehensive nuclear-free zone agreement under which the United States, the Soviet Union, China, the North, and the South would pledge not to use nuclear weapons against either of the two Korean states nor to deploy them on the peninsula.

The United States has understandably objected to the North's proposals for a unilateral American no-use pledge, pointing out that Pyongyang's two military allies, Moscow and Beijing, both have nuclear arsenals. But a multilateral nuclear-free zone agreement would be desirable for the U.S. and South Korea if it could be used to draw Pyongyang into more meaningful verification machinery than the I.A.E.A. safeguards. This would not necessarily require a

0239 -51-8

0014

8

separate agreement but might take the form of American, Chinese and
Soviet endorsements of a North-South nuclear-free zone agreement.

Conventional Force Reductions

Now as in the past, the issue of conventional force
reductions is likely to be a pivotal issue in the North-South peace
process. It should be remembered that in May, 1972, as in December,
1991, the North and South agreed to establish operational
committees to deal with military, economic and cultural issues. But
an impasse quickly developed in the military committee over force
reductions. The North blamed this for the collapse of the North-
South Coordinating Committee, though there were clearly other
factors also involved.

In its formal negotiating posture, the South accepts the goal
of force reductions. Former Prime Minister Kang Young-Hoon,
presenting a five-point arms control formula at the first round of
talks between the Prime Ministers of North and South in September,
1990, specifically referred to "arms and force reductions based on
the principle of parity, with the superior side reducing its arms
and troops to the level of the inferior side." However, he refused
to put reductions on the negotiating agenda, declaring that this
issue should "be pursued only after political and military
confidence-building and a declaration of non-aggression have been
realized."

0239 -51-1

0015

9

Kang's insistence on the principle of parity contrasted with the North's concept of equal reductions by stages and reflected the South's belief that the North is the "superior side," with more than a million men under arms, as against its own figure of 650,000. The North, for its part, claims that its armed forces number 450,000. Thus, the first step in any force reduction process should be an attempt to agree on the facts concerning the military balance. As arms control experience in Europe has shown, such an effort would be difficult and should, therefore, be accompanied by confidence-building measures, mutual pullbacks of forward-deployed forces and reductions in offensive equipment. Nevertheless, a serious proposal for large-scale force reductions by the South would in itself be a basic 'confidence building measure' in the eyes of the North, and is a prerequisite for overall progress in reducing North-South tensions.

The Debate on Force Reductions

Is Seoul ready for serious movement toward force reductions? Entrenched vested interests in the South, centered in the armed forces and a politically powerful military-industrial complex, have so far resisted a positive response to the North's force reduction proposals. To be sure, there is also a military-industrial complex in the North, allied with hard-liners in the ruling Workers Party. Force reductions are not popular with this hard-line faction in Pyongyang. In the case of the North, however, economic factors have made such reductions imperative and have tipped the scales in the

0016

10

intra-party debate. By contrast, since the South spends so much less of its GNP on defense, the pressures for reductions are not as great as in the North. The South's rapid economic growth has enabled successive regimes to avoid increasing the proportion of GNP allocated to defense while, at the same time, steadily raising the actual level of defense expenditures. Another factor making force reductions less urgent than in the North is the economic subsidy provided by the American military presence. It should be emphasized, however, that the middle and low-income majority of the populace in the South would benefit greatly from the diversion of resources now going into military spending to civilian welfare needs.

Professor Lee Chang of Seoul National University has pointed to the urgent need for increased expenditures on health, welfare and social security, comparing what South Korea spends on these programs (2.6 percent of GNP) with comparable outlays in Sweden (33.3 percent), the United States (13.8 percent), and Japan (12 percent). Less than 2 percent of the elderly receive any form of social security. According to Lee, the government spends only $390 million per year on all forms of welfare and would have to spend $1.3 billion "for every citizen to have a minimally adequate income" (defined as $32 per month). He estimates that there are 4.3 million "poor and near poor" people earning less than $64 per month. ("Setting National Priorities: Welfare vs. Defense, Korean Social Science Journal, Vol. 16, 1990, pp. 27-47.)

Until recently, some observers argued that the South, with a

0239 -51-11

0017

11

labor surplus, would find it more difficult to reduce its armed forces than the North, which has long had a labor shortage, especially in its critical mining sector. But to some extent, changing life-styles in the South have now blurred this contrast. The major opposition to reductions in the South now appears to come not from government technocrats concerned about their economic impact but mainly from defense contractors whose profits would be reduced and from a bloated military elite fearful of losing jobs and perquisites.

With South Korean workers shifting from blue collar to white collar jobs, the government reported a shortage of 190,000 workers in key manufacturing industries in 1990. To deal with the problem, it has offered to permit up to 15,000 members of the armed forces to fulfil their 18-month requirement of military service by working five years in specified industries. Many industrialists anxious to contain rising wages would welcome a larger labor pool resulting from large-scale force reductions. But significant movement toward force reductions would undoubtedly require a sweeping reappraisal of government economic planning to forestall dislocations.

The economic impact is only one of the objections put forward by opponents of force reductions. Jong Youl Yoo, Director of Ideology Studies at the Institute of National Policy Studies of the Democratic Liberal Party, offered a variety of arguments against the idea of such reductions on November 8 at a conference on Korean security in Washington under the chairmanship of retired General Richard Stilwell, former commander of U.S. Forces in Korea.

0238 -51 -12

0018

12

"Military industries would go bankrupt because of the sudden cut of their production," Yoo contended. "The bankruptcy of military industries would detonate a chain of bankruptcy disrupting the established socio-economic order in both North and South Korea."

Calling for a freeze on existing force levels and limitations on future increases in place of reductions, Yoo argued that this approach is "necessary for Korean arms control since post-unification Korean security should be considered vis-a-vis a militarily strong Japan and China. We do not want to cut our military might so deeply that we could not effectively counter external threats to our national security." Japan, in particular, he warned, is "becoming a military giant." The purpose of arms control, he said, should be the reduction of North-South tensions, and this can be accomplished through the "freeze and limitation" approach.

In deciding its policy on force reductions, South Korea must first make a judgement concerning whether a German-style unification-by-absorption would be desirable, apart from the larger question of whether it is possible.

Comparing the German and Korean cases, it is clear that the costs of absorbing the North could wreck the South economically. The burden of reunification has already been staggering for Bonn, which is spending $55 billion to rebuild EASt Germany in 1991 alone, one-quarter of its total budget. Yet as a Lucky-Goldstar study has pointedly observed, "the relative costs of unification are likely to be much heavier for South Korea than they were for

0239 — 51 — 13

0019

13

West Germany. This prediction is based on a comparison of demographic factors and per-capita income in the two cases. East Germany, the study pointed out, has a population and a per-capita gross development product (GDP) that is one-fourth as large as West Germany's. North Korea, by contrast, with a population half that of the South, has a per-capita GDP only one-fifth as large. (Lee Woo Sik, "The Path Toward a Unified Korean Economy," a monograph prepared for a symposium on "The Comparative Analysis of German Reunification and the German Case," sponsored by the International Cultural Society of Korea, Seoul, November 5, 1990, p.5).

Despite these forebodings, the Lucky-Goldstar study concluded on a relatively sanguine note. Its author expressed confidence that the South could handle the "inevitable" responsibilities of reunification if it prepared adequately by stepping up its growth and savings rates. The only thing to worry about, the study suggested, is that a crisis might develop before Seoul is ready. President Roh has also voiced a similar concern, declaring on July 3, 1991, that "our people do not want accelerated unification."

In the foreseeable future, the possibility of a collapse in the North appears to be marginal. To the extent that it exists, it arises from two factors: a crushing defense burden that breeds economic unrest and the dangers of factionalism following Kim Il Sung's death. For the South, therefore, the best way to avert a repetition of the German experience would be to do business with Kim Il Sung by pursuing large-scale mutual force reductions and a loose confederation.

0237 -51 -14

0020

PREPARED STATEMENT BY DR. WILLIAM J. TAYLOR, JR.
VICE PRESIDENT, INTERNATIONAL SECURITY PROGRAMS

THE CENTER FOR STRATEGIC AND INTERNATIONAL STUDIES
WASHINGTON, D.C.

BEFORE THE SENATE COMMITTEE ON FOREIGN RELATIONS

SUBCOMMITTEE ON EAST ASIAN AND PACIFIC AFFAIRS

JANUARY 14, 1991

0239 -51.-15

0021

TRENDS IN NORTH KOREAN BEHAVIOR;
IMPLICATIONS FOR U.S. POLICY

Mr. Chairman; members of the subcommittee; it is a distinct
privilege to be here to contribute to your important
deliberations concerning an international security issue of vital
importance -- North Korea's march toward acquiring nuclear
weapons, its recent apparent willingness to accept IAEA
inspections and to enter a conference dialogue on nuclear
weapons, and U.S. policy alternatives to keep the North on this
positive track. Let me begin with a few general observations
about North Korean foreign policy behavior.

Since World War II and the division of the Korean Peninsula,
the behavior of the Democratic Peoples Republic of Korea (DPRK)
is best characterized as erratic and periodically violent.
Erratic behavior has been seen repeatedly, for example, in the
on-again, off-again DPRK approaches to North-South dialogue,
reunification, arms control and nuclear inspections by the
International Atomic Energy Agency (IAEA). Periodic violence has
manifested itself in the June 25, 1950 invasion which started the
Korean War; in military incidents along the DMZ such as the 1976
axe murders; in the 1983 Rangoon bombing which practically wiped
out South Korea's leadership; in the 1968 and 1974 assassination
attempts against President Park Chung Hee; and in the 1987
bombing of KAL flight number 858, killing more than 100 people.

But there is no denying that there have been important, if
not yet fundamental, changes in the behavior of the DPRK over the

2

0239 -51.-16

past two years. Let's catalogue them perhaps in ascending order
of importance. First, there have been agreements to participate
in united Korean sports teams, and to send the DPRK soccer team
to Washington, D.C. to compete against the U.S. team. In both
cases they risk the ideological "pollution" of their coaches and
athletes. Second, the DPRK entered a direct barter deal with the
Republic of Korea (ROK) to trade coal and cement for rice, an act
which is not only another sign of food shortages in the North,
but also a chink in the armor of "Juche," the DPRK philosophy of
"self-reliance." Third, a rapidly-increasing number of foreign
scholars and retired officials have been invited to North Korea.
This includes last year's visit by a group of retired U.S.
military officers and academics led by General Stilwell and four
scholars from The Center for Strategic and International Studies
(CSIS); three in late October and I, alone, in mid-November 1991.
This may be a relatively significant signal that the DPRK is
trying to move up the learning curve concerning U.S. policy and
polity. It is hard to believe that anyone in the DPRK government
would believe that they could propagandize the Stilwell-Group or
a CSIS political-military scholar who has published many pieces
critical of North Korean behavior. Fourth, in a total reversal
of policy, the DPRK accepted dual, simultaneous entry into the
United Nations. President Kim Il Sung has delivered public
speeches as late as mid-1990 saying that the DPRK would never
accept U.N. entry with separate seats for North and South Korea.
Fifth, despite some earlier cancellations based on the U.S.-ROK

3

0231 - 51 -17

"Team Spirit" military exercises, the DPRK has conducted five
ministerial meetings with the South in both Pyongyang and Seoul,
with a sixth scheduled for February 19, 1992. Sixth, the DPRK
has accepted de facto the legitimacy of the South by concluding
with the ROK last month an agreement of reconciliation, non-
aggression, cooperation and exchange. Seventh, the DPRK has
pledged to sign the IAEA accords soon, permitting inspections of
its nuclear facilities. Eighth, last week the DPRK agreed with
the United States to participate in a historic nuclear weapons
conference to be held in the next few days, perhaps in New York.
Change in North Korean behavior is coming with lightning-like
speed. Why?

Plausible Explanations of Change

The reasons for North Korea's new flexibility become clear
when we look at its economic situation. The North's economy
appears to be in dire straits. Per capita GNP is barely $1,000,
one-fifth as great as in the South. North Korean economic growth
ran at only two to three percent during the late 1980s and by
1989 had apparently shifted into reverse, with the economy
contracting by nearly six percent in that year according to
recent figures from Seoul's Korean Development Institute (KDI).
Like most socialist countries, the North also labors under heavy
foreign debt: nearly $3 billion total, half of which is owed to
Russia.

There are widespread reports of regional food shortages;

4

0239 - 51 -18

outside the elite class in the North (which may account for as
much as 25 percent of the population), many North Koreans may get
meat only once or twice a year. Even basic staples reportedly
are in short supply. South Korean experts on the North have
reported that 1990 was a disastrous year for the North's rice
harvest, with agricultural production plummeting 30 percent in
one year. The North was forced to use scarce foreign currency to
purchase hundreds of thousands of tons of rice from Thailand.
Lack of motivation and a shortage of fuel and tires partly
account for the drop in food availability; defectors report that
cattle are increasingly used in farming in the North. These are
generally accepted perspectives on the food situation in the
North. I caveat them only by saying that in my travels in
Pyongyang, Kaesong, to the DMZ, and east about 30 km toward
Wonson, the people I saw did not appear malnourished or ill. But
my observations were geographically limited.

Meanwhile, military leaders in the North must know that they
no longer possess a viable military option for unification. The
U.S. commitment to the South remains strong, which in itself
might cause the North to abandon any thoughts of an attack. But
now the North has lost one potential sponsor and ally in such a
war (the former Soviet Union). Its remaining ally (China) is
intent on economic development and peaceful relations with the
West, and would have no interest in supporting the North in a war
on the Peninsula. Any rational leader in Pyongyang must know
that, whatever option the North chooses to escape from its

5

economic and social malaise, it cannot be a military one.

In my view, this situation confronts Kim Il Sung with a fundamental choice: whether to maintain the North's isolation from the world community and court economic disaster, or whether to open up to outside trade and investments and hope that he can maintain control. Based on existing research and my recent personal observations and discussions in Pyongyang, I believe Kim Il Sung and his officials have made the second choice. The primary evidence for this is in the stunning way in which by Pyongyang has reversed long-standing positions as stated above, in order to promote improved relations with the South and the United States.

What does Kim expect to obtain by opening up? First and foremost, a closer economic relationship with Japan, who has promised billions in reparation payments for its World War II-era occupation and has expressed interest in investing in the North. The Japanese are currently, however, holding off pending resolution of the DPRK nuclear weapons issue. Second, Kim also believes that joint ventures with South Korean companies can provide jobs for his people and profits in convertible currencies for his government. Finally, an opening would allow Kim to achieve a long-standing goal: direct negotiations and improved diplomatic relations with the United States.

Change and Risk for the DPRK

There can be no doubt that Kim Il Sung, his son Kim Jong Il

6

0219 - 51 - 20

0026

and other senior government leaders view change with great
apprehension. There are many reasons for this, the most
important of which hinges on the prevailing juche ideology; let
me explain. Juche is not Marxism-Leninism writ large, and it is
not Stalinism. A variant of Marxism-Leninism, it is a "corporate
philosophy" which has produced a totalitarian political system
ruled by the "enlightened despot" who created it. Basically, the
"corporate philosophy" is that individuals, like the cells of a
living organism, have meaning only as parts of the organic whole
-- the state. It is the ruler of the state who has unlimited
authority to decide what is best for the state. This is
totalitarianism pure and simple. But, given years of propaganda,
Kim Il Sung probably is perceived by his people as the northern
hero in the struggle against the brutal Japanese occupation of
1910-1945; as the great defender who stopped U.S.-ROK aggression
during the Korean war; and as the strong, but benevolent leader
who, against all the odds, has led a successful struggle to
protect the nation against the forces of imperialism. The Kim Il
Sung "epic political myth" has been building since the 1920s and
has been thoroughly developed over the past 46 years since World
War II. Epic myths have often been the political dynamic of
various cultures and their force, perpetuated through political
symbolism, is not to be dismissed lightly. In the case of the
DPRK, which for years has almost hermetically sealed off its
society, the Kim Il Sung myth and the juche philosophy of self-
reliance has been thoroughly propagated among the people. The

7

0239 -51-21

political power of President Kim and his son is based on juche, the idea that Kim Il Sung in his benevolence knows what is best and can provide what is best for his people.

Although we deplore it, it is not difficult for me to believe that Kim Il Sung believes deeply that he knows best how to protect the interests of his people and that he is ultimately responsible for their collective welfare as he sees it. No challenge to his wisdom and authority can be permitted. His symbol is everywhere -- on the red pin with his picture worn by everyone; on billboards at main intersections; in films proclaiming his greatness and his political, social, and economic exploits, and in messages which are blared everywhere -- often from loudspeakers atop vehicles moving around cities and towns (in Pyongyang, one does not need a wakeup call; the loudspeakers start early).

Juche is a seamless cultural, social and political web. Significant breaks in the strands could cause the web to snap apart. My conversations with North Korean officials and researchers lead me to believe that they know this. And they know now, if they did not before, that they are in desperate economic straits. They are fully aware of the demise of most communist governments, but they believe, for example, that the Soviet Union fell apart because of foreign imperialist influences and pressures, not because the communist system is fundamentally flawed.

During my November trip to North Korea, I often heard about

8

0239 -51-22

0028

Kim Il Sung's strong desire to modernize his country, but also about his fears that the necessary tools of modernization -- infusions of foreign capital, technology and management expertise -- bring with them all kinds of corrupting social influences. Officials deny that the DPRK has the corruption which typifies imperialist models of rapid economic modernization, such as crime, drugs, prostitution and environmental degradation. They say that The Great Leader is dedicated to "metered" economic reform which he, and when the succession comes, his son can control. Obviously, this presents a dilemma for the two Kims, and one that U.S. and ROK policymakers need to ponder.

A second risk for the DPRK arises in the clear need to dramatically reduce defense spending (perhaps now at 23 percent of GNP) at a time when their economic growth rate probably is negative 2 percent. Yet, the North has been near paranoia about the threat of military aggression and subversion from the South. It has been typical for them to cut off all dialogue with South Korea and the United States when the annual Team Spirit exercises have been held. They express fear that the increased readiness and reinforcements involved could turn into an attack north at any time. Of the five invitations I have had to visit North Korea, two have been cancelled at the last minute because Team Spirit was about to begin (two other invitations were cancelled, as DPRK Ambassador Ho Jong told me, because his government was upset by some of my publications). The continuing perceived military threat, combined with the necessity to reduce defense

9

0239 -51-23

spending, presents another dilemma for the Kims.

There are many explanations offered for the oft-reported North Korean decision to develop nuclear weapons. Selig Harrison who is testifying today, can explain all of them. Others far more expert than I will testify about the extent and pace of DPRK nuclear development. But I find it persuasive that the DPRK leadership long ago became paranoid about the reported presence of U.S. nuclear weapons in South Korea, concluded that their best deterrent against an attack from the South resided in a credible threat to retaliate with nuclear weapons, and believe that nations acquire international prestige and leverage by the possession of weapons of mass destruction, to include chemical and biological weapons (which should remind us that there is much more at stake in our policy toward North Korean than stopping their nuclear weapons program).

Progress toward nuclear weapons has created for the DPRK leadership a third dilemma. They have long believed in the imminence of the ROK-U.S. military threat, and believe that their conventional and unconventional military deterrent must be augmented by a nuclear capability. But as the evidence of their march toward a nuclear weapons capability has mounted, they have incurred the serious and increasing concern of major international actors who believe that the DPRK will soon acquire at least crude nuclear weapons, which might be used intentionally or through miscalculation in a time of crisis. And this international concern, among other factors, has led to the

10

0239 -51-24

0030

increasing isolation of the North both politically and, more important, economically, with increasing talk about multilateral economic embargoes. The DPRK leadership worries also about reports that some foreign officials, especially ROK Defense Minister Lee Dong Bok (who has recently been replaced), have been considering preemptive military strikes against the North's nuclear facilities. But both Kim Hyong U, a deputy to the Korean Peoples Assembly and Major General Kim Young Chul, senior military spokesmen to the ministerial talks, told me explicitly that such attacks, whatever the source, would mean the start of a second Korean war. If this situation has not presented the DPRK with a real "dilemma," it certainly has presented their leaders with some heavy requirements for cost-benefit analysis in regard to nuclear weapons development.

Clearly, if the DPRK follows through with the changes of the past year, concludes all the agreements it has pledged (and honors them), it will be incurring some serious potential risks to the solidarity of its prevailing political system.

U.S./ROK Policy Toward North Korea

Much of what I have to say here is drawn directly from the conclusions of an important conference held under the auspices of CSIS and the Korean Institute for Defense Analyses and the resulting publication, Korea 1991: The Road to Peace. No matter how one looks at it, ROK and U.S. policies toward North Korea over the past few years have so far been a stunning success. The

11

0219 -51-25

speed of change in DPRK policies toward the South and the United States is almost breathtaking. President Roh's Northern policy has been a stunning success. President Bush's declaratory nuclear policy of September 1991 was a brilliant stroke in relation to the Korean Peninsula. One could cite many other aspects of U.S./ROK policies which deserve high praise. We have coordinated our policies well, keeping our repeated pledge not to get out in front of our South Korean allies. But where do we go from here?

First, we should continue to promote inter-Korean dialogue. The basic objective of inter-Korean dialogue is tension reduction and confidence-building, leading ultimately to national unification. Unification, of course, will take time -- some say a generation. I disagree, given the accelerating factors of change. How about 3-5 years? Reunification can take many forms, including South Korea's "Korean Commonwealth" proposal, which envisages elections at the final stage, and some variant of the North's "confederation" plan, which calls for the retention of both present Korean governments as partially sovereign states under a central authority, purportedly leaving the existing political or economic systems intact.

Any process of unification, however, will contain a transition period of expanding North-South ties and political, military, and economic confidence-building. Even North Korea's various proposals, which display expectations of rapid change, envisage mutual arms and force reductions and military confidence

12

0239 -51-26

0032

building as the South does. Such a transition period could be
relatively brief but will hold risks of instability as well as
opportunities for enhancing security on the Korean Peninsula.

One possible response to the current situation would be to
use accords achieved in a "transition period" as a delaying
tactic and await the demise of the North Korean regime. Despite
the economic problems stated above, it is not yet clear whether
or how the regime in Pyongyang will respond -- by attempting to
muddle through, by selecting the military option or clamping down
even more tightly on its people, or by pursuing meaningful
detente and an opening to the outside world. None of these
approaches is likely to solve North Korea's problems in the short
term. And another crisis may loom in the form of the succession
to Kim Il-sung.

One of the primary goals of South Korean and U.S. policy, of
course, is to encourage change in the North Korean system. If
such change were to come rapidly - and peacefully - it might be
all to the good. Attempts to isolate North Korea and await its
sudden collapse, however, would be risky. Conditions for smooth
transitions, which exist to a limited extent in Eastern Europe,
do not now exist in North Korea. Convulsions in the North would
carry risks of armed conflict. Moreover, South Korea would face
real difficulties and exorbitant financial costs in "absorbing"
the North, playing the role of West Germany to Pyongyang's East,
under any circumstances. The present ROK leadership understands
this. If the North were to collapse quickly, it would exacerbate

13

0235-51-27

the problem. Although metered pressure on the North should be maintained, a policy of further isolation it could lessen the prospect for gradual, rather than catastrophic, change.

Rather than isolation, the basic policy for the transition period ought to be one of defense and dialogue. The overriding objective of the U.S.- ROK relationship will remain deterrence of northern aggression, and for this reason the South and the United States must maintain a strong defense. In a time of enormous uncertainty and pressure on the North, with the dangerous prospect of an unstable transition of power looming on the horizon, South Korea and the United States must follow prudent policies. The elements of prudence include continued military preparedness by the South, supported by a continued U.S. security commitment and a militarily significant troop presence during the transition.

There are political risks inherent in a policy of concurrent efforts at both defense and dialogue. The two might not always be in harmony; measures designed to bolster military security might be treated by the North as barriers to negotiations. Washington and Seoul must explain this "two-track" policy carefully to their respective publics and, in doing so, can point to the success of similar tactics in Western negotiations with the Soviet Union. In the end, there is no real alternative to a policy that combines vigilance with a willingness to seek tension reduction. What must be recognized, however, is that South Korea and the United States can afford to signal flexibility on a few

14

0237-51-28

0034

non-central defense issues for the purpose of dialogue.

To fulfill the dialogue half of the two-track policy, South Korea's northern policy has focused on securing diplomatic recognition for the South from current or former Communist governments, but also includes engagement with North Korea. Since July 1988, South Korean President Roh has proposed various cooperative measures, beginning with a six-point "policy on reunification" to encourage trade, cultural, and scientific exchanges, and other contacts between the two Koreas. He also pledged to help the North develop its relations with the United States and Japan. President Roh and his government subsequently declared that the North is not an adversary; have argued that North Korea ought to be drawn into the world community, not isolated; have declared that here are no nuclear weapons in South Korea; have offered to establish a non-aggression agreement; have offered to agree to a nuclear free Korea, and more.

Roh's northern policy deserves praise and encouragement. Through selective agreements and contracts, improved North-South ties can continue the process of change that Pyongyang will be powerless to stop. The primary lesson of the East European experience with reform, and of the Soviet one as well, is that reform once begun assumes a life of its own.

Expanded contacts have the potential to allow Seoul and Washington to keep diplomatic fingers on the pulse of official and, to some extent, public (or at least elite) opinion in the North; at a time of extreme tension for the North, the value of

15

such contacts should not be underestimated. Moreover, a Mao-like
nod to reform by Kim Il-sung may provide a necessary basis for
stable change occurring both before and after he passes from the
scene.

Of course, lines of contact with North Korea must be
established very carefully. We should emphasize those areas of
cooperation calculated to promote change in the North Korean
system, to pry open its hermetically sealed economic, military,
economic, and cultural realms. Pyongyang is undoubtedly groping
for ways out of its dilemmas that would render any reform
unnecessary; we must seek to deny it such a course. For this
reason among others, an immediate rapprochement with North Korea
would be premature. Broad-based economic aid or barter
agreements would do little to foster systemic change. The
planned economic relations between North Korea and Japan, for
example, must be examined carefully to ensure that they do not
make reform unnecessary. Just as the DPRK wants "metered"
economic development for their own reasons, we and the other
major actors in Northeast Asia, should prefer "metered"-provision
of capital, technology, and management expertise tied first to
DPRK follow-through on IAEA inspections, then tied to such
matters as the North's policies on human rights for its own
people.

We should work with our South Korean allies to consider
objectively what ROK priorities ought to be in inter-Korean
dialogue. Military tension reduction leaps out as the obvious

16

0239-51-30

0036

primary goal. The recent decision to cancel this year's Team
Spirit exercise is an excellent start. For the South, the goal
means transparency of military activities in the North and then a
reduction of the North's offensive military capability to create
a more stable military situation. An eventual objective should
be the redeployment of Pyongyang's land forces, now dangerously
deployed near the DMZ.

The analysis so far suggests that the primary South Korean
near-term goal in inter-Korean talks ought to be the alleviation
of military tension and mutual reduction of arms and forces,
accomplished in a manner designed to spur systemic change in the
North. Of course, it is up to the ROK government to determine
which agreements it wishes to seek and in what order.

The security issues fall into two broad categories: those
concerning a lack of confidence and worries about surprise
attack, and those concerning military asymmetries of various
types. To deal with the former category, North and South Korea
have proposed various confidence-building measures (CBMs):
notifications of movements and military exercises, a "peace zone"
in the DMZ, a military hot line, exchanges of various forms of
data about military deployments, exchanges of observers,
agreements to expose covered military materiel, and others. In
addition, both have proposed various arms and force reduction
options, including reductions to parity in offensive weapons and
units, cuts in paramilitary forces, and the like. The phased
reduction would ultimately be included in any arms and force

17

0239-51-31

reduction plan, linked to North Korean reciprocation. Small cuts in U.S. forces, however, will begin at the outset, if only because a 3-phased unilateral reduction is already under way for reasons of economy. The continued presence of a substantial USFK could provide the South Korean government with leverage as negotiations progress.

In early negotiations with North Korea, the South might wish to avoid requesting reciprocal measures from Pyongyang that are very expensive and time consuming. Major redeployments of troops, for example, can take some time and require the construction of new bases and housing. Certain measures from the category of military CBMs might be more appropriate as first steps toward tension reduction. The planned mutual nuclear inspections will be an excellent first step. Exchanging observers might be an especially promising idea: if their rules of operation were negotiated carefully, observers could help the South penetrate the North's secretive military establishment, while allowing the North to make up for its lack of other means of verification.

A promising longer-term idea is to negotiate a "Limited Deployment Zone" between Seoul and Pyongyang, an area in which military forces, especially in North Korea, would be thinned to reduce the chances of surprise attack. As noted, however, such a move would be expensive - unless an outside sponsor offered to make up the costs, or unless the steps were combined with cuts in military forces to make redeployment unnecessary. Another

18

0239 -51-32

0038

potential arms control measure is the notion of a standing
commission or other mechanism for continuing North-South military
consultations and other data. Still another issue is some form
of "open skies" agreement. Any of these measures could help
reduce tensions and improve stability on the Korean Peninsula.

The field of confidence-building and arms and force
reduction between the two Koreas is thus a potentially fertile
one. Both sides possess strong incentives to reach agreements,
and many areas of parallelism exist between the two sides'
proposals. A variety of arms control measures, both CBMs and
arms and force reductions, would be in the interest of both
Koreas, and particularly the South. Once South Korea has
established arms control and military tension-reduction as its
top priority in inter-Korean talks, there is a wide menu of
potential agreements from which it can choose in adopting a
specific negotiating strategy.

As it formulates such a strategy, South Korea must seek out
basic principles to guide its thinking. Three such principles
seem particularly appropriate: specificity, the advancement of
specific and, initially at least, small-scale, low-cost steps;
conditionality, or the creation of specific quid pro quo
situations; and phasing, moving through logical stagings or
progressions. In employing these ideas, moreover, South Korea
and the United States must recognize that they are dealing from a
position of strength, and they should structure any initiatives
in ways that play to and maximize this strength.

19

A fourth principle, or more accurately an operating
assumption, is the admission that North Korea possesses
legitimate security concerns. South Korea's technologically
superior military is growing and is backed by the overwhelming
strength of the U.S. military. In fact, many estimates suggest
that within several years South Korea's burgeoning gross national
product (if current levels are sustained and inflation is kept
under control) will provide it with military superiority -- just
as the Soviet Union and China are backing away from the North.

This situation means, first of all, that the South cannot
expect the North to take all the initiatives, or even very many
of them. Seoul must be ready to compromise if it expects
Pyongyang to do the same; it cannot claim that Pyongyang knows
very well that the South and the United States harbor no
aggressive intentions. Perhaps just as important, the existence
of very real concerns in Pyongyang creates a powerful incentive
to negotiate candidly in the hope of reaching agreements that
moderate or reverse the military competition on the peninsula.
Although the intrusive verification components of arms control
might be distasteful to the North, if the alternative is
perpetual and worsening military inferiority and an unsupportable
military burden, arms control might seem the lesser of two evils.

How should United States - North Korean relations proceed?
U.S. ties with North Korea consist only of low-level discussions
in Beijing. The U.S. government has established preconditions
for establishing diplomatic relations with Pyongyang. The chief

20

0239-51-34

0040

condition is IAEA inspection of North Korea's nuclear facilities in accordance with Pyongyang's adherence to the Non-Proliferation Treaty (NPT). A second is the renunciation of terrorism as a state instrument by the DPRK. We should seek the latter without expecting reference to any previous terrorist acts, just as the ROK announced that there are no nuclear weapons in the South without reference to previous conditions. If these two conditions are met, the United States should recognize and establish diplomatic relations with the DPRK, in full consultation with South Korean and Japanese allies. Then, in constant dialogue, we can get on with the serious matter of North Korean policies on human rights.

There are many reasons to be hopeful about inter-Korean relations. The two Koreas are now talking seriously and both sides possess very real incentives to compromise and reach agreements aimed at building trust and winding down their military competition. But further major progress must await first and foremost the DPRK acceptance of intrusive and, hopefully effective, IAEA inspections and review of their results. We are at a cross-roads in U.S./ROK/DPRK relations which has major implications for peace and stability in Northeast Asia.

Mr. Chairman, I think that think tanks such as CSIS and KIDA have an important role to play in all this. For example, it is important to note that arms control is a complex business. It properly focusses on much more than numbers; it deals with

21

0239 -51 -35

0041

complicated calculations on such matters as force/space ratio,
relative technological capabilities, terrain, obstacles, weather,
time/rate/distance figures, etc. Out of my conversations with
North Korean officials, I conclude that the DPRK is not very
familiar with this kind of analysis. I am told that the North
Koreans lack basic literature on arms control, a notion partially
confirmed by a report I received that a DPRK team was recently
sent to The Stockholm International Peace Research Institute
(SIPRI) to acquire relevant materials. It is in our interest
that the North Koreans understand the complexities of arms
control. Toward this end, CSIS has recently agreed to mutual
exchanges with both the DPRK Institute on Disarmament and Peace
and the DPRK Institute on International Affairs.

As a related matter, I think that the North Koreans have not
been exposed to the military lessons of the Gulf War. It is in
ROK/U.S. interests that they understand fully what happened in
Desert Storm, especially about the capabilities of U.S. high-tech
equipment in the hands of highly trained military personnel
against the same kinds of Soviet equipment now in the hands of
the DPRK military. Given the differences in terrain between
Kuwait/Iraq and the Korean Peninsula, and given the undoubted
differences in quality between the Iraqi and North Korean
military personnel, some lessons do not apply, but many do. I
have already sent the recent CSIS study, The Gulf War: Military
Lessons Learned, to two DPRK institutes. Perhaps the
unclassified version of the Pentagon's interim report should also

22

0239-51-36

0042

be provided to the DPRK.

And there are other major areas where think tanks can contribute. For example, we have discovered the importance of teaching the basics of democratic legal systems in Russia, East European and Latin American countries. If North Korea begins to change for the better, its officials will need basic education in the fundamentals of democracy and free enterprise economy. Think tanks such as CSIS, working with their ROK think tank counterparts, can play a major role in this important kind of endeavor. In many ways, non-profit research institutes can accomplish tasks which government cannot or should not undertake.

Mr. Chairman, thank you for this opportunity to share my personal views at this important time in your deliberations.

23

0043

NUCLEAR CONTROL.
INSTITUTE
1000 CONNECTICUT AVE. N.W. SUITE 704 WASHINGTON DC 20036 202-822-8444

Testimony of Paul Leventhal, president
Nuclear Control Institute
Hearing on the Threat of North Korean Proliferation
Subcommittee on East Asian and Pacific Affairs
U.S. Senate Committee on Foreign Relations
January 14, 1992

Mr. Chairman, I appreciate your invitation to comment
on current efforts to halt North Korea's nuclear weapons
program and thereby avert what President Bush calls "the
single greatest source of danger to peace in Northeast
Asia."

Today I will concentrate on what I regard as the single
greatest danger to these efforts---a problem that lies just
below the horizon but threatens to sabotage the U.S.
initiative to make the Korean Peninsula free of nuclear
weapons and of the essential materials for building them.
The problem is Japan and the 100 tons of weapons-capable
plutonium it plans to acquire over the next 20 years---as
much plutonium as in the entire U.S. nuclear arsenal.

Plutonium is a man-made element that is created in
nuclear reactors. After irradiated uranium fuel is removed
from a reactor, its plutonium content can be extracted
either for use as a nuclear explosive in bombs or as fuel in
reactors. Japan's pledge to use all of its plutonium
peacefully in reactors to generate electricity is of little
comfort to the North and South Koreans who share deeply
etched memories of Japanese occupation and fears of renewed
Japanese militarism.

Although the two Koreas recently initialed an agreement
pledging not to possess plants for manufacturing plutonium
or the other nuclear-weapon material, highly enriched
uranium, each is keeping its options open. South Korea,
while committed not to extract plutonium at home, recently
followed in Japan's footsteps by signing an agreement with
Britain that allows this service to be performed on spent
reactor fuel shipped there.

North Korea finally has agreed to accept international
inspections but is unlikely to cooperate with the
International Atomic Energy Agency to the extent necessary
for the agency's inspectors to be able to verify that the
North Korean plutonium-extraction and bomb-building
operations have not been moved from the presently suspected
sites to other secret quarters. At a meeting of the IAEA

0239-51-38

0044

Board of Governors last month, before North Korea finally
succumbed to diplomatic and economic pressures, its
representative to the IAEA expressed fears of a Japanese
nuclear weapons program and specifically cited Japan's
plutonium program. It is my understanding, based on an
account by an IAEA official who was present, that the North
Korean said his nation might not agree in the future to
international inspections of all nuclear facilities until
Japan agreed to forgo separation and use of plutonium.

        There is now some hope the Bush Administration is
coming to terms with how dangerous bomb-grade nuclear fuels
are in world commerce. During his trip to the far east in
November, Secretary of State Baker declared that "(T)he only
firm assurance against a nuclear arms race in the Korean
Peninsula would be a credible agreement by both Seoul and
Pyongyang to abstain from the production or acquisition of
any weapons-grade nuclear material." He also said the
United States had "learned from the case of Iraq" that IAEA
safeguards "cannot ensure that a renegade regime will not
seek to acquire nuclear weapons." Thus, the Administration
is working hard to establish the Korean Peninsula as well as
the Middle East as regions free of nuclear explosive
materials and the plants needed to manufacture them.

        But to be successful, this approach must be
broadened to encompass Japan and Europe. Otherwise, Japan
soon will acquire massive nuclear weapons potential from
plutonium extracted in Europe from reactor fuel supplied to
Japan by the United States. Japan is shipping spent fuel to
Britain and France where plutonium will be recovered in
reprocessing plants and shipped back to Japan. The first
plutonium shipments from European reprocessors are scheduled
to proceed by sea later this year. Japan is also about to
build its own large reprocessing plant, capable of
recovering about eight tons of plutonium a year---equivalent
to at least 1,000 nuclear weapons.

        The two Koreas cannot reasonably be expected to abstain
from plutonium indefinitely in the face of Japan's
insatiable appetite for it---especially now that the myth of
"effective" international safeguards has been exploded. The
reality of ineffective safeguards is what prompted Japan to
call on North Korea to dismantle its reprocessing plant, not
simply open it to international inspectors. The basic
inability of safeguards to detect or prevent determined
bombmaking also prompts Korean anxiety about Japanese
plutonium.

        Unfortunately, the Bush Administration is saddled with
a "plutonium use policy" devised a decade ago by President
Reagan's ambassador for non-proliferation, Richard T.
Kennedy. Kennedy still holds the job, and the policy
remains in effect. It declares that the United States will
go along with use of plutonium recovered from U.S.-supplied
reactor fuel by any nation whose advanced nuclear power
program "does not constitute a proliferation risk"---namely
Japan and the European Community. Four years ago,
Ambassador Kennedy renegotiated the U.S. nuclear-cooperation
agreement with Japan to accommodate Japanese demands for a

carte blanche to acquire all the plutonium it wants from
U.S.-supplied nuclear fuel. South Korea, with its own large
U.S.-built and -fueled nuclear power program, is now lining
up for similar treatment.

The United States cannot reasonably hope to divide the
world into plutonium "haves" and "have-nots" as contemplated
in the present misguided policy. Since plutonium and highly
enriched uranium are not essential for running nuclear power
or research reactors, but are essential for making bombs,
their further production and use in civil programs should be
prohibited everywhere. There is no need for these dangerous
fuels because cheap, low-enriched uranium that is unsuitable
for weapons is in ample supply.

The one veto the United States still retains over
Japanese plutonium is to suspend U.S. approval of its
recovery and use if these are found to be inimical to U.S.
security interests. The U.S.-Japan nuclear-cooperation
agreement specifically provides that either party can
suspend "activities or facility operations" authorized by
the agreement if "actions of governments of third countries
or events beyond the territorial jurisdiction of a
party....would clearly result in a significant increase in
the risk of nuclear proliferation or in the threat to the
national security of the suspending party."

Given the high stakes on the Korean Peninsula, if we
cannot persuade Japan to suspend its plutonium program in
its own security interests, we should suspend it in ours.

The Bush Administration should end its discriminatory
plutonium-use policy, which directly conflicts with U.S.
security interests on the Korean Peninsula and other
troubled regions. It should work instead toward a universal
ban on nuclear explosive materials. Inevitably this
approach must include a halt in production of these
materials for nuclear weapons and the disposal of materials
recovered from weapons being dismantled by the United States
and the former Soviet republics---a goal that is finally
attainable. There then would be a solid technical
foundation for devising effective national and international
political controls barring any commerce in bomb-grade
nuclear materials and in the industrial equipment needed to
produce them.

A global prohibition on civilian and military
production of nuclear explosive materials is long overdue
and would come not a moment too soon. These materials are
inherently unsafeguardable once possessed by a nation
determined to have the bomb. Since these materials last
thousands of years, they will pose an indefinite threat,
even in the hands of nations that have no weapons intentions
today.

Finally, a much more rigorous international safeguards
system must be developed---one capable of detecting and
thwarting secret bomb programs on a timely basis. This can
be accomplished by transferring safeguards authority from
the IAEA to the UN Security Council where it would be

0239 -51-ko

0046

exercised by a permanent version of the Special Commission
now overseeing dismantlement of Iraq's nuclear weapons
program.

0239 -51-K1

Testimony submitted by Lawrence Scheinman
to the Senate Committee on Foreign Relations
Subcommittee on East Asian and Pacific Affairs
Hearing on "Threat of North Korean Proliferation"
January 14, 1992

The IAEA has administered a safeguards system for nearly 30 years, the last 20 of them involving a comprehensive or full-scope system involving implementation of the Nuclear Nonproliferation Treaty which came into force in 1970. This system applies to all non-nuclear weapon states party to the NPT and involves verification that all nuclear material in peaceful use can be accounted for through a system of records, reports and on-site inspections in which IAEA inspectors independently verify the accountability of all nuclear material under safeguards. The system makes extensive use of material accountancy but also relies on containment and surveillance to verify compliance. It normally determines compliance or non-compliance after a period of time and is to be distinguished from a policing system that roams the countryside looking for evidence of possible cheating on the part of the safeguarded state.

It is often remarked that locks are made for honest people. In the same way, the safeguards applied by the IAEA are designed to provide assurance of compliance by states with their international undertakings. They are entered into voluntarily as a consequence of national decisions to forego the acquisition of nuclear weapons or explosive devices and they provide a means by which well-intentioned states can demonstrate their peaceful nuclear bona-fides to neighboring states, thereby reducing or eliminating incentives of others to consider acquiring nuclear weapons for their own security.

Of course, to be effective in doing this the safeguards system must be credible in terms of its ability to detect diversion of nuclear material should it occur and to sound a warning to other states. To this end the IAEA has established a system which provides for the timely detection of the diversion of significant quantities of nuclear material, with significant quantity and timeliness being defined in terms of the length of time it would take for given quantities of nuclear material in given form and composition to be converted into the metallic components of a nuclear explosive device. Timely detection is not timely warning, a term used in the US Nuclear Nonproliferation Act of 1978 and which considers timeliness to be adequate time for diplomatic efforts to be undertaken to prevent the production of a nuclear explosive device, a

0239 —51-42

0048

2

truly challenging task if one considers that conversion time for separated PU, highly enriched uranium or U-233 metal is gauged to be on the order of 7 to 10 days. Nevertheless, in a number of situations it has real time deterrent capability and it can sound the diversion alarm on a timely basis.

I emphasize timely detection and timely warning because they bear on a critical perspective of international safeguards, namely the expectation in many quarters that safeguards somehow serve to <u>prevent</u> proliferation. Would that they could; but they do not and cannot. It is well to recall the admonition of the Acheson-Lilienthal report of March, 1946 that "systems of inspection cannot by themselves be made 'effective safeguards...to protect complying states against the hazards of violations and evasions'." Somewhere along the line, as the notion of safeguarded international nuclear cooperation and commerce gained over the earlier hope for international ownership and control of the dangerous aspects of the nuclear fuel cycle, public expectation developed that safeguards were somehow interchangeable with the more far-reaching notion of international control. Nevertheless, as the last two NPT Review Conferences demonstrate, there is at the political level a high confidence that safeguards, as practiced, do contribute to national security and international stability and that limitations notwithstanding, security ends where safeguards end.

<u>Iraq introduced a new dimension into our thinking. The Iraqi experience bared many of the limitations of safeguards as currently practiced and brought to the fore the reality that, as good as safeguards may be, they do not cover all of the bases.</u> As already mentioned, safeguards have primarily been a mechanism for providing assurance of compliance by states firmly committed to nonproliferation and seeking a means of objective, third party certification of their peaceful use of nuclear technology. They have not been designed to, nor have they focussed on, the malevolent NPT party who with malice aforethought pursues a dual track program and relies on clandestine nuclear activity to achieve what it has foresworn in joining the NPT, although with some additional support and a more robust implementation there is more they could do in that direction as well. In the post cold-war environment when the two superpowers no longer pay as much attention to, nor have as much influence over, clients and dependents in the various regions of the world, aspirants for regional hegemony, aggressively inclined governments, and even governments deeply concerned that they may soon confront nuclear armed neighbors and no longer enjoy the implicit or explicit protection of a superpower, are or may be inclined to

0239 -51-83

─ 0049

3

hedge their bets. But at the same time they do not wish to do so overtly because of the risk of preemption, or the possibility that the international community will confront them while they are still in a pre-nuclear state of being. Iraq turned out to be one of these bad apples; there is good reason to be concerned that North Korea is intent on following suit. Still others may be waiting in the wings.

This raises the broad question of what can be done to constrain these kinds of develop-ments, to gain sufficiently early warning that the international community can react in time to prevent the outcome of proliferation. There are various approaches to questions like this. Some would argue for dealing with proliferation by seeking to stabilize the situation regionally through offsetting help to the most affected neighbors. Some would argue for managing proliferation through a variety of means once it has occurred, building firebreaks that limit the scope and depth of the proliferation in question. Still others would argue that while we may be forced into the latter position, our primary goal should be to prevent proliferation in the first place. This in turn involves probing the issue of what motivates countries to proliferate (a question that must be addressed not only generically, but on a case by case, region by region basis), what are the legitimate security concerns of states, and how those legitimate concerns can be met in ways that lead governments to reject acquisition of nuclear weapons, and so on.

From the point of view of safeguards, what can be said? Are safeguards an appropriate mechanism for dealing with these issues? Is the IAEA, as the only truly international safeguards organization and one that has enjoyed considerable international confidence, in a position to deal with the threat of the clandestine approach to nuclear weapons? If not, are there measures that can be taken to put it in a position to effectively meet this kind of a situation? The answer, in my view is both yes and no. Let me take the no part first. Safeguards, rightly or wrongly, are widely perceived as intrusions on national sovereignty. To the extent that they are applied by international organizations to states that voluntarily accept through treaty commitment to submit to safeguards there is relatively little room for discriminatory treatment, for international secretariats to say "A is good, B is bad so we will train our resources on B". So there are real limits here. Secondly, no international organization is likely to be given the roaming rights that are implicit in an international policing arrangement, which safeguards are really not; and limited random roaming rights are not likely to give that much added advantage over what the IAEA already does. It is well to recall how the United States has backed away from anytime, anyplace

0239 —51—44

0050

4

surprise inspections in the context of the chemical weapons convention, and how in the past the United States, having proposed such open ended verification arrangements has balked when push came to shove. Whether this is the result of consideration of 4th amendment implications, or derives from military or industrial reactions is irrelevant. The point is we have been reluctant to ourselves adopt such an open-ended and far-reaching arrangement. Imposing this on countries other than those to whom one is dictating terms after winning a war, as in the case of UNSC Resolution 687 and other following resolutions related to Iraq is another matter.

On the other hand there is much that can be done. It is, however, important to recognize the limits of the achievable and to plan on additive measures to take up where international safeguards inevitably must leave off. The NPT and the correlative IAEA safeguards document INFCIRC/153 are more rich in terms of verification opportunity than in practice has been done. Unfortunately the NPT emphasized that verification would apply to the issue of the diversion of nuclear material and did not cover all of the obligations that non-nuclear weapon states undertook in signing the Treaty. This is not something that can be reinterpreted, although it could be managed by protocols to the Treaty. But insofar as nuclear material (and the related facilities and activities) are concerned, there is room for improvement, and these measures are already being promulgated:

- full implementation of the concept of special inspections by the IAEA;

- enforcement of the requirement for early notification of design information to the IAEA to mean notification from the moment of decision to construct a facility so as to provide increased transparency of the national nuclear fuel cycle and activities, and not just 180 days before nuclear material is introduced into such a facility (as is now the practice);

- consideration of a universal reporting system centered on the IAEA which would add to transparency of national nuclear activities and provide a current record of the movements, locations and status not only of nuclear materials, and also relevant plants and components and activities.

Let me focus on just one of the above aspects, the special inspection, since it has been the most newsworthy in recent months, and has been called out by the Fourth NPT Review Conference (1990) as an area deserving particular attention by the Agency. IAEA special inspections traditionally have been conducted in order to clarify anomalies arising out of routine inspection activities which for one reason or another have not been resolved through normal

0239 —51-45

0051

5

procedures of consultation and further inquiry. They have been conducted, as provided by the safeguards system, with the concurrence of the state in question. Indeed in some cases it is the state that initiates the call for a special inspection because, for example, of a change of the containment of nuclear material. But they also can be called for by the Agency because information otherwise available is insufficient to allow the inspectorate to fulfill its obligations to verify the status and location of safeguarded nuclear material. In such circumstances the limitations that apply in the case of routine inspections such as the designation of strategic points to which inspector access is normally limited fall away and the inspectorate has the authority to access any location where information makes it reasonable to conclude that the IAEA would otherwise be unable to meet its obligation to ensure that safeguards are being applied to all nuclear material in peaceful use in the state. It has been argued before, affirmed by the legal advisor of the Agency, and the position adopted by the Director General in a paper informing the Board of Governors in December, 1991 how he intends to implement special inspection rights, that this access is not confined to other points in a declared nuclear facility but extends to other locations as well including undeclared facilities. This is not a claim of a new authority, but spelling out the scope of existing authority. The Director General, Hans Blix, has made clear his view that successful implementation of the right to inspect even undeclared facilities is dependent on three factors: plausible information resulting from safeguards or other Agency activities or from an outside source that indicates the existence of undeclared nuclear material; assured access by the Agency to such locations; and the backing of the United Nations Security Council where necessary to enable the IAEA to fulfill its responsibilities.

Fully implemented this kind of arrangement will go far toward providing more effective and credible safeguards in which the international community could have continued confidence and it would also serve as a further deterrent to would be proliferators. But it has its limits. Determined cheaters will presumably still seek to pursue their furtive schemes. Safeguards inspectors cannot, as noted, comb the countryside looking for telltale signs of cheating. A robust special inspections regime would, however, improve the current system, hone in more effectively on the missing element in the current system, namely the undeclared facility, make even more difficult the task of determined cheaters to go about their nefarious business, and contribute to enhanced national and international security. All of this has obvious relevance to the case of North Korea.

023p -51-46

0052

6

Despite the fact that the IAEA can do more with the information resources already at its disposal, it surely could profit substantially from the timely and consistent cooperation of national intelligence services in providing information upon which the IAEA could credibly act to ensure the full coverage of safeguards. Information is the grist of the safeguards mill and there are limits to what can be gleaned by even the most professional inspectors. In addition, as the Director General of the IAEA has pointed out assured support from the United Nations Security Council to guarantee that access where required will be demanded and supported is an essential element of a successful implementation of a safeguards system, especially the regime of special inspections. The UN Security Council could go far toward providing assurance by making a clear and unequivocal statement that it views violations of nonproliferation treaty commitments and of safeguards agreements as threats to international peace and security to be dealt with by any and all means available under chapter VII of the UN Charter. And finally, it must be understood that without adequate resources, the best intentions and most finely honed system cannot meet expectations. The member states of the IAEA, who have pursued a policy of zero growth budget for more than eight years, have increased the work load of the safeguards system, but have demanded service at a level that will provide the basis for continued confidence in the findings of the system, must reverse course. Resources must be commensurate with authority if expectations are to be met.

This says something about a US agenda for IAEA safeguards and nonproliferation, particularly since we have historically played a leading role in preventing the spread of nuclear weapons and in fostering and supporting the IAEA and international safeguards. The world has changed dramatically in the past few years, and our relative weight may have diminished at least in the economic and political arenas, but no one has come forward either individually or collectively to take our place and so the mantle of leadership still remains in our charge.

First, we surely do not want a haphazard and ad hoc approach to nonproliferation verification. We want system and continuity and the embedding of as strong and liberal a norm as possible vis-à-vis what states should be prepared to accept as legitimate international verification activity. We must exert continued leadership toward this end.

Second, we must be ready to provide not only moral and political support for an invigorated IAEA, but financial, manpower and, where needed, intelligence resources.

Third, we must either seek to curb public expectations in order to bring them into line

0239-51-87

0053

with authority and resources or, if, as we should, we endorse and promulgate higher expectations, bring the latter two into line with those expectations.

Fourth, we should be realistic about what a technically-anchored international organization can do and develop and support other multilateral and international approaches and instruments to support a credible international safeguards system. A good place to start is with the rejuvenated United Nations by ensuring through leadership and suasion that it is both committed and poised to assist and where necessary take active measures to help enforce implementation of the IAEA safeguards system.

We also should be prepared to go further and to support the development of additive measures in support of nonproliferation and safeguards at the regional level. In light of changes in the international political environment, the declining influence of superpowers and the rise of regional issues on the global security agenda, mentioned earlier, it is more important than ever to consider how regionally-based approaches to nonproliferation can be promoted and supported. We have seen substantial progress in Latin America as Argentina and Brazil have proceeded to endorse nonproliferation, accept full-scope IAEA safeguards and build a system designed to provide mutual reassurance. Mutual reassurance is also in some evidence in Indo-Pakistani relations and is a condition sine qua non for serious progress in achieving a zone free of weapons of mass destruction in the Middle East. In the case of the Korean peninsula there is a strong case to be made that much could be gained from encouraging and promoting regional nonproliferation arrangements including mutual inspection and other confidence building measures which are nested in the broader nonproliferation regime. These would not be substitutes for global nonproliferation or for international safeguards applied by the IAEA, but additive measures that are incorporated in the broader regime. There is, of course, an absolute need for independent and effective IAEA verification of any regional Korean arrangements. But in the final analysis it is perhaps a combination of approaches, mutually reinforcing and logically integrated, that may offer the best hope for making international safeguards optimally effective and nonproliferation a realistic outcome.

023p -51 -K8

0054

Testimony of William A. Hignbotham before the Subcommittee on
East Asian and Pacific Affairs of the United States Senate
Foreign Affairs Committee, January 14, 1992

As I understand it, I have been invited to testify because I have
some understanding of the technologies involved in safeguards and
verification. Before discussing the verification techniques, let me say
a few words about my background which may be relevant.

During World War Two, I devloped electronic circuits for radar at
M.I.T. and then for nuclear instruments at the Los Alamos Manhattan
District site. When I saw the first nuclear explosion in the early
morning of July 16, 1945, I was very frightened. Ever since then I have
been concerned about the nuclear arms race and nuclear proliferation.

Soon after the war ended, the scientists at Los Alamos and at other
Manhattan District sites formed associations to explain that "There is
no secret; There is no defense, and; We must have world control of the
atom". I was elected chairman of the Los Alamos Association.

I spent 1946 and 1947 in Washington, first as chairman and then as
executive secretary of the Federation of American Scintists.

In December of 1947 I went to Brookhaven National Laboratory, where
I was associate head and then head of the Instrumentation Division for
twenty years.

In 1968, I was one of the founders of a safeguards group at
Brookhaven which provided technical assistance to the safeguards offices
of the U.S. Atomic Energy Commission and, later, to its successors. This
involved systems studies and the development of safeguards techniques
for the International Atomic Energy Agency and for the protectioon of
nuclear materials and facilities in the U.S. Since my retirement at the
end of 1984, I have been a consultant on Nuclear materials Management.

In this activity, I have had the opportunity to visit nuclear
facilities in the United State, Europe, and Japan, to visit the
International Atomic Energy Agency many times, and to get acquainted
with safeguards people at professional meetings and at their facilties.
Since 1973 I have been the technical editor of the Journal of the
Institute of Nuclear Materials Management, an international
organization for those involved in developing and applying IAEA
safeguards and national systems to protect nuclear materials from theft
or dispersal.

In addition to these activities, I have been involved recently in
two projects which may be of interest to the committee. The Federation
of American Scientists has provided technical assistance to scientists
in Brazil and Argentina who were attempting to persuade their
governemnts to halt their nuclear weapons programs and agree to bilateral or international inspection. As you knowm they have just agreed
to the former. David Albright and I visited Brazil several times and
brought a few of the scientists from the two countries to the U.S. to
learn how our government controls its nuclear facilities, a necessasry
preliminary to any agreement on inspection by others. I have also been a
member of a committee of the Federation which has been working with
colleagues in what was, until recently, the Soviet Union on verification
techniques for future arms control agreements. The most recent product
of this cooperation was the release last May of our report: "Ending the
Production of Fissile Materials for Weapons and Verifying the

0251-51-49

Dismantlement of Nucl — warheads", an unofficial —esponse to the
Congressional request for such a report by the President.

Now for North Korea: Although North Korea signed the Nuclear Non-
proliferation Treaty (NPT) in 1985, it has not yet agreed to negotiate
the facility attachments, to declare all of its nuclear materials, or to
accept safeguards except, as previously agreed, to a 2 to 4 megawatt
research reactor, supplied long ago by the Soviet Union. These were also
supplied to Yugoslovia, Iraq, and others. I carefully looked over the
one that is near Belgrade in 1963. These are normally loaded with
natural uranium. A few kilograms of high enriched uranium may be added
to provide higher neutron fluxes in a few locations, in order to produce
radioactive isotopes or more intense external neutron beams for
research. I am told that the North Koreans have constructed a 30
megawatt reactor, which is operating, and a larger one, which may be
operational. A 30 megawatt reactor can produce as much as 30 grams of
plutonium each day. In 300 days, this would amount to 9 kilograms (kg),
enough for one Nagasaki type bomb.

One question, then, is: Would it be possible to verify the state's
declaration of how much plutonium in spent fuel had been produced by the
time when it might agree to accept IAEA safeguards? That would depend on
the reactor operating history and on whether it had been operated to
produce the maximum quantity of low burnup plutonium or operated
primarily as a research reactor. All information which might provide
useful information would have to be carefully studied in order to
determine how such a verification might be performed and how sensitive
it might be.

Other questions are: Might the country have constructed a facility
to extract plutonium from the reactor fuel or might it secretly
construct such a facility ? If so, how might such a facility be
detected?

It seems likely to me that a 30 megawatt reactor should be
detectable from satellite surveillance using infra-red detectors. A
small reprocessing plant would not be detectable in this manner.

The kind of a facility we are talking about is not a large,
efficient, and expensive reprocessing plant, such as those which have
been built here and in other countries to recover the plutonium and
unburned uranium from commercial reactor spent fuel. A good reference on
this subject is the report by the General Accounting Office: "Quick and
Secret Construction of a Plutonium Reprocessing Plant: A Quick Way to
Nuclear Proliferation?", EMD-78-104, Oct.6,1978. For processing a few
tons of irradiated reactor fuel a year, the operations would be
performed batch-wise in a few hot cells with remote control instruments.
The fuel rods or elements would be chopped up, under water in a pool,
using bolt cutters. The pieces would be transferred to another vessel
and dissolved in nitric acid. The dissolver solution would be
transferred to other vats where the plutonium would be separated from
the uranium and fission products. 90% efficiency would be acceptable and
the uranium could be discharged with the fission products.

While the fission products are highly radioactive, they don't
produce much heat, and the pool and hot cells should contain the gamma-
rays and neutron emitted by them.

Unless one knows where such a facility might be located, it would be
very difficult, if not impossible, to detect it by searching for the

0251—51—50

0056

radiations. The extraction process would consume a lot of nitric acid,
which is widely used industrially. The other extraction materials might
be kerosene and tri-butyl-phosphate or resin beads. The latter two might
be traced. There are some other possible things to look for. Unless the
reprocessing facility is located near the reactor, the several tons of
highly radioactive irradiated fuel must be transported to the expraction
facility in heavy shielded containers. When the fuel elements are
chopped up and dissolved, the noble fission product isotopes of krypton
and xenon probably will escape to the surrounding atmosphere. The
krypton 85 isotope is a beta emitter with a half life of 11 years. The
xenon isotope is stable. I have not estimated how difficult it might be
to detect these isotopes near such a facility; though it may be
possible. As we know from our experience, it is easy to make mistakes in
storing or disposing of high level radioactive wastes. If they leak into
the environment, they might be easy to detect.

Once the IAEA safeguards begin, I believe that they should be
capable of detecting diversion of the several tons of <u>declared</u> spent
fuel which would contain 8 kg of plutonium.

The answers to the above questions may be "possible" or "very
difficult to achieve", depending on the degree of cooperation of the
North Korean government, information obtained from "national technical
means" and defectors, and the types and intensity of the verification
activities that may be possible at the time.

0239-51-51

0057

北韓 核問題 關聯 美上院 外交委 聽聞會

1992. 1. 16(木)

外 務 部

> 美上院 外交委 東亞.太 小委員會(委員長 : 「크랜스턴」上院 議員)는 1.14(火) 北韓의 核開發 問題에 관한 聽聞會를 開催 하였는바, 그 主要內容을 아래 報告 드립니다.

1. 討議要旨

가. 證言人士 發言

(「해리슨」 카네기財團 先任 研究員)

o 北韓 核問題와 미.북한 關係改善 問題의 關聯性 고려, 미.북한 外務長官 또는 次官會談 開催를 권유함.

o 北韓의 安保憂慮 除去를 위해 美國의 대한국 核雨傘 保護 中斷이 필요함.

(「테일러」 國際戰略 問題研究所 副所長)

o 北韓의 態度變化는 國內經濟의 惡化및 武力 統一의 비현실성에 대한 指導部의 自覺에 起因함.

- 1 -

0058

250 북한 핵문제 미국 동향

o 韓國과 美國은 對北韓 政策에 있어 北韓의 體制
   變化를 誘導하되, 國防力과 對話의 維持등 兩面
   戰略을 適用해야 함.

o 美國및 日本의 對北韓 關係改善은 北韓의 核查察
   受容및 人權問題등과 段階的으로 連繫, 推進해야함.

(「레벤탈」 核統制研究所 所長)

o 韓半島에서의 진정한 核開發 防止를 위하여는
   日本의 플루토늄 生産 中斷이 必要함.

o 日本은 向後 20년간 100톤의 플루토늄을 保有할
   計劃임.

(「쉰만」 코넬 大學教授)

o IAEA 查察 制度 强化를 위해 美國은 政治的. 財政的.
   人的 支援 및 情報를 提供해야함.

o 北韓 核問題 解決에는 IAEA 查察이외에 남. 북한간
   相互查察이 實施되어야 함.

나. 質疑應答

o 北韓은 最近 IAEA 核安全協定 署名을 發表하였으나,
   核查察에 實際 응할것인지는 불확실함

o 北韓은 현재 食糧不足, 분배 體制의 脆弱 및
   蘇聯援助의 中斷등으로 經濟的 困境에 처해있음.

- 2 -

2. 評價

o 美議會 휴회기간중 聽聞會가 開催된 것은 北韓
   核開發 問題에 대한 美國의 깊은 憂慮와 關心을
   反映한 것임.

o 남.북한간 合意書 採擇 및 비핵화 共同宣言
   合意에 대해서는 肯定的으로 評價하나, 北韓의
   核開發 抛棄 實踐 與否에 대해서는 懷疑的

o 미.북한 外務長官會談 및 미국의 대한국 核雨傘
   保護 除去 提議등은 미국의 北韓 核開發 沮止에
   대한 강박감을 代辯 .

o 美國, 日本의 플루토늄 大量 保有 計劃등 核開發
   潛在力 警戒 및 韓半島 非核化에 미칠 影響에 留意
   必要

- 끝 -

외 무 부

종 별 : 지 급

번 호 : USW-0228

일 시 : 92 0115 1728

수 신 : 장 관(미일,미이,동구일,아일) 사본:주미대사(주라성 경유-직송필)

발 신 : 주 미국 대사대리

제 목 : 솔라즈의원 보좌관 접촉

연: 1) USW-0203, 2) 6484

1. 금 1.15 당관 임성준 참사관이 접촉한 솔라즈 의원실 STANLEY ROTH 수석
전문위원에 의하면, 하원이 1.22 개회 예정이어서 솔라즈 의원이 내주초에는 워싱턴
귀환 예정이었으나, 선거구조정(REDISTRICTING) 문제로 지역구를 떠날 형편이 못되는
데다가, 내주중 부표에 회부될 만한 중요 안건도 없어 뉴욕에 계속 체류키로 금일
결정되었다 함. 따라서, 장관님 방미시 연호 (1) 솔라즈 의원 면담 추진은 어렵게
되었음.

2. 동 접촉 기회에 임 참사관이 북한 핵개발 문제 관련, 의회 결의안 추진 문제에
대한 연호 (2) 방침 변경 여부에 관해 문의한 데 대해, 동 전문위원은 북한이 기
약속한대로 1 월말까지 IAEA 안전협정을 서명하고 조속한 비준조치를 취할 준비가
되어있을 경우 동 결의안 추진은 불필요한 압력이 될 것이므로 이 문제는 북한의
태도와 6 차 남북고위급회담 결과등 진전사항을 좀더 지켜본 후 추진 여부를 결정해야
할 것이라는 연호 입장에 변함이 없다고 말함.

3. 동인은 또한 금년도 선거정국과 관련, 정치권의 논의는 주로 국내경제 문제에
집중될 것이므로 대외 문제에 관한 미 의회의 관심은 상대적으로 줄어들 것이나,
부쉬대통령의 아시아 순방을 전후하여 JAPAN BASHING 의 분위기가 고조되어 있는
상황이어서 대일관계는 앞으로도 계속 주요 쟁점이 될 것으로 보며, 북한의 핵개발
문제도 북한의 태도에 별다른 변화가 보이지 않을 경우 의회내 주요 관심사로 부각될
것으로 본다는 견해를 피력함.끝.

(대대대리 김봉규-국장)

예고: 92.6.30 까지

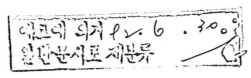

미주국 분석관	장관 청와대	차관 안기부	1차보	2차보	아주국	미주국	구주국	외정실

PAGE 1

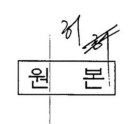

외 무 부

종 별 :

번 호 : USW-0244   일 시 : 92 0115 1916

수 신 : 장 관(미이,미일,동구일,정안,정북,중동일,기정,국방부)

발 신 : 주 미 대사

제 목 : 미상원 무기확산 관련 청문회

1. 상원 정부문제 위원회 (위원장: JOHN GLENN)는 금 1.15 ROBERT GATES CIA 국장을 출석시킨 가운데 무기확산에 관한 청문회를 개최함. GLENN 위원장은 개회사에서 CIS 의 핵무기통제 이완 우려를 비롯, 남아시아 (인도, 파크스탄), 중동 (이락,이란, 시리아), 북한 등에서의 핵무기 및대량 살상 무기확산 위협을 지적하고 무기확산의 방지를 미국가 안보의 절대 불가결한 목표로 삼아야한다고 강조하면서 금번 청문회는 핵무기를 비롯한 대량살상 무기의 확산과 이에 따른 안보위협에 대해 미국민의 관심을 환기시키는데 주목적이 있다고 밝힘.

2. GATES 국장 증언 요지

가. 무기확산 이유

. 현재 20여개국이 핵무기, 생화학 무기 및 동 무기발사 장치를 보유 또는 개발중에 있으며, 이러한 대량살상 무기의 확산 추세가 계속 되고 있는바, 이는 다음과 같은 요인에 기인함.

- 제3세계 국가들에 의한 무기제조 기술 습득의 용이화
- 대부분의 무기제조 관련 기술이 군수
- 민간의이중용도를 갖고 있어 기술이전의 제약에 한계
- 일부 가인, 기업 및 국가들이 불법판매를 통한 부당이익 추구
- 이락 등 제3세계 국가들의 독자적인 무기개발추세
- 대량 살상 무기 보유국의 인접국들이 정치적 이유및 억지력 유질 위해 상응한 무기 보유 추진

나. CIS 의 핵확산 위협

. 소련의 와해로 핵무기에 대한 중앙 통제체제가 취약해지고 있으며 핵기술 및물질의 확산위협이 증대됨.

미주국 안기부	1차보 국방부	미주국	구주국	중아국	외정실	외정실	분석관	청와대

PAGE 1   92.01.16   09:54 WG

외신 1과 통제관

0062

. 엘친이 작년말 핵통수권을 이양받은 이후 효과적인 중앙 직업의식 (PROFESSIONAL INTEGRITY)에도 달려 있는바, 핵무기 감사, 운영, 유지관련 요원들을 포함한 군부인사들의 불만팽배는 우려요인이 되고 있음.

. 소련 핵무기 해체협조, 핵물질, 핵무기 및 핵기술자의 하외유출 방지를 위해 CIS 측과 긴밀히 협조하고 있으며, 현재 BARTHOLOMEW국무차관이 모스크바를 방문중에 있음.

다. 북한의 핵개발 위협

. 북한의 핵계획은 동아시아에서 가장 급박한 안보위협이 되고 있음. 북한의 핵개발은 동북아의 안정을 위협함은 물론 핵무기 및 동 제조기술을 국제적 확산을 우려케하고 있음.

- 북한은 외화가득을 위해 무기판매에 의존
- 이란, 시리아 등 중동국가에도 스커드 미사일 판매
- 사정거리 천키로 이상의 장거리 미사일을 개발판매할 단계 임박.

. 북한은 핵무기 개발을 위한 모든 하부시설을 갖추고 있음. 플로토늄 추출만을 모적으로한 원자로 2기를 건설, 1기는 이미 4년전부터 가동중에 있으며, 보다 대규모의 1기는 금년중 가동시작예정임.

. 남북한은 작년 12월 한반도 비핵화에 관한 역사적 합의를 한바, 동 합의의 실효성은 북한이 앞으로 핵사찰을 어느정도로 수용하느냐에 따라 판단될 수 있음. 북한은 2월중 안정협정에 서명할 것임을 약속한 바, IAEA 에 의한 사찰책임을 북한이 어떤식으로 해석할지가 관심사임.

3. 이어 진행된 질의응답 과정에서 북한 관련주요 토의 내용은 아래와 같음.

. 구소련 보다는 북한이나 큐바, 이란, 이락, 파키스탄과 같은 나라를 봉한 핵확산 위험이 더클것으로 보느냐는 GLENN 위원장 질의에 대해 GATES 국장은 큐바, 알제리, 시리아 및 기타 2,3개국을 대사국가로 거론할 수 있다고 말하고, 상호 과학자 교류 및 접촉이 빈번한 국가들이 주요위험 대상이라고 부언함. GATES 국장은 또한 생화학 무기 확산 위험국가로 북한을 제일 먼저 거론하고, 북아프리카에서 서남아시아에 걸친 지역이 모두 요관찰 대상이라고 언급함.

. 북한이 이락, 이란, 시리아 등 중동국가들의 핵무기 및 생화학무기 개발에 필요한 주요물질을 공급하고 있다는 주장에 대해, GATES국장은 북한이 유일한 공급원은 아니나 주요지원 국가임은 확실하다고 답함. 배석한 OEHLER정보담당관은

PAGE 2

부연설명에서 북한의 대중동지원은 주로 BALLISTIC MISSILE 과 관련된 거이며
화학무기나 핵무기는 아니라고 언급함.

    (대사 대리 김봉규- 국장)

     첨부: USWF-0263

주 미 대 사 관

USW(F) : 0263   년월일 : 920115   시간 : 19:00

수 신 : 장   관 (미이, 미일, 청안, 정특, 중동일, 개방) 　부 안
　　　　　　　　　　　　　　　　　　　　　　 풍 제

발 신 : 주 미 대 사 (

제 목 : 상원 정부분네히 증언을 (북한핵관련 38매)　　(출처 :　　　　)

外信 1과
通 　　제

HEARING OF THE SENATE INTERNMENTAL AFFAIRS COMMITT   SUBJECT: WEAPONS
PROLIFERATION IN THE N   WORLD ORDER   CHAIRED BY: SENATOR JOHN GLENN,
(D-OH);   WITNESS: ROBERT GATES, CIA DIRECTOR
6-3-3 page# 1   WEDNESDAY, JANUARY 15, 1992
     dest=fnc11102,hill,sengovaf,cia,nucweapon,weapons,armscont,intarms
     dest+=fnc00652,fnc10000,ussr,thdwd,pharm,budgus,defense,prc,europe
     dest+=asia,mideast,africa,nkor,kazak,ukra,byel
     dest+=biol,chemwar,asia,iraq,nkor,skor
     data

          MR. GATES: Thank you very much, Mr. Chairman. I welcome the
     opportunity to talk today about a subject of critical importance, as
     you have indicated.

          The intelligence community has been concerned about the
     proliferation of weapons of mass destruction for a number of years. In
     that time, our resources for tracking and combating the problem have
     grown substantially, and we have recently made the organizational
     changes you have just described to deal with it more effectively,
     specifically, the creation of our Interagency Nonproliferation Center.
     **As Director of Central Intelligence, I intend to continue to make the
     proliferation problem a top priority for US intelligence.**

          The intelligence community has also conveyed consistently its
     concerns to policymakers, to the Congress and to the public. For
     example, Judge Webster addressed the subject in open session of this
     committee in February 1989 and again in a public speech in May of
     1989. I believe the policy community has taken our concerns seriously
     and has done a good deal to address them. Agreements like the Missile
     Control Technology Regime and formation of consultative bodies on the
     spread of chemical and biological weapons like the **Australia Group** are
     just two examples of this effort.

          There are many individual US initiatives under way or planned.
     I'll touch on a few of those in my remarks today, but I would urge the
     committee to get a more complete picture from the administration of
     these diplomatic efforts under way.

          In the wake of Desert Storm, after we discovered just how far Iraq
     had gotten in its nuclear weapons program, we have succeeded in further
     energizing the international community to combat the proliferation
     effort. The cooperation that has existed between traditional allies
     has spread to include other members of the world community and even
     includes now new republics formed from the **old Soviet Union.**

          With those preliminaries, let me now provide an overview of the
     problem. First I'll speak generally and then address the concerns
     raised by the dissolution of the Soviet Union, and then turn to the
     problems that we face in other regions.

          We continue to witness a steady and worrisome growth in the
     proliferation of advanced weapons. Today, over 20 countries have, are
     suspected of having, or are developing nuclear, biological or chemical
     weapons and the means to deliver them. There are several reasons for
     the proliferation of weapons of mass destruction. First and perhaps
     foremost, the technologies used in these weapons are simply more
     available and more easily absorbed by Third World countries than ever

                              0262 - /

before. Nuclear and ballistic missile technologies are, after all,
1940s technologies by US standards. Biological and chemical weapons
technologies are even older, and they are easier and cheaper to
develop.

Second, most of these technologies are so called dual use
technologies. That is, they have legitimate civilian applications. This
makes it difficult to restrict trade in them because we would be limiting
the ability of developing nations to modernize. For example, much of the
technology needed for a ballistic missile program is the same as
that needed for a space launch program. Chemicals used to make
nerve agents are also used to make plastics and process foodstuffs.
Moreover, a modern pharmaceutical industry could produce biological
warfare agents as easily as vaccines and antibiotics.

A third reason for the increase is that individuals, companies,
and in some cases countries facing stiff economic competition in
legitimate business look for quick profits in illicit sales.

Fourth, Gerald Bull and the supergun he was building for Iraq
illustrate another disturbing trend. Countries like Iraq are no
longer satisfied with hand-me-downs from the larger powers.
Instead, they want state of the art weapons that will give them
prestige as well as first-class capabilities. If this trend
continues and as budget reductions and arms control agreements limit
our advances, we will increasingly see weapons in the Third World
with technical capabilities that could challenge **US defenses.**

Fifth and finally, as some countries acquire weapons of mass
destruction, their neighbors feel compelled to develop comparable
capabilities for reasons of politics, pride and deterrence.

Now, let me review the threat in some detail. Only **China** and
the Commonwealth of Independent States, the former Soviet Union,
have the missile capability to reach US territory directly. We do
not expect increased risk to US territory from the special weapons
of other countries in a conventional military sense for at least
another decade. However, the threat to **Europe, the Middle East and
Asia** is real and growing.

US or multinational forces deployed abroad could face an
increased threat of air-delivered nuclear weapons before the end of
the decade. Several countries now have missiles and rockets that
could carry nuclear warheads, and others are likely to field some
ballistic missiles with nuclear warheads in coming years. If any of
those countries could acquire even a few nuclear warheads, it could
soon become a nuclear threat.

Most of the major countries in the Middle East have chemical
weapon development programs, and some already have stockpiles that
could be used against civilians or poorly defended military targets.
Most countries have not yet equipped their military --- their
delivery systems to carry weapons of mass destruction, but over the
next decade, many countries will, from **North Africa** through South

0262 - 2

Asia, if international efforts to -- curtail these efforts fail.

China and **North Korea** may sell other countries longer-range
missiles and technology to produce them. Countries with special
weapons that succeed in buying these missiles will further expand
and accelerate the special weapons arms race already under way in
the Middle East and South Asia.

Now, let me turn to the CIS -- the Commonwealth of Independent
States. The decade of the 1990s is just beginning, but we already
have a new dimension to the proliferation problem. The breakup of
the Soviet Union threatens the stability of Moscow's centralized
command and control system and threatens to unleash technologies and
materials that had been carefully controlled.

Russia and the other new republics face multiple internal
crises -- the possible collapse of authority, potentially
large-scale civil disorder, and the unraveling of social discipline
-- while they still have about 30,000 nuclear weapons, the most
powerful of which are aimed at us. Moscow's centralized nuclear
command and control system continues to function as -- even as
control of conventional begins to shift to the republics.

Russian Federation President Yeltsin assumed control of CIS
strategic nuclear forces from Gorbachev on Christmas Day. Under
current and foreseeable circumstances, we believe the -- new
national command authorities will be able to maintain effective
control over their nuclear arsenal. However, this elaborate and
centralized system was designed to rely in part on professional
integrity. As we watch the breakup of the center and the military,
we must worry about the growing dissatisfaction of military
personnel, including those responsible for guarding, operating, and
maintaining nuclear weapons.

Traditionally, the Soviets had three nuclear briefcases. They
were held by the President, the Minister of Defense, and the Chief
of the General Staff. Today, there appear to be only two, interim
Commander and Chief of Commonwealth Armed Forces and formerly
Minister of Defense Shaposhnikov said two weeks ago that he and
President Yeltsin are the only ones with nuclear briefcases. The
third is apparently in reserve.

We are still looking to see how Russia and the other republics
will sort out the ownership of nuclear weapons and what procedures
they establish to maintain and control them. The leaders of
Kazakhstan, Belarus, and Ukraine all have said that they want to
return the nuclear weapons that are on their soil to Russia for
dismantlement and destruction. They all have said that they want to
share nuclear decisionmaking with Russia,

CONTINUED

0263-3

dest=nsil1102,hill,=gov81,cia,nucweapon,weapor=rmscont,intarms
dest+pfnsopebi,insi____,fns13897,ussr,thdwd,def===,europe
dest+=asia,mideast,kazak,un
dest+=biol,chemwar,iraq,cuba,india,alg,egypt,syria
data

but the extent to which they can influence decisions is not yet
clear. In particular, building a nuclear command and control system
that allows leaders outside Moscow to participate in the timely
execution of orders will be difficult.

With respect to the capability to dismantle nuclear weapons,
Russian officials have claimed that they can dismantle about 1,500
weapons per year. We have a moderate degree of confidence that they
can do this, but at that rate it would still take well over ten
years to dismantle the 15,000 weapons they say they will destroy.

Turning to the proliferation question resulting from the Soviet
breakup, we face a range of troubling possibilities, potentially
including the sale of materials, weapons, or a brain drain to
weapons programs abroad. In response, an international effort is
taking place, led by the United States but with the cooperation of
many Europeans and the republics of the CIS, which clearly should
mitigate the danger. Boris Yeltsin and most of the other republic
leaders are serious about preventing this, and have announced
policies to prevent this hemorrhage. Undersecretary of State
Bartholomew is in Moscow as we speak, recommending concrete actions
and offering US assistance.

We expect to see attempts by the former Soviet Union's defense
industrial sector to market dual-use technologies of concern,
notably for nuclear power and space launch vehicles. For example,
the space organization, Glav Kosmos, has reorganized to market a
joint Russian-Kazakhstan space launch services, and Russia is
offering SS-25 boosters as space launchers. Other nations with
ambitious weapons development programs are certain to try to exploit
the opportunity to get some of the world's most advanced weapons
technology and materials at bargain basement prices.

We have seen a number of the press reports that Soviet nuclear
materials have already been offered on the black market. Thus far
we have no independent corroboration that any of these stories are
true, and all that we have been able to check out have turned out to
be false. Because of the great demand for these materials, the
difficulty in determining the authenticity of nuclear materials, and
the widespread availability of small quantities of uranium and plutonium
in research facilities, we can expect to see many scams and hoaxes.
This will make our job even more difficult.

Smuggling in Central Asia and the Transcaucasus is an ancient
and highly developed art. Because these republics are near states
that are deeply interested in acquiring special weapons, traders, no
doubt, are acutely aware of the potential value of sensitive

                                        OMMITTEE SUBJECT: WEAPONS

materials and technologies and would be eager to act as middlemen.
Even when the KGB and the armed forces were controlling the borders
in these areas, local communities conducted largely uncontrolled
cross-border trade. Now, the borders are under local control.
Despite the rules of the Commonwealth, some republics or regions may
become more closely aligned with their non-CIS neighbors. Trade
that earns hard currency is likely to be encouraged and inhibitions
against trade in special weapons materials or equipment may weaken
and disappear.

We are closely watching for a brain drain from the Soviet
republics. We've seen these same Soviet scientists on television
and watched those reports. The sheer number of people associated
with Soviet weapons programs gives some idea of the potential size
of the drain. We estimate that nearly one million Soviets were
involved in the nuclear weapons program in one way or another, but
probably only a thousand or two have the skills to design nuclear
weapons.

A few thousand have the knowledge and marketable skills to
develop and produce biological weapons. The most worrisome problem
is probably those individuals whose skills have no civilian
counterpart, such as nuclear weapons designers and engineers
specializing in weaponizing CW and BW agents. They were well
treated under the Soviet system and will find it hard to get
comparable positions now.

Most Soviet scientists who want to emigrate probably would
prefer to settle in the West, but the West probably cannot absorb
them all. Based on Soviet scientific collaboration in the 1980s,
Cuba, India, Syria, Egypt, and Algeria are most likely to have the
contacts and resident scientists to assist emigrating Soviets.
There presumably is a point beyond which Russia and the other
republics would want to staunch the outflow of talent, but
scientists need not leave at all to pass on specifications or advice
to agents of another country.

I should add that we may also see leakage of highly
sophisticated, but less controlled, conventional military
technologies and weapons from the former Soviet republics.
Technologies of concern include stealth, counter-stealth, thermal
imaging, and electronic warfare. Weapons could include fuel-air
explosives, precision guided munitions, and advanced torpedos.

As a result of the proliferation of new weapons technologies,
conventional or special, I expect that foreign military capabilities
will expand and become considerably more complex to deal with.
Some, we will not have anticipated. The range of conditions under
which these capabilities might be used is much wider than we were
accustomed to in the past when the main threat was from the Soviet Union
and we understood it well. Keeping track of burgeoning foreign military
capabilities will be one of our greatest challenges in the years
ahead. The potential for technological surprise in the Third World
is growing as some international restrictions on foreign access to

Having discussed proliferation generally and in the CIS, I will now review the problem region by region. In the Middle East, Iraq is still a great challenge. Saddam has built formidable programs in all four areas of weapons of mass destruction. The UN Special Commission has worked diligently to eliminate Saddam's programs, but as the episode in the parking lot in Baghdad illustrates, Saddam digs in whenever the Commission gets close to something he particularly wants to protect.

There is no question that Desert Storm significantly damaged Iraq's special weapons productions programs. It will take varying lengths of time for Baghdad to recover. Nuclear weapons production is likely to take the longest time. Although the technical expertise is still there, much of the infrastructure for the production of fissile materials must be rebuilt. However, we measure the time required in a few, rather than many, years.

The chemical weapons production infrastructure also was severely damaged and will have to be rebuilt. Much of the hard-to-get production equipment was removed and hidden before the bombing started, however, and would be available for reconstruction. If UN sanctions are relaxed, we believe Iraq could produce modest quantities of chemical agents almost immediately, but it would take a year or more to recover the CW capability it previously enjoyed.

The biological weapons program also was damaged, but critical equipment for it, too, was hidden during the war. Because only a small amount of equipment is needed, the Iraqis could be producing BW materials in a matter of weeks of a decision to do so.

We believe a number, perhaps hundreds, of Scud missiles and much Scud and Condor production equipment remain in Iraq. The time and cost of reviving the missile program depend on the continuing inspection regime, and then on how easily the regime can get critical equipment from abroad.

In our opinion, Iraq will remain a primary proliferation threat at least as long as Saddam Hussein remains in power. The cadre of scientists and engineers

CONTINUED

0263 — 6

0071

PROLIFERATION IN THE NEW WORLD ORDER CHAIRED BY: SENATOR JOHN GLENN,
(D-OH); WITNESS: ROBERT GATES, CIA DIRECTOR
G-3-5 page# 1 WEDNESDAY JANUARY 15, 1992
```
dest=fns11182,hill,govaf,cia,nucweapon,weapc___armscont,intarms
dest+=fns00652,fns10000,fns13597,user,thdwd,defense,europe
dest+=asia,mideast,kazak,un,iran,nkor,cruisems,prc,abm,libya,skor,pak
dest+=biol,chemwar,iraq,cuba,india,alg,egypt,syria,milair,uranium
data
```

trained for these programs will be able to reconstitute any dormant program rapidly. Saddam clearly hopes his intransigence will outlast the international will for sanctions. Fortunately, international resolve to maintain those sanctions, including UN inspections, remains strong. As long as that is so, Saddam will be severely hampered from rebuilding his weapons program.

If the Iraqi government ever becomes serious about giving up its capacity to produce weapons of mass destruction, as mandated by UN Resolution 687, we should see a full accounting for its past actions. This would include an inventory of Iraq's nuclear materials, a description of its missile and warhead production infrastructure, admission that Baghdad did indeed have an offensive biological weapons program, including the production and weaponization of biological agents, and most important, an accurate list of the critical personnel and the programs and outside suppliers so the UN can better monitor any cessation of prohibited activities.

Iraq is not our only concern in the Gulf and the Middle East. Iran has embarked on an across-the-board effort to develop its military and defense industries. This effort includes programs in weapons of mass destruction not only to prepare for the potential reemergence of the Iraqi special weapons threat but to solidify Iran's preeminent position in the Gulf and Southwest Asia. Iran continues to shop Western markets for nuclear and missile technology, and is trying to lure back some of the technical experts Tehran drove abroad in the

Increasingly, however, Iran has turned to Asian sources of military and technical aid, and it probably hopes that its contacts in Kazakhstan will allow it to tap into Soviet weapons technology. Tehran's principal sources of special weapons since the Iran-Iraq war have been North Korea for long-range Scuds, and China for battlefield missiles, cruise missiles and nuclear-related technologies. China, for example, is supplying Iran with a miniature neutron source reactor and an electromagnetic isotope separator. This equipment has legitimate peaceful purposes, but Iranian public statements that it should have nuclear weapons suggest they intend otherwise.

Iran also says it has a right to chemical weapons in light of Iraq's use of chemical weapons against them, and we believe it has exercised this option. We also have good reason to believe that Iran is pursuing collaborative arrangements with other would-be special weapons developers in the region.

Syria, too, has turned to North Korea. Because Damascus has been unable to get SS-23s from the Soviet Union and now the CIS, it acquired an extended-range missile from Pyongyang. It also

appears to be seeking assistance from China and Western firms for an
improved capability with chemical and biological warheads. In the
nuclear area, Damascus is negotiating with China for a reactor.

Other countries in the region have -- seemed to have decided
recently to strengthen their own deterrent and defensive
capabilities as a hedge against long-term threats from Iran and a
resurgent Iraq. The Israelis continue to invest in the development
of the Arrow anti-tactical ballistic missile and test and maintain
their own ballistic missile force. The Saudis are expanding their
CSS-2 missile support facility, and Egypt has a missile production
facility that could begin operations at any time.

In North Africa, despite international outcries, Libya's CW
program continues. We estimate that the production facility at
Rabta has produced and stockpiled as many as a hundred tons of
chemical agents. The Libyans have cleaned up the Rabta plant,
perhaps in preparation for the long-awaited public opening of the
facility to demonstrate its supposed civilian pharmaceutical
purpose. But they have yet to reconfigure the plant to make it
incapable of producing chemical agents. Even if Rabta is closed
down, the Libyans have no intention of giving up CW production.
There have been a number of reports the Libya is constructing
another chemical weapons facility, one they hope will escape
international attention.

For several years, the Libyans have made a concerted effort to
build a BW facility, but this has not progressed very far. We
believe they need assistance from more technically advanced
countries to build one and make it work. Persistent efforts to deny
Libya access to nuclear, biological, and delivery system technology
have undoubted stalled these programs to a great extent by forcing
Qadhafi to turn to less advanced technology and less trustworthy
sources available in grey and black markets in the developing world.

Libya has by no means abandoned its long-term goal of extending
its military reach across the Eastern Mediterranean. Setbacks have
limited it to the relatively short-range SCUDs Libya now produces --
possesses. Both Russia and China have rejected Libyan purchase
requests. Tripoli is now shopping diligently throughout the world
for an alternative source, and recent South Korean allegations
suggest Libya has found a seller in North Korea.

As you know, Algeria is nearly finished building a nuclear
reactor it bought from China.

Both the Algerians and the Chinese have assured us the reactor will
be used for only peaceful purposes. But we are concerned about the
secrecy of the original agreement and the lack of inspections.
According to the International Atomic Energy Agency, Algeria
finalized an agreement with the IAEA to safeguard the reactor. The
IAEA Board of Governors will review the agreement at its meeting in
February. We hope this will lead to a quick inspection and allay
some of our concerns.

In South Asia, the arms race between India and Pakistan is a
major concern. Not only do both countries have nuclear weapon and
ballistic missile programs, they recently have pursued chemical
weapons as well. These programs are particularly worrisome because
of the constant tensions and conflict in Kashmir. We have no reason
to believe that either India or Pakistan maintains assembled or
deployed nuclear bombs. But such weapons could be assembled quickly
and both countries have **combat aircraft** that could be modified to
deliver them in a crisis. Both have publicly agreed to certain
confidence-building measures, such as not attacking each other's
nuclear facilities, and we are hopeful that the continuing dialogue
will bear fruit.

The United States continues to oppose exports of space launch
vehicles or advanced computer technology to either country by the
CIS, China, or MTCR partners because of the high probability that
such technology would end up in a nuclear long-range ballistic
missile program.

North Korea's programs are our most urgent national security
threat in East Asia. North Korea has invested heavily in the
military and depends on arms sales for much of its hard currency
earnings. It has produced and sold copies of the Soviet scud
missile to several Middle Eastern countries. It has also modified
its scuds, giving them longer range than Iraq's, and has sold them
to Iran and Syria. Pyongyang is not far from having a much larger
missile for sale, one with a range of at least 1,000 kilometers --
enough to reach Osaka, Vladivostok or Shanghai if deployed on North
Korean soil.

The North's nuclear program is our greatest concern. Pyongyang
has an entire infrastructure that can support the development of
nuclear weapons, from the mining of the **uranium** to the reprocessing
of reactor fuel to recover plutonium. It has constructed two
nuclear reactors whose sole purpose is to make plutonium. One of
these reactors has been operating for four years, and a second and
much larger reactor will start up this year.

In December, North and South Korea negotiated a historic
agreement in principle for a nuclear-free Korean Peninsula. Each
side has committed itself, and I quote, "Not to test, manufacture,
produce, receive, possess, store, deploy, or use," end quote,
nuclear weapons. Both sides also agreed not to have nuclear
reprocessing or uranium enrichment facilities. Verification, to
include on-site inspections, remains to be worked out, however.

We believe the significance, and indeed the value of the
North-South nuclear accord can be judged only by the inspection
regime Pyongyang ultimately accepts. North Korea has not been
forthcoming in this area until very recently. It signed the nuclear
nonproliferation treaty back in December 1985, and was thereby
obligated to declare and place all nuclear facilities under
safeguards. Pyongyang, however, only this month finally pledged to

0074

sign a safeguards agreement by February. We remain concerned with how the North will interpret its responsibility to permit IAEA inspections. The North has not yet even admitted the existence of, much less declared, its plutonium production reactors and reprocessing facility at Yongbyong (sp) Nuclear Research Center. It has consistently missed deadlines for completion of the agreement procedures, and several times has tacked on additional conditions to acceding to the agreement.

Overall, our concerns about the North's nuclear effort extend well beyond the Peninsula. We worry not only about the consequences for stability in northeast Asia if the North acquires nuclear weapons, but also about the possibility of Pyongyang putting these weapons and nuclear technology into the international marketplace.

As for North Korea's neighbor, China, they have made several -- several important public commitments that suggest an intention to honor international agreements on both missile and nuclear proliferation. Beijing is developing two solid fuel short-range ballistic missiles, the M-9 and M-11, that exceed the range and payload limits of the missile technology control regime, that is, a 500-kilogram payload and a range of 300 kilometers. It has offered to sell these missiles in the past, but indicated that its conditional commitment to abide by MTCR guidelines and parameters would apply to both missiles.

Last August, China pledged that it would sign the NPT, and its National Peoples Congress has now ratified the agreement. China is now obligated to require all recipients of its nuclear equipment to adhere to IAEA safeguards. This development is important because

CONTINUED

0263 - 10

HEARING OF THE SENATE GOVERNMENTAL AFFAIRS COMMITTEE SUBJECT: WEAPONS
PROLIFERATION IN THE NEW WORLD ORDER CHAIRED BY: SENATOR JOHN GLENN,
(D-OH); WITNESS: ROBERT GATES, CIA DIRECTOR
G-3-6 page# 1 WEDNESDAY, JANUARY 15, 1992

dest=fne11182,hill,sengovaf,cia,nucweapon,weapons,armscont,interna
dest+=fns00052,fns10000,fns13597,user,defense,europe,israel,intel
dest+=asia,mideast,un,iran,nkor,austral,prc,libya,swcy,pak
dest=biol,chemwar,iraq,fortr,safr,arg,braz
data

China has long been a supplier of nuclear technologies in the Third
World. While China has claimed that all such exports were for
peaceful purposes, it has not always required recipients to adhere
to safeguards. Despite its accession to the NPT we remain concerned
that Beijing could claim existing contracts are grandfathered and
therefore exempt from IAEA safeguards.

Unhappily I must report that commercial enterprises in the West
continue to sell sensitive technologies to countries developing
weapons of mass destruction. Some of this trade goes through front
companies or third countries to innocuous sounding consignees. Most
of the sales are of equipment that has some legitimate end use,
justifying the claims of exporting firms and export control
autorities that they had no way of knowing a particular shipment was
designed for a special weapons development program. In all too
many cases however, exporters knew very well who they were dealing
with. They may even have sought the business and collaborated with
the purchaser to evade export regulations. Libya, Iran and India
for example, are continuing to obtain advanced materials such as
specialty steels, high purity graphite and composite materials for
rocket motors from West European suppliers. The sale of precision
machine tools with missile and nuclear applications are of
particular concern.

There is good news on the non proliferation front, much of it
the result of United States leadership. Since the Gulf War and
revelations about Saddam Hussein's programs, many responsible
countries have expanded export control laws, increased penalties for
violators and stepped up enforcement regimes. International
organizations and agreements such as IAEA and the Missile Technology
Control Regime have taken on a new life. The governments of several
key countries have assured our State Department that they have
abandoned nuclear weapons or ballistic missile programs. For
example, South Africa has signed the NPT and Argentina and Brazil
have taken real steps away from their nuclear options. South Korea
and Taiwan, who once had entertained the thought of developing
nuclear weapons in the past have both walked away from this option.

The recent reunification talks with North Korea have shown that
the South is serious in its efforts to achieve a nuclear free
peninsula. Israel has publicly announced that it will abide by the
MTCR guidelines, and according to the Israeli press will not
cooperate any longer with South Africa on ballistic missile
development. Brazil has announced its space launch program has
been placed under civilian control, and the Argentine government has
said that it is investigating the suspended Condor II program.

Although the members of the MTCR and the Australia Group, the

0076

regime to control ▦ mical and biological weap — technology have been actively aiding new members -- adding new members to their rosters and refining specifications of equipment and materials covered, there are limits to what we can expect multilateral control regimes to accomplish. Some countries will find it -- never find it in their interest to join. Even membership is no guarantee of good behavior. Trade and other incentives conditioned to membership can force some countries to accede, even though they have little intention of enforcing the regulations.

Despite the greater awareness and interest in doing something about the proliferation problem, the greater availability of relevant materials and technologies, the difficult economic times in many potential supplier countries, and enduring regional animosities suggest that the problem will get worse.

I believe American intelligence plays a critical role in this nonproliferation effort. As I said in my opening remarks, proliferation is a top priority of the intelligence community. We recently formed a nonproliferation -- center, with senior officials from several agencies to better formulate and coordinate intelligence actions in support of US government policy. This center will coordinate the extensive and detailed information that all intelligence community components provide to arms and export control negotiators and to technical experts throughout the government. We are continuing to strengthen and add resources to this effort.

As the foregoing suggests, we have accumulated considerable information. At the same time, we're aware of our shortcomings. For example, while we correctly warned of Sadeam's nuclear program, we clearly underestimated its scope and pace.

We also have worked closely with the State Department, which in turn has worked closely with the IAEA and the UN Special Commission in implementing UN Resolution 687, and we have, and will where appropriate, share intelligence with other countries working to stem the proliferation threat, including the governments of the new republics of the Commonwealth of Independent States.

In addition to supporting the efforts of the US and other like-minded government in stemming proliferation, we have a responsibility to defense planners to assess the status of special weapons programs abroad and to forecast dangers in the long term. We can hope that there will be no further transfers of special weapons or delivery systems to potential enemies. We can hope that the countries that have said they will abandon development programs will do so, and we can hope that illicit -- technology transfers will stop. But we cannot assume that they will. In fact, it is likely that those countries that have special weapons or those developing them will keep what they have and try to make progress surreptitiously.

Advances in special weapons are extraordinarily difficult to

0263 — 12

monitor. We will do everything we can to unearth and examine all relevant
cases, and when we uncover dangerous developments we will present our
findings to the decision makers in the administration and to the Congress.

In closing, I would like to say that non-proliferation efforts
have had a positive affect. There is strong international support
for both the MTCR and the Australia Group, and the level of
attention to export controls among all civilized countries has never
been greater. Despite this, however, we have our work cut out for
us. As this presentation notes, there are still disturbing trends.
This message may be unpleasant, it may require difficult actions,
but as I pledged to the House Defense Policy panel last month, we
will continue to describe the world as it is, not as we or others
would wish it to be.

I hope that these comments will serve as a useful overview. I
would be happy to answer any questions that you have, Mr. Chairman,
on the subjects I've covered today. I'll answer all that I can, but
I know that you recognize that much of our information on this
subject is derived from sensitive intelligence sources and methods.
To jeopardize these would jeopardize obtaining information in the
future. Accordingly, when I believe answering publicly will
endanger those sources, I would be happy to respond either in a
closed session or for the classified record.

I would also add, before beginning to take your questions, that
I am far from an expert on most of these matters and may well turn
to my colleagues that I have with me here.

SEN. GLENN: Fine. Anytime you wish to call them up to the
table there, that's fine. And I appreciate your broad overview of
this whole situation.

One of the first questions I would have is on one of your
statements on the last page there, from the top of page 13 of your
testimony: "We have and will, where appropriate, share intelligence
with other countries working to stem the proliferation threat,
including the governments of the new republics of the CIS." Are we
sharing any intelligence information with the CIS intelligence
people now?

MR. GATES: No, sir, I don't think we are. But we prepared to
do so.

SEN. GLENN: Have there been -- is that in the offing? Have we
talked to them about this?

MR. GATES: There have been some very preliminary contacts. I
think that most of the discussion of this has taken place at the
policy level up to this time.

SEN. GLENN: Are the Soviets going ahead now with new nuclear
warhead development?

0763- 13

HEARING OF THE SENATE GOVERNMENTAL AFFAIRS COMMITTEE SUBJECT: WEAPONS
PROLIFERATION IN THE NEW WORLD ORDER CHAIRED BY: SENATOR JOHN GLENN,
(D-OH); WITNESS: ROBERT GATES, CIA DIRECTOR
6-3-6 page 4 WEDNESDAY, JANUARY 15, 1992

        MR. GATES: I think that their R&E programs are continuing.
But -- Gordon, do you want to answer that?

        MR. OEHLER: Yes, they are continuing.

        SEN. GLENN: Just identify yourself for the record here, and
then go ahead and use the mike. Pull those mikes up close,
incidentally. They're not very good, they're very directional.

        MR. OEHLER: My name is Gordon Oehler and I'm the National
Intelligence Officer for science, technology and proliferation.

        There is still some continuing ongoing work, but it's a much
lower level. The funding for these programs has been drastically
cut and therefore the programs themselves have been retarded quite a
bit.

        SEN. GLENN: Well, I know it's hard to turn around big programs
like that instantaneously. It's something that I think we should be
watching very, very closely because it might signal a long-term
intent. If those programs are not turned around

                        CONTINUED

dest=fns11:82,hill,sengovai,cia,nucweapon,weapons,armscont,intarms
dest+=1059,ntcliab,ltr,12ah,arop,skep,pak,defense,nuclear
dest+=biol,chemwar,iraq,fortr,icbm
data

expeditiously as we think they should be, it would indicate perhaps
intent that we wouldn't like particularly. How about in chemical
weapons and biological weapons? Are their programs in developing
those continuing?

MR. GATES: We are beginning to see on the biological front,
for example, that the new government in Russia takes much more
seriously than apparently its predecessor our concern about
continuing biological programs. And we are beginning to get some
information that suggests that those programs are being turned off.
They are turning their attention on the chemical side to the
destruction of chemical weapons problem. They now have some -- we
estimate something like 40,000 tons of agent, chemical agent. A
good deal of that is old, represents a safety hazard, and they're
working on technologies for its destruction.

(ASIDE.) Do you want to add anything to that?

MR. OEHLER: No, that's fine.

SEN. GLENN: How good -- how much do we know about, and how
good do we think their system is for coping with this taking weapons
down, dismantling them, and disposing of the material? Do they have
adequate systems to even do that? It's an enormous problem. It's
not easy. We think you just destroy them, but you can't just
destroy them like that.

MR. GATES: No, sir.

SEN. GLENN: I got with the staff one day, was going through
just what would be required for us to go ahead and say, "Okay, we're
going to take down 10,000 nuclear weapons." Well, then you start
going through the process of how you transport them, where you store
it, what you do with the material after it's over. We have Pantex
down there that can do work on this that everybody knows about, of
course. Do we need more? And then, you talk about the Soviets that
probably have gone into the disposition problem less than we have
and you wonder how fast we're going to be able to get these things
done. Do you have any estimates on those?

MR. GATES: Not very fast, Mr. Chairman. As I indicated in the
testimony, the Soviets themselves, or the Russians -- and they have
the only dismantlement, nuclear dismantlement, facility in the CIS
-- their people say they have the capability to dismantle about
1,500 warheads a year. They claim they're going to take down about
15,000, so that's ten years for that amount, and that's half their
stockpile. I would say, based on the variety of problems that
they're having internally right now, that 1,500 warheads a year is

probably an optimistic assessment on their part.

On the chemical side, they are just beginning to investigate
the technologies for the destruction of chemical weapons, and we
estimate that it would take them several years to develop those
technologies and then a few more years to actually carry out the
destruction of the weapons. So, it's not a near-term solution at
all.

SEN. GLENN: I was concerned enough about this, I've asked OTA
to look at this, as to what's involved with this taking down
thousands of nuclear weapons and trying to dispose of them or make
them safe or store -- however we're going to do this. And it's
going to take them some time to do the study. They've got men in
too, as time goes along.

So it is something that is not easy. We think that, you know,
the danger's going to be over right now, and yet the weapons are out
there, still targeted, still there -- not going to be able to be
pulled down for a lengthy period of time.

Let me get into the command and control problems here that
we've all been concerned about during this transition period. You
mentioned that you think there are two footballs, or whatever, right
now that are ready to go. With what you've known about their
command and control in the past, is that adequate? How does it
compare with ours?

MR. GATES: Well, I think that what I can say in an
unclassified form -- I'm certainly no expert on our own, and I think
everybody is familiar with the football that accompanies the
President. So what we are seeing is a situation in the CIS where
the command has gone from the three that I indicated, where both the
-- beyond the President of the then-Soviet Union and the Chief of
the General Staff and the Defense Minister to two: the President of
Russia and the Chief of the General -- Chief of the --
Commander-in-Chief of the CIS force -- strategic forces.

We don't have any indication that there are any problems or
concerns associated with this reduction from three to two, and, in
fact, I think one of the things people have found reassuring just in
the last few weeks has been the relative harmony with which the
commonwealth members have addressed themselves to the question of
the disposition of nuclear weapons and the command and control of
nuclear weapons. They've got lots of differences on many issues,
including the disposition of conventional forces, that we've been
reading about in the newspapers, but I think most of the people who
are following this closely have been greatly encouraged by the level
of responsibility that's been brought to bear by the leaders on
this. So we don't really -- I think we do not see that as a source
of concern.

SEN. GLENN: Well, there's concern to everybody, including some

0081

that are written about in the press or on TV -- it concerns me, too -- is whether a dissident military person off at some remote post where there are nuclear weapons, and whether it's in one of the four republics or wherever they might be -- whether they have it within their capability to make a launch. If they would become a dissident "Hunt for Red October" type dissident of some kind or other, might launch one for whatever reasons. Is it possible -- could you tell us whether it's possible for them to do that, or are these codes and interlocking codes and permissive links and PALs and all this sort of thing -- permissive action links -- are these sufficiently good that we don't need to worry about a single person launching something that would still be targeted at the United States?

MR. GATES: Mr. Chairman, on an unclassified level I would confine myself to saying that I think that the experts in our community do not believe that there is a concern about an y -- of the older much less sophisticated very small tactical devices might be stolen or slip out of control -- out of control of the central authorities.

They are aware of this and they are engaged in a major effort, or they are aware of this possibility and they are engaged in a major effort in consolidating their -- the storage of these tactical nuclear weapons. They are -- they have for several years been consolidating these weapons and withdrawing them into fewer and fewer areas of the Soviet Union, and now they are working to bring all of them back into the Soviet -- back into Russia where they can be controlled prior to their dismantlement. So they have -- I would say that our confidence level is strong on command and control and we are further heartened by the measures that they are taking to strengthen their command and control over even all of the tactical weapons that they have.

SEN. GLENN: Well I was talking primarily about the ICBMs and SLBMs, things like that, but you bring up the tactical and I was going to get to that too, me of these are actually in their territory, could they be used without the coding having to come from Moscow?

MR. GATES: On an unclassified level, Mr. Chairman, let me just say that we don't have perfect knowledge about this matter but I would say that we have good confidence in their control of these tactical weapons as well in the manner that you describe. Now

CONTINUED

0263-17

destmfns111A7,h-1),c ■ovaf,cia,nucweapon,weapoil,armscort,intarme
dest+=fns00652,fns10000,fns13597,ussr
dest+=mideast,un,iran,cuba,nkor,iraq,pak,alg,syria,africa,asia
dest+=biol,chemwar,iraq,germany,easteur,libya,thdwd
data

some of these people have no alternative employment or see their
families in desperate circumstances, they may be induced to emigrate
to some of these countries, or they may remain in place and, in
exchange for cash, provide information. This is, again, a problem
that I think that Under Secretary Bartholomew is addressing with the
republic leaders right now in Moscow.

As I say, we don't -- part of the problem with some of these
scientists in these research centers is that they are at the end of
a very long supply network. They are in remote areas, and they fall
into the same category as the military and hospitals and others --
those that have been in the past dependent on a -- on the
centralized supply system for their day-to-day supplies -- food and
so forth. And it's precisely these networks that are breaking down
the fastest in the Soviet Union.

So I would say that, of all of the possibilities that we have
addressed here with our discussion of command and control and so
forth, it is this concern about the scientists and their future --
particularly given the large numbers of them -- that concerns us the
most.

SEN. GLENN: What are your views as to who is the most likely
nuclear proliferator around the world? Some place like North Korea
at this point, or the Soviet Union? And we read in the papers from
time to time about Cuba, Iran, Iraq, Pakistan's development, of
course, we've known about for a long time. Is the likely
information supply point more likely to be some place like North
Korea now, as they develop their program, more than the Soviet
Union?

MR. GATES: Well, as I indicated in the statement, I think our
best guess -- and it's really no more than that -- would be that --
would be the first place these people would turn would be to those
countries where there have been the greatest contacts between
scientists or among scientists in these different areas. I think I
mentioned Cuba and Algeria, Syria, two or three others along those
lines where there have been, over the past decade or decade and a
half, a fair number of these contacts.

SEN. GLENN: Yeah. You concentrated in your statement more on
the nuclear end of things, which we are certainly concerned about.
Could you go through some of those same countries and give us a
little information on what their chemical and biological
capabilities are, because that, to me, is almost more important
than the nuclear. I won't say it's more important, but you get the
same effect out of -- eventually, perhaps, out of a biological

0083

weapon. You can almost have the same effect you can out of a nuke.
It just doesn't occur quite as fast.

And the developing countries, if they were looking to have a
weapon of mass destruction, it seems to me it's far more likely at
this point to be developments along the biological or chemical --
particularly biological line, though, which are much easier for them
to get.

I know we had Judge Webster here one day testifying a couple of
years ago, and he sat where you're sitting and I asked him what, if you
wanted to set up a biological plant or a chemical plant what would be the
size of the area that you would need. And he turned to one of the people
he had brought along with him and I think the reply was it could be in
an area about the size of this hearing room, which indicates the
difference in level of technology also, as well as just the space.
And so that makes your job in intelligence, of course, far more
difficult, to find that sort of thing.

But what nations are likely to be the biggest proliferators of
chemical and biological weapons?

MR. GATES: I would say that -- acknowledging North Korea as
one -- that in broad terms that the problem is focused in the region
from North Africa to Southwest Asia, and there are a number of
countries in that area that we know have worked on or are developing
or have chemical weapons. I mentioned in the hearing -- or in the
testimony, where we have certain knowledge, Libya, Syria, Iran and
Iraq. There may be others as well.

SEN. GLENN: Is there any Soviet or former -- CIS now
cooperation with Iran in Iran's efforts to get nuclear weapons?

MR. GATES: Not to my knowlege.

SEN. GLENN: Where are they getting their major information
from? Are they developing it indigenously?

MR. GATES: Yes, they could easily, on the chemical side.
That's the problem, as you've identified it, on both the chemical
and the biological side these weapons have been with us since the
beginning of the century, and the technologies involved in mustard
or sarin or some of those things are pretty primitive.

SEN. GLENN: How good a handle do we have on the Soviets'
storage or their supplies and where they're stored for chemical
weapons and biological weapons and what they're doing, particularly
with biological?

MR. OEHLER: Well, they have not admitted to having a
biological weapons program. You remember we have accused them of
having one because of the Sverdlovsk incident in 1979. So they have
not made any statements on that.

0084

On the chemical weapons, of course, you know there is an agreement, a treaty with the United States, and they have declared their chemical facilities and have taken a number of steps to centralize them.

SEN. GLENN: Do we inspect those, or does IEA. They don't inspect the chemical or biological --

MR. OEHLER: It's not the IAEA but it is a --

SEN. GLENN: A UN organization?

MR. OEHLER: -- a unilateral, I believe US-USSR treaty arrangements. Bi-lateral, pardon me.

MR. GATES: We or the State Department can get back to you with a specific answer on it.

SEN. GLENN: All right. Good.

One of the difficulties you pointed out has been the difficulty in trying to get the free world's businessmen not to do business with countries that are trying to develop weapons of mass destruction. The Germans in particular have had a problem because they didn't have a law that would prevent their businessmen from exporting and so some of them did that. I talked personally to Helmut Kohl when he over here once about this, and he said that they -- he told me he

CONTINUED

0263-20

0085

dest=fns:1182,hill,sengovaf,cia,nucweapon,weapons,armscont,intarms
dest+=fns0652,fns0000,fns13517,ussr,austral,india
dest+=mideast,iran,nkor,iraq,pak,
dest+=biol,chemwar,iraq,germany,easteur,libya
date

knew the question was going to come up and they were going to take care
of this two weeks after he went back, gave me a date when it was
going to be before the bundestag, and that it was going to be corrected
so they would have that authority. But I understand that what has
happened is they've had enough problem with some of their civil
liberties people and so on that they didn't want to put these
restrictions on. So, some of the restrictions we thought were going to
go on businesses over there just have not occurred yet. So some of
this — the proliferation, while we're concerned about it, coming out
of places of Soviet — former Soviet Union and China and North Korea or
wherever, some of it is enhanced, certainly, by just the fact that we
haven't had adequate export controls in places like Germany and, to
some extent, some of our own people in this country.

MR. GATES: I would just mention in that connection, Mr.
Chairman. I think that the Germans have, in fact, passed a number of —
have passed legislation that strengthens their export controls, but it
is an interesting phenomenon that in the wake of the end of the Cold
War, there is tremendous pressure around the world for easing export
controls, not strengthening them, because most of those export controls
in the past were aimed at the Soviet Union and the countries of Eastern
Europe and were not written or formulated in the first instance to
apply to proliferation-related problems. So, other than where you have
voluntary arrangements such as MTCR and Australia Group, you're really
beginning at the beginning in terms of a body of legislation in a
variety of countries for having to deal with this kind of problem.

SEN. GLENN: Well, we've tried to deal government by government
and tried to do things that way, and that's fine. I think it was a
good effort. But I think it has not worked the way we should have it
— it should be working. I put in legislation. It was referred to the
Foreign Relations Committee and it's now been passed — I think it was
19 to nothing — over there in their vote on it. It would say that we
would take a little different approach and say that where we know that
companies, whatever their nationality, are supplying materials like
that and we disagree with that, that we could restrict their sales and
their business in this country, either government or private, and I
hope we can get that passed. That would put some teeth in this, I
think, and make some of these companies think twice.

MR. GATES: One thing that has helped our capabilities from the
intelligence standpoint on this, Mr. Chairman, has been the
intelligence effort to monitor the implementation of the sanctions
against Iraq. We've developed a variety of sources and approaches to
dealing with these kinds of problems that I think will enhance our
ability in the future to be able to help the policymakers in terms of
making demarches or doing business with foreign governments that may be

0086

involved or where there may be companies involved in violating either
sanctions or export controls.

We came up with the material for something like 1,000 demarches
during the war of violations of the sanctions against Iraq.

In the process of doing that, we also developed some new procedures
in terms of how we can make intelligence information available to
policymakers, that they then can use with foreign governments.

Part of the problem we've had in the past has been taking
intelligence information and making it available in a way that can
be used with a foreign government so that they have some specifics
in hand. It's not good enough just to go to them and say "One of
your companies is involved in a violation," unless you can say what
the company is. And during the period leading up to the war with
Iraq and during the war and subsequent to it, we were able to
develop information that basically said we not only know this
country, but this company and sometimes these individuals. And so I
think our ability to support that kind of an effort has been
improved substantially over the last year.

SEN. GLENN: You keep lists of firms that are doing the nuclear
trafficking, then?

MR. GATES: Yes, sir.

SEN. GLENN: Yeah. All over the world.

MR. GATES: We're watching.

SEN. GLENN: As best you can. All right, good. Well, that
would fit in perfectly with the legislation I'm talking about, if we
wanted to really clamp down on this.

In regard to Pakistan, which countries have been the key
suppliers of Pakistan's nuclear programs?

MR. GATES: That's a long list, Mr. Chairman. There have been
a -- (laughs) -- there have been a variety of countries that have
provided support to Pakistan. I think we might be able to provide a
list on a classified basis.

SEN. GLENN: Okay. Good. Would there be a list available that
could be provided to us of the companies specifically?

MR. GATES: Let me -- let me check and see.

SEN. GLENN: All right, fine.

MR. GATES: If we have it we might be able to do that on a
classified basis.

SEN. GLENN: All right. Good. Tensions seemed to have eased between Pakistan and India over the past several months, but it doesn't lessen my concern about both countries efforts in the nuclear area. Are these countries both stockpiling nuclear weapons now? Is a South Asian nuclear arms race under way? Have they both gotten to the point of stockpiling existing weapons? Or maybe they're not all put together but they could be within a matter of hours or days.

MR. GATES: Yeah. I think that I'm certainly far from expert and I'll refer to Dr. Oehler, but I think that the view of our people is that they do not actually stockpile the weapons for safety reasons. It is clear that -- it is our judgment that we gave to the President in the summer of 1990 that we could no longer certify that Pakistan -- or that we could no longer provide information that suggested Pakistan did not have a -- or possess a nuclear device. But let me defer to Gordon on that.

MR. OEHLER: I think that it is our judgment that both countries have all of the parts or can make the parts on very short notice. And so we are very careful of stating it that way. They could have nuclear devices in a very short period of time, but we believe that they would not want to assemble them for safety reasons.

SEN. GLENN: How about delivery systems? Is there any evidence

CONTINUED

0263-23

  dest=fns11182,hill,sengovaf,cia,nucweapon,weapons,armscont,intarms
  dest+=fns00652,fns10000,fns13597,un
  dest+=mideast,iran,iraq,
  dest+=biol,chemwar,germany,syria,nkor
data

Some Middle East states will have nuclear, chemical, and biological
weapons in ten years if they continue to acquire armaments. These
nations included by his statement: Iraq, Iran, and Syria. And
Porzner claims the chief supplier of material has been North Korea.
He says further that if Iraq is not strictly controlled, it will
re-achieve its former technological standard within about two years.
He also says that Iran will be able to build a nuclear weapon by
2000 and Syria already has poison gas factories. Would you comment
on those remarks and do you agree with his assessment?

     MR. GATES: I don't think we have any reason to disagree with
that overall assessment.

     SEN. GLENN: It's correct. Okay. And that's coming basically
from North Korea, then?

     MR. GATES: They've gotten help from North Korea --

     SEN. GLENN: It was his statement.

     MR. GATES: -- but not just North Korea. The Syrians and
others have gotten help from others as well.

     MR. OEHLER: Well, the North Korean assistance in the Middle
East has been to date primarily ballistic missiles, not CW or
anything else -- nuclear.

     SEN. GLENN: Back to Iraq again. What's the likelihood Saddam
may already have nuclear materials for bomb making? If he does, how
long would it take, under today's conditions, for him to make one or
more weapons? Do you think it's advanced to that point?

     MR. GATES: It is -- I think it's our judgment, and Gordon can
correct me if I'm mistaken -- I think it's our judgment that he does
not have the fissile material yet to assemble a nuclear device.

     Had the war not taken place, it is our view that he would have
had a device probably by the end of this year. It is our view that
if the sanctions were lifted and there were -- and he basically
could run his program the way he did before the war, that it would
only be a few years before he would be back where he was.

     You want to add anything?

     MR. OEHLER: That's correct. No, nothing additional.

     SEN. GLENN: Yeah. We were all -- we were depending, perhaps,

0263~24

HEARING OF THE SENATE GOVERNMENTAL AFFAIRS COMMITTEE SUBJECT: WEAPONS
PROLIFERATION IN THE NEW WORLD ORDER   CHAIRED BY: SENATOR JOHN GLENN,
(D-OH);   WITNESS: ROBERT GATES, CIA DIRECTOR
G-S-12 page# 2 WEDNESDAY, JANUARY 15, 1992

too much on IAEA and that 28 pounds of French weapons-grade material
that was in there, that they went in -- as I recall, it was 28
pounds -- that they checked every six months under normal IAEA
inspections.

We found afterwards that there was an enormous industrial or
nuclear complex in Iraq that we really didn't know that much about.
How confident are we that we know everything about Iraq right now?
Has all that now come out?

MR. GATES: Well, we certainly know a great deal more than we
did before the war, thanks to the intrusive inspections that have
taken place. I think our intelligence is better in addition to what
the inspectors have uncovered.

I think one of the things that we've learned is -- there have
been a number of lessons learned out of all of this. One is, I
think, that this experience has been a real eye-opener for the IAEA
and other international bodies themselves about what was going on, even at
a time that -- when they were conducting inspections.

I think, also, what we have learned in terms of what I
mentioned earlier on our own shortcomings on -- with respect to the
pace and scale of the program is that we had inadequate human
intelligence about what actually was going on. And one of the
reasons for some of the initiatives that I have described in terms
of strengthening our human intelligence capability is that,
particularly with respect to chemical and biological weapons, but
also with respect to early identification of nuclear programs, it's
very difficult for us to get at these, to learn about them through
technical intelligence means. We need somebody who is aware of
these programs early on. And so we need to improve in that area;
and I think that that's an important reason why we -- while we were
aware of the fact of the program, we underestimated its pace and
scale.

SEN. GLENN: Well, every time that we think that the UN
inspectors have uncovered the last thing over there, or we hope
they've uncovered it, something new seems to turn up. How confident
are you that we now really have a handle on what Saddam Hussein's
at he
had going on. For example, we are fairly confident that he, as I
indicated in the testimony, has got several hundred Scud missiles,
but we sure are having some difficulty finding them.

SEN. GLENN: Yeah.

MR. GATES: And so we have, I think, a pretty good handle on
what we think he's doing, and what he has preserved, but in terms of
where everything is, and whether we have identified everything, no,

0263-25

0090

HEARING OF THE SENATE GOVERNMENTAL AFFAIRS COMMITTEE SUBJECT: WEAPONS
PROLIFERATION IN THE NEW WORLD ORDER. CHAIRED BY: SENATOR JOHN GLENN,
(D-OH); WITNESS: ROBERT GATES, CIA DIRECTOR
A-A-17 page 5 WEDNESDAY, JANUARY 15, 1992

I don't think we can be totally confident of that. I would note in
reference to the newspaper story this morning, though, on these
the parts for these centrifuges that's just been revealed -- in
fact, we were aware that this was a problem as early as the summer
of 1990 when there was -- a number of these things were seized in
Frankfurt Airport. So -- and we -- but by the same token, I would
say we were not able to identify this alternative site that was
being described for this enrichment process, although we had several
candidate sites and were looking at them kind of one by one in terms
of trying to identify where they might have been. I don't know, do
you want to add anything?

MR. OEHLER: That's right.

SEN. GLENN: Can we say with considerable confidence that we
think he does not have a weapons-making capability right now?

MR. GATES: Yes, sir, I think we can.

MR. OEHLER: I think, certainly. His infrastructure is on hold
right now.

SEN. GLENN: Okay, well, if the UN -- those special inspection
teams that are over there, if they halt, will the existing IAEA
safeguards be sufficient to verify he wasn't -- is not again
working on the bomb?

MR. OEHLER: Well, the UN measure allows for inspections on
into the future. And as long as those inspections continue, the
will of the UN is to continue with the sanctions, and if they do
take place, I think that we will retard his nuclear program.

CONTINUED

    dest=fns11162,hill,sengovaf,cia,nucweapon,weapons,armscont,intarms
    dest+=fns00652,fns10000,fns13537,un,cuba,safr
    dest+=mideast,iran,iraq,jordan,alg,uranium,prc,france,intel,russia,ussr
    dest+=biol,chemwar,germany,syria,nkor,libya,soamer,arg,braz,caribb,centamer
    data

SEN. GLENN: I guess it makes us all nervous when -- there's a
lot of things there in Iraq we did not know in the past.   I know you
can't know everything, you don't have a crystal ball out there
that's perfect but there are an awful lot of things that were not
known over there and we wonder if all that information is now out so
we are not going to get blindsided in the future?

There were reports earlier this month that suggested that over
10 metric tons of uranium were shipped by truck through Jordan to
Algeria from Iraq.   Can you tell us anymore about this?

MR. OEHLER: I know nothing about it.

MR. GATES: We'll have to check on that.

SEN. GLENN: The London Sunday Times reported that Western
intelligence now believes the Iraqis and Algerians may have formed a
nuclear axis, as they termed it, to build a nuclear weapon.   The
report indicates that Algeria may have enough plutonium to build a
primitive bomb by 1995.   For all of the UN's efforts to restrict and
ultimately end Iraq's nuclear ambitions how can we protect against
multilateral efforts with the Iraqis to produce a nuclear weapons?
First, I guess, how accurate do you think that Times report is?

MR. GATES: We don't have anything that would verify what that
London Sunday Times article said.   The possibility of collaboration
among these governments, I think is a real one and it's one that
both through intelligence sources and diplomatic means we need to
watch very closely, but we don't have anything that would suggest
that that sort of thing has happened yet.

SEN. GLENN: The French intelligence reportedly learned of the
supply of a research reactor to Algeria by China again, as early as
1987.   Did they share that with us or when did we learn about that
transition -- or that transaction?

MR. OEHLER: In my view that information is wrong, sir.   I
don't believe to my knowledge that they had information of that back
at that time.   I may be wrong, that's my knowledge.

SEN. GLENN: Libya.   A press report from last week indicates
that two Russian scientists were approached by Libya to work in
their nuclear energy program.   Obviously the scientists skills could
be used in a nuclear weapons program as well.   Now you have
commented briefly on this.   Specifically with regard to Libya, have
they gone out on a recruitment program as far as you know?

0263-27

MR. GATES: We have seen the rumors but we don't have an
corroboration.

SEN. GLENN: An article in the Christian Science Monitor a
couple of weeks ago asserts that some White House officials were
quoted in December saying that the US government is convinced that
Iran has launched a secret effort to build an atomic bomb, we
mentioned that earlier. It further asserts that we have already
identified a number of possible undeclared nuclear facilities in
Iran. Meanwhile, a recent op-ed in the Washington Post further
allege that Iran now has enough enriched uranium for a bomb. Are
these charges correct, and if so what are we doing to encourage the
Iranians to provide full disclosure about their activities to the
IAEA.

MR. OEHLER: We do not believe that they have any significant
quantities of enriched uranium. They do have nuclear research
facilities, as I mentioned before, which they haven't necessarily
announced to the world. There isn't a need to declare those
because they don't have nuclear materials in them necessarily.

SEN. GLENN: **South America, in Argentina and Brazil**, what can
you tell us about their programs? They've signed and are supposedly
putting into force an agreement to open their nuclear facilities to
mutual inspection. Neither country, however, has signed the NPT,
and neither has yet fully implemented the Treaty of Tlatelolco,
which would prohibit nuclear weapons in **Latin America**. In light of
these facts, how confident are you that the Brazilians and
Argentinians are serious about their earlier pledge to use nuclear
energy exclusively for peaceful purposes?

MR. GATES: Let me respond first and then invite Dr. Oehler to
add. I think we take seriously the commitment on the part of the
leaders of both Brazil and Argentina to not pursue nuclear weapons
programs. By the same token, Argentina remains an active vendor of
nuclear technologies for peaceful purposes all over the world and
sort of end to end in terms of equipment and material and so forth.
But we don't have any indication that that is for weapons purposes
at this point. I think that, as I said at the outset, that we take
seriously the commitments on the part of the leaderships of these
two countries with respect to not having nuclear weapons and to
implementing those diplomatic accords that you've described.

But do you want to add anything?

MR. OEHLER: I think just maybe a little balance, that Brazil
has been marketing nuclear technologies, peaceful nuclear
technologies, as well.

SEN. GLENN: Coming a little farther north up to **Cuba**,
according to a recent -- to a report in the Journal of Commerce,
which was in November of last year, DIA reported in a study that the
Cubans have shown an interest in acquiring nuclear weapons material.
And a Cuban defector, Jose Oro (sp), also reportedly has said that

HEARING OF THE SENATE GOVERNMENTAL AFFAIRS COMMITTEE SUBJECT: WEAPONS
PROLIFERATION IN THE NEW WORLD ORDER CHAIRED BY: SENATOR JOHN GLENN,
(D-OH); WITNESS: ROBERT GATES, CIA DIRECTOR
5-3-13 page# 3 WEDNESDAY, JANUARY 15, 1992
Cuba has launched a program to develop its own reprocessing plant.
Could you comment on that?

MR. GATES: No, I can't comment on that. I simply don't know
much. Let me say that their economy is in very bad shape right now,
and probably any program, if they do have one, would be very slow in
maturing. As you know, they have no reactors. They have contracted
to build some pressurized water reactors, which are not the best
reactors for producing plutonium for nuclear weapons. And it will
be — (inaudible) —

SEN. GLENN: How about South Africa? They recently became a
party to the NPT. How confident are you that all of their sensitive
nuclear materials have been fully declared to IAEA? Do we have
independent estimates on that?

MR. GATES: I have not seen the full declaration yet. And so,
there has not yet been an intelligence community judgment on that.

SEN. GLENN: Okay. Back to the Soviet Union again, or the CIS
now, do we know where the CIS chemical weapons and biological
weapons, if they have them, are stored?

MR. GATES: Well, I think we have a pretty good idea on the
chemical weapons. They've had to declare those sites. And we have
raised sites with them. So, I think we have a pretty good fix on
that.

I think we do not have anything like that kind of information
on their biological weapons. We have a number of places where we
think the biological program, where the biological agents are
produced, and where we are suspicious that they have biological
agents. But,

CONTINUED

0263—29

0094.

HEARING OF THE SENATE GOVERNMENTAL AFFAIRS COMMITTEE SUBJECT: WEAPONS
PROLIFERATION IN THE NEW WORLD ORDER CHAIRED BY: SENATOR JOHN GLENN,
(D-OH);   WITNESS: ROBERT GATES, CIA DIRECTOR
S-3-14 page# 1 WEDNESDAY, JANUARY 15, 1992
     dest=fns11182,hill.senqovaf,cia,nucweapon,weapons,armscont,interms
     dest=fns00652,fns10000,fns13537,terr,icbm,thdwd,easteur
     dest=midreast,iran,irau,intel,russia,ussr
     dest=biol.chemvar,soamer,arg,braz,caribb,centamer
     data

     I don't think we have a good idea on their storage facilities.

     SEN. GLENN: Are those facilities you say we do have a good
handle on, are those all in Russia per se or are they in some of the
other republics, too?

     MR. GATES: All in Russia.

     SEN. GLENN: They're all in Russia. Okay.

     Do we know whether any of the weapons have been sold or
exported to other -- to any of the other republics?

     MR. GATES: I don't think we have any evidence of that.

     SEN. GLENN: And not outside the former Soviet Union I presume.

     MR. GATES: No.

     SEN. GLENN: No, okay.

     (Pause.)

     Back to their nuclear weapons per se, do we know the extent to
which CIS' nuclear weapons are equipped with disabling devices, if
they're tampered with?

     MR. GATES: Can we --

     SEN. GLENN: Getting back to the terrorist thing and a stealing
of a weapon or something like that and whether it would be usable or
not. Do they have disabling devices that would inactivate the whole
thing if they were -- unless somebody knew exactly what they were
doing?

     MR. GATES: I'd like to respond to that on a classified basis,
Mr. Chairman.

     SEN. GLENN: All right, good. Yeah.

     (Pause.)

     You mentioned the possibility of sharing intelligence -- back
to that one, too -- with the CIS. What kind of intelligence do you
think that we would be able to share with them and get from them?
Could you elaborate a little more on what you would expect out of
that in the future?

EARING OF THE SENATE GOVERNMENTAL AFFAIRS COMMITTEE SUBJECT: WEAPONS
ROLIFERATION IN THE NEW WORLD ORDER CHAIRED BY: SENATOR JOHN GLENN,
D-OH); WITNESS: ROBERT GATES, CIA DIRECTOR
-3-14 page# 3 WEDNESDAY, JANUARY 15, 1992

MR. GATES: It's hard to be precise because we haven't really
gotten into it at this point. It seems to me that if we learned --
if we were to receive independent evidence of some of the press
stories that we have seen or perhaps even wanted to pursue some of
the press stories, that talking with them would provide an
opportunity for them to conduct their own independent check to see
if these stories were true, or work with them to identify
vulnerabilities in their control system if we had reports that there
might have been leakage, or if we had information that perhaps
certain scientists or military officers were contemplating some
kind of action, I think we could find ways to share that kind of
information so they could pursue it.

SEN. GLENN: We spoke earlier about the ICBMs and SLBMs that
still are targeted on this country, still have the latitudes and
longitudes of our major sites all targeted, even as we speak here
today. But branching out to other places, how many Third World
ballistic missiles will be able to reach the US, say in the decade
or say by the year 2000?

How fast do you see those programs developing, and how much of a
threat do you see them being to this country?

MR. GATES: Well, as I indicated, I think that we do anticipate
that at least some will have the capability of reaching the United
States by the end of the decade. I don't know in terms of the
numbers.

MR. DEHLER: Not any of the major Third World countries that
we're interested in.

SEN. GLENN: Can you tell us what those countries might be.

MR. DEHLER: I think what you would say -- what I would say
would be the countries with the more advance space-launch vehicle
programs can also, if they so choose, use those same boosters for
military purposes.

SEN. GLENN: Okay, which would be what countries?

MR. DEHLER: Well, I would just as soon not name all of the
names here --

SEN. GLENN: All right.

MR. DEHLER: But I think that you can make up the list from
that.

SEN. GLENN: Yeah, okay. (Pause.) Have you run any analysis
that would indicate what you think the chances are that there could
possibly be a seizure of nuclear weapons -- what the likelihood of
that is, or fissile material that could be developed by some of
these countries that might be a danger to us?

0263 — 3/

0096

HEARING OF THE SENATE GOVERNMENTAL AFFAIRS COMMITTEE SUBJECT: WEAPONS
PROLIFERATION IN THE NEW WORLD ORDER CHAIRED BY: SENATOR JOHN GLENN,
(D-OH);   WITNESS: ROBERT GATES, CIA DIRECTOR
3-3-14 page# 9 WEDNESDAY, JANUARY 15, 1992

        MR. GATES: Seizure of whose fissile material?

        SEN. GLENN: Of -- in other words, if any of these tactical
nuclear weapons fell into anyone else's hands, what are the chances
of that happening, do you think? Are they under good enough
control that the chance would be very remote, or is it --

        MR. GATES: I think --

        SEN. GLENN: Likely.

        MR. GATES: I think the view of the intelligence community of
the likelihood of these weapons -- of any of these weapons falling
into the hands of people not authorized to have them is very low,
but not negligible, and that's the source of our concern.

        SEN. GLENN: How do you see the military cohesion in the Soviet
Union right now? Is it breaking down to where there is no longer
the same centralized control we once had, or is that holding up
pretty well?

        MR. GATES: Well, particularly on the conventional side, it is
beginning to break down as the different republics lay claim to
parts of the -- what was the Soviet army and the Soviet armed
forces, other than the strategic forces -- air defense and parts of
the navy. The morale of the military is low. They're having
difficulty getting supplies of food and housing. There is -- for
those who are coming back from **Eastern Europe**, there is difficulty
in finding jobs and schools for their children.

                        CONTINUED

0263—32

HEARING OF THE SENATE GOVERNMENTAL AFFAIRS COMMITTEE SUBJECT: WEAPONS
PROLIFERATION IN THE NEW WORLD ORDER CHAIRED BY: SENATOR JOHN GLENN,
(D-OH);   WITNESS: ROBERT GATES, CIA DIRECTOR
G-3-13 page# 1 WEDNESDAY, JANUARY 15, 1992
    dest=fns11182,hill,sengovaf,cia,nucweapon,weapons,armscont,interms
    dest+=fns00652,fns10000,fns13597,terr,icbm,thdwd,easteur
    dest+=mideast,iran,iraq,intel,russia,ussr,envrmt,dopten
    dest+=biol,chemwar,
    data

    They are confronted with very difficult choices about taking loyalty
oaths, whether to take a loyalty oath to the Commonwealth or to
Russia or to one of the republics, we have commanders of certain
units declaring their allegance to republics, but uncertainty about
the loyalty of the troops in their units. So it is a very difficult
time for the Soviet military.

    It is -- it is a time in which we think that the command links
at the local level, at the lower levels, are not too bad because
they have a greater likelihood of being fed in the unit than if they
were released and just sort of turned out on the economy without a
job. I don't think that contradicts what I said about the
difficulties of getting proper food and housing and so on for the
military as a whole.

    So it is -- it's a tough time, and that's one of the reasons
that we have elaborated our concern in terms of the state of the
military with respect to some of the problems we've been talking
about today.

    SEN. GLENN: Can you give us a figure on what percent of their
military forces are Russian, per se? Because if they stayed under
Yeltsin's command, say, are they big enough that they're going to be
the 400 pound gorilla no matter what happens off in the other
republics? Do you have a figure on that?

    MR. GATES: I'll have to get back to you on that, Mr. Chairman.
I think it is on the order of two-thirds or so. It may be higher.
I'm just not certain.

    SEN. GLENN: What's the agency's estimate on the prospects of a
coup against Yeltsin in the next several months? Do you hold that
out as a real possibility, or is it remote?

    MR. GATES: I think the intelligence community's view is that
the likelihood of a military or security services coup against
Yeltsin is not particularly high. What you are more likely to see
is action on the local level to obtain necessary food and supplies.
The Soviet military may be in a time of troubles, but they're still
smart enough to realize they don't want to take on responsibility
for running that country right now.

    SEN. GLENN: Our ability to monitor -- in the wake of the 1986
Chernobyl accident we have come to learn that the Soviet Union
experienced other accidents and serious radiological contamination
problems such as the 1957 high-level nuclear waste explosion at
Kistim (ph) in the Ural Mountain region, large radiation doses

                        0163- 33

                                                            0098

290 북한 핵문제 미국 동향

HEARING OF THE SENATE GOVERNMENTAL AFFAIRS COMMITTEE SUBJECT: WEAPONS
PROLIFERATION IN THE NEW WORLD ORDER CHAIRED BY: SENATOR JOHN GLENN,
(D-OH); WITNESS: ROBERT GATES, CIA DIRECTOR.
G-G-15 page# 2 WEDNESDAY, JANUARY 15, 1992

received by nuclear workers and residents living near Soviet nuclear
test sites. In this regard, has CIA performed any comprehensive
review of ES&H -- environment safety and health problems at former
Soviet nuclear sites which you can share with the Committee?

    MR. GATES: We have not been able to do this on a comprehensive
basis yet, Mr. Chairman, but we have been tracking what we've been
able to learn about **serious environmental problems** growing out of the
nuclear and chemical and biological programs over time. We know, for
example, thanks to glasnost, that in the same site that you're talking
about near the village of Mayak (ph), which is in the southern Urals also,
that the water supply was contaminated with -- badly contaminated with
radioactive material. We know that the Yenisei River was badly
contaminated -- this is near Krasnoyarsk -- badly contaminated by a
plutonium production facility in that area. We know that in a small
village or small town near St. Petersburg, that the local residents
were able to get a BW -- what we think was a BW program closed -- plant
closed down because several people fell ill. So, there are a number of
sites like this, and I would assume that as we go along and are able to
learn more, that that list will grow considerably.

    SEN. GLENN: In our ability to monitor these things, it is my
understanding **Department of Energy** is actively pursuing the use of
remote sensing and imaging technologies to aid in the characterization
of contamination at DOE nuclear weapon sites. Their goal has been to
attempt to go to some new technologies that would leapfrog past the
expensive and time-consuming conventional ES&H measuring techniques,
even using satellites, airborne, surface remote sensing technologies.
Have you followed that? Are you working with Jim Watkins on that? And
the idea being could these be applied to international monitoring,
which would let us have a better handle on these things when they
happen?

    MR. GATES: I assume that they could be applied.

    MR. OEHLER: I have no idea. I think right now our best approach
is that the Soviets and now the Russians themselves are very interested
in finding out what the total contamination is. And they've been quite
forthcoming in talking about a number of sites that have been polluted
this way. And that's going to be far better data than I would imagine
it would be possible to get from remote means.

    SEN. GLENN: The Soviets have not done nuclear testing for a
while. Are they still doing any missile testing? In other words, are
they doing any firing out of Tyura Tam --

    MR. GATES: Yes.

    -- out to the Kamchatka Peninsula? Are they continuing their ICBM
testing?

    MR. GATES: Yes, sir.

    SEN. GLENN: And out of Plesetsk, also, up north?

                         0263~ 34

HEARING OF THE SENATE GOVERNMENTAL AFFAIRS COMMITTEE SUBJECT: WEAPONS
PROLIFERATION IN THE NEW WORLD ORDER CHAIRED BY: SENATOR JOHN GLENN,
(D-OH); WITNESS: ROBERT GATES, CIA DIRECTOR
S-3-15 page# 3 WEDNESDAY, JANUARY 15, 1992

MR. GATES: I don't know if there have been any launches --

MR. DEHLER: Yes, there have been at Plesetsk because they've also
tested, I think, some of their -- they're looking to test some of their
ICBM boosters in an application for space launch vehicles, and, in
fact, have talked about sales of some of these.

SEN. GLENN: When these occur, do we send any demarches to the
Soviets on their continued testing, or what do we do? Do we just do
nothing? Do we just monitor it and that's it?

MR. GATES: I think we just monitor it as long as they're in
compliance with the arms control agreements.

CONTINUED

0263-35

0100

HEARING OF THE SENATE GOVERNMENTAL AFFAIRS COMMITTEE SUBJECT: WEAPONS
PROLIFERATION IN THE NEW WORLD ORDER CHAIRED BY: SENATOR JOHN GLENN,
(D-OH);   WITNESS: ROBERT GATES, CIA DIRECTOR
5-3-16-E page# 1 WEDNESDAY, JANUARY 15, 1992
   dest=fns11182,hjll,sengovaf,cia,nucweapon,weapons,armscont,intarms
   dest+=fns00652,fns10000,fns13597,icbm
   dest+=intel,russia,ussr,septen
   dest+=biol,chemwar,defense,dod
   data

        SEN. GLENN: How effective are demarches? Do you have any
confidence in demarches changing anybody's mind anywhere around the
world? We send them out by the basket full, I understand.

        MR. GATES: Well, I think that they do have an effect.
Certainly not in every case and maybe not even in most cases, but I
think that there are two aspects to it.

        The first is sometimes it's enough for a foreign government to
know that the United States has them in its figurative crosshairs on
one or another particular problem, whether it's a proliferation
problem or something else, a violation of economic sanctions that we
have identified that they are not playing by the rules and sometimes
that does bring them to change their behavior. Sometimes it causes
them to be more careful about that behavior but it may also serve to
retard it.

        Other times I think that the behavior of nations is — of
governments is affected when some of their behavior or activites are
brought into the glare of publicity or have the glare of the public
spotlight, particularly if they are engaged in practices that while
economically profitable may be contrary to international norms or
the general view of the international community. So I think you
can't — just as I think you cannot generalize too much about
sanctions and embargos and things like that, the same thing is true
of demarches.   There are plenty of instances in which they have been
successful, to make them worth doing.

        SEN. GLENN: Richard Perle testifying here one day called them
demarche-mallows, that was his view of them, but Richard had his own
view on things.   What role do you play in whether something like
that is going to be sent or not? Do you just furnish background
information for it? I would think there would be a little problem
because some of those things might tip off some of your intelligence
gathering methods that you wouldn't want revealed.

        MR. GATES: We work very closely with the State Department and
the National Security Council and the **Defense Department** and the
Arms Control Agency in putting together those demarches precisely so
that we can protect our sources and methods.

        SEN. GLENN: At Tyuratam the testing is still continuing there
you indicated a moment ago. How many launches have they had over
the last say six months or so? Can you give us a rundown on that?

        MR. OEHLER: No, I cannot.

                    0263-36

HEARING OF THE SENATE GOVERNMENTAL AFFAIRS COMMITTEE SUBJECT: WEAPONS
PROLIFERATION IN THE NEW WORLD ORDER CHAIRED BY: SENATOR JOHN GLENN,
(D-OH);   WITNESS: ROBERT GATES, CIA DIRECTOR
1-3-16-E page# 2 WEDNESDAY, JANUARY 15, 1992
         MR. GATES: We can get that information for you.

         SEN. GLENN: Are there a number of them though? This wasn't
just one thing to keep the launch pad operating was it? There was a
number of them? It's a real testing program?

         MR. OEHLER: We have not seen much of a slowdown in the testing
programs.

         SEN. GLENN: Well how do you account for that? Because I would
think that if they are serious about all of the things that they are
talking about doing and their own internal concerns that some of
those things that are -- those tests are very expensive to conduct
for them as well as for us, I would think that they would be pulling
down on that rather rapidly.

         MR. GATES: I don't think that there's a precise answer to
that, Mr. Chairman, but I think that there are probably several
factors involved.

         One may well be inertia. These programs have been going for
quite some time. They probably have a test schedule that they've
had for a long period of time. Missiles are available to them, and
so on. I think that also, as Dr. Oehler indicated earlier, they are
interested increasingly in marketing space launch services, and so
they would want to continue testing for reliability and testing
these capabilities.

         Third, I think that there is continuing interest on the part of
even -- of the reform leadership of maintaining the strategic
capabilities of Russia -- of the CIS, even though that may be at a
considerably smaller level or a considerably lower level of launch
vehicles and warheads in the future. There is every indication that
they intend to keep those programs viable.

         SEN. GLENN: Who do they see as a threat to them now?

         MR. GATES: Well, I don't know --

         SEN. GLENN: Here we are trying to help them, sending food and
everything else. We can't possibly be viewed as a threat, and yet
we're still the targets of the ICBMs, the SLBMs. Who else in the
world would they see as a threat --

         MR. GATES: I'm not entirely --

         SEN. GLENN: -- that would require a continual testing and
continual development program?

         MR. GATES: I'm not entirely convinced that all of the Soviet
military see us as a great friend and benefactor at this point. But
I think it may be as much as anything a guarding against uncertainty
in the future as well as the status of a greater superpower.

0162-37

0102

294 북한 핵문제 미국 동향

외 무 부

종 별 : 지 급

번 호 : USW-0362　　　　　　　　　　일 시 : 92 0122 2223

수 신 : 장 관(미이,미일,정안,정특)사본:국방 장관

발 신 : 주 미 대사

제 목 : 국제 안보 문제 관련 상원 청문회

1. 상원 군사위 (위원장: SAM NUNN 의원)는 금 1.22 GATES CIA 국장, CLAPPER 국방정보처장을 증인으로 출석시킨 가운데, 향후 10년간 국제 안보 환경에 관한 청문회를 개최하였는바, 동 청문회시 한반도 관련 언급 요청 아래임.

가. NUNN 위원장

0 한반도 긴장 완화를 위한 최근의 남북한간 구체적 합의서 채택은 WARSAW PACT 의 해체, 걸프전에서의 승리, 엘살바도르 평화 협정등과 함께 지난 수년간 국제 안보 환경을 변화시킨 주요 사건임.

나. GATES 국장

0 북한의 핵개발 계획은 동북아 안보에 최대의 위협 요인임. 한반도 비핵화를 위한 남북한간 협의는 역사적인것이나, 북한이 IAEA 안전 협정의 신속한 이행을 포함, 국제 사찰을 수락해야만 한반도 핵확산에 대한 우려가 해소될수 있음.

0 미국은 북한이 핵무기를 보유할 경우 동북아안보에 미칠 영향과 북한 핵무기 개발 기술을 제 3국에 판매할 가능성을 특히 우려하고 있음. 북한은 이미 스커드 미사일을 이란, 시리아등 중동제국에 판매 하였음.

0 김일성 사후 북한 체제 안정 여부도 우려 요인의하나임.

다. CLAPPER 처장

0 향후 3-4년은 한반도 안보에 가장 중요한 시기임. 북한은 아직 무력 적화 통일의 OPTION 을 버리지않고 있음. 북한이 실제로 이 OPTION 을 선택할것인지 아니면 대남 협상의 지렛대로 활용하는데 그칠 것인지는 확실치 않으나, 남북한 간군사력 균형 유지와 대북한 경제 압력등을 통해 이를 견제할수 있을것임.

0 향후 10년간 남북한간 군사력 균형은 북한에 유리한 상황이 지속될것임. 남한은 자체 방위증강 노력에도 불구하고 독자적인 방위 능력을 확보하기 어려울 것이며,

---

미주국　　1차보　　미주국　　외정실　　외정실　　분석관　　청와대　　안기부

PAGE 1　　　　　　　　　　　　　　　　　　92.01.23　　13:48 WG

외신 1과 통제관

0103

정보, 군수, 해전, 공군지원과 같은 주요 분야에서 미국의 지원에 계속 의존하게
될것임.

0 북한은 2-3년내 핵 무기를 보유할수 있을것으로 판단되며, 효과적인 사찰 제도가
마련되지 않는한 북한이 핵무기 개발 계획을 포기할 것으로 보이지 않음.

2. 이어 진행된 공개 질의시 한반도 문제 관련 특기할만한 사항은 없었으나 중국.
북한등의 대중동 무기 판매등 일부 민감한 무기 확산문제가 비공개리에 논의되었음.

(대사 현홍주-국장)

관리번호 92-254

외 무 부

종 별 :

번 호 : USW-0540

일 시 : 92 0131 1759

수 신 : 장관(미일,미이,정안,정특,국기,외교안보)사본;통일원,국방부

발 신 : 주 미 대사

제 목 : 북한관계 상원 청문회

상원 외교위 동아태 소위 (위원장; CRANSTON 의원)는 2.6 미국의 대북한 정책에 관한 청문회를 개최할 예정인바, 당관 박흥신 서기관이 접촉한 ELIZABETH LAMOIRD 전문위원에 의하면, 동 청문회에는 KANTER 국무부 차관이 증인으로 출석, 최근 미.북한 고위급 접촉 결과및 북한 핵 문제등 미국의 대북한 정책에 관해 증언 예정이라함. 동 청문회 내용 추보 위계임.

(대사 현홍주-국장)

92.6.30 까지

미주국 국방부	장관 통일원	차관	미주국	국기국	외정실	외정실	정와대	안기부

PAGE 1

외　무　부

(Richardson 의원은 누구?)

종　별 :

번　호 : USW-0541　　　　　　　　　　일　시 : 92 0131 1759

수　신 : 장관(미일,미이,정북,기정,외교안보)사본;국방장관

발　신 : 주 미 대사

제　목 : 하원 정보위 전문위원 접촉

연;USW-5821

1. 하원 정보위(위원장; MCCURDY 의원)은 2.6 북한의 특수 무기 개발 (SPECIAL WEAPONS PROGRAM)문제에 관한 비공개 청문회를 개최할 예정임.

2. 금 1.31 당관 조태열 서기관이 접촉한 CALVIN HUMPHREY 전문위원에 의하면 동 청문회에는 SOLOMON 국무부 동아태 차관보를 비롯, 국방부, CIA, NSC 등 행정부 인사들이 증인으로 출석, 북한의 핵무기 개발 문제(특히 핵 안전 협정 서명, 이행 문제)와 탄도 미사일등 특수 무기 개발, 수출 문제등에 대해 브리핑 예정이라함.

3. 동 전문위원은 의회 규칙상 비공개 회의 내용의 대외 유출이 엄격히 금지되어 있어 상세 내용을 DEBRIEFING 해줄수는 없으나 이문제에 관한 미 행정부의 시각등 개괄적인 내용은 알려줄수 있다하였기, 2.12 오찬을 함께 하기로 하였는바, 특기사항 있을시 추보 하겠음.

4. 연호 RICHARDSON 의원의 방북 계획 관련 질의에 대해, 동인은 북한 유엔대표부 허종 대사와 계속 접촉중이며, 북한측이 동의원원 방북을 환영하는 입장이므로 방북에 별 문제는 없을것으로 본다고 말하고, 2 월 중순 또는 4 월경 방북이 가능할것이라고 부연함. 동인은 또한 방북 계획이 확정되면 아측 요청대로 서울을 먼저 방문할 예정이며, 당관에도 사전 통보, 일정주선등을 요청하겠다하였음. 상기 오찬시 동의원의 방북 여부 재확인 예정이며, 진전 사항 있을시 함께 추보 하겠음.

(대사 현홍주-국장)

예고:92.6.30 일반

예고에 의거 92.6. 일반문서로 재분류

미주국	장관	차관	미주국	외정실	청와대	안기부	국방부

외 무 부

종 별 :

번 호 : USW-0606   일 시 : 92 0205 1858

수 신 : 장 관(미이,미일,정안,해외)

발 신 : 주 미대사

제 목 : SOLARZ 의원 아시아 협회 연설

작 2.4 STEPHEN SOLARZ 하원 외무위 동아태 소위원장은 당지 소재 ASIA SOCIETY워싱턴 센터에서 자신의 최근 북한, 한국, 인도 차이나 방문결과에 대한 설명회를 가졌는바, 방북과 관련한 주요 내용을 하기 보고함.

1.북한 핵문제

O SOLARZ 의원은 방북 기간중 김일성 주석과2시간 30분,김영남 외교 부장과 5시간에 걸쳐 회담을 가졌으며, 자신은 동 면담들을 통해 북한이 핵보유국이 되기위해대단한 노력을 이미 기울이기 시작했으며, 따라서 북한의 핵문제를 평화적으로 해결할 수 있는 가능성에 대해서 상당히 회의적인 (PESSIMISTIC) 생각을 갖게 되었다고말함.

O 동의원은 상기 면담중 북한의 핵문제 해결을위한 진실성(SINCERITY) 을 시험해 보기 위해 여러 질문을 하였던바, 김일성은 이에 대해 한반도핵 철수에 대한 미국의 보증, 남북 핵 시설 사찰을 위한 미.북한 직접 협상등을 들고 나오는등 성실성을보이지 않았다고 함.

O SOLARZ 의원은 자신의 방북후 2 주만에 북한이 IAEA 안전협정 서명, 남북 동시 핵사찰, 한반도 비핵화 선언등에 동의한 것을 매우 놀라운 것으로 받아들인다고면서, 이런 갑작스런 북측태도 변화의 동기를 1) 북한의 핵 개발 완전 포기 결정,2)국제적인 경제 제재 조치나 무력 사용 압력을 우선 회피하고, 사찰을 계속 미루면서시간 벌기, 또는 3) 영 변이나 기타 소규모 핵 시설에 대한 사찰을 허용하면서 은밀한 장소에서 계속 핵개발을 하려는것 등으로 분석하고, 자신은 세번째 동기를 가장가능성이 높은것으로 보며, 따라서 북한에 대해서는 -의심하고, 검증해봐야 한다(WE SHOULD MISTRUST,BUT VERIFY)- 고 강조하였음.

O 이와관련, SOLARZ 의원은 북한이 IAEA핵 사찰에 응하는데 시한을 두어야 하지

미주국   1차보   미주국   외정실   분석관   청와대   안기부   공보처

0107

PAGE 1   92.02.06   10:31 WH

외신 1과 통제관

않겠느냐는 질문(W.P의 OBERDORFER 기자)에 대해, 자신이 정확한 시한을 제 시할수는 없으나 북한은 신속히 남북 동시 사찰에 응하여야 하며, 이를 위한 한국은 북한이 IAEA 안전협정을 비준하고 실행하기 이전가지는 남북화해, 불가침 및 교류 에관한 협정을 비준하지 말아야 할것이라고 주장하고, 북한의 진정한 의도를 알수 있는 진실의 시간이 급속히 다가 오고 있으므로 현재로서는 무력 사용을 포함한 어떠한 해결 방법도 배제하지 않는것이 중요하다고 강조하였음.

  2.기타 사항

  O 솔라즈 의원은 김일성 면담 관련하여, 김일성에 대한 인상은 그가 매우 건강하며, 활동적이고, 정신적으로도 흐트러짐이 없다(MENTALLY QUITE ALERT)는 것이었으며, 매우 친절하게 대하면서 BNA 상세한질문에 대해서 답변을 외교 부장에게 모두 미루었다고 함.

  O 동 의원은 김일성 사후의 북한 전망에 대한 질문에 대해, 자신은 김일성 사망직 후에는 김정일이 지도자가 될것이라는 강한 인상을 받았으나, 그가 얼마나 권력을유지할수 있을런지에 대해서는 의문시 된다고 관찰함.

  (대사 현홍주-국장)

솔라즈,北韓 비밀시설서 핵폭탄 제조가능성

(워싱턴 AP=聯合) 北韓은 핵사찰 수락에도 불구하고 숨겨진 시설에서 핵폭탄 제조를 시도할것 같다고 최근 北韓의 金日成주석과 회담한 스티븐 솔라즈 美하원 외교위 아시아 태평양소위원회 위원장이 4일밤 말했다.

작년 12월 北韓과 캄보디아를 방문한 솔라즈 의원은 이날밤 아시아 협회에서 美國이 北韓과 캄보디아에서 "진실의 순간"에 직면하고 있다고 말했다.

그는 金주석과 만나본 결과 경제문제 때문에 과연 北韓이 핵무기 보유국이 되려는 야심을 버리게 됐는지 의심을 갖게 됐다면서 北韓이 국제원자력기구(IAEA)와 핵안전협정을 체결한 이상 "우리는 급속히 진실의 순간에 접근하고 있다"고 말했다.

솔라즈 의원은 北韓이 IAEA의 사찰을 허용하면서 지하 시설에서 핵무기 개발을 계속할 "가능성이 크다"고 말하고 걸프 전쟁당시 이라크가 이같은 일이 가능하다는 것을 입증했다고 덧붙였다.

그는 美國과 기타 국가들이 北韓 핵연료재처리시설의 해체를 주장하고 유엔 안보이사회의 제재위협을 곁드린 IAEA의 기습사찰을 고집해야 한다면서 "세계에서 가장 전제적인 정권"이 핵무기를 보유한다는 것은 많은 나라에게 불안하고 수락할수 없는 일일 것이기 때문에 韓國은 그같은 조건이 이루어질 때까지 北韓과의 화해합의 문서의 교환을 보류해야 할것이라고 말했다.

솔라즈 의원은 캄보디아의 "취약한 평화"를 굳건히 하고 새로운 파국을 막기 위해서는 美國의 지도역량과 돈이 필요하다고 지적하고 앞으로 조지 부시 대통령의 美행정부가 의회에 유엔 캄보디아 평화유지군에 대한 美國의 첫 부담금 3억5천만달러의 승인을 요청하게 되면 "이는 美國과 의회에 대한 진실의 순간"이 될것이라고 말했다.

그는 "만일 우리가 이 돈을 내지 못하면 국제공동체의 지도자로서의 우리의 책임을 전적으로 저바리는 일이 될것"이라고 말했다.(끝)

0109

관리
번호 92-322

외 무 부

종 별 :

번 호 : USW-0623   일 시 : 92 0206 1712

수 신 : 장관(미이,미일,정안,정북,국기,아일,아이,동구일,외교안보,봉일원)

발 신 : 주 미 대사

제 목 : 미상원 외교위 아태소위 북한 핵관계 청문회

1. 미 상원 외교위 아태소위(위원장: ALAN CRANSTON)는 금 2.6 ARNOLD KANTER 국무차관을 출석시킨 가운데 "북한의 핵 확산과 미국의 정책" 제하의 청문회를 개최함.(당관 임성준 참사관, 박흥신 서기관 참석)

CRANSTON 위원장은 모두발언에서 한반도에서의 핵확산 봉제를 위한 한. 미 양국정부의 노력을 치하하고 북한의 1.30 핵 안전협정 서명에도 불구, 북한의 의무이행 여부에 대해 아직 의문을 갖고 있다고 말함. 동 위원장은 이어 이락의 경험에 비추어 IAEA 안전조치가 불완전함을 지적, IAEA 의 사찰 및 감시기능 강화 필요성을 강조함.

2. KANTER 차관 증언요지(증언문 FAX 송부)

가. 북한 핵 문제에 대한 미국의 입장

. 구소연방의 해체, 북한 경제의 정체, 북한내 세대교체 및 북한 핵무기 개발에 대한 광범한 국제적 반대등의 영향으로 북한은 잠정적이나마 국제적으로 책임있는 행동을 보이기 시작하고 있으나, 북한의 상금 모호한 태도에 비추어 한반도에서의 핵확산 위협에 대한 미국의 우려는 가시지 않고 있음.

. 북한 핵 문제에 대한 미국의 정책은 한. 미 동맹관계 및 남. 북 분단이라는 큰 테두리 안에서 검토 되어야함. 이런 맥락에서 한반도 상황에 주요한 영향을 미치는 세가지 요인, 즉 북한 핵무기 계획, 남북한 관계, 미국및 주변 열강(러시아, 중국, 일본)과 북한과의 관계가 함께 다루어져야함.

나. 북한 핵무기 계획

. 북한은 60 년대 중반 소련으로 부터 소규모 연구용 원자로 도입을 시작으로 지난 20 년 이상 핵기술을 축적해 왔으며, 87 년 이래 플루토늄 생산용 10-30메가와트의 원자로를 자체 개발, 가동해 왔음. 북한은 또한 보다 대규모의 원자로와 핵 재처리

| 미주국 | 장관 | 차관 | 1차보 | 2차보 | 아주국 | 아주국 | 미주국 | 구주국 |
| 국기국 | 외정실 | 외정실 | 분석관 | 정와대 | 안기부 | 통일원 | | |

시설로 추정되는 공장을 건설중에 있는 것으로 파악되고 있는바, 재처리 시설은 거의 가동 단계에 이른 것으로 보임.

. 북한은 85.12. NPT 협정 서명후 18 개월내에 실시해야 하는 안전협정 서명을 미루어 오다가 국제적 압력에 못이겨 지난 1.30. 에야 IAEA 와 핵 안전협정에 서명하고 가능한 가장 빠른 시일내에 비준조치를 하겠다고 공표한바 있음. 미국은 동 비준조치가 2.19. 남. 북 총리회담 이전에 이루어지기를 희망함.

다. 미국의 대한반도 정책

. 미국의 대한반도 정책의 기본은 확고부동한 대한방위 공약과 더불어 한반도 문제의 항구적인 해결책이 남. 북한 당사자간에 이루어져야 한다는 것임. 따라서 미국은 한반도에서 긴장완화와 화합을 위해 남북대화가 가장 중요한 수단이라고 간주하고 있음.

. 제 2 단계 감군(93-95)의 동결 결정은 한국을 안심시킴과 동시에 북한에 대한 경고의 의미가 있음. 3 단계 감군(95-2000) 계획은 당시 한반도 안보상황의평가에 기초할 것임.

. 한반도에서의 핵확산 문제와 관련 미국은 지난 2 년간 한국과 긴밀한 협의를 유지해 왔으며, 9.27. 부쉬 대통령의 육상및 해상 전술핵무기 배치 중지 선언, 노대통령의 11.8. 한반도 비핵화 정책 선언, 12.18. 남한 핵무기 부재 선언등 한. 미 양국 정부의 일련의 정책 선언을 통해 핵확산 위협 저지및 폭넓은 신뢰 구축 실현을 위한 기초를 마련함.

.12.31 한반도 비핵화 선언에 따라 남북한은 핵무기 보유 및 재처리 등의 포기와 상화 핵 사찰에 합의하였으며, 동 합의서는 2.19 남북 총리회담에서 발효예정임. 미국의 남북한이 효과적인 사찰 방식에 조속 합의, 이행할 것을 강력히 촉구중에 있음.

라. 한반도 주변국과의 협조체제

1) 일본

. 일본은 북한의 핵 위협에 대해 미국과 인식을 같이하고 있으며, 6 차에 걸친 일.북한 수교협상을 통해 수교와 원조를 북한의 핵문제 해결과 연계시킬 것임을 분명히 하였음.

. 지난 11 월에는 최초의 한. 미.일 3 개국 정책협의회를 서울에서 개최, 3 개국간의 협조체제를 다진바 있음.

2) 러시아

. 러시아는 핵확산 문제와 관련 미국과 인식을 같이 하고 있음. 85 년 북한의 NPT 가입도 당시 소련의 압력에 힘 입은바 크며, 90 년말 세바르드나제 외상의 북한 방문시 대북압력 및 한. 소 수교가 북한의 계산에 중요한 영향을 미친 것으로 보임.

. 러시아는 91.9 IAEA 의 북한에 대한 조속한 안전조치 이행을 촉구하는 91.9 IAEA 결의안을 지지한바 있으며, ROGACHEV 러시아 특사의 92.1 평양 방문시에도 북한의 NPT 의무와 관련 강력한 메시지를 전달한바 있음.

3) 중국

. 미국은 그간 한반도 핵확산 위협 저지를 위해 중국의 협조를 촉구해 왔으며, 작년 11 월 베이커 국무장관 방중시에도 동 문제가 주요 의제중의 하나였음.

. 한. 중 양국은 준외교관계로 발전, 양국 경제관계가 북한을 훨씬 앞지르고 있는바, 작년 남북한의 UN 동시 가입시에도 중국이 북한에 영향력을 행사한 것으로 확인되고 있음.

. 중국은 최근 핵확산 방지와 관련 협조적 자세를 견지하고 있음. 중국은 최근 NPT 가입 결정과 더불어 북한의 IAEA 핵안전 조치 이행에 더욱 단호한 입장을 취하고 있으며, 이러한 메시지는 분명히 북한측에 전달 되었음.

. 중국은 또한 북한의 경제 개혁과 개방을 권유해 왔는바, 지난달 북한의 경제특구 및 자유항 지정 발표도 이러한 중국의 영향을 반영하는 것임.

4) 다자협력

. 남. 북한 및 주변국과의 협력외에 IAEA 및 유엔 안보리 등을 통해 북한의핵 위협에 대한 국제적 CONSENSUS 를 제고해 나가고 있음.

. 한반도 핵 문제에 대한 다변외교(MULTIFACETED DIPLOMACY) 는 BAKER 장관이 말한 집단개입 (COLLECTIVE ENGAGEMENT) 의 좋은 예중의 하나임.

. 마. 미.북한 접촉

. 1.21 뉴욕에서의 미.북한 고위접촉시 핵심 의제는 북한 핵문제였는 바, 이 기회에 북한 핵 문제에 대한 미국의 우려를 전하고 동 우려 해소와 미.북한 관계 발전을 위해 북한이 취할 조치들을 명백히 하였음. 또한 미.북한 관계의 발전이 남. 북 대화의 진전과 밀접히 연관될 것임을 밝히고, MIA, 미사일 확산, 인권분야에서의 북한의 협력과 개선 문제를 논의하였음.

. 북한은 핵안전 협정의 1 월내 서명과 조속한 비준을 약소하고, 한국과의 합의 및

PAGE 3

양자 핵사찰 합의를 이행할 의사를 표명하였는 바, 이에 대해 미국은 미.북한 고위급 접촉의 계속 여부가 IAEA 안전협정 및 남북 비핵화 합의에 의한 조속하고 실효적인 사찰 실시에 달려 있음을 강조하였음.

. 동 회담결과 북한은 국제사회의 책임있는 일원으로 참여하기 위해서는 핵문제 관련 약속이행이 절대 불가결 함을 이해하기 시작한 것으로 평가됨.

바. 결론

. 최근 남북한간의 합의 및 북한의 IAEA 안저협정 서명은 매우 희망적인 진전인바, 북한의 조속한 실천을 기대함.

. 이락의 예에서 사찰 제도의 불완전함이 드러나기는 했으나 IAEA 안전협정과 관련 사찰 제도의 이행시 북한이 핵무기 제조용 물질을 은닉하기는 극히 어렵게 될 것이며 북한의 핵관련 활동 정보를 크게 늘일수 있을 것임.

3. 질의 응답 및 당관 평가 추보함.

첨부: USWF-672(19 매)

(대사 현홍주-국장)

예고 :92.12.31 까지

외 무 부

종 별 :

번 호 : USW-0630   일 시 : 92 0206 1900

수 신 : 장관(미이,미일,정안,정특,국기,아일,동구일,외교안보,사본;통일원)

발 신 : 주 미 대사

제 목 : 미 상원 외교위 아태소위 북한 핵관계 청문회

    연: USW-0623 의 계속분

    3. 이어 계속된 질의 응답에서는 CRANSTON 위원장이 단독 질의에 나선바, 요지는 다음과 같음. (북한의 안전협정 서명 추속조치 및 비준 절차를 문의한데 대해)

    . 한국은 북한이 비준 이전에라도 IAEA 사찰을 기다릴것 없이, 남북한간의 상호 시범 사찰을 조속 실시할 것을 촉구중에 있음. 비준은 김일성의 서명으로 족한 것으로 아는바, 그간 남북한 합의서 비준 속도에 비추어 비준에 시간을 끌 이유는 없다고 봄.

    . 영변에서의 활동 감소 징후는 없음.

    (북한의 IAEA 기준 준수 의사 관련)

    . 북한은 85 년도 NPT 가입후 안전협정 서명을 지연하는 등 과거 국제적 의무를 제대로 이해치 않은 선례가 있음. 그러나 지금은 국제적 압력의 가중과 고립심화 위협에 비추어 핵안전 의무를 이행치 않을 수는 없을 것임.

    . 미국은 북한의 의무이행 상황을 면밀히 추적할 것임.

    . 영변에서 핵관련 활동이 진행되고 있다는 증거가 있다는 1.15 GATYES CIA국장의 증언에 대한 평가를 요청한데 대해 북한도 영변이 사찰대상에 포함될 것임을 알고 있다고 말하고 기다려봐야 알게될 것이라고 답변

    (미.북한 고위접촉 관련)

    . 미.북한 고위촉시 한. 미 합동사찰팀 문제를 거론했느냐는 질의에 대해, 북한의 의도에 대한 평가가 단순히 IAEA 안전협정의 비준 뿐 아니라 합동 사찰팀의 수락 여부에 기초할 것임을 밝혔다고 답변

    . IAEA 특별사찰 문제도 동 고위접촉시 가장 크게 다루어 졌다고 답변

    . (북한이 지하터널에 핵무기 시설을 은닉할 가능성에 대해) 지하시설을 판별하기는 훨씬 어려울 것이나, 그러한 시설이 있을 경우 밝혀 낼수 있을 것으로

미주국 국기국	장관	차관 외정실	1차보 외정실	2차보 분석관	아주국 정와대	미주국 안기부	구주국 통일원	

자신함.

. (북한이 몰래 핵 폭탄을 제조할 가능성에 대해) IAEA 사찰이 완전하지는 않으나, 동 사찰과 양자 사찰제도 병행시 웬만한 핵관련 활동은 밝혀질 것으로 확신함.

(제 2 단계 주한미군 감축 동결의 해저 조건)

. 주한미군 감축 동결 조치는 북한 핵 개발에 대한 우려 때문에 취해진 것이브[84f. IAEA 에 대한 추가 기금 필요에 대해, 추가 기금 문제는 UN 의 테두리에서 검토되어야 한다고 말함.

4. 당관 관찰 및 평가

. KANTER 차관은 북한의 핵 안전협정 서명등 최근의 진전에 대해 조심스러운 환영의 뜻을 표시하면서도 북한의 실제 의도에 대해서는 계속 의구심을 가조있는 것으로 감지되었으며, IAEA 사찰 및 남북한 시범 사찰의 조속한 이행등 실제 행동에 의해 북한이 핵개발 포기의 증거를 보여야 한다는 입장을 견지 하였음.

. 그간 두차례의 학계인사 증언 및 금번 행정부 인사의 증언을 통해 북한의핵 문제에 대한 미 조야의 관심과 우려를 수렴하고 북한의 핵 확산 위협에 대한 미국정부의 강령한 대처 의사를 공개적으로 표명했다는 데 의의가 있음.

(대사 현홍주 - 국장)

92. 12. 31 까지

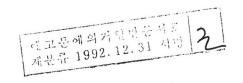

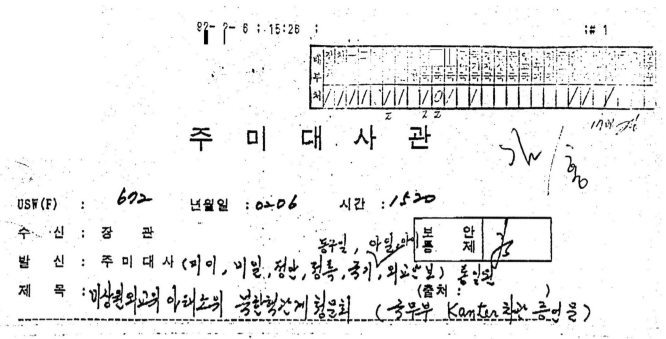

주 미 대 사 관

USW(F) : **672**　　년월일 : 0206　　시간 : 1520

수 신 : 장 관

발 신 : 주미대사 (미이, 비일, 정반, 렴록, 국기, 외교안보) 통일원

제 목 : 비상원외교위 아태소위 북한핵건계 청문회 (국무부 Kanter 차관 증언 문)

NORTH KOREA, NUCLEAR PROLIFERATION, AND U.S. POLICY:

COLLECTIVE ENGAGEMENT IN A NEW ERA

STATEMENT OF ARNOLD KANTER

UNDERSECRETARY OF STATE FOR POLITICAL AFFAIRS

February 6, 1992

BEFORE THE SENATE FOREIGN RELATIONS COMMITTEE

SUB-COMMITTEE ON EAST ASIAN AND PACIFIC AFFAIRS

(672 -17 -1)

외신 1과
통 제

0116

Introduction

Mr. Chairman, members of the committee, I appreciate
this opportunity to discuss the North Korean nuclear
program and our efforts to halt the threat of nuclear
proliferation on the Korean Peninsula.

Meeting the global challenge of nuclear and missile
proliferation is one of the administration's highest
national security priorities. As our knowledge of North
Korea's unsafeguarded nuclear activities has grown, our
concern has mounted over the past two years. During
visits to Seoul last November Secretaries Baker and Cheney
both stressed that the very real danger of nuclear
proliferation on the Korean Peninsula is now the number
one threat to security in northeast Asia. President Bush
reinforced this theme in the strongest possible terms
during his visit to Seoul last month.

Mr.Chairman, let me be frank about the stakes here.
If North Korea attained nuclear weapons capability, we
could eventually face the risk of proliferation not only
on the Peninsula, but in the worst case, grave instability
in northeast Asia. We could also face the danger of the
covert export of nuclear materials and/or technology by
the DPRK to unstable areas of the world. Such a harrowing
scenario is in no nation's interest, but it is
unfortunately not the stuff of mere science fiction.

672-11-2

Overview of U.S. Strategy

We have developed a broad strategy aimed at removing
DPRK pretexts for uncooperative behavior, drawing the
North out of its self-imposed isolation, and encouraging
it to address our nuclear concerns. Through a mix of
incentives and disincentives we are trying to persuade the
DPRK to enter into the mainstream of history and behave as
a responsible international actor.

The combined weight of the dissolution of the Soviet
Union (until recently the DPRK's major trade partner and
aid provider), the stagnation of the North Korean economy,
generational changes within the DPRK, and broad international opprobrium resulting from the pursuit of a nuclear
option appears to be moving the DPRK, albeit modestly and
tentatively, towards responsible international behavior.

But let me be clear: there is still a very long way to
go before we can have any confidence that our concerns
about nuclear proliferation on the Korean Peninsula are
close to being met. The writer Ernest Hemingway once said
that one should never confuse action for movement. In
light of North Korea's still ambiguous behavior, that is a
useful axiom for judging progress on the nuclear issue.

Our policies toward the North Korean nuclear issue

672-10-3

0118

- 3 -

must be viewed in the larger framework of our alliance
with the Republic of Korea and the enduring reality of a
divided Korean Peninsula. It is in this context that we
consider the three inter-related factors which have a
major impact on the situation on the Korean Peninsula.
These are: the North Korean nuclear weapons program;
North-South Korean relations; North Korean relations with
the U.S. and other great powers in northeast Asia (Russia,
China and Japan).

North Korean Nuclear Program

     The starting point is North Korea's nuclear program.
Pyongyang has sought to accumulate nuclear expertise for
more than two decades. It acquired a small research
reactor from the USSR in the mid-1960s that has operated
under IAEA safeguards which the USSR required as a
condition of sale. This demonstrates that the DPRK is
familiar with the routine of IAEA inspections and knows
how to comply.

     Since 1987, the DPRK has operated an unsafeguarded,
indigenously developed, 10-30 megawatt reactor of a type
suitable for producing plutonium. Available information
also indicates it is constructing another, larger reactor,
and a probable reprocessing plant. The latter may be
nearing operational status. These facilities could
constitute the essential elements of a nuclear weapons

672-17-4

program.

North Korea has no civilian nuclear power program,
though it has an agreement with Russia to construct four
nuclear power reactors. For some time, the Soviets had
made fulfillment of that arrangement conditional on North
Korean acceptance with IAEA safeguards as required for
adherence to the NPT. Russia continues to follow this
policy.

In December 1985, the DPRK signed the nuclear
non-proliferation treaty (NPT). This act obligated
Pyongyang to place all of its nuclear activities under
IAEA safeguards within eighteen months. North Korea's
failure to meet its freely assumed obligations under the
NPT fueled growing suspicion about its unsafeguarded
nuclear activities. North Korea is the only NPT signatory
with a significant nuclear program that has not fulfilled
its NPT safeguards responsibilities.

As international pressure mounted, North Korea cited a
variety of preconditions to be met before it would comply
with the IAEA. These have included at various times: the
removal of the U.S. nuclear threat, the withdrawal of U.S.
forces from the ROK; demands for security guarantees from
the U.S.; and demands for withdrawal of the U.S. nuclear
umbrella from the ROK.

672-19-5

0120

- 5 -

It was not until a week ago that North Korea took the
first step towards compliance. On January 30 -- more than
six years later and amidst dramatically altered
circumstances on and around the Peninsula -- North Korea
signed a nuclear safeguards agreement with the IAEA. The
agreement now must be ratified and implemented by North
Korea.

Under the DPRK constitution, President Kim il Sung has
the power to ratify the agreement by executive order.
North Korean officials have stated publicly that they will
ratify it "in the shortest possible time." We hope that
the IAEA agreement could be ratified before the next round
of North-South Prime Ministerial talks now scheduled to
begin on February 19.

U.S. policies: ROK Alliance

Fundamental to our policies towards the Korean
Peninsula is our unshakable commitment to the security of
the ROK and our belief that any lasting solution to the
problems of the Korean Peninsula must be achieved by the
Koreans themselves. Thus, we and the ROK view the
North-South dialogue as the principal means for reducing
tensions and facilitating reconciliation on the Korean
Peninsula. We are in the process of transforming what has
been largely a military alliance with the ROK into a more
balanced defense, political and economic partnership.

- 6 -

In the realm of security, this entails a three-phased process outlined in our East Asia Strategy Initiative presented to the Congress in April 1990. We are currently implementing an approximately 15% reduction of the 43,000 U.S. troops (to 36,000) in Phase I (1990-92), with the ROK moving towards assuming the lead role in its own defense capability and the U.S. towards a support role.

As a result of our assessment of the security situation on the Korean Peninsula, Secretary Cheney announced during a trip to Seoul last November that the U.S. would freeze further force reductions envisioned for Phase II (1993-95) pending clarification of the situation on the Peninsula. This reassurance of our security commitment to the ROK enhances alliance confidence and sends a signal to the DPRK. Phase III (1995-2000) planning would depend on our assessment of the security situation on the Peninsula at that time.

Our security consultations with the ROK, of course, also include the issue of nuclear proliferation on the Korean Peninsula. Indeed, we have developed a pattern of intensified, effective consultation with Seoul over the past two years. Our own experience both in nuclear matters and in arms control has proven valuable to the ROK as it has developed initiatives for a non-nuclear Korean Peninsula and an agenda for tension-reduction, confidence

building, and ultimately, arms-reduction measures as an
intrinsic part of the process of reconciliation and
eventually, reunification.

A sequence of policy initiatives by the U.S. and the
ROK last fall laid the groundwork for halting the threat
of nuclear proliferation and provide a basis for a broader
confidence-building process and eventually, arms reduction
initiatives. On September 27 President Bush announced a
global policy to end the deployment of tactical nuclear
weapons at sea and on land. On November 8, President Roh
Tae Woo announced a bold non-nuclear policy by which the
ROK committed itself not to "test, produce, possess,
store, deploy or use" nuclear weapons and to forego any
nuclear reprocessing or enrichment.

Then, on December 18, President Roh announced that as
of that date, there were no nuclear weapons in the ROK.
Shortly thereafter, President Bush stated at a press
conference that while we have a "neither-confirm-nor-deny"
policy, he "would not argue" with President Roh's
statement on nuclear weapons. While in Seoul last month,
President Bush said, "to any who doubted that (President
Roh's) declaration, South Korea, with the full support of
the United States, has offered to open to inspection all
of its civilian and military installations, including U.S.
facilities."

This chain of events created the circumstance for the two Koreas to conclude an agreement on a Non-Nuclear Korea on December 31. Under the agreement, both parties pledged to foreswear nuclear weapons, reprocessing and enrichment, and agreed to verify their respective compliance by establishing verification procedures. Implementation will follow entry into force at the next Prime Ministerial meeting scheduled for February 19.

We are strongly urging both the North and South to quickly agree on and implement an effective inspection regime. As Secretary Baker wrote recently in <u>Foreign Affairs</u>, "The only firm assurance against nuclear proliferation in Korea is a credible agreement by both Seoul and Pyongyang to abstain from the production or acquisition of any weapons-grade nuclear material on the Korean Peninsula."

Japan

The second element of our efforts to meet the challenge of Korean proliferation is our close cooperation with Japan. In late 1990, North Korea suddenly offered to normalize relations with Japan. This was a major policy shift which implicitly accepted the reality of two Korean governments. The DPRK has historically sought to deny the legitimacy of the ROK. Its motive in moving towards Japan was clearly to seek massive transfers of hard currency as reparations from the colonial period.

However, the DPRK's hope for a quick injection of much
needed foreign currency has not been realized. Japan
fully shares our view of the dangers of North Korea's
nuclear program. In six rounds of normalization talks
with the DPRK -- most recently, last week -- it has made
normalization -- and aid -- contingent upon North Korea's
resolution of the nuclear proliferation problem. This
tough stance by a potentially major benefactor has been a
major factor in sending North Korea a clear message about
its nuclear activities. It is also an important example
of the value of the U.S.-Japan partnership.

We have also initiated trilateral consultations
between the US, ROK and Japan. Last November, we held the
first trilateral policy planning talks in Seoul. These
discussions covered cooperation on the nuclear issue as
well as a broad range of issues relating to reducing
tensions on the Peninsula and stability in northeast Asia.

Russia

The third part of our approach to the Korean
proliferation problem is our dialogues with the other
major powers in the region, Russia and China, about the
North Korean nuclear issue. We have consulted closely
with the Soviets, now with Russia, who have shared our

0125

views on proliferation. As was the case during the Iraq
conflict, the Soviets have proved an important partner in
meeting such regional security challenges.

    In addition to halting delivery of the four nuclear
power plants they agreed to build in 1985, we believe
Soviet pressure was an important factor behind the DPRK's
accession to the NPT that year. In high-level meetings,
particularly during then Soviet Foreign Minister
Shevardnadze visit in late 1990, the Soviets applied
direct pressure on North Korea. The dramatic Soviet
opening to South Korea, evidenced in then President
Gorbachev's meeting with President Roh in San Francisco in
1990 also had a major impact on North Korean calculus.

    Moscow also supported a September 1991 IAEA resolution
calling on North Korea to promptly implement safeguards.
Just last month, Russian Ambassador-at-large Igor Rogachev
made an important visit to Pyongyang where he delivered a
similarly strong message about North Korean obligations to
the NPT.

China

    As the country closest to the quixotic and fiercely
independent DPRK regime, China can play a key -- though
clearly limited -- role. Cooperation on regional
conflicts -- particularly Cambodia and Korea -- is an
important aspect of our engagement with the PRC.

0126

We have urged the Chinese to cooperate in halting the
threat of proliferation on the Korean Peninsula. This was
a central concern raised by Secretary Baker with his
Chinese counterpart during his visit to Beijing last
November. And China has been playing a positive role in
several respects. In recent years they have developed
booming economic ties with South Korea, substantially
larger than those with the North. In the past year the
PRC and ROK have established quasi-diplomatic ties by
exchanging trade offices in each others' capitals. And
Chinese influence was apparent in urging North Korea to
accept the simultaneous entry of both Koreas into the U.N.
last September.

China has also announced readiness to accede to the
NPT treaty itself. We believe that with this decision,
China also adopted a firmer stance, pressing North Korea
to implement IAEA safeguards. This message has been
authoritatively communicated to Pyongyang by Beijing.
China also helped facilitate our contacts with North
Korea.

More broadly, for some time, China has sought to
persuade North Korea to pursue economic reforms and an
opening to the West as it has done. North Korea's
announcement last month that it would establish special
economic zones and free ports on its east coast may be one
reflection of China's impact.

672-1712

0127

Multilateral Efforts

In addition to our activities with the two Koreas, the
three other major powers in northeast Asia, and our close
ally, Australia, we have pursued an activist diplomacy
worldwide. We have sought to build consensus and raise
consciousness of the danger of proliferation on the Korean
Peninsula, not only amongst our friends and allies, but
also with many others, including countries with amicable
ties to the DPRK. We have shared our assessment of the
North Korean program and the implications on both regional
and global security.

We have been pleased to see a strong international
consensus emerge evident in multilateral fora such as the
United Nations and the IAEA. There have been informal
discussions of the North Korean nuclear issue among U.N.
Security Council members. And last September Japan and
Australia initiated a successful resolution urging North
Korea to fulfill its obligations in the IAEA.

In my view, our multifaceted diplomacy on the Korean
nuclear issue is precisely what Secretary Baker means when
he uses the term "collective engagement." This sort of
multilateral exercise in consultation and
consensus-building is a model for U.S. foreign policy in
the post-Cold war world.

0128

<u>U.S.-DPRK</u>

Finally, let me say a few words about my own meeting with the North Koreans on January 22nd, the first such high-level contact between U.S. and North Korean officials.

We initiated a low level dialogue with North Korea in 1988, in tandem with President Roh's "Nordpolitik" opening to the communist world. In addition, we allowed the commercial trade in items meeting "basic human needs and have encouraged academic and cultural visits. At the official level, we have held 18 official meetings at the embassy counselor level in Beijing since 1988. We have discussed our nuclear proliferation concerns as well as other issues of interest, particularly, Korean War Missing-in-Action, DPRK support for terrorism, and North Korean missile sales. These meetings have not proven very fruitful.

However, as the North-South dialogue began to gather momentum in late 1991, we and the ROK discussed the utility of a direct meeting between U.S. and DPRK officials at a sufficiently high level to deliver an authoritative message about our concerns that would reach their top leadership in unfiltered form. On January 22 in New York, I met with Kim Young Sun, Korean Workers Party (KWP) Secretary for International Affairs.

USW(天) -672-17-14

The focus of the talks was the North Korean nuclear
program. We indicated to the North Koreans both our
concerns and North Korean actions which could allay those
concerns and lead to an improvement in U.S.-DPRK
relations. At the same time, we stressed the fundamental
importance of North-South dialogue in resolving the
problems of the Korean Peninsula, and the necessity for
its continued progress if U.S.-DPRK relations are to be
enhanced. We also discussed other areas of concern where
North Korea could take steps we would regard as positive
including Korean War-era missing-in-action American
troops, missile proliferation, and human rights.

The North Koreans affirmed their earlier public
declarations that whey would sign a safeguards agreement
by the end of the month -- which they have since done --
and bring it into force shortly thereafter. They also
said they intend to implement their agreements with the
ROK to develop and implement a bilateral inspection regime.

We welcomed their commitment to follow through on
these commitments with both the IAEA and the ROK. We
emphasized the importance of early implementation, and
said that the continuation of our dialogue at a high level
depends on their prompt implementation of effective
inspections under both an IAEA safeguards regime and the
North-South Agreement on a Non-Nuclear Korea.

0130

Our assessment of the meeting is that the North Koreans are beginning to understand the absolute necessity of meeting their commitments in the nuclear area if they are to enjoy the benefits of responsible membership in the international community. We do not underestimate, however, the potential difficulties in the implementation phase that lies ahead.

Conclusion

In the recent agreements reached between North and South Korea and the DPRK's signing on January 30th of an IAEA safeguards agreement we see hopeful signs of progress. We believe this progress is related to the multifaceted diplomatic activity I have outlined which has sought to create a political climate conducive to responsible North Korean behavior. The U.S. is prepared to reciprocate positive DPRK behavior. We do see preliminary signs that North Korea has begun to make some of the decisions necessary to become a responsible international actor. We believe such behavior is in the best long-term interest of the DPRK and hope that Pyongyang takes timely action to prove us right.

At the same time, we have been disappointed before by North Korean behavior. And as we have seen in the case of Iraq, no inspection regime can provide absolute

certainty. But we believe that the implementation of IAEA
safeguards and the associated inspection regime will make
it extremely difficult for North Korea to conceal
significant quantities of nuclear weapons grade materials,
substantially increase our knowledge about North Korean
nuclear activities, and increase our confidence in
detecting any proliferation activity. An effective
North-South inspection regime could clearly enhance the
ability to detect and thwart any illegal nuclear
activity. Thank you.

672-17-17

외 무 부

종   별 : 지 급

번   호 : USW-0638   일   시 : 92 0206 1858

수   신 : 장관(미일,미일,정특,아일)

발   신 : 주 미 대사

제   목 : 하원 외무위 미 외교 정책 관련 청문회(아국 관계 요지)

　　연;USW-0604

　　1. 연호 상원 외교위 청문회에 이어 하원 외무위(위원장; DANTE FASCELL 의원)도 금 2.6 BAKER 국무장관을 출석시킨가운데 미 외교 정책에 대한 별도 청문회를 개최하였는바, 동 청문회 베이커 장관의 증언 내용은 연호와 동일함.

　　2. 동장관의 증언에 이어 진행된 질의 응답과정에서 HOWARD WOLPE 의원(민-미시간)은 북한에 대한 핵 사찰 및 아국과 일본의 핵 재처리 능력 문제와 관련, 몇가지 문제점을 제기하고 아래 언급함.

　　가. 남북한간 역사적 비핵화 합의에도 불구, 북한이 과연 핵사찰에 관한 모든 합의를 성실히 이행할것이며, 또한 IAEA 가 이를 적절히 감독할수 있을것인지는 이락에서의 경험에 비추어 의심스러움.북한이 핵 재처리 및 기타 핵 시설을 은밀한 장소로 이전, 비밀리에 무기 개발 계획을 계속 추진하지 않을것이라는점을 어떻게 확신할수 있을것인가

　　나. 한국은 핵 재처리 능력 포기 선언에도 불구하고 최근 영국, 카나다등과별도의 핵관련 협정을 체결한바, 동 협정 체결을 통해 한국은 핵 재처리 기술이나 플루투늄 생산능력을 획득하게 될지도 모름. 한국은 최근 영국 회사인 BRITISH NUCLEAR FUEL 과 핵 재처리 관련 협정(UMBRELLA AGREEMENT)을 체결하였고, 카나다와는 소위 TANDAM FUEL CYCLE(미국산 경수 원자로로부터 수거된 연료를 재처리, 카나다산 중수 원자로 연료로 사용) 연구 검토를 위한 협정에 서명하였음. 이러한 협정은 핵 재처리 능력 포기 정책에 위배되는것이 아닌지 의문시됨. 또한미국은 영국및 카나다 정부로부터 이런 문제에 관해 사전협의도 받은적이 없는것으로 알고 있음.

　　다. 일본은 북한에 대해 핵 재처리 시설 폐기를 요구하면서도 100 본 가량의 산업용 플루토늄 생산을 계획하고 있음. 미국의 핵 정책(NO-PLUTONIUM POLICY)은 동

미주국 정와대	장관 안기부	차관	1차보	2차보	아주국	미주국	외정실	분석관

아시아 지역뿐 아니라 전세계적으로 무차별적으로 적용 되어야함.

3. 상기에 대해 베이커 장관은 북한 핵 사찰 문제에 관해서만 아래 답변하고, 아국과 일본 관련 사항에 대해서는 추후 문서로 답변하겠다면서 즉답을 회피하였음.

가. 미국은 최근 뉴욕에서 북한측과 차관급 접촉을 가졌음. 동 접촉시 미국은 북한측에 대해 12.31 남북한간 합의의 조속 이행을 촉구하고, 협정서명만으로는 불충분하며, 효과적이고 검증 가능한 사찰 제도에 따라 합의가 이행되어야함을 강조한바 있음. 미국은 이점을 한국측에도 분명히 하였음.

나. 북한의 핵 관련 시설 은폐 여부를 여하히 확인할것인가에 관하여는 IAEA 측이 적절한 사찰 권한과 제도를 먼저 갖추어야한다고봄. 미국은 NPT 조약 의무 이행과 IAEA 핵 사찰 문제를 북한측과 논의하는 과정에서 이문제에 관한 미측의 관심을 분명히 전달하였음.

4. 상기 2. 나 항의 영국, 카나다와의 핵관련 협정 체결에 관한 WOLPE 의원언급 내용의 진위 여부등 당관 참고 사항이 있을시 회시 바람.

5. 상기 질의 응답 내용 TRANSCRIPT 팩시편 별송함.

첨부; USW(F)-0684

(대사 현홍주-국장)

92.12.31 까지

주 미 대 사 관

USW(F) : 0684   년월일 : 920206 시간 : 1858
수 신 : 장 관 (미안.미이).정특.아일)
발 신 : 주 미 대 사
제 목 : 하원외무위 청문회 (아측관께질의응답내용) (출처 :   )

보 안
통 제 七8

외신 1과
동 제

REP. HOWARD WOLPE (D-MI): Thank you very much, Mr. Chairman.

And, Mr. Secretary, we're delighted to be welcoming you today. And I wanted to take advantage of the Hamilton-Solarz precedent and ask you a three-part question. I think the world has come to understand that the key security issue in the aftermath of the Cold War is the question of the proliferation of nuclear weapons. And that is the subject of my questions.

During your trip to the Far East in November, you stated, and I'm quoting, "The only firm assurance against a nuclear arms race in the Korean peninsula would be a credible agreement of both Seoul and Pyongyang to abstain from the production or acquisition of any weapons-grade nuclear material," end of quote. And since then, North and South Korea have entered into an historic agreement to forego the development of nuclear weapons and the possession of the reprocessing and enrichment plants needed to produce plutonium and uranium for weapons. And I certainly applaud your initative in these areas and the encouragement we have given to secure those agreements.

My first question relates to our confidence that North Korea will in fact cooperate in this process ultimately and our degree of ensuring that we will be able to adequately police any agreements finally implemented. Specifically, what are we doing to ensure that the IAEA will be in a position to adequately police the agreements, particularly in light of their failed record with respect to Iraq? And more generally, how can the United States ensure that North Korea does not remove its reprocessing and other nuclear capabilities to secret locations and does not operate a clandestine weapons program?

(0684 - 3 - 1)

My second question relates to the South Korean side of the equation. Although South Korea has agreed not to build reprocessing plants, it has, I understand, recently entered into separate nuclear arrangements with Great Britain and Canada that could result in it acquiring reprocessing technology or plutonium itself. It signed an umbrella agreement with Britain's reprocessing company, British Nuclear Fuels, for as yet unspecified spent fuel services, including the recovery of plutonium from South Korea and spent fuel shipped to Great Britian. South Korea has also recently signed an agreement with Canada to study the so-called tandum fuel cycle, in which spent fuel from South Korea's US-supplied light-water reactors would be reprocessed for use as fuel in South Korean's Canadian-supplied heavy-water reactors.

So my second question is whether or not these arrangements are in fact inconsistent with the policy that you enunciated earlier that both Koreas should abstain from the production or acquisition of any weapons-grade nuclear material and how will we be responding to those new arrangements, which I understand were entered into without the Canadian government at least consulting or the British consulting with the United States -- the British government, not the Canadian government.

And then finally, as you know, Mr. Secretary, Japan is calling on North Korea to dismantle its reprocessing plant at the same time that it is preparing to build on of its own, and Japan plans to acquire some 100 tons of plutonium for use by its utility industry. Will this not also complicate other diplomatic objectives in South Asia? And isn't it not time that the United States pursue a non-discriminatory, no-plutonium policy in the East Asian region and worldwide?

Those are my questions. I do want to say finally that I continue to be very disturbed by the administration's continuing opposition to those provisions of the Export Administration Act now in conference committee to close significant loopholes in our own nuclear non-proliferation law. I simply can't understand how we can be credible in our efforts worldwide if we're not prepared to close those loopholes in our own nuclear non-proliferation law.

SEC. BAKER: Mr. Wolpe, let me answer question one of the three you posed and tell you I will get you an answer for the record to questions two and three.

CONTINUED

0684-3-2

0136

With respect to question one, we've just rec\|\.\|y had a meeting
with the North Koreans ourselves at the level of the Undersecretary
for Political Affairs who met with the North Koreans in new York.
And we encouraged them during the course of that meeting to promptly
implement that December 31st agreement with South Korea. And we
encouraged them to do so on the basis of a very effective
inspections regime. And we told them that just signing the
agreement's not going to be enough, as far as we're concerned.
We've told the South Koreans the same thing.

    We want to see an agreement that contains an effective and
verifiable inspection regime. That would be my answer to your first
question, and particularly as it relates to how -- how will the IAEA
know that they're not hiding some capacity in a cave? They'll have
to satisfy themselves that they have adequate inspection rights and
an adequate inspection regime, and we've made known to the North
Koreans our interest in that specific issue of the broader issue of
their signing onto the NPT and accepting IAEA safeguards and
inspections.

    I'll have to get you an answer to your question about the South
Koreans and France and the United Kingdom -- and the Japanese
question.

068K - 3 - 3

0137

北韓 核關係 美議會 聽聞會 結果

1992. 2. 8.

外 務 部

> 아놀드 캔터 美國務部 政務次官은 2. 6(木) 美上院 外交委
> 亞. 太小委 聽聞會에 出席, 北韓의 核擴散과 美國의 政策에
> 관해 證言한 바, 同 要旨 및 評價를 報告드립니다.

(위원장 : 앨런 크랜스톤 의원)

1. 캔터次官 證言要旨

(北韓 核問題에 대한 美國의 立場)

o 北韓이 舊 蘇聯邦의 解體와 더불어 經濟의 沈滯, 世代
   交替問題, 核開發에 대한 광범위한 國際的 壓力 等으로
   一應 責任있는 姿勢를 보이고 있음.

o 그러나 北韓이 實際行動에 있어서는 계속 모호한 態度를
   취하므로써 北韓 核에 대한 美國의 憂慮는 사라지지 않고
   있는 바, 北韓이 具體的 行動을 취할 경우 美國은 相應
   하는 措置를 취할 準備가 되어 있음.
   - 美國은 北韓이 2. 19. 南. 北 高位級會談 以前 IAEA
      核安全協定을 批准하고, 南. 北韓間 合意에 의한 相互
      查察을 早速 履行할 것을 강력히 促求中

0138

o 美國의 政策은 韓.美 同盟關係 및 南北 分斷이라는 큰
   테두리 안에서 北韓 核武器 計劃, 南.北韓 關係, 美國 및
   周邊列强과 北韓과의 關係를 考慮하여 다루어져야 함.

   ~~- 美國의 對韓半島 政策의 基本은 확고부동한 對韓防衛~~
   ~~公約과 南北對話를 통한 韓半島問題의 恒久的인 解決~~
   ~~原則임.~~

   - 駐韓美軍 第2段階 減縮(93-95) 凍結 決定은 韓國을
      安心시키는 한편, 北韓에 대한 警告를 意味함.

〈韓半島 周邊國과의 協調體制〉

o 日本: 6次에 걸친 日.北韓 修交協商을 통해 修交와
   援助를 北韓의 核問題와 連繫시키고 있음.

o 러시아: 北韓의 核安全措置 履行을 促求하는 IAEA
   決議案(91.9)을 支持하는 한편, 로가쵸프 特使의 평양
   訪問時(92.1) 北韓에 대해 核非擴散條約 義務 遵守를
   促求함.

o 中國: 北韓이 IAEA 核安全措置 義務를 履行해야 된다는
   立場을 北韓側에 傳達함.

   - 最近 北韓의 經濟特區 및 自由港 指定 發表도 經濟
      改革과 開放을 勸誘하는 中國의 影響力 反映 結果

0139

o 한편 IAEA 및 유엔 安保理等을 통해 北韓 核問題의 解決을
   위한 國際的 合意를 提高中임.

   - 北韓 核開發 沮止를 위한 多邊外交는 베이커長官이
     闡明한 「集團介入 政策」의 좋은 事例

(美.北韓 뉴욕 高位接觸)

o 同 接觸結果, 北韓은 國際社會에 責任있는 一員으로의
   參與를 위해서는 核問題에 대한 約束履行이 不可避하다는
   점을 理解하기 始作한 것으로 評價함.

2. 評 價

o 금번 聽聞會는 지난 1. 22. 뉴욕 高位接觸時 美 行政府가
   北韓側에 傳達한 멧세지 內容을 議會에 報告하는 性格
   으로서, 核問題 解決을 위한 北韓의 조속한 行動을
   公開的으로 促求하는 것임.

   - 베이커 國務長官도 2. 6. 美 下院 外務委 聽聞會에서
     美國이 美.北韓 뉴욕 高位接觸時 北韓側에 대해
     南.北韓間 合意書 署名만으로는 不充分하며, 效果的
     이고 檢證 가능한 査察制度 마련을 통해 南.北韓間
     合意를 早速履行할 것을 促求한 바 있음을 밝힘.

o 캔터次官은 北韓의 核 安全協定 署名等 최근의 進展에
   대해 조심스러운 歡迎의 뜻을 表示하면서도 北韓의 實際
   意圖에 대해서는 계속 疑懼心을 갖고 있음을 表明함. 끝.

0140

北韓 核關係 美議會 聽聞會 結果

1992. 2. 8.

外 務 部

> 아놀드 캔터 美國務部 政務次官은 2.6(木) 美上院 外交委
> 亞.太小委(委員長 : 알랜 크랜스턴 議員) 聽聞會에 出席,
> 北韓의 核擴散과 美國의 政策에 관해 證言한 바, 同 要旨
> 및 評價를 報告드립니다.

1. 캔터次官 證言要旨

   (北韓 核問題에 대한 美國의 立場)

   o 北韓이 舊 蘇聯邦의 解體와 더불어 經濟의 沈滯, 世代
   交替問題, 核開發에 대한 광범위한 國際的 壓力 等으로
   一應 責任있는 姿勢를 보이고 있음.

   o 그러나 北韓이 實際行動에 있어서는 계속 모호한 態度를
   취하므로써 北韓 核에 대한 美國의 憂慮는 사라지지 않고
   있는 바, 北韓이 具體的 行動을 취할 경우 美國은 相應
   하는 措置를 취할 準備가 되어 있음.
   - 美國은 北韓이 2.19. 南.北 高位級會談 以前 IAEA
   核安全協定을 批准하고, 南.北韓間 合意에 의한 相互
   査察을 早速 履行할 것을 강력히 促求中

0141

o 美國의 政策은 韓.美 同盟關係 및 南北 分斷이라는 큰
  테두리 안에서 北韓 核武器 計劃, 南.北韓 關係, 美國 및
  周邊列强과 北韓과의 關係를 考慮하여 다루어져야 함.

    - 駐韓美軍 第2段階 減縮(93-95) 凍結 決定은 韓國을
      安心시키는 한편, 北韓에 대한 警告를 意味

(韓半島 周邊國과의 協調體制)

o 日 本 : 6次에 걸친 日.北韓 修交協商을 통해 修交와
  援助를 北韓의 核問題와 連繫시키고 있음.

o 러시아 : 北韓의 核安全措置 履行을 促求하는 IAEA
  決議案(91.9)을 支持하는 한편, 로가쵸프特使의 평양
  訪問時(92.1) 北韓에 대해 核非擴散條約 義務 遵守를
  促求함.

o 中 國 : 北韓이 IAEA 核安全措置 義務를 履行해야
  된다는 立場을 北韓側에 傳達함.

    - 最近 北韓의 經濟特區 및 自由港 指定 發表도 經濟
      改革과 開放을 勸誘하는 中國의 影響力 反映 結果

o 한편, IAEA 및 유엔 安保理等을 통해 北韓 核問題의
  解決을 위한 國際的 合意를 提高中임.

    - 北韓 核開發 沮止를 위한 多邊外交는 베이커長官이
      闡明한 「集團介入 政策」의 좋은 事例

0142

(美.北韓 뉴욕 高位接觸)

ㅇ 同 接觸結果, 北韓은 國際社會에 責任있는 一員으로의
  參與를 위해서는 核問題에 대한 約束履行이 不可避하다는
  점을 理解하기 始作한 것으로 評價함.

2. 評   價

ㅇ 금번 聽聞會는 지난 1.22. 뉴욕 高位接觸時 美 行政府가
  北韓側에 傳達한 멧세지 內容을 議會에 報告하는 性格
  으로서, 核問題 解決을 위한 北韓의 조속한 行動을
  公開的으로 促求하는 것임.
  - 베이커 國務長官도 2.6. 美 下院 外務委 聽聞會에서
    美國이 美.北韓 뉴욕 高位接觸時 北韓側에 대해
    南.北韓間 合意書 署名만으로는 不充分하며, 效果的
    이고 檢證 가능한 査察制度 마련을 통해 南.北韓間
    合意를 早速履行할 것을 促求한 바 있음을 밝힘.

ㅇ 캔터次官은 北韓의 核 安全協定 署名等 최근의 進展에
  대해 조심스러운 歡迎의 뜻을 表示하면서도 北韓의 實際
  意圖에 대해서는 계속 疑懼心을 갖고 있음을 보여줌.   끝.

0143

관리 번호	92-201

외 무 부

종 별 :

번 호 : USW-0724　　　　　　　　　　일 시 : 92 0212 1832

수 신 : 장 관 (미일,<u>미이</u>,정북,기정,국기)

발 신 : 주 미 대사

제 목 : 하원 정보위 전문위원 접촉

　　연: USW-541, 612

　　1. 당관 조일환 참사관은 금 2.12. CALVIN HUMPHREY 하원 정보위 전문위원과 오찬 기회에(조태열 서기관 동석), 연호 북한 특수무기 개발 문제에 관한 비공개 청문회 일정및 RICHARDSON 하원의원의 방북 계획을 탐문한바, <u>의회측 사정으로 연기된 동 청문회는 2.26(수) 오전 10 시에 개최될 예정이며,</u> RICHARDSON 의원의 방북은 4 월중순 휴회기간에 이루어질 가능성이 많으나 아직 확정되지는 않았다함. 동인은 항공일정에 문제가 없는한 동경 경유, 서울 방문후 북경을 거쳐 방북할 생각이며, 방북전 아측과 사전 협의및 사후 DEBRIEFING 계획에 변함이없다고 부언함.

　　2. 동인은 RICHARDSON 의원 방북 문제 협의를 위해 접촉한 주유엔 북한대표부 허종대사는 상당히 서구화된 인물이라는 인상을 받았으며, 핵사찰 문제를 포함, 북한이 처해있는 국제적 상황에 대한 인식도 제대로 갖고 있는 것으로 보였으나, 핵사찰 문제는 북한 정부내부의 문제(PROBLEMS IN THE GOVERNMENT)로 조속한 이행이 어려울 것이라는 반응을 보였다고 말하고, 국제적으로 고립이 심화되고 있는 상황에서 핵 문제를 당장 해결할 경우 더 이상 활용할 카드가 없어 진다는데 북한의 고민이 있는 것으로 본다고 부언함. 　검토필(19□□. 6. 30.) 1□

　　3. 이에대해, 조참사관은 우리정부가 남북대화와 핵문제 해결을 병행 추진하고 있는 배경을 상세 설명한바, 동인은 현재 진행중인 남북 대화의 MOMENTUM 을 유지하고자 하는 한국 정부의 입장은 이해하나, 상대방이 강경한 입장을 포기하지 않을 경우에는 똑같이 강경한 태도로 임하는 것이 가장 효과적일 것이라고 사견을 피력함.

　　4. 상기 청문회 내용은 동인을 재차 접초, 가능한 범위내에서 파악, 보고 위계이며, 금일 동인으로 부터 입수한 국방정보국(DIA) 발간 북한 군사력 평가

미주국	장관	차관	1차보	2차보	미주국	국기국	외정실	분석관

청와대 안기부
예고문에 의거 재분류(19 92.12.31)

PAGE 1　　　　　성 명

　　　　　　　　　　　　　　　　　　　　　　92.02.13　　09:09

　　　　　　　　　　　　　　　　　　　　　외신 2과　통제관 BA

　　　　　　　　　　　　　　　　　　　　　　　　0144

보고서를 파편 송부함. 끝.
　(대사 현홍주-국장)
　예고: 92.12.31. 일반

| 관리
번호 | 92-90 |

분류번호	보존기간

발 신 전 보

번 호 : WUS-0693   920214 1712 DW   종별 :

수 신 : 주   미   대사. 총영사

발 신 : 장 관   (미이)

제 목 : 상원외교위 아.태소위 청문회

대 : USW-630

　　　최근 국내언론은 표제 청문회에서의 Kanter 차관의 증언내용을 인용,
미국이 남.북한 상호 핵사찰에의 참여를 주장하고 있어 한.미간에 이견이
있는 것으로 보도하고 있는바, Kanter 차관의 표제 청문회에서의 질의응답
transcript를 지급 송부바람.　　끝.

　　　　　　　　　　　　　　　　　　　　(미주국장 반기문)

검토필(19○○. 6. 30.) ○○

	보 안 통 제	

| 앙
고
재 | 92
년
2
월
14
일 | 북
미
2
과 | 기안자
성명 | 오 | 과 장 | | 국 장 | 전결) | 차 관 | 장 관 | | 외신과통제 | |

0146

외 무 부

관리 92
번호 -91

종 별 :

번 호 : USW-0757　　　　　　　　　　일 시 : 92 0214 1629

수 신 : 장 관 (미이)

발 신 : 주 미 대 사

제 목 : 상원외교위 아태소위 청문회

　　대: WUS-0693

　　1. 대호, KANTER 차관의 청문회 답변 내용에 대해 당관 유명환 참사관이 SCHMIEL 국무부 한국과장 대리에게 확인한바, 동인은 KANTER 차관의 언급은 다소 오해의 소지가 있는 것도 사실이나, 실제 문맥상으로 보면 북한에 의한 IAEA 안전협정의 서명이나 비준보다는 효과적인 사찰의 중요성을 강조한데 불과하다고 말하고, 실제로 뉴욕 회담에서 그러한 제의가 이루어지지 않았음을 분명히 하였음.

　　2. 한편, HASTINGS 한국과 북한담당관은 당관 박흥신 서기관과의 접촉시 남북한간에 핵사찰에 관한 구체적인 협의도 이루어지지 않은 상황에서 사찰팀의 구성 문제가 거론된다는 것은 어불성설이라고 말하고 언론에 대해서도 이러한 논리로 대응해 나가면 될 것이라는 견해를 피력하였음.

　　3. 질의 응답 관련 부분은 FAX 송부함.

　　첨부: USW(F)-0838(1 매). 끝.

　　(대사 현홍주-국장)

　　예고: 92.12.31. 까지 고문에 의거 일반문서로 재분류됨

검로필(19 02 6.30.)

미주국　　장관　　차관　　1차보　　외정실　　분석관　　정와대　　안기부

주 미 대 사 관

USR(F) : *0838*   년월일 :214.   시간 : *1400*

수 신 : 장 관 (버이) | 보안 |
                        | 통제 | *1/13*

발 신 : 주 미 대 사

제 목 : 상원 외교위 아태소위 청문회 (Kanter 차관 증언)(출처 :   )

SENATOR CRANSTON: What you said in response to
these particular questions is not particularly encouraging
in regard to the degree of confidence we might have about
their adhering to IAEA accords. Certainly exporting poison
gas violates the spirit, if not the letter, of the 1925
accord, I would think.

In your meeting, did you raise the issue of the
North permitting joint South Korean and American inspectors
of their facilities in return for inspecting American
military and civilian facilities in South Korea?

MR. KANTER: Yes, Senator, I did. And let me be
clear. The heart of our estimate of whether the North
Koreans are following through on their obligations with
respect to their nuclear program will be effective
inspections, not whether they simply sign and ratify the
IAEA safeguards agreement, but the results of those IAEA
inspections, complemented and reinforced by a separate,
effective inspection regime under the North-South non-
nuclear agreement, inspections of their military and
civilian facilities which would be reciprocated by North
Korean inspections of military and civilian facilities in
South Korea, including U.S. military facilities in South
Korea. And I went over that ground in considerable detail
with my North Korean counterpart.

SENATOR CRANSTON: In your meeting, did you raise
the issue of whether or not the North would permit IAEA
challenge inspections where we can go where we wish at any
time?

MR. KANTER: I did not explicitly raise that
subject in my meeting, but the IAEA's right to conduct
special inspections is extant. I mean, it's there. North
Korea must be aware of it.

(   ) | 몽 제 | --

배부처	장관실	차관실	一차보	二차보	기획실	의정실	분석관	의전장	아주국	미주국	구주국	중아국	국기국	경제국	통상국	문협국	영재국	총무과	감사관	공보관	의연원	청외실	총리실	안기부	공보처	경기국	상공부
	/	/	/		/		/	O														/	/				

0148

관리 번호	92-300

원 본

외 무 부

종 별 :

번 호 : USW-0762   일 시 : 92 0214 1807

수 신 : 장관(민의, 미일, 정북, 국기, 외교안보,사본;통일원,국방부장관)

발 신 : 주 미 대사

제 목 : SOLARZ 하원 아태소위 위원장 보좌관 접촉

대: WUS-0685

당관 임성준 참사관은 금 2.14 조일환 참사관과 함께 STANLEY ROTH 하원 아태 소위 수석전문위원을 방문, 대호 이동복 성명 내용과 6 차 남북 고위급회담에임하는 우리 정부의 입장을 설명한 바, 동인의 반응을 아래 보고함.

1. 솔라즈 의원은 그동안 북한의 핵개발 문제에 대해 계속 강경입장을 취해왔음. 한국 정부의 여사한 입장표명이 1 개월 정도 빨리 이루어졌더라면 하는 아쉬움은 있으나, 현명한 선택을 했다고 생각하며, 이를 환영함. 솔라즈 의원도 기쁘게 생각할 것임.

2. 솔라즈 의원은 이 문제의 해결없이 남북한 관계가 진전될 경우 북한에 대해 WRONG SIGNLAL 을 보낼 수 있다는 점을 우려하고 있으며, 이러한 입장을 국무부 KANTER 정무차관에게 서한으로 기표명한바 있음.

3. 북한의 핵개발 의도와 관련, 현재 미 조야의 시각은 1)북한이 핵시설을 은폐, 계속 핵무기를 개발할 것이라는 강경입장(HANKISH SCHOOL) 2) 일본의 경협자금 확보, 김정일의 권력승계,미.북한 관계개선등의 목표달성을위한 BARGAIN CHIP 으로 핵문제를 활용키 위해 전술적으로 문제해결을 지연시키고 있다는 두가지 입장으로 갈려 있는바, 지금까지의 북한 태도로 보아 자신은 전자의 시각이 맞는것이 아닌가 생각됨.

4. 남북한 핵통제 위원회도 1 개월내 구성키로 합의되어 있으나 원만히 구성될런지 의심스러우며, 설사 구성된다 하더라도 실질적으로 운영될 수 있을지 우려됨. 결론적으로, 북한의 핵개발 문제 해결에 대한 솔라즈 의원과 자신의 입장은 아직 회의적이며, 향후 진전 추이를 계속 관심을 가지고 지켜보겠음.

(대사 현홍주-국장)

예고:일반 92.12.31,에 핵고문제 의거 일반문서로 재분류됨

해제필(19 02. 6. 30.)

미주국	장관	차관	1차보	2차보	미주국	국기국	외정실	분석관
정와대	안기부	국방부	통일원					

PAGE 1

관리 번호	92-101		원 본

외 무 부

종 별 :

번 호 : USW-0919

일 시 : 92 0224 1858

수 신 : 장관(미이, 미일, 정특)

발 신 : 주 미 대사

제 목 : 솔라즈 의원 보좌관 접촉

대;AM-32, WUS-798

연;USW-762

1. 당관 조일환 참사관은 금 2.24 솔라즈 하원 아태소위원장실 STANLEY ROTH 수석 전문위원을 방문, 대호 6 차 남북 고위급 회담 결과를 설명한바(조태열 서기관동석), 동인은 회담 결과에 대하여는 신문 보도를 통해 대략 파악하고 있었으나, 상세 내용을 알려주어 감사하다고 말하고, 아래 언급함.

가. 예상했던대로 회담 결과가 매우 실망스러운(DISCOURAGING)것이어서 유감임. 솔라즈 의원이 회담전 KANTER 정무차관에게 연호 서한을 보낸 이유도 이러한 결과를 우려해서였던바, 지금까지 취해온 대북한 유화 정책(CARROT)을 더이상계속한다면, 북한은 아마도 핵문제 해결 없이도 남북간 합의를 통해 경제적 이득을 얻을수 있다고 판단, 핵문제와 관련한 모든 조치를 계속 미루게 될것으로 봄(VERY LIKELY SCENARIO).

나. 더우나, 금번 회담시 북한이 주한 미군 철수와 T/S 훈련 중지 문제등을 다시 거론한것은 그간의 북한 태도보다 오히려 후퇴한것이며, 솔라즈 의원 방북시 김일성이 언급한 내용과도 상충하는것임. 북한이 7 차 남북 고위급 회담 개최 이전까지 IAEA 핵안전 협정을 비준하지 않을경우에도 한국측이 동 회담에 응할것인지 궁금함. 남북 대화의 MOMENTUM 을 살려가는것도 중요하지만 문제는 대북한 유화책을 어디까지 끌고갈것이냐에 있다고 봄.

검토필(19?2. 6.30.) 명

2. 동인은 또한 금일 NYT 사설 내용에 언급, 동 사설은 사실관계에서의 오류뿐만 아니라 미국내 여론을 오도하는것으로서 솔라즈 의원이 이를 매우 불쾌하게 생각하여 동지 편집인을 직접 접촉, 오류를 지적할 계획이라고 말하고, 북한에 대해 온건한 입장을 갖고 있는 인사들 조차 그런 잘못된 정보를 제공할리는 없다고 보기 때문에, 아마도 북한 대표부 허종 대사가 제공한것이 아닌가 생각한다고 부언함.

미주국 안기부	장관	차관	1차보	2차보	미주국	외정실	분석관	정와대

PAGE 1

92.02.25   09:58

외신 2과 통제관 BX

0150

(대사 현홍주-국장)

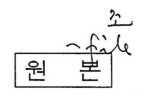

관리
번호 92-105

외 무 부

종 별 : 지급

번 호 : USW-0969

일 시 : 92 0226 2021

수 신 : 장관(미일,민의,정안,국기)

발 신 : 주 미 대사

제 목 : 하원 외무위 청문회

1. 하원 외무위는 2.25(화) GATES CIA 국장을 출석시켜 -냉전 시대 이후의 정보 기구의 역할- 제하의 청문회를 개최하였는바, 동 청문회시 GATES 국장의 한국관계 언급 내용을 아래 보고함.

가. 북한은 소련제 SCUD 미사일을 복제, 이란 시리아등 중동 국가에 수출 하는등 대량 살상 무기 운반 체제의 세계 확산에 큰 위협 요소가 되고 있는바, 현재는 사정 거리가 최소 1,000 KM 에 이르는 대형 미사일을 개발중에 있음.

나. 특히 북한은 국내에 우라늄 광산을 갖고 있기 때문에 외부 세계의 도움없이도 무기 수준의 핵분열 물질을 생산할수 있는 시설을 건설중에 있는바, 플루토늄 생산만을 위한 핵발전기 2 기를 영변에 건설, 1 기는 4 년전 부터 가동중에있으며, 1 기는 금년중 가동이 시작될것으로 알고 있음(MAY START UP THIS YEAR). 또한 영변에는 핵 재처리 플루토늄 생산을 위한 시설도 거의 완공 단계에 있음. 충분한 플루토늄 생산을 하더라도 핵무기를 만드는데는 또다른 기술적 절차가 필요한것인데 일반의 경우 수개월 내지는 수년간의 시간이 걸릴것으로 봄(REQUIRE MONTHS OR EVEN YEARS)

검토필(19?2.6.30)

다. 북한이 지난달에야 비로서 IAEA 핵안전 협정에 서명은 하였으나 외부 세계의 의심을 불식시킬만큼 의미있는 현장 검증을 받아들일것인가 하는것은 미지수이며, 핵 검증을 지연시켜 보려는 북한의 일련의 행동은 북한이 대외적으로 한반도 비핵지대화를 위한 남한과의 협력 제스쳐를 취하고 있는것과는 달리 실제로는 주요 핵시설을 은폐시키려는 의도에서 비롯된것으로 보임. 북한이 향후 수개월내 핵처리 시설 보유 사실을 인정하고 사찰 절차에 합의를 할것인가의 여부가 북한의 진의를 판단할수 있는 관건이 될것임.

라. 미국은 북한의 핵 개발이 동북 아시아 안보 유지에 심대한 결과를 초래할뿐

미주국 분석관	장관 청와대	차관 안기부	1차보	2차보	미주국	국기국	외연원	외정실

92.02.27 13:28

외신 2과 통제관 BN

0152

아니라 핵물질 및 관련 기술을 국제시장에 내다놓을 위험이 높다는 점에 대해 큰 우려를 하고 있는바 이는 북한이 외화 획득을 위해서는 무슨일이든 할수 있기 때문임.

　　마. 리비아는 핵무기, 생화학무기 및 동 운반을 위한 미사일 개발에 혈안이되어 주로 소련과 중국의 지원을 시도해왔으나 미국등 서방의 효과적인 봉쇄로뜻을 이루지 못하자 암시장으로 눈을 돌려 조금 낮은 수준이긴 하지만 북한과의 거래를 적극 추진하고 있는것으로 알고 있음.

　　2. 이와 관련 동 청문회종료후 당관에서 청문회에 참석한 주요 의원들로부터 파악한 반응은 아래임.

　　가.STEPHEN SOLARZ 의원(민주, 뉴욕)

　　0 북한이 핵무기 제조 계획을 진정으로 폐기할것이라고 보기는 어려운바, IAEA 핵안전 협정 서명및 한반도 비핵화 선언등은 경제 제재등 각종 제재를 피해보자는 술책(RUSE)으로 보임.

　　0 IAEA 가 이락의 핵 시설을 수차례 사찰하였음에도 불구하고 핵무기 개발 계획을 발견치 못하였던 경험에 비추어 IAEA 가 북한 핵 시설을 사찰하더라도 그결과를 전적으로 신뢰할수는 없음.

　　나.HOWARD BERMAN 의원(민주-캘리포니아)

　　0 북한의 핵 개발에 우려를 갖지 않을수 없는바, 이는 한국에 대한 우호적 입장에서라기 보다 핵 확산을 방지하여야 한다는 우선적 관심 때문임.

　　다.HENRY HYDE 의원(공화-일리노이)

　　0 북한이 핵문제에 명확한 입장을 취하지 않는것은 용이하기 어려운바, GATES 국장의 증언은 북한의 의도에 대한 의구심을 깊게 하였음.

　　라.ROBERT LAGOMARSINO 의원(공화-캘리포니아)

　　0 북한은 전혀 신뢰할수 없다고 보는바 미국은 북한의 위협에 대응하기 위해 한국에 가능한한 모든 지원을 하여야 하며 나아가, 한. 미 양국은 한국의 안보에 영향을 미치는 어떠한 조치에도 공동 보조를 취하여야 함.

　　(대사 현홍주-국장)

관리번호 92-347

외 무 부

종 별 : 지 급

번 호 : USW-0970

일 시 : 92 0226 2021

수 신 : 장관(미일,미이,정안,국기,국연,기정)

발 신 : 주 미 대사

제 목 : 하원 정보위 북한 핵무기 청문회

연;USW-0624

하원 정보위는 금 2.26(수) 10;00 연호 북한 핵무기에 관한 비공개 청문회를 개최하였는바, 동 청문회 내용과 관련 당관 박인국 서기관이 CALVIN HUMPHREY정보위 전문위원으로부터 파악한 내용을 아래 보고함.

1. 회의 개요

0 금일 청문회는 DAVE MCCURDY(민주, 오클라호마)위원장의 주재로 7 명의 하원 정보위 소속 의원들이 참석했으며, 행정부에서는 북한 핵과 관련된 정보를 가지고 있는 관련 부처의 차관보급 인사들이 참석했음(HUMPHREY 전문위원은 위원장의 특별 보안 유지 지시가 있었음으로 증언 인사에 대한 이 이상의 확인은 곤란하다고 설명)

0 참석 의원들은 비교적 강한 대북한 강성 발언과 함께 행정부의 구체적 대응책과 GATES 국장 증언 내용에 대한 근거에 관심을 표명하였음.

2. 주요 증언 내용

가. 하원 외무위 청문회 평가

0 작일(2.25) 개최된 하원 외무위 청문회시의 GATES 국장의 발언 내용에 대하여 금일 증언 인사들은 대부분이 사실로 받아들였으므로 동국장 발언 내용을 주목할 필요가 있음.

나. 북한의 핵 폭탄 제조 시점.

(박서기관이 동 청문회에서 GATES 국장이 북한의 핵폭탄 제조 가능 시점을 향후 -수개월에서 수년간-으로 다소 광범위한 개념으로 잡았는데 보다 정확한 시점에 관한 논의가 있었는지 문의한데 대해)

0 북한의 핵폭탄 제조 능력은 두가지로 나누어 지고 있는바 첫째는 1960 년대 수준의 DELIVERY SYSTEM 이 없는 초보단계(RUDIMENTARY FORM)의

미주국 외정실	장관 분석관	차관 청와대	1차보 안기부	2차보	미주국	국기국	국기국	외연원

0154

PAGE 1

92.02.27   13:29

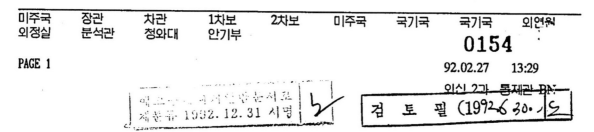

외신 2과 통제관 BN

검 토 필 (1992. 6. 30. 16)

핵폭탄(YOUNGBOMB)으로서 동 수준의 핵폭탄은 수개월내 (A FEW OR SEVERAL MONTHS)생산 가능하다는데 증인들의 의견이 근접하였으며, 두번째 단계는 DELIVERY SYSTEM 을 갖춘 핵무기로서 SCUD 등 MISSILE 장착 핵무기 개발은 고도의 기술이 요구되어 향후 수년간의 시일이 걸릴것으로 보고 있음.

0 참석증인들은 SWCUD 장착 미사일 개발이 고도의 기술을 요하기는 하나 쏘련등으로부터의 두뇌 유출 등으로 북한의 기술 축적 능력은 시간문제일뿐 동 가능성에대해서는 의심의 여지가 없다고 보았음.

다. IAEA 핵안전 협정 비준 시점

0 북한은 상기 초기 단계 핵 폭탄 제조 가능성등과 관련, 경험 축적과 관련시설 및 핵물질의 은폐를 위해 최대한의 시간을 벌기 위해 진력하고 있으며, 일부 증인은 북한이 6 월을 INSPECTION 시점으로 보고 있는것으로 보았음.

라. 대북한 제제 방안

0 참석증인들은 아직은 현재의 행정부 외교적 조치외에 특별한 제제를 생각하고 있지는 않지만 북한이 계속 불성실한 자세를 보일경우에는 우선 유엔 안보리를 통한 압력 행사를 고려할수 있다는 입장을 취하였음.

마. IAEA 조기 사찰 가능성

0 작일 일부 지상에 보도된 IAEA 핵안전 협정 비준전 사찰 실시 가능성 문제에 대해서는, 청문회시 토의 내용을 다 밝힐수는 없으나, 북한측의 진의가 어디있는지는 좀더 두고 보자는 반응이 많았음(HUMPHREY 보좌관은 다소 부정적인 분위기 였음을 시사하였음)

바. 추가 청문회 개최 여부

0 단기간내 추가 청문회 개최 계획은 없으나, 북한의 핵안전 협정 비준 여부등 향후 진전 사항에 따라 필요시 재개 예정임.

(대사 현홍주-국장)

92.12.31 일반

PAGE 2

정 리 보 존 문 서 목 록

기록물종류	일반공문서철	등록번호	2020010126	등록일자	2020-01-21
분류번호	726.64	국가코드	US	보존기간	준영구
명 칭	북한 핵문제 : 미국 의회 동향, 1992. 전3권				
생 산 과	북미1과/북미2과	생산년도	1992~1992	담당그룹	
권 차 명	V.2 3-4월				

내용목차	* 3.27 하원 군사위원회, 중동 및 한반도의 정세에 관한 청문회 개최
	  4.8 미국 의회 조사국, 북한 핵개발계획에 관한 보고서 제출
	  4.23 미국 회계감사국, 상하 양원 군사위원회에 보고서 제출				

0001

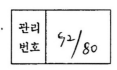

외 무 부

종 별 :

번 호 : USW-1065   일 시 : 92 0303 1839

수 신 : 장 관 (미일,미이,~~정총~~) 사본: 주미대사

발 신 : 주 미 대사대리

제 목 : 하원 외무위 대량 살상무기 확산 관련 청문회

하원 외무위 군비통제, 국제안보 및 과학소위(위원장: DANTE FASCELL 의원)는 금 3.3(화) 표제 청문회를 개최한바, 동 요지 하기 보고함.(김형진 서기관 참석)

1. 증언요지

가. ELISA HARRIS(BROOKINGS 연구소 연구원)

- 생.화학 무기는 소련의 붕괴에 따른 핵무기 위협의 상대적 감소, 걸프 전쟁시 IRAQ 의 사용위협, 북한(화학무기 생산시설 최소 8 개소 및 화학무기 물질 250 톤 보유) 및 리비아등의 생.화학무기 생산 능력에 대한 정보확보 등으로 최근 더욱 주목을 받고 있으나 UN 에 의한 IRAQ 의 화학무기 파괴, 미.러시아의 자발적 화학무기 해체등으로 생.화학무기 확산은 오히려 감소하는 추세임.

- 생.화학무기 확산 감소 추세를 유지, 강화하기 위하여 하기 정책을 제의함.

. UN 의 IRAQ 내 대량 살상무기 해체 활동지원

. 러시아의 생.화학무기 축소 지원

. CIS 및 동구제국의 생.화학무기 수출통제

. 생.화학 무기 사용국가에 대한 응징및 피해 국가에 대한 지원

나. JANNE E. NOLAN(BROOKINGS 연구소 선임연구원)

- 탄도미사일 및 기타 대량 살상무기의 확산이 상대적으로 등한시 되어 있는바 효과적인 탄도미사일 통제 체제를 개발, 유지하기 위하여 하기 정책을 건의함.

. 18 개 선진국이 합의한 미사일 기술 통제제제(MISSILE TECHNOLOGY CONTROL REGIME)의 신뢰도 제고

. PATRIOT 미사일등 대미사일 방어체제 및 적성국 군사시설을 목표로 하는 대무기 파기 전략에 대한 과대 의존 지양

. 상대적으로 관리가 소홀한 재래식 군비의 확산 통제

미주국 청와대	장관 안기부	차관	1차보	2차보	미주국	미주국	외정실	분석관

PAGE 1   92.03.04   10:42

외신 2과 통제관 BX

0002

. 군사용 산업용 양면으로 사용이 가능한 기술이전 통제를 위한 산업계의 협조

다. LOUIS V. NOSENZO(MERIDIAN CORPORATION 국방정책 소장)

- 핵무기의 확산을 통제하기 위하여는 핵무기 및 관련기술 확산 통제를 강화하는 범세계적 차원의 노력과 함께 지역분쟁의 소지를 축소하기 위한 정치대화개발, 신뢰구축 조치등 지역적 노력이 병행되어야함.

2. 질의 응답시 파악된 주요 참석의원의 군비확산 방지를 위한 의견은 하기와 같음.

가. FASCELL 위원장

- IAEA 에 대한 미국의 재정적 지원등 새로운 안보지원 계획의 방편으로 대외원조 법안내 군비확산 금지및 군비축소 기금을 만들 것을 희망함.

- 핵무기 확산 금지를 위해서는 이를 위한 정치적 의지가 관건이 되는바, 피사찰 대상국의 투명성(TRANSPARENCY)를 강화하기 위한 노력이 필요함.

나. STEPHEN SOLARZ 의원(민주, 뉴욕)

- IAEA 의 사찰이 형식적 사찰에 그치지 않고 핵무기 제조 움직임을 사전에파악, 저지할 수 있는 실질적 조치가 되도록 IAEA 에 신고된 시설외에도 사찰을 할수 있게 하는 강제사찰(CHALLENGE INSPECTION)및 필요시 모니터를 통한 24 시간 사찰도 가능토록 IAEA 의 권한을 강화하여야함.

- 북한은 핵안전 협정에 서명하였음에도 불구하고 협정이행을 위한 조치를 취하고 있지 않은바, UN 안전보장 이사회를 통한 강제조치등도 강구됨이 필요함. 끝.

(대사대리 김봉규-국장)

예고: 92.12.31. 까지

검토필(199 2. 6. 30)

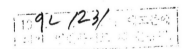

PAGE 2

0003

북한 핵문제 : 미국 의회 동향, 1992. 전3권 (V.2 3-4월) 351

주 미 대 사 관

USW(F) : 1247   년월일 : 92. 3. 3. 시간 : 18:50

수 신 : 장 관 (미 안)

발 신 : 주 미 대 사

제 목 : 상원 외교위 청문회시 Kissinger 증언문 (출처 :   )

보안통제 제 83

(1247 - 20 - 1)   외신 1과 동 제

0004

As prepared for Delivery

STATEMENT OF
THE HONORABLE HENRY A. KISSINGER
BEFORE THE
SENATE COMMITTEE ON FOREIGN RELATIONS

FRIDAY, FEBRUARY 28, 1992
10:00 AM

ADAPTED FROM PREVIOUSLY PUBLISHED MATERIAL

0005

—   1

Mr. Chairman. It is a pleasure to be with you today for
these important hearings on American policy toward the former
Soviet Union.

It is the essence of revolutions that they seem to
contemporaries like a series of unrelated incidents.
Especially a country like the United States, which takes
stability for granted, has a tendency to consider upheavals as
a temporary deviation from the familiar. This is why Yeltsin
is treated as the linear descendant of Gorbachev and the so-
called Commonwealth of Independent States as if it were the
old Soviet Union with a different name.

These attitudes, understandable as they may be, overlook the
most important consequence of the second Russian revolution:
the collapse of an imperial state that from the time of Peter

0006

1247 - 20 - 3

2

the Great brought pressure on all its neighbors, started more

wars than any other European state and culminated in a

Communist monolith. Because of the emergence of new national

states on the territory of the former Soviet Union, Yeltsin

cannot be dealt with as if he were Gorbachev. The Russian

Republic is the largest of the successor states and comprises

three fourths of the former Soviet territory and half its

population. But there are also 11 other republics; the

largest, Ukraine, has a population nearly as big as France's.

The evolution of the new Commonwealth is bound to be long,

painful and possibly violent. The various republics were glued

together forcibly over four centuries under the aegis of what

is today the Russian Republic, which stifled local initiative

and filled the key governmental posts with Russians.

Inevitably, the new Commonwealth reflects a melange of

motives. Most Russian leaders see it as a way to keep alive

0007

3

what can be salvaged of the traditional union and perhaps of

Russia's historic domination. The larger republics such as

Ukraine, Belarus and Kazakhstan consider the Commonwealth a

regrettable halfway house on the road to full independence;

this is why Ukraine prefers the term "community." The smaller

republics, especially in Asia, view the Commonwealth as a

modest improvement over the old Union which, given their

fragile economies, is the best they can hope for. It also

gives them a certain amount of maneuvering room with respect

to Turkish and Iranian designs.

The ambiguity of the Founding Document reflects these

crosscurrents. Neither the competencies nor the composition of

the Commonwealth ministerial committees, which are supposed to

"coordinate" the republics, have been spelled out. The Council

of Heads of States of the republics is to make decisions by

0008

4

consensus, which sounds unworkable. Ukraine has so far refused

to consider a Commonwealth constitution.

The Commonwealth economic policy is equally ambiguous and

pptentially more explosive. The parties have declared an

interest in creating an "economic space" and have forsworn

economic coercion against each other. Yet they have neither

defined what that term means nor do they practice what it

implies. Russian President Boris N. Yeltsin has asserted that

all the republics will use the ruble. Ukrainian President

Leonid M. Kravchuk is committed to introducing a separate

currency in the spring. In the meantime, Ukraine has already

introduced a separate coupon system to keep products inside

its borders.

The Commonwealth agreement declares the borders of each

republic to be inviolable. But it does not explain how these

borders are to be demarcated or who is responsible for

0009

5

security. Yeltsin and the Defense Ministry have spoken of a

commonwealth responsibility. The president of Ukraine insists

that the republics should control their own borders.

There is no agreement on how citizenship in the Commonwealth

is to be defined. If economic progress in the various

republics continues unevenly, citizenship will become a

crucial privilege. It will also prove central to the

definition of what constitutes a "minority."

A recent trip to the former Soviet Union brought these

clashing perspectives home to me. No Russian I met accepted

that Ukraine can be truly independent; no Ukrainian wanted any

central organs to survive. To a man, the Ukrainians spoke of

the threat of Russian imperialism - a view shared by the

leaders of several other republics I have since met. The

Russians argued that Ukraine agreed to an "economic space" but

then immediately issued its own currency. The Ukrainians

0010

—   6

insisted that Russia accepted their independence but

immediately challenged Ukraine's borders by raising questions

about the status of the Crimea. The Russians see the

Commonwealth as a mechanism to preserve as much of the central

machinery as they can. The Ukrainians envision it as having no

permanent status or organs - not even a secretariat to prepare

foreign-minister meetings. They totally reject any concept of

a united armed force.

   The practical disagreements are concentrated in three areas:
① nuclear weapons, ② the future of the Black Sea Fleet, and
③ command and control over conventional weapons. But the deepest

issue is the future of the Army. Russia sees Ukraine's armed

forces as a militia to protect politicians and buildings and

wants the Commonwealth to defend Ukraine's borders. I met no

Ukrainian who would tolerate that view. They would consider

such a defense establishment an army of occupation.

0011

1247-20-8

7

Over all this floats the General Staff in Moscow, now for the first time effectively without political control by Party, KGB or government. It represents the Commonwealth, which has neither political institutions nor personnel. The political vacuum has left the General Staff with unprecedented independence, though in practice it has put itself at the service of Yeltsin.

What does this mean for the United States? What do we want from any state located on the territory which was once the Soviet Union? In my view, our goal should above all be peaceful, non-threatening conduct. That is what the neighbors of the Russian Empire have never had, under tsars or commissars, in 400 years of modern Russian history. America should encourage institutions which guarantee that goal.

The Soviet Union is the heir of the tsarist empire, which started as the duchy of Muscovy and in the course of 250 years

0012

8

spread to the center of Europe, to the shores of the Pacific,

and to the gates of India, inundating entire countries and

peoples like the sea. Many of the republics that are now

seeking independence have been Russian less than 150 years.

There was never any act of free choice that created the

"union" that the coup plotters, and many officials still in

power in Moscow, wanted to preserve. Not a single republic

voluntarily joined the Russian Empire.

Creating obstacles to this relentless expansionism is the

most desirable outcome for the peace of the world. Ideally,

the republics on the territory of the former Soviet Union -

other than the Baltics - should be strong and cohesive enough

to defend themselves but not so centralized as to be able to

launch attacks abroad. Confronted with an overwhelming danger,

the republics would have the means to cooperate, but not to

mobilize a consensus for foreign aggression. American support

0013

9

for this degree of decentralization should not be viewed as a

matter of Machiavellian self-interest. Rather, such an outcome

would benefit the Soviet people above all by allowing them to

. concentrate for the first time on improving their own well-

being.

U.S. policy toward CIS

The United States faces two challenges that may seem

contradictory but are in fact quite complementary. On the

international scene, this country should work closely with the

Russian Republic, because a non-expansionist Russia would have

nary a clashing interest with the United States.

But the welcome vista of close cooperation on the

international scene should not lure us into inadvertently

encouraging Russian domination of the other peoples of the

former USSR. A lasting structure of peace requires close

cooperation between Washington and Moscow, but this will work

only if it is made compatible with the existence of

0014

10

independent republics on the territory of the former Soviet

Union. For attempts to recentralize would require methods,

policies and justifications bound to rekindle tensions

reminiscent of the Cold War.

American officials must understand that some of our

sacramental language may incur quite another meaning in the

context of Soviet and Russian history. When American

officials, in fulfilling their own criteria, bestow the

appellation "democratic" on particular leaders, they often

confer a courtesy title that reflects a hope rather than the

actual record. Almost without exception, the leaders of the

new republics achieved high office as cadre of the Communist

Party. Their adaptability to nationalist slogans and

democratic rhetoric is a tribute to their finely honed skills

for survival; it would be a mistake to treat anti-Stalinism as

a fundamental conversion to democracy.

0015

11

All factions in the former Soviet Union, within as well as

between the republics, are fighting their battles in the name

of democracy. It is important for America to encourage

genuinely democratic forces. But do we really know enough

about the players to take stands in all the political contests

now developing in faraway republics? We should be wary of

encouraging efforts to recentralize the former Soviet Union in

the name of loosely and perhaps cynically applied democratic

rhetoric.

Similarly, anyone brought up in the American tradition will

support the principle of protection for minorities. But in the

Soviet context, the issue of minorities merges with

territorial claims - especially by the Russian republic in the

Baltics, Ukraine and elsewhere. We must take care that a

precious American constitutional principle not legitimize the

0016

12

forcible takeover of disputed territories on the Yugoslavian

model.

The window of opportunity for supporting pluralism in the

former Soviet Union may turn out to be very fleeting. In

addition to fostering relations with the Russian Republic, we

should therefore accelerate diplomatic, economic and cultural

contact with at least the larger republics.

The United States should deal with the republics of the new

Commonwealth as it has dealt with the nations of Europe, and

it should treat Commonwealth institutions as it has those of

the European Community. This country has been meticulous about

avoiding the principle of a dominant European country. The

Russian Republic, as the most powerful of the successor

states, will always have a major international role, an

important place in American foreign policy and a leadership

position in the Commonwealth. But it should be encouraged to

0017

- 13

do so from within its boundaries and consistent with the

spirit of the institutions it has helped to create.

The following principles seem to me important:

- Russia is the heir of a proud and heroic tradition and

recent events have been a devastating blow to its self-esteem.

It is essential that Washington make clear in actions and in

words that it considers Russia an appropriate partner in world

affairs and a major country with legitimate security

interests. Russia extending from St. Petersburg to Vladivostok

and possessing thousands of nuclear weapons no longer needs

the territorial buffers for security it considered so

essential throughout its history. And it needs to devote

resources hitherto spent on imperial expansion to economic

recovery.

- At the same time, Russia must be given to understand that

new expansionism - by force or blackmail - will exact a heavy

0018

/247-20-/5

14

price. It would clash with US principles and frighten Russia's

neighbors. And it would reactivate the cycle of confrontation

between Russia and the world.

- The United States should rapidly expand its economic and

cultural contacts with the key new republics. We must remember

that an imperial heritage has left most of them little

experience in international affairs. They need sensitive

encouragement. We must balance the attention Yeltsin deserves

with the support the new republics require. We must find

subjects to talk to them about other than nuclear control.

- If Russia respects the new situation and remains within

its borders, a significant Western aid program would be in

order. This should be balanced with commensurate programs

toward the other republics. Such an aid program can, however,

be at best of an emergency nature. No democratic government or

combination of governments has the resources, and the former

15

Soviet Union lacks the appropriate institutional framework for

a Marshall-type program.

There is no short-cut to a domestic restructuring that can

attract the largest pool of available capital, which is

private investment. This requires two steps: the adoption of a

constitution which establishes a predictable environment for

investment; and, an intermediate step between emergency and

long-term aid such as assistance in the field of energy. The

Soviet Union has vast energy resources. The world is heading

into an energy shortage. The Western democracies have an

interest in reducing their dependence on Mideast oil. It

should be possible to generate foreign capital rapidly to

modernize the infrastructure for exploring, mining and

transporting Soviet deposits of oil and gas.

Finally, the United States and its allies must not become

totally preoccupied with events in the Soviet Union. In

0020

16

Eastern Europe, the nightmare is resurgent Russian

imperialism. The Western countries must now move decisively to

ease those fears. The fate of the democracies of Eastern

Europe must be linked rapidly to that of the West. The

European Community should end its petty haggling over East

European associate membership in the Common Market. The United

States should assist with some aid in a part of the world

where substantial governmental assistance can make a

difference. Allies on both sides of the Atlantic should

consider appropriate security arrangements, short of moving

NATO forces to the Soviet frontier.

If the former Soviet Union evolves in the direction foreseen

here, Russia's neighbors will be freed of a threat that has

been part of their landscape since Peter the Great. With new

republics along the Soviet western border, with the Ukraine

declaring itself independent and Belarus part of a loose

0021

1247-20-18

17

confederation, the institutional basis for Russian westward

expansion will diminish, if not disappear. This would lay the

basis for linking Russia to Europe in a way that has always

been thwarted by Russia's scale and the ambitions of Russian

rulers.

Such a realignment will also bring about a shift in the

center of gravity of Russian foreign policy. At this point, it

is too early to tell whether the Muslim republics with their

65 million people will opt for independence or association. In

either case, they will be very sensitive to developments in

the Islamic countries along their borders. That will make it

likely that Russia, whatever its new frontiers, will become an

increasingly active player in the Middle East.

As the Russian center of gravity moves toward the Urals,

Moscow may resume a historic activism in Asia. It was within

this century, after all, that Russia and Japan fought a war

1247-20-17   0022

—   .   18

over which country should govern Manchuria and Korea. It is

far too early to speculate about the long-term initiatives of

the new leadership in Moscow. But it is not too early to begin

reflecting about the nature of a new world order in conditions

that now seem quite foreseeable. This should be a subject of

intense consultation with all friendly countries, our allies

as well as China. Above all, it should be on the agenda of US-

Russian dialogues.

   The great historic opportunity for peace resides in

pluralism among the republics of the former Soviet Union side

by side with a close and confident US relationship with a

Russian Republic that is non-expansionist for the first time

in its history. Such an architecture would open up

unprecedented prospects for all the peoples of the world, and

especially for the long-suffering populations of the former

Soviet Union.

1247 - 20 - 20   0023

외 무 부

종 별 :

번 호 : USW-1066   일 시 : 92 0303 1840

수 신 : 장 관 (미일,미이,봉일,정총) 사본: 주미대사

발 신 : 주 미 대사대리

제 목 : 미상원 핵감축 관련 청문회

　　　연: USW-1018

　　1. 금 3.3.(화) 상원 외교위원회는 연호 전략무기 감축문제에 관한 청문회를 속개하고 SIDNEY DRELL, STANDORD 대 교수, RICHARD PERLE, AMERICAN ENTERPRISE INSTITUTE 선임연구원 및 TEDWARNER, RAND CORPORATION 선임 연구원을 증인으로 채택하여 의견을 청취하였음.

　　2. 상기 증인들은 모두 조속한 시일내 전략무기감축 조약 (START) 의 비준 필요성에 동감하면서 단지 START 규정 이상의 추가 감축 방법론에 대해서는 WARNER 연구원이 전통적인 협상채널의 유용성을 언급한데 반해 여타증인은 구쏘련과의 협상이 많은 시간이 소요된 경험에 비해 일방적 선언등 혁신적인 방법을 통해 현상 타개를 주장하였음. 특히 PERLE선임 연구원은 쏘련의 GNP 대비 군사비 지출비율이 미국 전문가들의 예측보다 높은 25-30프로에 달하는 것으로 밝혀지고 있어 보다 적극적인 감축노력을 촉구해야 한다고 언급하였음.

　　3. 지금까지의 관.학계 증인들의 START 비준긍정론에도 불구하고 금일 청문회시 JOE BIDEN상원의원은 보다 많은 감축을 위해 START내용을 수정해야 한다는 종래 주장을 되풀이함으로써 상원 외교위내 의견 봉일이 아직 이루어지지 않고 있음을 보여 주었음.

　　4. 금일 청문회중 PERLE 연구원은 북한의 핵개발과 관련 군사적 제제를 고려하지 않은것은 잘못된 것이며, 북한에 대해서는 평화적 목적의 핵개발 지원도 어리석은 발상이 될것이라고 지적하였음.끝.

　　(대사대리 김봉규-국장)

미주국	1차보	미주국	미주국	통상국	외정실	분석관	청와대	안기부

관리 번호	92-539

원 본

외 무 부

종 별 :

번 호 : USW-1128   일 시 : 92 0305 1931

수 신 : 장관(미일,동구일,정총) 사본:주미대사

발 신 : 주 미 대사

제 목 : 상원 외교위 전략핵무기 감축 청문회

연: USW-1106

상원 외교위원회(위원장: CLAIBORNE PELL, 민주,-로드아일랜드)는 연호 전략핵무기 감축청문회를 속개한 바, 주요 내용을 하기 보고함.(당관 김형진 서기관 참석)

1. 증언요지

가. JONATHAN DEAN,(MBFR 회담(MUTUAL AND BALANCED FORCE REDUCTION TALKS시) 미측 대표)

. 소련방의 붕괴에 따라 냉전의 원인이 해소되었음에도 불구하고 구소련방내 2 만 7 천기의 핵탄두가 그대로 남아 있다는 새로운 위협이 등장한바, 이의 해결책은 미.소의 핵탄두 보유를 부시대통령 제의(미.소 각각 4,500 기 의 핵탄두 보유) 보다 훨씬 적은 각각 1,000 기 이하로 줄이고 유엔 안보리의 기능을 강화, 핵무기의 여타국으로의 확산을 막는데 있음.

나. SPURGEON M. KEENY, JR.(U.S. ARMS CONTROL AND DISARMAMENT AGENCY 전부소장)

. START 조약은 러시아 배치 전략 핵탄두를 30%이상 감축시키고 미.러시아 양국간 신뢰구축 첫 단계이므로 가능한한 조속 비준이 되어야 함. START 조약의 비준은 러시아를 소련의 유일한 핵무기 승계 국가로 인정함으로써 카자크스탄, 우쿠르이나 벨라루스의 핵무기를 봉제하는 데도 도움이 될것임. START 체제가 정책되면 미.소의 핵탄두를 각각 3,000-4,000 기로 감축하는 방향으로 나아갈 수 있을 것임.

다. FRANK VON HIPPEL (PRINCETON 대 교수)

. START 조약은 미국과 CIS 의 저략핵무기를 추가로 감축할 수 있는 기준은제시하여 주나 그 자체로는 부족하며 또한 감축되는 핵탄두를 궁극적으로

미주국 청와대	장관 안기부	차관	1차보	2차보	미주국	구주국	외정실	분석관

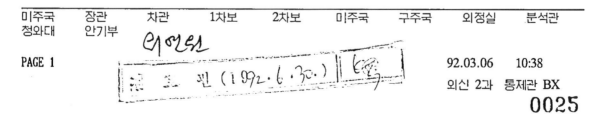

PAGE 1   92.03.06   10:38

외신 2과 통제관 BX

0025

어떻게 처분할 것인가에 대하여 답을 주지 못하는 바, 핵무기의 추가 감축이 필요함.

라. KJAY KOSMINSKY (HERITAGE 재단 국방정책 연구소 부소장)

. START 의 비준에 앞서 STARET 조약의 상대방이 누구인가를 확실히 하고(CIS 내부에서도 합의가 되지 않고 있다고 지적) 러시아 정부가 조약에 따라 핵실험 겨로가를 공개(NO ENCRYPTION) 한다는 보장을 받아야함. 현재 가장 중요한 문제는 러시아를 민주화시키는 것임.

2. 질의응답에서 PELL 위원장은 미국과 CIS 가 공동으로 핵 방위체제를 개발하는데 대한 의견을 문의한바, 참석자들의 답변은 하기와 같은

가. DEAN: 반대. 핵공격에 대한 유일한 방위책은 장거리 미사일을 최대한 줄이는 것임.

나. KEENY: 미국과 CIS 가 핵방위 체제를 공동 개발한다는 것은 비현실적이므로 반대함.

다. VON HIPPEL: 반대. 단, 우발적 발사를 막기위하여 발사 후에도 자체 폭파시킬 수 있는 장치를 폭탄에 부착할 것을 제의함.

라. KOMINSKY: 야국이 세계 평화를 위해할 수 있는 **가장** 중요한 공헌으로 적극 찬성함.

(대사대리 김봉규-국장)

92.12.31 까지

美國은 北韓을 철저히 믿지않는다

美의회 잇단 청문회

"核개발 속셈 여전" 4월 이후 단계적 응징

부시, 北韓核제거를 대외정책 제1목표삼아

행정부-言論서도 저지 총력전

〔워싱턴=丁海榮기자〕 요즘 美행정부와 의회, 언론이 북한 핵개발 저지에 쏟는 열의를 보면, 미국 전체가 북한 핵개발을 저지하기위해 「총력전」을 펴고있다는 느낌을 갖게된다.

지난 1월28일 부시대통령의 연두교서 발표에서 예산문제를 다루고있는 상원의 경우 외교위·군사위, 하원의 경우 세임위·세입위, 외무위·군사위, 정보위 등에서 북한의 核개발관련 청문회가 이례적으로 빈번하게 열리고있다.

...본문 전체가 흐려 판독이 어려움...

행정부-言論서도 저지 총력전

92. 3. 10 (화)

KOREA TIMES 1면

New York Times Says

Pentagon Wants US As Sole Superpower

NEW YORK (Reuter-AFP) — The U.S. mission in the post-Cold War era will be to ensure that it remains the world's sole and unrivalled superpower, according to a Defense Department document quoted by the New York Times on Sunday.

The newspaper said the Pentagon, in the policy statement to be released next month, warned the United States to guard against the emergence of any challenger from Western Europe, Asia or the former Soviet Union.

Part of the U.S. mission will be to convince potential competitors "that they need not aspire to a greater role or pursue a more aggressive posture to protect their legitimate interests," the newspaper quoted the document as saying.

The Times said the 46-page document, which had been circulating at the highest levels of the Pentagon for weeks, sees a world dominated by a single superpower whose military might and "constructive behavior" would deter any challenger.

In its opening paragraph, the document said the end of the Cold War led to "the integration of Germany and Japan into a U.S.-led system of collective security and the creation of a democratic 'zone of peace'."

The newspaper said it had been giv-

en the document by an official "who believes this post-Cold War strategy debate should be carried out in the public domain."

It said the document, with its concept of "benevolent domination" by a single power, was developed by the Pentagon in conjunction with the National Security Council and in consultation with President George Bush or his senior national security advisers.

To maintain its superiority, the United States "must sufficiently account for the interests of the advanced industrial nations to discourage them from challenging our leadership or seeking to overturn the established political and economic order," it quoted the draft document as saying.

On the subject of U.S. security in Asia, it quoted the document as saying the United States "must maintain status as a military power of the first magnitude in the area.

"This will enable the U.S. to continue to contribute to regional security and stability by acting as a balancing force and prevent emergence of a vacuum or a regional hegemony."

It warned that Cuba and North Korea were "entering periods of intense crisis" and urged the United States to be prepared for irrational behavior from either country.

0028

376 북한 핵문제 미국 동향

북한 核무기개발 時期 분석 싸고
美CIA·국무부 異見

【뉴욕=朴秀晩특파원】북한의 핵무기개발 능력에 대해 中央정보부(CIA)와 국무부간에 견해가 엇갈리고 있으며 국방부내에서도 견해가 대립돼있다고 뉴욕타임즈가 10일 행정부 관리들의 말을 인용해 보도했다.

로버트게이츠 CIA국장은 지난달 한의회증언에서 북한이 수개월내에 또는 그상당 기간내에 핵무기개발 능력을 갖게될것이라고 예측했다. 국방부의 한고위관리는 이보다 근기가 충분하며 북한의 상당수의 2년 임박한것이고 편향적이라고했다.

이상문은 국방부 관리들의 말을...

北의 「관광개방」에 담긴뜻
「交流」명분속 관광外貨 노력
核압력 초점흐리기 속셈도
걸림돌 제거되면 年內 成事가능성 높아

남북관광교류가 조만간 이루어질 것인가?

북한이 9일 비록 비공식적으로이긴 하지만 재미교포와 敎友회를 통해 金剛山, 白頭山관광을 오는 5월부터 남한주민에게 개방하겠다고 전격 제의해왔음에 따라 제의의 배경과 실현여부가 주목되고 있다.

그러나 최근 核문제가 현안으로 부각되면서 교류협력에 관한 논의자체가 일시중단상태에 있다.

⟨鄭仁和기자⟩

主要外信隨時報告

술라즈의원, 對北 무력사용 검토 주장

　　(워싱턴=聯合) 박정찬특파원=스티븐 술라즈 美하원 외무위원회 아시아 태평양소
위원회 위원장은 12일 美國은 북한의 핵개발을 제지하기위해 북한에 대한 양보를 중
단해야하며 유엔 안보리를 통해 북한에 대한 경제제재 조치를 취하고 무력사용도 검
토해야 한다고 주장했다.

　　술라즈의원은 이날 워싱턴에서 닉슨 도서관이 주관한 세미나에 참석, 이같이 주
장하고 "유엔을 통한 對북한 제재를 중국이 반대하거나 북한이 묵살할 우려가 있다
"고 전제하면서 미국은 이에 대비해 한국및 日本정부등과 협의를 거쳐 무력사용을
고려해야 한다고 말했다.

　　그는 또 북한의 핵시설에 대한 강제사찰이 이루어 질때까지 남북한 관계증진을
위한 노력이 보류돼야 한다고 말했다.

　　이날 "변천하는 세계와 미국의 역할"이라는 주제로 열린 세미나에서 아시아 문
제에 언급한 술라즈의원은 "북한은 핵무장을 위한 목표에 아주 근접해 있으며 핵사
찰을 앞두고 시간벌기 외고를 벌이고 있다"고 주장하고 "북한이 핵무장을 할 경우
남한에 대해 재래식 전쟁을 도발할 가능성이 높다"고 경고했다.

　　술라즈의원은 북한의 핵무장은 한국과 일본의 핵개발을 자극하는 압력으로 작용
할 뿐 아니라 북한은 실제로 핵무기와 기술을 제3국에 수출할 우려가 있다고 말했다

　　술라즈의원은 지난해 12월 핵문제를 논의하기 위해 남북한을 동시 방문한 적이
있다.(끝)

0030

관리
번호 92-623

외   무   부

종   별 :

번   호 : USW-1561   일   시 : 92 0327 1902

수   신 : 장관(미이, 미일, 중동일, 정특, 기정)

발   신 : 주 미 대사

제   목 : 하원 군사위 청문회

1. 하원 군사위 국방정책 연구반(반장: LES ASPIN 의원, 민주-위스콘신)은 "지역위협 및 1990 년대 국방 대책" 제하 일련의 청문회를 개최하고 있는바, 금3.27(금)에는 ROBERT GATES CIA 국장을 증인으로 출석시켜 중동 및 한반도의 정세에 관하여 청문회를 개최하였음. (당관 김형진 서기관 참석)

2. 동 청문회는 GATES 국장의 증언(증언문은 USWF-1863 로 FAX 송부함) 부분은 공개로, 이후 질의·응답은 비공개로 진행되었는바, ASPIN 의원과 BILL DICKINSON 의원(공화-알라바마)은 모두 발언에서 냉전이후 분쟁 발발의 위험이 가장높은 지역으로 중동과 한반도를 지적하고 동 지역에서의 안보위협 및 미군의 역할에 대한 GATES 국장의 견해를 요청한바, GATES 국장의 주요 증언 내용은 하기와 같음.

가. 중동은 향후 수년내 미국이 군사적으로 개입하게될 가능성이 가장 높은지역으로 특히 이락과 이란이 큰 위협이 되고 있는바, 이락은 걸프전 패배 및 UN 의 제재에도 불구하고 화학무기 원료 및 상당규모의 군사력을 보유하고 있으며, 제한낮적이나마 무기생산을 재개하고 있고 이란은 북한으로 부터의 스커드 미사일 구입등 90-94 년간 20 억불 상당의 무기를 외국으로 부터 구입할 계획으로 있으며 핵무기, 화학무기등 대량살상 무기개발 노력을 강화하고 있음.

나. 한반도는 미군의 실제의 적과 대치하고 있는 유일한 지역으로 북한은 병력의 전투준비도, 공군력, 병참등에는 약점이 있으나 남한에 대한 대규모 기습공격에 적합한 병력을 휴전선 바로 이북에 유지하고 있으며, 최근 기동력을 증강시켜 더욱 큰 위협이 되고 있음.

다. 더우기 북한은 핵무기 원료를 자체 생산할 수 있는 시설을 개발중에 있으며, 영번에 플로토늄 생산만계획위한 것으로 보이는 원자료 2 기를 건설, 1 기는 4 년전부터 가동중이며 보다 용량이 큰 1 기는 금년도 가동예정인바, 플로토늄 추출을

미주국 청와대	장관 안기부	차관	1차보	2차보	미주국	중아국	외정실	분석관

PAGE 1

위한 핵연료 재체리 시설도 거의 완공단계에 있음.

　라. 북한은 91.12 월 한반도 비핵화 선언에 합의하였음에도 불구하고 영변의 원자료 및 핵재처리시설의 존재 자체를 부인하고 있고 핵안전 협정을 상금 비준하지 않는등 핵개발을 계속할 조짐이 있어 제 3 국의 의심을 불식시킬만한 사찰을 받아들일 것인가에 대하여는 의구심이 있는바, <u>북한의 핵무기 개발은 임박하였으며 그것도 매우 임박(CLOSE, PERHAPS VERY CLOSE) 하였다고 봄</u>. <u>북한의 핵무기 개발은 동북아 안보에 위협이 될뿐 아니라 북한이 외화를 얻기위해 핵물질 및 관련 기술을 외국에 수출할 가능성이 있기 때문에 더욱 우려가됨.</u>

　마. 장기적으로는 북한에 대해 과거 소련이 공급한 신무기 및 연료공급의 중단, 경제적 어려움등으로 북한의 남한에 대한 군사적 우위가 감소될 것이나, 단기적으로는 북한의 전략가들이 북한이 우위에 있을 때 남한을 공격하도록 권고할 수 있고 북한이 재래식 무기의 유지 및 현대화의 어려움으로 오히려 핵무기및 미사일 개발 노력을 강화할 수 있으므로 더욱 위험한 상황을 맞이하게 될 것임.

　(대사 현홍주-국장)

　92.12.31 까지

일반문서로 재분류(1992.12.31.)

검토필(1992.6.30.)

군사소위 ~~Defense~~ Defense Policy Panel
하원   CIA 국장 발언중 한반도 관련 ('92. 3. 27)

1. Status of the negotiations

○ 합의서 발효이후 남북 대화의 구체적 성과로 핵통제공동위 발족 (3.19) 평가

○ 남북화해를 위한 틀만 만들었고, 실질적 진전 (substance) 무
   - 사찰규정 미합의, 인적교류 및 군사 신뢰조치 이견

2. The threat from the North

○ 비무장지대 북쪽지역에 서울에 대한 기습공격에 적합한 대규모 지상군 배치
   - 합의서 서명에도 불구, 수적 우세의 북한군 위협은 실제적이며 심각

○ 북한군의 훈련, 전투준비, 방공, 군수능력 취약

○ 미국의 대한 군사지원 (공군등)은 국경접경 북한군에 대한 억지력

3. North Korea's Nuclear Weapon Program

○ 북측, 국내우라늄으로 독자적인 핵무기 개발 시설 건설 의심
   - 영변지역 두개 원자로 (1개 4만KW 가동, 금년가동예정) 및 핵재처리시설 (거의 완성단계).
   - 플루토늄 생산용원자로 및 재처리 시설로써 미사인은 핵개발 의심.

○ 핵안전 협정 비준 약속에도 불구, 상기 이슈로 의미있는 현장사찰 수용여부 의심.

○ 핵무기 능력 보유 단계 접근 확신
   - 핵무기 보유시 동북아안전 저해 및 핵물질·관련기술의 해외판매 가능성 우려

4. Trends unfavorable to the North

○ 경제난, 불확실한 권력승계문제 등이 대남 전략 및 대외전략 (미·일·유엔) 수정 야기

○ 국내경제, 전통우방국의 자원감소 등으로 90년대에 대남군사력 우위 되기 곤란
   - 무기구식화 (60년대기술), 경화부족으로 최신 기술도입 실패, 89년이후 소무기 불구입.
   - 연료부족 (신년원유도입격감), 특히 군사부문 타격

○ 그럼에도 불구, 가까운 장래 위협상황 초래 가능성
   - 북한 인적·무기수 우위에 있을때 대남공격 가능 (북한조전략가들 공유)
   - 재래식 군사력유지 및 현대화 어려움으로 핵무기·탄도마사일 개발격량 가능성. 끝

0033

STATEMENT OF

THE DIRECTOR OF CENTRAL INTELLIGENCE

BEFORE

THE U.S. HOUSE OF REPRESENTATIVES

ARMED SERVICES COMMITTEE

DEFENSE POLICY PANEL

27 MARCH 1992

(*1863 - 26 - 1*)

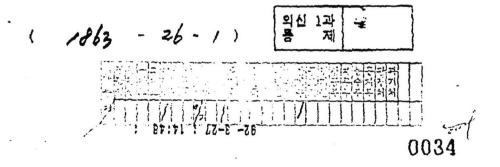

0034

Mr. Chairman, and members of the Defense Policy Panel:

I am happy to come before you again to discuss emerging trends in parts of the world where the United States has manifest and enduring security interests. You have suggested I focus on the Middle East and Persian Gulf, as well as on the Korean peninsula, and I will do so. I would be remiss, however, if I did not first at least allude to other parts of the world where our interests are at stake and our military forces might be needed, though not necessarily to fight.

When I was here last December, I ended my statement with a caution about the unpredictability of the future. I suggested we think about:

--- How fast events are moving.

--- The prospects for turbulence and instability in heavily armed Central Eurasia.

--- The problematic disposition of nearly the 30,000 nuclear weapons of the former Soviet Union.

--- The volatility of the Middle East and South Asia.

--- The proliferation of weapons of mass destruction, particularly the nuclear development programs in countries hostile to our interests.

--- The centrifugal forces of nationalist and ethnic hostility that threaten instability or even civil war on several continents.

During the ensuing three and a half months some disquieting trends have been evident. Unrest is worse, for example, in parts of the former Soviet Union than when I last stood here before you. Conflict is deepening between Soviet successor states such as Armenia and Azerbaijan. While the CIS has helped cushion the collapse of the Soviet empire, it is facing increasing strains that it may not survive. It is not hard to find other disquieting news:

--- Ukraine has suspended the transfer of tactical nuclear weapons to Russia for dismantling.

--- Ratification and implementation of the CFE Treaty appears increasingly complex and problematic.

1863- 26-3

--- Arms races are heating up in the Middle East and Southeast Asia, among other regions.

--- Despite significant -- and costly -- counternarcotics achievements, narcotics trafficking shows no sign of abating.

--- The devastating explosion in Buenos Aires shows that international terrorism is still of grave concern.

On the other hand, I can point to some positive developments and trends, as well:

--- White citizens in South Africa voted strongly in favor of continuing political reforms. A cease-fire is in effect in El Salvador, and the prospects that the contending factions can work out their differences peacefully have improved. Democracy has begun to make progress even in Albania and Romania. The unrest in Yugoslavia has abated, if perhaps only temporarily.

--- Transforming centrally planned economies into market economies continues to be wrenching and destabilizing. But the worst predictions -- about massive starvation,

0037

hypothermia, and civil unrest in Russia, for example -- have so far failed to materialize. And Yel'tsin is still holding firmly to the course of economic reform.

We may no longer need to fear a nuclear holocaust, but the famous Chinese curse appears to have come true. We are truly living in interesting times. With those thoughts in mind, I will devote the balance of my presentation to the regions you have asked me to cover.

THE MIDDLE EAST AND PERSIAN GULF

If in the next few years it again becomes necessary to deploy US combat power abroad, the strategically vital region encompassing the Middle East and Persian Gulf is at the top of the list of likely locales.

Among the several countries in this region that are hostile to US interests, two -- Iraq and Iran -- continue trying to rebuild their military power to enhance their influence. Let me say a few words about each, starting with Iraq.

IRAQ: WEAKENED BUT STILL FORMIDABLE

Operation Desert Storm greatly reduced Iraq's ability to conduct large-scale offensive military operations. The UN sanctions have impeded Saddam's efforts to reequip his forces. Preoccupied with defending the regime and putting down local insurgencies, the Iraqi military is currently capable of conducting only small-scale offensive operations with limited objectives.

Nevertheless, the size and equipment of Iraq's military forces remain formidable, especially in comparison with those of most of its neighbors. Let me give you some figures:

--- Iraq's ground forces number about two dozen divisions, though they are on the whole smaller and much less capable than the prewar divisions. The Army still has more than 3,000 armored personnel carriers, 2,000 tanks, and 1,000 artillery pieces.

--- We believe Iraq also retains some mobile Scud missile launchers and as many as several hundred missiles.

--- The Iraqi Air Force probably still has about 300 combat aircraft, though many are not operational. Because the Air Force has been grounded for over a year, it would need at least a month of intensive training and maintenance to become even minimally combat-ready.

--- Although a large quantity of Iraqi nuclear-related equipment has been identified and destroyed, we suspect Iraq has managed to hide some equipment from the UN inspectors. And, of course, Iraq's nuclear scientists and engineers retain their expertise.

--- Baghdad surrendered thousands of chemical munitions, tons of chemical agents, and considerable production equipment, but we believe the regime still has more of everything -- more precursor chemicals, more bulk agent, more munitions, more production equipment.

--- The regime never admitted having a biological weapons program and never surrendered any toxins or weapons. But we know the Iraqis had such a program, and we are convinced they have been able to preserve some biological weapons and the means to make even more.

HOW LONG TO RECOVER?

The restoration of Iraq's defense industries is one of Saddam's main postwar goals. Notwithstanding UN-imposed inspections and sanctions, Iraq claims to have partly repaired nearly 200 military-industrial buildings and to be in the process of repairing many others. We can confirm that significant reconstruction has been taking place at least two dozen military-industrial sites.

Limited production of artillery and ammunition has resumed at some weapon production facilities damaged during the Gulf war. Despite these efforts, total arms production will remain significantly below prewar levels as long as sanctions remain in force and inspections continue.

If the sanctions were removed, we estimate it would take Iraq at least three to five years to restore its prewar conventional military inventories. Long before then, Iraq's forces could be strong enough to threaten its neighbors.

More important, however, is how fast we think Iraq could restore its special weapons capabilities. We believe Baghdad has been able to preserve significant elements of each of its special weapons programs. Once it is free to begin rebuilding them, its scientists and engineers will be able to hit the ground running.

--- The nuclear weapon development program would need the most time to recover, because much of the infrastructure for the production of fissile material would need to be reconstructed. (This judgment would be reinforced if equipment at certain only recently identified nuclear research sites is destroyed, as UN inspection teams have demanded.) The time Iraq would need to rebuild its nuclear capability could be shortened dramatically if it could somehow procure fissile material from abroad.

--- Much of the chemical weapons production infrastructure would have to be rebuilt before the Iraqis could reestablish the prewar level of production. However, we believe they could quickly resume limited production of such weapons using covert stocks of precursor chemicals, undeclared chemical process equipment, and unfilled munitions.

--- Because it doesn't take much equipment to make biological warfare agents, we estimate the Iraqis could resume production within weeks. They have retained microbial fermentation equipment and pathogen cultures; we remain convinced they also have a stockpile of biological weapons.

--- Finally, we judge that the Iraqis could soon restore their capability to produce Scud-type missiles, though they might need some help from abroad.

WHAT IF SADDAM WENT AWAY?

How might Iraq's internal politics and external behavior change if Saddam Hussein left the scene?

As Saddam's decades of repressive rule demonstrate, he will do whatever it takes to cling to power. No succession mechanism is in place, nor are there any obvious candidates to replace Saddam -- Iraq is one of those countries where being the number-two man is unnerving, not to say life-threatening.

Consequently, we judge that if Saddam left the scene, it would be because of a coup or other violent act. How likely this is to happen, I cannot say, though we have evidence that Saddam's power base is shrinking and that dissatisfaction with his leadership is growing even among his core supporters -- chiefly, among Iraq's Sunni Muslims.

A likely successor to Saddam would be someone from the current, Sunni-Arab-dominated ruling circle -- someone who shares Saddam's perspectives, especially his belief in the political efficacy of ruthless violence. Such a successor might think pretty much like Saddam. Even so, whoever Saddam's successor was, he would lack a broad power base and could face immediate and serious challenges from other contenders.

A successor regime might be a little less hardnosed, both toward Iraqi Shi'ites and Kurds and toward Iraq's external adversaries. While it would continue efforts to restore Iraq's military capability, it might shift some resources from military to civilian reconstruction. The new regime could anticipate a quick end to the UN sanctions as well as recognition and support from the international community. In the short run, then, Iraq might present a lower threat to its neighbors. Still, any successor to Saddam is likely to share his regional aspirations, and over the longer term we could expect Iraq to try to regain its position as the dominant Arab military power.

If a successor regime begins to have trouble maintaining Iraq's unity or territorial integrity, its immediate neighbors, particularly Iran, Turkey, and Syria, will be strongly tempted to intervene. They all fear that an unstable Iraq would threaten their own national interests and might lead to an undesirable shift in the regional balance of power. None wishes to see Iraq break apart into independent Kurdish, Shi'ite, and Sunni states.

IRAN'S REARMAMENT PROGRAM

While Iraq struggles to recover from the Gulf War, Iran is determined to regain its former stature as the preeminent power in the Persian Gulf. Tehran's reformulated national security policy has three main goals:

--- Guarantee the survival of the regime.

---- Project power throughout the region.

--- Offset US influence in the Middle East.

To achieve these goals, Iran has undertaken diplomatic measures to end its international isolation, is purchasing weapons from a variety of foreign suppliers, and is developing a capability to produce weapons of mass destruction. During the period 1990-94, Iran plans to spend $2 billion in hard currency annually on foreign weapons.

--- Already, Tehran has purchased significant numbers of advanced warplanes and antiaircraft missiles from Russia and China. It has bought some extended-range Scud missiles from North Korea and is building a factory to manufacture its own.

--- As part of its upgrade of naval forces Iran has also contracted to buy at least two Kilo-class attack submarines from Russia.

--- Even after Operation Desert Storm, Iraq still has three times as many armored vehicles as Iran. To reduce that gap, Tehran is attempting to purchase hundreds of tanks from Russian and East European suppliers.

In the Iran-Iraq war, Iraq's chemical weapons were decisive factors in several important engagements, a lesson not lost on Iran.

--- We judge that Tehran is seeking to acquire a nuclear weapon capability. Barring significant technical input from abroad, however. the Iranians are not likely to achieve that goal before the year 2000.

--- Although extensive and improving, Iran's chemical weapon program remains relatively crude. Nevertheless, we expect Iran to develop chemical warheads for its Scud missiles within a few years.

--- We also suspect that Iran is working toward a biological warfare capability.

IRAN AND THE ARAB STATES

Tehran is rebuilding its military strength not only to redress the military imbalance with Iraq but also to increase its ability to influence and intimidate its Gulf neighbors -- though in the near term Tehran's desire to reduce US involvement in the region will probably lead it to court the Gulf States rather than bully them.

1863 -26- 14

0047

UNCLASSIFIED

Tehran is also trying to improve its relations with Arab states outside the Gulf, stressing Muslim solidarity and Islamic principles. In countries with Islamic opposition movements, Iran hopes to increase its influence among local fundamentalists without damaging its relations with these governments. For example, in Algeria Tehran wants to maintain ties with the new regime but continue its political and financial support for the Front for Islamic Salvation, which the Algerian Government is in the process of banning. Trying to have it both ways has been difficult: Algiers recalled its Ambassador in Tehran recently to protest Iran's continued support for the FRONT.

Iran's growing support of radical Palestinian groups may bring it closer to some Arab states, such as Libya. This support reflects Tehran's antipathy toward Israel, which it regards as both a US ally and a strategic threat. We expect Iran to continue to strongly oppose the peace process and probably to promote terrorism and other active measures aimed at undermining progress toward Israeli-Palestinian reconciliation.

Tehran's main surrogate in the Arab world will continue to be the radical Lebanese Shi'ite group Hizballah, which is the leading

UNCLASSIFIED

0048

396 북한 핵문제 미국 동향

ASSIFIED

suspect in the recent horrific bombing of the Israeli Embassy in Argentina. To ensure that its links to Hizballah are preserved, Tehran will be careful to stay on the good side of the Syrian Government, which controls access to the territory occupied by Hizballah.

IRAN AND THE NEW ISLAMIC REPUBLICS

Tehran considers developments in the region to its north to be vital to its national interests. It wants both to fill the void caused by the collapse of the Soviet Union and to prevent the United States and regional rivals, especially Turkey, from gaining dominant influence there. Tehran's diplomatic efforts to improve its own influence in the new Islamic states of the region have included sponsoring them for membership in various regional and international organizations.

In addition, Tehran is trying to forge cultural and religious ties to the new republics. It remains to be seen how successful Tehran will be, given that these peoples are mostly Turkic, not Persian, and mostly Sunni Muslims, not Shi'ites.

182- 26-16
UNCLASSIFIED
: 92- 3-27 : 14:54 :

0049

북한 핵문제 : 미국 의회 동향, 1992. 전3권 (V.2 3-4월) 397

UNCLASSIFIED

We see no evidence of Iranian efforts to subvert the secular governments of the new states or to alienate them from Russia and the other non-Muslim members of the CIS. For now, at least, Iran seems to want to preserve amicable relations with Russia, which has become a major source of its arms. Furthermore, Iran must be cautious about instigating instability along its northern border, lest nationalist sentiment be aroused among its own Azeri and Turkmen minorities. Indeed, with regard to the conflict between Azerbaijan and Armenia, Tehran has tried to exert a moderating influence on the Azerbaijani Government.

While pursuing military reconstruction, President Rafsanjani is trying to create an Iranian image of responsibility and respectability -- both to reassure foreign investors and the Gulf Arab states and to maximize Iran's leverage in Afghanistan and the Central Asian republics. Moreover, Tehran wants to avoid providing the United States with an excuse to extend its presence in the Gulf. Tehran's current approach appears pragmatic and patient, but its clerical leadership has not abandoned the goal of one day leading the Islamic world and reversing the global dominance of Western culture and technology.

0050

UNCLASSIFIED

HAS CHANGE PASSED BY THE MIDDLE EAST?

What about the impact of recent military, political, and economic trends in the region? Haven't these trends reduced the capability and inclination of Iran, Iraq, Libya, and Syria for military conflict and terrorism?

It is true that these states have suffered some major setbacks:

--- Iraq's military forces were devastated during the Gulf War and are encountering difficulties in rebuilding because of international sanctions. The Iraqi regime is likely to find itself in nearly continuous military conflict, at least against Kurdish and Shi'ite dissident groups.

--- Iran has still not recovered from the destruction suffered during its long war with Iraq, and its military reconstruction is being hampered by the poor state of its economy.

--- Meanwhile, having seen its hope of achieving strategic parity with Israel dashed by the collapse of its Soviet sponsor, Syria may have difficulty finding a reliable source of

0051

advanced conventional weaponry. Damascus will find it even harder to pay for such weaponry.

--- The Libyan regime is currently preoccupied with the fear of UN sanctions and the possibility that the United States and Britain will launch military action in punishment for its bombing of Pan American Flight 103. As a consequence, its perpetual subversion machine is barely ticking over.

Still, such developments have not led these governments to abandon their objectives -- we see no evidence of that -- only to alter their strategies and timetables. In particular, the escalating cost and difficulty of building first-rate conventional forces have increased the attractiveness of weapons of mass destruction. The evident determination of all four states to acquire special weapons suggests that they view such weapons as force multipliers capable of compensating for inadequacies in conventional forces and perhaps deterring future Desert Shield/Desert Storm campaigns.

THE KOREAN PENINSULA

I'll turn now to the second part of the world you asked me to focus on, namely the Korean peninsula -- the one place in the world where US forces remain deployed opposite the forces of an avowed adversary.

STATUS OF THE NEGOTIATIONS

Since initialing agreements on Nonaggression/Reconciliation and the denuclearization of the Korean peninsula last December, North and South Korea have engaged in a series of negotiations and discussions, some at very high levels, to implement the accords. These discussions have achieved some concrete results, particularly the formation on 19 March of a Joint Nuclear Control Commission with a mandate to set up bilateral inspections of nuclear facilities.

For the most part, however, the two sides have so far produced a framework for but not the substance of reconciliation. They remain far apart on critical issues, such as frequency, thoroughness, and basic ground-rules for nuclear inspections. They also have major differences about the people-to-

1813-

24-20

UNCLASSIFIED

92-3-27 ; 14:55 ;

0053

북한 핵문제 : 미국 의회 동향, 1992. 전3권 (V.2 3-4월) 401

people exchanges and military confidence-building measures called for in the reconciliation agreement.

THE THREAT FROM THE NORTH

Until they are much farther along in this process, we must continue to be wary and respectful of the military threat from North Korea It is hard for me to say very much about this in open session, however. North Korea is the most secretive state on earth. Much of what we know about that country and the threat it poses to South Korea comes from sensitive sources, and I must wait until we get into closed session to go into some details.

I can say this much, however. The North maintains enormous ground forces just north of the Demilitarized Zone. They are in formations optimized for a sudden, massive strike southward toward Seoul. In recent years, these forces have increased their mobility and flexibility, improving their capability to threaten prepared defenses. They considerably outnumber the opposing Southern forces in both men and weapons. Notwithstanding the recently signed Korean nonaggression pact, until these forces go away, the threat they present is real and serious.

It is not a question of fearing an attack from the South. The South Korean forces are deployed to defend Seoul. They present no countervailing threat to North Korea -- and P'yongyang knows it.

I don't want to exaggerate this threat. North Korea's armed forces suffer from many deficiencies. Their training and, consequently, combat readiness are questionable. They have weaknesses in air defense and logistics. They could not count on much if any support from erstwhile allies.

Furthermore, as Operation Desert Storm demonstrated, US airpower is highly effective against massed ground forces. The prospect that South Korea would receive extensive combat air support as well as other support from US forces is a potent deterrent, even to forces as strong as those North Korea has concentrated along the border.

NORTH KOREA'S NUCLEAR WEAPON PROGRAM

P'yongyang has been building an infrastructure that, without input from abroad, will be able to produce weapons-grade fissile material from scratch. It has domestic uranium mines. At

Yongbyon it has constructed two nuclear reactors whose sole purpose appears to be to make plutonium. One of these reactors has been operating for four years; the second, much larger reactor, may start up this year. Nearly completed is another facility at Yongbyon that will be able to reprocess reactor fuel to recover the plutonium.

Last December, North and South Korea negotiated an agreement-in-principle for a nuclear-free peninsula. Each side has committed itself not to "test, manufacture, produce, receive, possess, store, deploy, or use" nuclear weapons. Both sides also agreed not to have nuclear reprocessing or uranium enrichment facilities. There are grounds for questioning the North's intentions, given that it has not yet even admitted the existence of, much less declared, the plutonium production reactors and reprocessing facility at the Yongbyon nuclear research center.

Moreover, verification procedures remain to be worked out -- agreement was reached only this month that a joint committee should be formed to do that. The validity of the North-South nuclear accord depends on the inspection regime P'yongyang ultimately accepts.

Historically, North Korea has not been forthcoming in this area. It signed the Nuclear Nonproliferation Treaty in December 1985, and was thereby obligated to declare and place all nuclear facilities under safeguards. We are still waiting for P'yongyang's promised ratification of a safeguards agreement. Because some aspects of P'yongyang's behavior so far could be interpreted as an effort to continue nuclear weapon development, we wonder whether the North Koreans will accept meaningful on-site inspections that could allay our suspicions.

We believe P'yonguang is close, perhaps very close, to having a nuclear weapon capability. Where North Korea is concerned, moreover, we have to worry not only about the consequences for stability in Northeast Asia if it acquires nuclear weapons, but also about the possibility that P'yongyang might put nuclear materials and related technologies on the international market. In the past, the North Koreans have been willing to sell anything that could earn hard currency.

TRENDS UNFAVORABLE TO THE NORTH

The straitened economic circumstances in the North, coupled with uncertainties associated with the looming dynastic change of leadership in P'yongyang have led the North Koreans to modify their confrontational strategy toward the South, as well as toward the United States, Japan, and the United Nations. Tensions between North and South have decreased somewhat, though the actual military threat to the South has not changed significantly.

We expect that many of the North's military advantages over the South will erode throughout this decade, largely because of decreasing support from the North's traditional allies, coupled with its continuing economic problems:

-- North Korea's large inventory of weapons is becoming obsolete. The North's defense industry is based on 1960s technology and beset by quality problems. P'yongyang lacks the hard currency to purchase more advanced technology. We have seen no deliveries of major weapons from the Soviet Union or its successors since 1989. China cannot provide the types of weapons, such as modern aircraft or surface-to-air missile systems, that the Soviets supplied.

--- Fuel shortages -- principally a result of drastically reduced imports from the former Soviet Union -- are having a broad cumulative impact on all sectors, including the military.

Nevertheless, in the near term we could be entering a more dangerous period:

--- North Korean strategists could recommend an attack on the South while the North retains its substantial edge in numbers of men and weapons.

--- Difficulties in maintaining and modernizing P'yongyang's conventional forces could reinforce the North's determination to develop nuclear weapons and ballistic missiles.

That concludes my remarks in open session. I will have a little more to add about some of these issues when we resume in closed session.

0059

관리
번호 92-783

외 무 부

종   별 :

번   호 : USW-1616   일   시 : 92 0331 2152

수   신 : 장 관(미일, 미이, 아일, 아이, 국기)

발   신 : 주 미국 대사

제   목 : 상원 외교위 SOLOMON 차관보 증언

   상원 외교위(위원장 CLAIBORNE PELL 상원의원)는 금 3.31 INDOCHINA 관련 청문회를 열고 RICHARD SOLOMON 국무부 동아. 태차관보로부터 증언을 청취하였는바 SOLOMON 차관보는 최근 인도차이나 3 국 문제에 국한하지 않고 북한 핵문제등주요 지역문제에 대해서도 언급하였으며 주요 발언내용 아래 보고함.

   (당관 박인국 서기관 참석).

   1. 기조발언중 아국관계 부분(TEXT 는 낭독하지않고 간략히 요약설명, 동 TEXT 팩스기송부).;

   O 3.24 총선거결과는 한국에서 민주주의가 깊이 뿌리를 박고있다는 증거가 되었음.

   - 북한이 핵개발을 포기하지 않고 있다는 의심에 대해서 한. 미양국 정부는의견을 같이하고있으며 IAEA 사찰과 더불어 남. 북한간의 동시사찰을 병행실시하는것은 매우 적절한 조치임.

   O 북한이 성실한 자세로 임한다면 4 월 비준, 5 월 목록제출, 6 월 말 이전IAEA 및 동시 사찰이 이루어질것으로 기대하며 북한은 이번 기회를 세계무대 진출을 위한 호기로 적극 활용하기 바라며, 그렇지않을 경우 긴장과 고립만이 계속될것임.

   2. 아국관계 주요 질의 응답 내용

   가. IAEA 사찰 신뢰도

   O CRANSTON 상원의원

   -IAEA 가 강제사랄 기능을 가졌음에도 불구하고 이락의 핵개발 저지에 실패한 점에 유의할때 북한이 IAEA 안전협정에 서명했다고 해서 핵무기 개발 계획을 포기했다고 보기는 지극히 의심스러움, 이에대한 미국의 입장은 ?

   O BIDEN 상원의원

   - IAEA 의 사랄 능력에 대한 행정부의 평가는 ?

미주국 외정실	장관 분석관	차관 정와대	1차보 안기부	2차보	아주국	아주국	미주국	국기국

0060

PAGE 1   92.04.01   14:39

외신 2과 통제관 EC

O SOLOMON 차관보

- 남북한간 동시사찰 은 IAEA 능력을 강화시켜줄것이며 미국등 서방은 IAEA의 현장에서의 시행착오등 경험을 십분 활용하고있음.

- IAEA 능력 문제에 대한 행정부의 평가를 언급할 입장은 아니나 현 IAEA 사찰능력이 대폭 강화되어야한다는 견해가 광범위하게 제기되고있음을 시인함.

나. 미국 검증 전문가의 동시사찰 참여문제

- CRANSTON 상원의원

- 한국측 핵무기 전문 수가 극히 제한되어 있을것이므로 미국 전문가의 한국검증팀 참여가 허용되어야할것으로 생각하는바 이에대한 현황은 ?

OSOLOMON 차관보

- 한국전문가의 핵사찰 능력은 괄목할 성장을 보이고있어 매우 인상적임. 미국 사찰팀이 IAEA 사찰과정이나 양자간 사찰절차에 직접 관여하느냐하는 문제는아직도 결론이 내려지지 않고있음(STILL OPEN TO ISSUE).

북한 핵에 관한 일본 입장.

O BIDEN 상원의원- 북한이 핵사찰을 교묘하게 호피할 가능성에 대한 이본의 우려가 어떠한지?

- SOLOMON 차관보

- 최근 북한의 핵개발문제에 대한 일본의 우려는 점증하고 있으며 특히 재처리 시설에 대해 민감한 반응을 보이고있음.

핵사찰에 대한 일본의 경험이 일천한 상태이므로 북한의 핵개발 은폐 문제를 일본과 상의하지는 않고있음.

라. 북한의 미사일 수출 전박 규제 문제

O CRANSTON 상원의원

- 북한이 대흥호와 같은 미사일 선적 선박을 다시 이란으로 보내면 이를 저지할것인지 ?

O SOLOMON 차관보

- 아마 또다시 선박을 보낼것으로 생각되나 이락이 목적지인 경우에만 유엔결의에 의거 저지가 가능함. 만약 해협을 (호르뮤즈 해협지칭) 지나 이락을 향해 항진하면 정선과 화물검색이 이루어질것임.

3. 기타문제에 관한 언급내용

가. 인도지나 문제

0 부시대통령과 베이커 장관의 캄보디아 유엔 평화유지군 기금 확보를 위한노력에 대해 의회가 적극적인노력을 해줄것을 당부하며 유엔에 의한 캄보디아 문제 해결은 캄보디아의 마지막이자 유일한 희망임을 유념바람.

0 현재 조사가 진행중에 있는 POW/MIA 문제에 관한 월남 당국의 협조에 감사하며 특히 즉석에서 요청한 특정완계자 면담이나 5 개지역 사찰에 적극적인 자세로 응해준것은 매우 큰 진전으로 평가함.

0 (HELMS 의원이 금번 인지 방문을 계기로 미-월남 관계는 ROAD MAP I 에서II 단계로 이동했다고 보아도 되느냐는 수차 집요한 질문에 대해).

단계 I 에서 II 로 언제 이동할지 예견할수 없지만 이동을 위한 제반 여건이 서서히 준비되고 있는것으로 생각함.

0 (PELL 위원장의 1-2 년내 미-월남 외교관계 수립 가능성 질문에 대해)

POW/MIA 문제에 달려 있으며 이번방문을 계기로 월남측이 매우 협조적인 자세임이 확인되었음.

나. 중국문제

(PELL 위원장의 중국 인권상황의 개선 여부 질문에 대해).

0 중국의 인권개선 여부는 아무도 확인할수없으며 시간이 걸리는 문제라고 생각함.

0 대부분의 서방여론은 북경 천안문사건에 집착하고있는데 여타 도시(광동등을 예로 들었음) 는 매우 자유로운 분위기를 보이고있으며 북한이나 버마와는 비교가 되지않음.

(BIDEN 상원의원의 미사일 기술수출 규제를 위한 중국의 노력여부 질문에 대해)

0 중국의 규제가 가시화되고있으며 특히 핵심부품 기술이전 규제는 잘 지켜지고있음.

(HELMS 의원이 대만의 GATT 가입을 중국의 GATT 가입과 연계시켰다는 FINANCIAL TIMES 3.25 자 보도에 대한 사실여부 질문에 대해).

0 양국의 가입은 별개의 문제로 중국의 가입은 GATT 가입요건 충족여부에 따라 결정될것임.

4. 평가 및 관찰

0 SOLOMON 차관보는 북한측에 대한 6 월말 사찰 시한에 대한 의회에서의 공개입장 표명과 경고 메세지를 통해 'WAIT AND SEE' 기간동안의 미국의 입장을 재천명한것으로

인식됨.

O 동시에 북한 핵문제, 인지문제, 미사일 기술이전 규제등 주요 지역현안 문제를 위요한 미국과 한. 중. 일. 인도지나 제국등 관계국간의 쌍무간 내지는 다자간 협조체제가 미국을 중심으로 긴밀하게 발전되고있음을 시사함으로써 부시 대통령의 외교치적 강조와 함께 동 지역에서의 미국의 확고한 LEADERSHIP 을 재확인하였음.

O 상원으원들의 집요한 대중국 규탄 분위기에도 불구하고 SOLOMON 차관보는북경을 제외한 여타지역에서의 분위기 소개와 미사일 수출규제 협조등을 강조함으로서 현행정부의 대중국 입장을 시사한 점과 지난번의 INDOCHINA 청문회때에인도지나 안정을 위한 중국 정부의 노력을 높이 평가를 한데 이어 금번에는 월남 정부에 대한 적극적인 평가가 특이하였음. 끝

(대사 현홍주-국장)

예고 92.12.31 일반

주 미 대 사 관

USW(F) : 1945　　년월일 : 0331　　시간 : 1520

수 신 : 장 관 (미일, 아이)

발 신 : 주 미 대 사

제 목 : Solomon 동아·태 차관보 상원증언문 (출처 :　　　　　)

보 안 통 제	

(아국관계 P16 - P19
Indochina 관계 P1 - P15)

배부처	장관실	차관실	1차보	2차보	[illegible]	[illegible]	[illegible]	[illegible]	[illegible]	[illegible]	[illegible]	[illegible]	[illegible]	[illegible]	[illegible]	[illegible]	안기부	공보처	경기원	상공부	재무부	농수부	동자부	환경처	과기처		
	/	/	/		/	/ ✓	/	0								/	/										

(1945 - 2기 - 1)

외신 1과 통 제	

0064

1 #:　　　　92-3-31 : 15:53 :

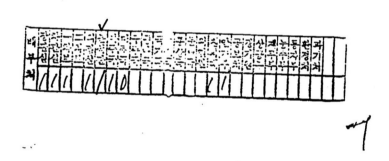

EAST ASIA TRIP REPORT AND POLICY UPDATE

TESTIMONY OF RICHARD H. SOLOMON

ASSISTANT SECRETARY OF STATE

FOR EAST ASIAN AND PACIFIC AFFAIRS

BEFORE THE SENATE FOREIGN RELATIONS COMMITTEE

MARCH 31, 1991

1945- 27-2
92- 3-31 : 15:53

0.065

INTRODUCTION

MR. CHAIRMAN, MEMBERS OF THE COMMITTEE, I AM PLEASED TO HAVE THIS OPPORTUNITY TO DISCUSS MY RECENT TRIP TO SEVERAL EAST ASIAN COUNTRIES AND THE RANGE OF ISSUES WHICH I PURSUED RELATED TO ADVANCING AMERICAN INTERESTS IN THE REGION.

DURING MY TRIP EARLIER THIS MONTH I VISITED THAILAND, VIETNAM, CAMBODIA, LAOS, THE REPUBLIC OF KOREA, JAPAN AND HONG KONG. AS THIS COMMITTEE WILL BE HOLDING A SEPARATE HEARING ON HONG KONG LATER THIS WEEK, I WILL NOT ADDRESS ISSUES RELATED TO THAT PORTION OF MY TRAVELS HERE TODAY.

LET ME SAY A FEW WORDS ABOUT THE BROADER CONTEXT OF THOSE TRAVELS. MY TRIP TOOK PLACE IN THE AFTERMATH OF THE PRESIDENT'S VISIT TO THE ASIA-PACIFIC REGION EARLIER THIS YEAR. MY CONSULTATIONS REFLECTED MANY OF THE CHALLENGES AND OBJECTIVES PRESIDENT BUSH EMPHASIZED ON HIS TRIP: REALIZING A JUST PEACE IN CAMBODIA AND ATTAINING THE FULLEST POSSIBLE ACCOUNTING OF POW/MIA'S FROM THE VIETNAM WAR ERA SO THAT WE CAN BEGIN A NEW ERA IN OUR RELATIONS WITH THE NATIONS OF INDOCHINA; MEETING THE CHALLENGE OF NUCLEAR PROLIFERATION ON THE KOREAN PENINSULA; AND FORGING A GLOBAL PARTNERSHIP WITH JAPAN BY ENHANCING OUR FOREIGN POLICY COOPERATION AND ATTAINING MORE BALANCED AND EQUITABLE ECONOMIC RELATIONS.

1945 - 27-3

92-3-31 : 15:54

0066

INDOCHINA

INDOCHINA WAS A CENTRAL FOCUS OF MY MISSION. MY VISIT
TO VIETNAM, LAOS, AND CAMBODIA MARKED THE FIRST TIME THAT
AN ASSISTANT SECRETARY OF STATE HAS VISITED ALL THREE
COUNTRIES IN THE SAME TRIP SINCE THE END OF THE VIETNAM
WAR; AND IT WAS THE FIRST TO CAMBODIA SINCE PHONM PENH
FELL TO THE KHMER ROUGE. AS PRESIDENT BUSH SAID IN
SINGAPORE LAST JANUARY, THE U.S. SEEKS TO IMPROVE ITS
RELATIONS WITH VIETNAM, LAOS AND CAMBODIA AND HELP
INTEGRATE ALL THREE COUNTRIES INTO THE DYNAMIC EAST ASIAN
REGION AND THE LARGER INTERNATIONAL ECONOMIC AND POLITICAL
SYSTEM. I WENT TO INDOCHINA TO ADVANCE THIS PROCESS OF
RECONCILIATION BETWEEN THE U.S. AND THESE THREE STATES; TO
HELP CREATE CONDITIONS IN WHICH WE COULD BEGIN TO BUILD AS
THE PRESIDENT SAID IN HIS SINGAPORE LECTURE, "LASTING TIES
OF INTEREST AND AFFECTION."

VIETNAM

AS I HAVE TESTIFIED HERE PREVIOUSLY, IN APRIL 1991 WE
PRESENTED TO THE VIETNAMESE A NORMALIZATION PLAN SOMETIMES
REFERRED TO AS THE "ROADMAP." THIS POLICY WAS DESIGNED TO
ALLOW THE U.S. TO PURSUE IN PARALLEL THE TWO PRIMARY
POLICY OBJECTIVES FOR INDOCHINA THAT WE HAVE MAINTAINED
OVER THE PAST 12 YEARS: ATTAINING THE FULLEST POSSIBLE
ACCOUNTING FOR OUR POW/MIAS; AND A NEGOTIATED PEACE
SETTLEMENT IN CAMBODIA WHICH WILL RESULT IN THE WITHDRAWAL

OF ALL VIETNAMESE FORCES, PREVENTION OF A RETURN TO POWER
OF THE GENOCIDAL KHMER ROUGE, AND FREE ELECTIONS FOR THE
FORMULATION OF A NEW CAMBODIAN GOVERNMENT.

OUR POLICY FRAMEWORK IS A STEP-BY-STEP PROCESS WHEREBY
THE U.S. AND VIETNAM WOULD TAKE A SERIES OF RECIPROCAL
MEASURES DESIGNED TO BUILD TRUST AND CONFIDENCE. IT WOULD
LEAD TO NORMALIZATION OF OUR ECONOMIC AND POLITICAL
RELATIONS AS THE CAMBODIA PEACE ACCORDS ARE IMPLEMENTED
AND AS POW/MIA ACCOUNTING ADVANCES. IT LEFT HANOI WITH NO
DOUBT AS TO WHERE WE STAND AND UNDER WHAT CIRCUMSTANCES WE
WOULD BE PREPARED TO MOVE AHEAD.

I WOULD NOTE THAT IN THE MONTHS SINCE THE PARIS
ACCORDS WERE SIGNED LAST OCTOBER, VIETNAM HAS — TO
VARYING DEGREES — ADDRESSED MANY OF THE CONCERNS EMBODIED
IN OUR POLICY, INCLUDING POW/MIA ACCOUNTING AND OTHER
HUMANITARIAN ISSUES.

AT THE SIGNING OF THE CAMBODIA PEACE AGREEMENT IN
PARIS LAST OCTOBER, SECRETARY BAKER ANNOUNCED THAT IN VIEW
OF THE COOPERATION FROM VIETNAM AND CAMBODIA ON THE U.N.
SETTLEMENT EFFORT AS WELL AS CERTAIN PROGRESS ON THE
POW/MIA ISSUE, THE U.S. WAS TAKING STEPS TO LAUNCH THIS
NORMALIZATION PROCESS. THE INITIAL ACTIONS IN THIS
PROCESS INCLUDED:

— CHANGING THE EMBARGO RULES TO PERMIT U.S.-ORGANIZED
GROUP TRAVEL TO VIETNAM,

92-3-31 ; 15:54

0068

-- LIFTING THE 25-MILE TRAVEL LIMIT FOR VIETNAMESE
DIPLOMATS ASSIGNED TO THE UNITED NATIONS,

-- BEGINNING TALKS WITH VIETNAMESE OFFICIALS IN NEW
YORK ABOUT THE ISSUES AND MODALITIES SURROUNDING THE
NORMALIZATION PROCESS,

-- ESTABLISHING A U.S. MISSION IN CAMBODIA,

-- STATING PUBLICLY OUR CONCERNS ABOUT GENOCIDE IN
CAMBODIA AND OUT DETERMINATION TO PREVENT ITS RECURRENCE,

-- AND LIFTING THE TRADE EMBARGO AGAINST CAMBODIA AS
SOON AS IMPLEMENTATION OF THE PEACE AGREEMENT BEGAN.

AT THE SAME TIME, THE U.S. HAS SUSTAINED OUR EFFORTS
TO ADDRESS VIETNAM'S HUMANITARIAN NEEDS, ESPECIALLY IN THE
HEALTH AND PUBLIC SERVICES SECTORS. VICE FOREIGN MINISTER
LE MAI AND I HELD THE FIRST ROUND OF NORMALIZATION TALKS
IN NEW YORK LAST NOVEMBER, AND VIETNAM'S PERMANENT
REPRESENTATIVE TO THE U.N., AMBASSADOR TRINH XUAN LANG,
MET WITH MY DEPUTY KEN QUINN IN JANUARY TO REVIEW VARIOUS
TECHNICAL ISSUES THAT WE AGREED WOULD BE ADDRESSED IN A
U.S.-SRV WORKING GROUP.

LAST SEPTEMBER, AND AGAIN IN LATE JANUARY, GENERAL
JOHN VESSEY, THE PRESIDENT'S SPECIAL EMISSARY TO HANOI FOR

0069

POW/MIA AFFAIRS, TRAVELLED TO HANOI AND MET WITH
VIETNAMESE LEADERS. DURING THESE VISITS HE OBTAINED
IMPORTANT NEW VIETNAMESE COMMITMENTS ON OUR POW/MIA
ACCOUNTING AS WELL AS SOME SPECIFIC VIETNAMESE ACTIONS TO
IMPLEMENT THOSE UNDERSTANDINGS. GENERAL VESSEY'S
IMPORTANT WORK -- IN CONJUNCTION WITH THE SIGNING OF THE
UN SETTLEMENT AGREEMENT FOR CAMBODIA -- HELPED SET THE
STAGE FOR US TO BEGIN THE NORMALIZATION PROCESS. HOWEVER,
ON HIS MOST RECENT VISIT AT THE END OF JANUARY THE GENERAL
WAS TOLD THAT THERE WAS SOME RELUCTANCE IN HANOI TO MOVE
AHEAD AS RAPIDLY AS WE PROPOSED TO ACHIEVE OUR POW/MIA
OBJECTIVES.

GENERAL VESSEY UNDERSCORED TO VIETNAMESE LEADERS OUR
INTENT TO ADHERE TO OUR POLICY OBJECTIVES, EMPHASIZING
THAT WE WERE PREPARED TO MOVE EITHER RAPIDLY OR SLOWLY
TOWARDS NORMALIZATION WITH VIETNAM: THE PACE AND SCOPE OF
THE PROCESS -- AS WE HAVE CONSISTENTLY MAINTAINED FOR
YEARS -- WILL DEPEND ON THE SPEED OF OUR PROGRESS IN
POW/MIA ACCOUNTING. AT THE SAME TIME, THE HANOI INDICATED
A STRONG DESIRE TO DISCUSS THE FULL RANGE OF OUR
COOPERATION ON HUMANITARIAN ISSUES, INCLUDING U.S. EFFORTS
TO MEET VIETNAM'S HUMANITARIAN NEEDS. IN SUM, THERE
APPEARED TO BE A REAL DANGER IN LATE JANUARY THAT THE
PROCESS WAS GRIDLOCKED.

FORTUNATELY, SUBSEQUENT DEVELOPMENTS HAVE BEEN MORE
FAVORABLE TO PROGRESS. ON MARCH 4-5 I LED A DELEGATION TO

0070

HANOI TO DISCUSS HUMANITARIAN ISSUES OF CONCERN TO THE
U.S. AND VIETNAM. TRAVELLING WITH ME WERE MR. ALAN PTAK,
THE NEW DEPUTY ASSISTANT SECRETARY OF DEFENSE FOR POW/MIA
AFFAIRS, MR. GEORGE LAUDATO, THE DEPUTY ASSISTANT
ADMINISTRATOR OF A.I.D. FOR ASIA, AND MRS. ANN MILLS
GRIFFITHS, THE EXECUTIVE DIRECTOR OF THE NATIONAL LEAGUE
OF FAMILIES. BRIGADIER GENERAL THOMAS NEEDHAM, COMMANDER,
JOINT TASK FORCE - FULL ACCOUNTING, JOINED US IN THE
REGION AFTER HAVING PRESENTED OUR PLANS FOR AN ACCELERATED
POW/MIA EFFORT TO HIS VIETNAMESE COUNTERPARTS THE PREVIOUS
WEEK. IN MY DISCUSSIONS WITH THE VIETNAMESE WE REACHED AN
IMPORTANT NEW LEVEL OF UNDERSTANDING ON HOW BOTH SIDES CAN
IMPROVE OUR HUMANITARIAN COOPERATION, PARTICULARLY ON
POW/MIA ACCOUNTING.

THE VIETNAMESE AGREED TO A FIVE-POINT PROGRAM TO
ACCELERATE THEIR COOPERATION WITH US ON POW/MIA
INVESTIGATIONS, UNDERTAKING TO DO THE FOLLOWING:

-- ALLOW US GREATER ACCESS TO THEIR CENTRAL RECORDS,
ARCHIVES AND MUSEUMS AND TO INDIVIDUALS WITH
INFORMATION ON POW/MIA ISSUES;

-- IMPLEMENT A MECHANISM FOR SHORT-NOTICE "LIVE
SIGHTING" INVESTIGATIONS;

-- BEGIN A TWO-YEAR PLAN FOR ACCELERATED JOINT
INVESTIGATIONS IN VIETNAM, TO INCLUDE FIVE SUCH

INVESTIGATION CYCLES OVER THE NEXT TEN MONTHS,
FOCUSSING ON THE 135 REMAINING HIGH PRIORITY
DISCREPANCY CASES;

-- CONTINUE TO WORK ON TRILATERAL COOPERATION WITH LAO
AND CAMBODIAN AUTHORITIES; AND

-- REAFFIRM VIETNAM'S INTENTION TO SEARCH FOR AND
RAPIDLY REPATRIATE REMAINS OF AMERICANS STILL
UNACCOUNTED FOR, AND TO HOLD TECHNICAL EXCHANGES IN
ORDER THAT WE UNDERSTAND CLEARLY WHY REMAINS WE
BELIEVE THEY MIGHT HAVE ACCESS TO ARE NOT AVAILABLE,
IF THAT IS INDEED THE CASE.

IF ALL FIVE AGREEMENTS ARE SINCERELY IMPLEMENTED THEY
SHOULD SIGNIFICANTLY ADVANCE US TO OUR GOAL OF ATTAINING
THE "FULLEST POSSIBLE ACCOUNTING" WITHIN A REASONABLE
PERIOD OF TIME.

VIETNAM SIGNALLED ITS INTENT TO DELIVER ON THIS
PROGRAM IN SEVERAL WAYS. FIRST, IT AGREED TO THE FIRST
SHORT-NOTICE INVESTIGATION OF A LIVE-SIGHTING REPORT ON
MARCH 5, THE DAY I COMPLETED MY TALKS IN HANOI. WITH ONLY
ONE HOUR'S NOTICE TO VIETNAM OF THE DESTINATION, A
HELICOPTER LIFTED OFF FROM HANOI THAT DAY WITH VIETNAMESE
AND U.S. EXPERTS ON BOARD AND FLEW TO A REMOTE PART OF
THANH HOA PROVINCE, WHERE THEY WERE ABLE TO CONDUCT A
THOROUGH INVESTIGATION. U.S. PERSONNEL WERE PERMITTED TO

0072

CONDUCT SPONTANEOUS INTERVIEWS WITH LOCAL VILLAGERS OF
THEIR OWN CHOOSING AND WERE PERMITTED TO MOVE ABOUT THE
AREA FREELY. AFTER THOROUGH INVESTIGATION, OUR EXPERTS
CONCLUDED THAT THE REPORT THAT LIVE AMERICANS WERE SEEN IN
THIS PARTICULAR AREA IN 1986 WAS NOT CREDIBLE.

ALSO ON THE DAY I DEPARTED HANOI, A VIETNAMESE
DELEGATION TRAVELLED TO PHNOM PENH TO PARTICIPATE IN THE
FIRST TRILATERAL TALKS WITH U.S. AND CAMBODIAN OFFICIALS;
THIS FOLLOWED THE U.S.-SRV-LAO TRILATERAL TALKS HELD IN
VIENTIANE LAST DECEMBER. WE THUS HAVE ESTABLISHED A
MECHANISM FOR PURSUING THE FULLEST POSSIBLE ACCOUNTING FOR
AMERICANS MISSING IN THE BORDER AREAS BETWEEN THESE
COUNTRIES. AS I LEFT VIETNAM, THE 16TH IN A SERIES OF
JOINT INVESTIGATIONS WAS TAKING PLACE IN VIETNAM. RESULTS
FROM THIS ACTIVITY, AS WELL AS THE DAY-TO-DAY COOPERATION
OUR POW/MIA OFFICE RECEIVES IN VIETNAM, WILL HELP CONFIRM
WHETHER VIETNAM CONTINUES TO IMPLEMENT THE STEPS WE
REACHED UNDERSTANDINGS ON IN HANOI. THE INITIAL
ASSESSMENTS OF THE 16TH ITERATION ARE ENCOURAGING.
GENERAL NEEDHAM IS IN HANOI TODAY TO ARRANGE THE 17TH
JOINT INVESTIGATION, WHICH BEGINS NEXT MONTH.

FINALLY, A FEW DAYS AFTER I LEFT HANOI, VIETNAM
INFORMED US THAT THEY HAD RECOVERED THREE SETS OF REMAINS
BELIEVED TO BE OF AMERICAN SERVICEMEN. WE HAVE
REPATRIATED THEM AND ARE EXAMINING THE REMAINS TO
DETERMINE WHETHER THEY ARE INDEED AMERICAN.

IN HANOI WE ALSO DISCUSSED U.S. EFFORTS TO ADDRESS VIETNAM'S HUMANITARIAN NEEDS. AS YOU KNOW, MR. CHAIRMAN, SINCE 1987 THE U.S. HAS URGED AMERICAN NON-GOVERNMENTAL ORGANIZATIONS (NGO'S) TO DONATE HUMANITARIAN ASSISTANCE TO VIETNAM UNDER AN INITIATIVE HEADED BY GENERAL VESSEY. IN 1990 WE ANNOUNCED THAT TREASURY DEPARTMENT LICENSING REGULATIONS FOR HUMANITARIAN DONATIONS WOULD BE STREAMLINED; IN 1991 WE MADE THE FIRST DIRECT DONATION OF U.S. AID, PROVIDING $1.3 MILLION FOR PROSTHETICS ASSISTANCE IN VIETNAM. THIS PAST JANUARY WE PROVIDED OUR FIRST DONATION OF DISASTER RELIEF FOR VIETNAM, GIVING $25,000 FOR TYPHOON RELIEF.

IN HANOI I TOLD OUR HOSTS THE U.S. IS PREPARED TO TAKE ADDITIONAL STEPS TO ADDRESS VIETNAM'S HUMANITARIAN NEEDS. I OUTLINED A HUMANITARIAN ASSISTANCE PACKAGE FOR 1992 THAT WILL INCLUDE ADDITIONAL FUNDS FOR PROSTHETICS ASSISTANCE, AID FOR DISPLACED CHILDREN, EXCESS MEDICAL EQUIPMENT MADE AVAILABLE BY THE DEPARTMENT OF VETERANS AFFAIRS, FULBRIGHT SCHOLARSHIPS, POSSIBLE ADDITIONAL DISASTER RELIEF, AND USE OF THE DENTON AMENDMENT PROGRAM TO TRANSPORT HUMANITARIAN ASSISTANCE DONATED BY NGOS. IN ADDITION, DOD MEDICS ACCOMPANYING OUR TEAMS DOING POW/MIA INVESTIGATIONS IN VIETNAM WILL NOW OFFER MEDICAL SERVICES TO LOCAL RESIDENTS.

LAOS

IN LAOS MY DELEGATION WAS RECEIVED AT AN
UNPRECEDENTEDLY HIGH LEVEL, MEETING FOR THE FIRST TIME
WITH PRIME MINISTER KHAMTAI AND MINISTER OF DEFENSE
CHOUMMALI, AS WELL AS FOREIGN MINISTER PHOUN AND
VICE-MINISTER SOUBANH. THE LAO GOVERNMENT AGREED TO
EXPAND ITS ALREADY CONSIDERABLE COOPERATION WITH US ON
POW/MIA INVESTIGATIONS, INCLUDING PROVISION OF LAO
PERSONNEL TO WORK WITH DOD OFFICIALS ASSIGNED TO VIENTIANE
FOR THIS PURPOSE. THEY INFORMED US THEY WOULD SOON BE
TURNING OVER TWO SETS OF REMAINS, APPARENTLY OF AMERICAN
SERVICEMEN, DISCOVERED BY LOCAL PEOPLE IN XIENG KHOANG
PROVINCE. THEY ALSO AGREED TO ACCEPT U.S. TRAINING OF
HELICOPTER PILOTS SO THAT THEY WILL EVENTUALLY BE
QUALIFIED TO FLY U.S. HELICOPTERS FOR OUR JOINT
INVESTIGATIVE WORK. FINALLY, THE LAO GOVERNMENT PLEDGED
TO CONTINUE THEIR COOPERATION WITH US TO COUNTER THE
NARCOTICS TRADE, PARTICULARLY IN THE ENFORCEMENT AREA.

I TOLD THE LAO THE U.S. IS GRATIFIED BY THEIR
COOPERATION ON THESE IMPORTANT ISSUES, AND URGED
CONTINUING EFFORTS. OUR RELATIONSHIP HAS IMPROVED
SIGNIFICANTLY OVER THE PAST SEVERAL YEARS, AND THE
PRESIDENT ANNOUNCED IN NOVEMBER THAT WE WILL RAISE THE
LEVEL OF OUR REPRESENTATION TO THE AMBASSADORIAL LEVEL FOR
THE FIRST TIME SINCE 1975. THE U.S. HAS RECENTLY

ESTABLISHED A POW/MIA OFFICE IN OUR EMBASSY IN VIENTIANE
AND WE LOOK FORWARD TO INCREASINGLY PRODUCTIVE EFFORTS TO
ACCOUNT FOR U.S. SERVICEMEN MISSING IN LAOS. DURING THIS
VISIT I ANNOUNCED OUR DECISION TO PROVIDE 4,000 METRIC
TONS OF RICE AND A $400,000 FAMINE MITIGATION PROGRAM IN
RESPONSE TO RECENT DISASTERS CAUSED BY FLOODS AND
DROUGHT. I ALSO TOLD THE LAO THAT WE WOULD BE BUILDING
MORE SCHOOLS IN REMOTE AREAS AND WOULD SEND AN A.I.D. TEAM
THIS SPRING TO SURVEY PROSTHETICS NEEDS WITH A VIEW TO
INCREASING OUR ASSISTANCE IN THIS FIELD.

CAMBODIA

ACHIEVEMENT OF THE COMPREHENSIVE POLITICAL SETTLEMENT
AGREEMENT FOR CAMBODIA LAST OCTOBER LAID THE GROUNDWORK
FOR REGIONAL PEACE AND NATIONAL RECONCILIATION FOLLOWING
DECADES OF WAR. I TRAVELLED TO CAMBODIA TO UNDERSCORE
CONTINUING U.S. SUPPORT FOR THE SETTLEMENT AGREEMENT
SIGNED IN PARIS LAST YEAR AND TO ASSESS PROGRESS SO FAR IN
IMPLEMENTING IT. JOINING MY DELEGATION WAS DEPUTY
ASSISTANT TO THE PRESIDENT SICHAN SIV, HIMSELF A SURVIVOR
OF THE KHMER ROUGE KILLING FIELDS. WE WERE RECEIVED BY
PRINCE SIHANOUK, AND MET WITH OFFICIALS OF THE UN ADVANCE
MISSION (UNAMIC) AND A NUMBER OF CAMBODIAN LEADERS
REPRESENTING THE STATE OF CAMBODIA AND THE NON-COMMUNIST
RESISTANCE PARTIES ON THE SUPREME NATIONAL COUNCIL (SNC).
ALL THE CAMBODIANS WE MET EXPRESSED THEIR STRONG SUPPORT
FOR THE SETTLEMENT PROCESS AND LOOKED FORWARD TO THE

0076

IMPENDING ARRIVAL THE FOLLOWING WEEK OF THE UN
TRANSITIONAL AUTHORITY IN CAMBODIA (UNTAC).

I FOUND THAT UNAMIC HAS DONE A GOOD JOB IN CARRYING
OUT ITS LIMITED MANDATE -- TO PREPARE THE COUNTRY FOR THE
ARRIVAL OF UNTAC -- BUT THAT IMPLEMENTATION OF THE
SETTLEMENT WILL DEPEND IMPORTANTLY ON A CREDIBLE, SIZEABLE
UN PRESENCE, ESPECIALLY DURING THE DIFFICULT TRANSITIONAL
PERIOD AS DEMOBILIZATION AND CANTONMENT OF FORCES IS
CARRIED OUT. UNTAC WILL ALSO HAVE AN IMPORTANT ROLE TO
PLAY IN ELICITING THE COOPERATION OF THE KHMER ROUGE. TO
DATE, WE HAVE BEEN DISAPPOINTED AND CONCERNED ABOUT
CREDIBLE REPORTS OF KHMER ROUGE MILITARY ACTIONS IN
KOMPONG THOM AND OTHER INSTANCES OF NON-COOPERATION IN
CONTRAVENTION OF THE REQUIREMENTS OF SETTLEMENT
IMPLEMENTATION. WE ALSO URRGED RESTRAINT ON THE PART OF
THE SOC DURING OUR MEETINGS WITH HUN SEN LAST WEEK.

EVERYTHING I WITNESSED IN CAMBODIA — FROM THE
ATROCITIES OF THE TUOL SLENG GENOCIDE MUSEUM TO THE NEWLY
BUILT REFUGEE REPATRIATION CENTER AT SIEM REAP —
CONVINCES ME IT IS ESSENTIAL THAT THE U.S. AND OTHER DONOR
COUNTRIES ACT QUICKLY TO PROVIDE FUNDING FOR THIS VITALLY
IMPORTANT UN MISSION. THE HORRORS INFLICTED ON THE
CAMBODIAN PEOPLE OVER THE LAST TWO DECADES MUST NEVER BE
ALLOWED TO RECUR. THE UN SETTLEMENT IS CAMBODIA'S LAST,
BEST -- PERHAPS ITS ONLY -- HOPE. THE VISIT OF SNC MEMBER
HUN SEN TO WASHINGTON LAST WEEK TESTIFIED TO THE HOPES OF

ALL CAMBODIANS THAT THE U.S. WILL DO ITS SHARE TO MAKE THE UN SETTLEMENT PROCESS SUCCEED.

THE PHNOM PENH AUTHORITIES CONTINUE TO COOPERATE WITH US FULLY ON POW/MIA WORK. THE FIRST FULL-SCALE JOINT RECOVERY AND EXCAVATION OPERATION WAS IN PROGRESS WHILE I WAS IN CAMBODIA, AND U.S. MILITARY HELICOPTERS WERE ALLOWED TO OPERATE WITHIN THE COUNTRY FOR THIS PURPOSE. THAT INVESTIGATION HAS UNCOVERED AT LEAST FOUR SETS OF REMAINS OF INDIVIDUALS MISSING SINCE 1970. MR. HUN SEN AND MR. CHEA SIM OF THE STATE OF CAMBODIA REAFFIRMED THE WILLINGNESS OF THEIR ADMINISTRATION TO CONTINUE COOPERATING WITH US ON THIS IMPORTANT ENDEAVOR.

IN CONCLUSION, I CAME AWAY FROM THIS PORTION OF MY TRIP WITH THE CONVICTION THAT WE HAVE FINALLY LAID IN PLACE POLICIES, PROCESSES AND PERSONNEL WHICH WILL HELP PUT THE PAST BEHIND US AND MOVE TOWARD A NEW RELATIONSHIP WITH ALL THREE COUNTRIES OF INDOCHINA. GOOD FAITH IMPLEMENTATION OF THESE PLANS BY THE LEADERS OF VIETNAM, LAOS AND CAMBODIA WILL BE KEY TO ACHIEVING THIS GOAL. THE ADMINISTRATION AND THE AMERICAN PEOPLE WILL NOW BE LOOKING FOR RESULTS.

IN PARTICULAR, WE WILL BE SEEKING TO ACCOUNT FOR AS MANY OF OUR MISSING SERVICEMEN FROM THE WAR AS POSSIBLE. ACHIEVEMENT OF THAT IMPORTANT GOAL -- IN THE CONTEXT OF CONTINUING PROGRESS IN CAMBODIA -- WILL ALLOW US TO MOVE

- 14 -

TOWARD THE OBJECTIVE ANNOUNCED BY PRESIDENT BUSH AND
SECRETARY BAKER OF RECONCILIATION WITH ALL THREE COUNTRIES
OF INDOCHINA. WITH RESOLUTION OF THESE PROBLEMS, WE LOOK
FORWARD TO THE DAY WHEN PROGRESS IN ALL THREE COUNTRIES
WILL ENABLE THEM TO JOIN THEIR SOUTHEAST ASIAN NEIGHBORS
AS PRODUCTIVE PARTNERS IN A MORE PROSPEROUS AND PEACEFUL
INTERNATIONAL COMMUNITY.

THAILAND/BURMA

    I MET WITH THAI LEADERS BOTH BEFORE AND AFTER MY TRIP
TO INDOCHINA. THE THAI WERE IN THE MIDST OF AN IMPORTANT
ELECTION CAMPAIGN THE RECENT RESULTS OF WHICH WE HOPE WILL
HERALD A RETURN TO DEMOCRACY TO THAILAND.

    WHILE OUR SUPPORT FOR CONSTITUTIONAL RULE AND
DEMOCRACY AS WELL AS BILATERAL ECONOMIC ISSUES WERE
MATTERS I PURSUED WITH VARIOUS THAI LEADERS, WE ALSO
FOCUSED ON REGIONAL ISSUES OF MUTUAL CONCERN: CAMBODIA,
VIETNAM AND BURMA. OUR CLOSE COOPERATION WITH THE RTG AS
A TREATY ALLY AND PROMINENT MEMBER OF THE ASSOCIATION OF
SOUTHEAST ASIAN NATIONS (ASEAN) HAS FACILITATED OUR
EFFORTS TO BRING PEACE TO CAMBODIA. THE THAI SHARE OUR
INTEREST IN ADHERING TO THE SCHEDULE FOR ELECTIONS IN
CAMBODIA NEXT YEAR, AND RECOGNIZE THAT OUR CONTRIBUTION TO
UNTAC WILL BE CRUCIAL TO MEETING THIS GOAL. FOR THEIR
PART, THE THAI ARE WORKING CLOSELY WITH THE UNHCR TO
ASSURE AN ORDERLY AND SAFE REPATRIATION OF CAMBODIAN
DISPLACED PERSONS, AND HAVE CONTRIBUTED PERSONNEL AND

- 15 -

FUNDS TO ROAD-BUILDING AND MINE-CLEARING PROJECTS IN
SUPPORT OF THE REPATRIATION EFFORT.

THE THAI ARE ALSO VERY INTERESTED IN THE PROGRESS OF
OUR RELATIONS WITH HANOI, AND ARE WORKING TO IMPROVE THEIR
OWN RELATIONS WITH VIETNAM. I EXPLAINED TO THE THAI THAT
I HAD HAD A SERIES OF CONSTRUCTIVE MEETINGS WITH THE
VIETNAMESE, AND THAT WE HOPED THAT IMPLEMENTATION OF THE
FIVE-POINT PROGRAM DISCUSSED IN HANOI WOULD ENABLE US TO
TAKE CORRESPONDINGLY POSITIVE STEPS. THE THAI WELCOMED
THIS NEWS, AND SHARED THEIR IMPRESSION THAT THE VIETNAMESE
ARE EAGER TO IMPROVE THEIR RELATIONS WITH THE OUTSIDE
WORLD.

I ALSO DISCUSSED OUR CONTINUING CONCERNS ABOUT THE
DETERIORATING SITUATION IN BURMA, WHICH HAS BEGUN TO SPILL
OVER INTO THAILAND AND BANGLADESH. LET ME ADD HERE THAT
WE WILL WORK WITH OTHERS AMELIORATE THE SITUATION OF THE
ROHHINGYA REFUGEES FLEEING BURMA FOR BANGLADESH, AND THAT
IN THIS CONNECTION, WE WELCOME THE FORTHCOMING VISIT BY A
REPRESENTATIVE OF THE UN SECRETARY GENERAL TO BURMA AND
BANGLADESH.

DURING MY DISCUSSIONS I NOTED THAT THE REFUGEE OUTFLUX
IS GROWING, AND THAT NARCOTICS OBVIOUSLY REMAIN A SEVERE
PROBLEM. I EXPLAINED THAT THERE WAS CONSIDERABLE INTEREST
IN THE U.S. IN THE SAFETY OF BURMESE REFUGEES IN THAILAND,
AND SUGGESTED THAT IF THE THAI DO SET UP A SAFE AREA FOR

BURMESE STUDENTS, WE BELIEVE THAT APPROPRIATE
INTERNATIONAL ORGANIZATIONS SHOULD HAVE REGULAR ACCESS.

ON BILATERAL MATTERS, I STATED THAT THE USG VIEWS
THAILAND AS A STAUNCH AND LONG-TERM FRIEND AND THAT WE
PARTICULARLY APPRECIATED THAILAND'S COOPERATION DURING THE
GULF WAR. I NOTED AS WELL THAT WE WELCOMED THE PASSAGE OF
THE NARCOTICS-RELATED ASSET FORFEITURE AND CONSPIRACY
LEGISLATION, AND THAT WE HAD MADE STRIDES IN PROTECTION OF
COPYRIGHTS AND PATENTS, AND HOPED TO MAKE FURTHER PROGRESS
ON OUR REMAINING CONCERNS. AND I STRESSED OUR SUPPORT FOR
THAI EFFORTS TO MOVE ASEAN TO BECOME A FREE TRADE AREA.

KOREAN PENINSULA

I ALSO HELD DISCUSSIONS IN SEOUL, WHICH, LIKE BANGKOK,
WAS CONSUMED BY ELECTION FEVER. AS WAS DEMONSTRATED BY
THE MARCH 24 NATIONAL ASSEMBLY ELECTIONS, DEMOCRACY IS
SINKING EVER-DEEPER ROOTS IN SOUTH KOREA. MOST OF MY
DISCUSSIONS, HOWEVER, CENTERED ON THE PROBLEM OF GETTING
PYONGYANG TO ABANDON ITS EFFORTS TO ACQUIRE A NUCLEAR
WEAPONS CAPABILITY, TO TAKE MEANINGFUL STEPS TO EASE
TENSIONS ON THE PENINSULA, AND TO BECOME A RESPONSIBLE
INTERNATIONAL ACTOR ON ISSUES SUCH AS THE PROLIFERATION OF
WEAPONS OF MASS DESTRUCTION AND THEIR DELIVERY SYSTEMS.
THESE DISCUSSIONS WERE PART OF A DEEPENING PATTERN OF
CONSULTATIONS WITH OUR ROK ALLIES WITH WHOM WE ARE WORKING
CLOSELY TO RESOLVE THE NUCLEAR ISSUE ON THE KOREAN
PENINSULA.

OUR MAIN CONCERN, AND THAT OF THE ROK AS WELL, IS RELATED TO THE INTERNATIONAL COMMUNITY'S SUSPICION THAT, DESPITE ITS AGREEMENTS WITH THE SOUTH AND WITH THE IAEA -- AGREEMENTS THAT REMAIN TO BE IMPLEMENTED -- THE NORTH KOREANS HAVE NOT ABANDONED THEIR QUEST FOR A NUCLEAR WEAPONS CAPABILITY. ONLY CREDIBLE INSPECTION REGIMES -- AND THEIR FULL IMPLEMENTATION -- UNDER BOTH THE BILATERAL AGREEMENT AND THE IAEA SAFEGUARDS AGREEMENT WILL BEGIN TO GIVE THE INTERNATIONAL COMMUNITY CONFIDENCE THAT THE NORTH KOREANS ARE GENUINELY HONORING THEIR COMMITMENTS AND ARE PREPARED TO MOVE BEYOND THE MILITARY CONFRONTATION THAT HAS POLARIZED THE PENINSULA FOR MORE THAN FOUR DECADES.

THERE ARE SOME HOPEFUL SIGNS. IN FEBRUARY THE NORTH AND SOUTH BROUGHT INTO FORCE TWO BILATERAL AGREEMENTS: ONE IS A BROAD-RANGING AGREEMENT ON RECONCILIATION AND NON-AGGRESSION, AND THE OTHER A NON-NUCLEAR AGREEMENT. SUBCOMMITTEES ON MILITARY MATTERS, POLITICAL MATTERS, AND ECONOMICS AND EXCHANGE HAVE ALREADY BEGUN MEETING UNDER THE RECONCILIATION AGREEMENT, AND THE TWO SIDES HAVE FORMED A JOINT NUCLEAR CONTROL COMMISSION, OR JNCC, UNDER THE NON-NUCLEAR AGREEMENT.

THE TWO SIDES HAVE PUBLICLY COMMITTED THEMSELVES TO WORK TO PRODUCE AN INSPECTION REGIME WITHIN ABOUT TWO MONTHS AFTER THE FIRST MEETING OF THE JNCC ON MARCH 19. THEY AGREED FURTHER THAT INSPECTIONS WOULD BEGIN WITHIN 20

DAYS OF AGREEMENT ON THE INSPECTION REGIME. WHEN
COMPLETED, THAT AGREEMENT WILL FORM THE BASIS FOR
BILATERAL INSPECTIONS TO VERIFY THE NON-NUCLEAR
AGREEMENT. THE NORTH HAS ALSO SAID IT WOULD RATIFY ITS
IAEA AGREEMENT IN APRIL, NOTIFY THE IAEA OF ITS LIST OF
RELEVANT FACILITIES IN MAY, AND THEN HAVE IAEA INSPECTIONS
IN JUNE.

THUS, THE DPRK NOW HAS BEFORE IT A GOLDEN OPPORTUNITY
TO ALLAY SUSPICIONS, DEMONSTRATE ITS CREDIBILITY, AND
ACCELERATE AN OPENING TO THE OUTSIDE WORLD, THEREBY
JOINING THE MAINSTREAM OF GLOBAL TRENDS TOWARDS
RECONCILIATION, REFORM, AND ECONOMIC DEVELOPMENT. IF
PYONGYANG ACTS IN GOOD FAITH, WE COULD SEE IAEA AND
BILATERAL INSPECTIONS UNDER BOTH REGIMES BY THE END OF
JUNE.

SUCH A DEVELOPMENT WOULD BE A HISTORIC STEP FORWARD IN
MOVING TOWARDS THE STATED GOAL OF BOTH KOREAS OF A SECURE,
DENUCLEARIZED KOREAN PENINSULA. FURTHER, IT WOULD GIVE
ADDED IMPETUS TO THE ONGOING NORTH-SOUTH DIALOGUE WHICH
REMAINS THE PRIMARY MEANS FOR RESOLVING KOREA'S PROBLEMS
AND ACHIEVING NATIONAL RECONCILIATION AND EVENTUAL
REUNIFICATION. RESOLVING THE NUCLEAR ISSUE WOULD ALSO
MAKE POSSIBLE MOVEMENT TOWARD A SIGNIFICANT IMPROVEMENT IN
U.S. RELATIONS WITH THE DPRK. WE HOPE THE NORTH WILL SEE
ITS INTERESTS SERVED BY TAKING ADVANTAGE OF THIS
OPPORTUNITY. THE ALTERNATIVE CAN ONLY BE HEIGHTENED
SUSPICIONS, RISING TENSIONS, AND SUSTAINED ISOLATION FOR
THE DPRK.

ANOTHER AREA OF CONCERN, OF COURSE, IS NORTH KOREA'S WEAPONS PROLIFERATION ACTIVITIES, ESPECIALLY ITS TRADE IN MISSILES WITH VARIOUS COUNTRIES IN THE MIDDLE EAST. WE HAVE URGED NORTH KOREA'S LEADERS TO REFRAIN FROM THIS PRACTICE, WHICH IS CLEARLY DESTABILIZING TO A HIGHLY VOLATILE REGION. WE HAVE TOLD THEM THAT THESE UNACCEPTABLE ACTIVITIES CAN ONLY WORSEN THEIR INTERNATIONAL REPUTATION AND FURTHER RETARD ANY PROSPECTS FOR IMPROVED DIPLOMATIC AND ECONOMIC RELATIONS WITH THE INTERNATIONAL COMMUNITY. WE ARE WORKING TOGETHER WITH OTHER CONCERNED COUNTRIES TO FIND WAYS TO LIMIT THE INTRODUCTION OF DESTABILIZING WEAPONS INTO AREAS OF CONCERN, ESPECIALLY THE MIDDLE EAST.

FOR THE MOMENT, HOWEVER, WE ARE IN A PERIOD OF WHAT MIGHT BE CALLED "WATCHFUL WAITING" TO SEE IF PYONGYANG WILL TAKE A NEW DIRECTION IN ITS SECURITY POLICIES — ESPECIALLY ON THE NUCLEAR ISSUE. THE NORTH HAS NOW MADE SEVERAL IMPORTANT COMMITMENTS ON PAPER, AND WE EXPECT THEM TO BE FULFILLED COMPLETELY IN THE TIMEFRAME PYONGYANG HAS PUBLICLY COMMITTED ITSELF TO. NOTHING LESS CAN ADEQUATELY REMOVE THE SUSPICIONS WE SHARE WITH THE REST OF THE WORLD. FURTHER DELAYS IN WHAT IS ALREADY AN UNREASONABLY PROTRACTED PROCESS WOULD BE CAUSE FOR GRAVE INTERNATIONAL CONCERN.

JAPAN

MY STOP IN TOKYO INVOLVED CONSULTATIONS ON THE EAST ASIAN
ASPECTS OF OUR GLOBAL PARTNERSHIP AND FOLLOW UP FROM THE
PRESIDENT'S TRIP ON A NUMBER OF TRADE AND FINANCIAL ISSUES
ESSENTIAL TO KEEPING THAT PARTNERSHIP ON A SOLID ECONOMIC
FOOTING.

OUR RELATIONS WITH JAPAN MUST REST ON EQUITABLE AND
MUTUALLY ADVANTAGEOUS POLITICAL, SECURITY AND ECONOMIC
FOUNDATION. THAT PARTNERSHIP OFFERS UNPRECEDENTED OPPORTUNIES
FOR SHAPING THE POST-COLD WAR INTERNATIONAL SYSTEM THROUGH
CLOSE COORDINATION OF US AND JAPANESE POLICIES TO ENCOURAGE
STABILITY, RESPECT FOR HUMAN RIGHTS AND POLITICAL PLURALISM,
ECONOMIC DEVELOPMENT, AND HALTING THE WORLDWIDE PROLIFERATION
OF WEAPONS OF MASS DESTRUCTION.

SINCE THE PRESIDENT'S VISIT, THERE HAS BEEN SIGNIFICANT
PROGRESS ON A NUMBER OF ASIAN FRONTS WHICH MY CONSULTATIONS
SOUGHT TO REINFORCE:

— VIETNAM: JAPAN HAS BEEN VERY HELPFUL IN URGING HANOI
TO BE RESPONSIVE TO OUR POW/MIA CONCERNS. A RECENT
LETTER FROM JAPAN'S FOREIGN MINISTER MICHIO WATANABE
TO HIS VIETNAMESE COUNTERPART SEEMS TO HAVE
FACILITATED HANOI'S DECISION TO AGREE TO THE
FIVE-POINT PROGRAM I MENTIONED EARLIER. AND JAPAN'S
VICE-MINISTER FOR PARLIAMENTARY AFFAIRS KOJI KAKIZAWA

STRESSED THE NEED FOR HANOI'S FULL COOPERATION IN
RESOLVING THE POW/MIA ISSUE DURING A VISIT TO HANOI
JUST LAST WEEK. WE ARE VERY APPRECIATIVE OF JAPAN'S
EFFORTS.

-- ON CAMBODIA, I DEBRIEFED MY JAPANESE COUNTERPARTS ON
MY ASSESSMENT OF THE SITUATION THERE AND DISCUSSED THE
CHALLENGES AHEAD FOR THE UNITED NATIONS TRANSITIONAL
AUTHORITY IN CAMBODIA (UNTAC) IN SUCCESSFULLY
IMPLEMENTING THE PARIS ACCORDS. THERE ARE INDICATIONS
THAT JAPAN WILL PROVIDE GENEROUS SUPPORT FOR UNTAC.
MRS. OGATA'S ACTIVITIES IN THE UNHCR AND MR. AKASHI'S
AS THE U.N. SECRETARY GENERAL'S SPECIAL REPRESENTATIVE
TO CAMBODIA UNDERSCORE JAPAN'S INCREASINGLY IMPORTANT
LEADERSHIP ROLE IN THE U.N. SETTLEMENT PROCESS.

-- KOREA: CLOSE COOPERATION WITH JAPAN HAS BEEN KEY TO
OUR DIPLOMATIC EFFORTS TO END THE NORTH KOREAN NUCLEAR
THREAT, AND I DEBRIEFED MY JAPANESE COLLEAGUES ON MY
DISCUSSIONS IN SEOUL AND OUR ASSESSMENT OF THE CURRENT
SITUATION ON THE PENINSULA. IN JAPAN'S NORMALIZATION
TALKS WITH NORTH KOREA, AND IN OUR LIMITED DIALOGUE
WITH PYONGYANG, WE BOTH HAVE MADE CLEAR TO THE DPRK IT
MUST MEET THE CONCERNS OF THE INTERNATIONAL COMMUNITY
ABOUT ITS NUCLEAR PROGRAM IF IT IS TO DEVELOP NORMAL
AND CONSTRUCTIVE INTERNATIONAL DEALINGS.

MORE GENERALLY, THERE HAVE ALSO BEEN CLOSE CONSULTATIONS
WEEN OUR TWO GOVERNMENTS ON REGIONAL ISSUES WITH GLOBAL

92-3-31 : 16:05 ;

0086

IMPLICATIONS INCLUDING THE MIDEAST PEACE PROCESS AND ASSISTANCE
TO THE REPUBLICS OF THE FORMER SOVIET UNION.

-- JAPAN HAS BEEN VERY SUPPORTIVE ON BOTH MIDEAST AND CIS
    INITIATIVES. TOKYO IS TAKING AN ACTIVE ROLE IN THESE
    DIPLOMATIC EFFORTS.

OF COURSE, MUCH REMAINS TO BE DONE ON A NUMBER OF ISSUES OF
MUTUAL CONCERN.

-- HAVING SEEN RECENT PROGRESS ON PRC PARTICIPATION IN
    THE GLOBAL NONPROLIFERATION REGIME, WE MUST CONTINUE
    TO ENCOURAGE CONSTRUCTIVE CHINESE INVOLVEMENT IN SUCH
    INTERNATIONAL SECURITY ACTIVITIES, AND TO ENCOURAGE
    IMPROVEMENTS IN CHINESE HUMAN RIGHTS PRACTICES.

-- WE MUST PRESS THE BURMESE REGIME TO AMELIORATE THE
    SITUATION OF THE ROHINGYA REFUGEES FLEEING BURMA FOR
    BANGLADESH, AND TO IMPROVE ITS RECORD ON HUMAN RIGHTS
    AND POLITICAL ACTIVITIES GENERALLY.

-- WE NEED TO CONTINUE OUR JOINT EFFORTS IN SUPPORT OF
    DEMOCRATIZATION AND DEVELOPMENT IN MONGOLIA. A SECOND
    MONGOLIA DONORS' CONFERENCE IS SCHEDULED THIS SPRING
    AS A FOLLOW ON TO THE TOKYO CONFERENCE HELD LAST
    SEPTEMBER.

ECONOMIC ISSUES

I ALSO FOLLOWED UP ON A RANGE OF ECONOMIC ISSUES RAISED
DURING THE PRESIDENT'S TRIP. PRESS REPORTS NOTWITHSTANDING, I
WOULD LIKE TO PROVIDE AN UPDATE ON SIGNIFICANT PROGRESS IN
TRADE-RELATED ISSUES OVER THE PAST THREE MONTHS:

--THE PRESIDENT'S VISIT TO JAPAN PRODUCED MARKET ACCESS
GAINS IN SECTORS IMPORTANT TO OUR EXPORTERS SUCH AS
COMPUTERS, GLASS, PAPER, AND AUTO PARTS. BUSINESS LEADERS
WHO ACCOMPANIED THE PRESIDENT REPORT POSITIVE RESULTS FOR
THEIR COMPANIES AND FOR US BUSINESS IN GENERAL.

--JAPANESE AUTOMAKERS AGREED TO MORE THAN DOUBLE THEIR
PROCUREMENT OF US-MADE PARTS BY 1994. THIS IS CONSISTENT
WITH MITI'S BUSINESS GLOBAL PARTNERSHIP PROGRAM, WHICH
ENCOURAGES JAPANESE FIRMS TO IMPORT MORE, SOURCE MORE
LOCALLY IN THEIR OVERSEAS OPERATIONS, AND TO ASSIST FOREIGN
FIRMS ENTERING JAPAN'S MARKET. WE WANT JAPANESE CARMAKERS
TO WORK WITH US PARTS SUPPLIERS ON PRODUCT DEVELOPMENT THE
SAME WAY THEY WORK WITH THEIR JAPANESE SUPPLIERS. US AUTO
PARTS MAKERS TELL US THEY NOW SEE CHANGED ATTITUDES AND
MORE INTEREST IN US PRODUCTS AMONG JAPANESE CARMAKERS.

--ON AUTOS, WE ARE GIVING FULL SUPPORT TO THE EFFORTS OF US
CARMAKERS TO SELL IN JAPAN.

--AS THE WASHINGTON POST REPORTED AFTER THE PRESIDENT'S
VISIT, THE US COMPUTER INDUSTRY WAS "STUNNED" BY HOW

92-3-31 : 16:06

0088

RAPIDLY WE NEGOTIATED THE PUBLIC SECTOR PROCUREMENT
AGREEMENT AND THE FACT THAT WE ADDRESSED EVERY MAJOR ISSUE
RAISED BY THE INDUSTRY TO ITS SATISFACTION. OUR COMPANIES
ARE NOW GEARING UP TO TAKE ADVANTAGE OF NEW OPPORTUNITIES.

--ON PAPER MARKET ACCESS ISSUES, NEGOTIATIONS ARE
CONTINUING TO GET MEASURES IN PLACE WHICH WOULD EXAND
ACCESS FOR U.S. FIRMS TO JAPAN'S DOMESTIC PAPER MARKET. WE
ARE FIRMLY COMMITTED TO SUPPORTING THE EFFORTS OF U.S.
PAPER COMPANIES TO SUCCEED IN JAPAN'S MARKET.

--WE ARE ADDRESSING THE IMBALANCES IN TRADE AND INVESTMENT
THROUGH THE URUGUAY ROUND, THE STRUCTURAL IMPEDIMENTS
INITIATIVE (SII) AND MARKET ACCESS TALKS. WHILE OUR
BILATERAL TRADE DEFICIT WITH JAPAN HAS FALLEN FROM $57
BILLION IN 1987 TO $42.3 BILLION IN 1991 -- AND OUR EXPORTS
TO JAPAN DOUBLED DURING THAT PERIOD -- THE DEFICIT REMAINS
UNSUSTAINABLY HIGH AND COULD INCREASE AS THE U.S. ECONOMY
STRENGTHENS. I MUST ADD THAT JAPAN'S CURRENT GLOBAL
ACCOUNT SURPLUS FOR 1991 OF $78 BILLION -- ALMOST DOUBLE
THE PREVIOUS YEAR -- INDICATES THAT ITS IMBALANCES ARE OF
GROWING CONCERN TO EUROPE AND OTHERS IN ASIA AS WELL. IF
JAPAN CANNOT GET THESE SURPLUSES UNDER CONTROL IT WILL
WEAKEN THE COUNTRY'S WELCOME IN MANY PARTS OF THE WORLD.

--SII IS AIMED AT ADDRESSING THE STRUCTURAL FEATURES IN THE
US AND JAPANESE ECONOMIES THAT BLOCK THE FREE FLOW OF
GOODS, SERVICES, INVESTMENTS, AND BALANCE OF PAYMENTS

ADJUSTMENT. LAST YEAR WE MADE GOOD PROGRESS ON REFORM OF
JAPAN'S DISTRIBUTION SYSTEM. THIS WILL MAKE US PRODUCTS
MORE WIDELY AVAILABLE TO JAPANESE CONSUMERS. IN 1992 WE
ARE FOCUSSING ON HOW THE JAPANESE BUSINESS ENVIRONMENT
AFFECTS THE ENTRY OF NEWCOMERS.

--- IN THE URUGUAY ROUND, AGRICULTURAL REFORM IS KEY, WHICH
MEANS TARIFFICATION FOR ALL COMMODITIES FROM ALL
COUNTRIES. FOR JAPAN THAT MEANS RICE. I SOUGHT TO
ENCOURAGE JAPAN TO DEMONSTRATE LEADERSHIP IN INCREASING
MARKET ACCESS FOR GOODS AND SERVICES AS WELL.

FINALLY, THE PRESIDENT AND PRIME MINISTER MIYAZAWA IN TOKYO
IN JANUARY PLEDGED TO WORK TOGETHER TO PROMOTE GROWTH IN THE US
AND JAPANESE ECONOMIES, WHICH TOGETHER ACCOUNT FOR 40 PERCENT
OF WORLD GNP. WE LOOK FOR POLICIES FROM JAPAN THAT WILL
STIMULATE ECONOMIC GROWTH THROUGH EXPANSION OF DOMESTIC DEMAND,
NOT THROUGH AN EVER-GROWING EXPORT SECTOR.

THANK YOU.

0090

北韓 지상군 「기습공격 포진」

게이츠국장 게이츠 국장

게이츠국장 美下院 증언 요지

검증절차 없는한 核協定 실효성 의문
北의 군사적 우위 90년대末돼야 해소

◇南北韓 대화 상황
지난해 12월 기본합의서를 체결한후 양측은 일련의 협의와 논의를 해왔으며 이과 정에서 지난 3월19일 핵공동 통제위구성을 몇가지 구체적인 결과를 얻었다. 그러나 대체로 양측은 화해의 기본 골격만을 도출했을뿐 그 내용에 대해서는 진전을 보이지 못하고 있으며 핵사찰의 회수·실시정도·기본규칙등과 같은 주요 이슈에 대해서는 이견을 보이고 있다. 인적교류나 신뢰구축조치등에도 이견을 보이고 있

◇北韓의 위협
南北대화가 진전을 보일 때 까지 北韓의 위협에 대해 조 심스럽게 주시해야 한다. 北韓은 비무장지대 바로 북

다.

금 제기되고 있는 위협은 실제 상황이며 심각한 것이 다.
그러나 北韓의 군사력은 자결집을 태고있고 이때문에 문제가 있

휴전선 일대에 집중 배치된 北韓의 강력한 군대에 대해서 매우 임박한 것으로 믿고있다. 北韓이 핵무기를 갖게되면 동북아의 안정이 저해될것이 우려되고 있으며 뿐만아니라 北韓이 핵물질과 관련기술을

◇北韓의 핵개발 계획
지난해 12월 南北韓은 한

쪽에 엄청난 지상군을 유지하고 있다. 이들은 서울에 대한 대규모 기습을 가할수 있다해도 과거의 동맹국들의 형태로 포진해 있다. 최근 몇년간 이 군대는 韓國의 방어태세를 위협할수 있는 정도로 능력을 개선하며 기동성을 증대해 왔다.
더욱이 「사막의 폭풍」작전 에서 과시됐듯이 美공군력은 대규모 지상군에 매우 효과적인 힘을 갖고 있다. 南韓의 美軍으로부터 공군력과 다른 지원을 받을수 있기 때문에 北韓이 군대가 완전히 사라질 때까지는 지

◇防空과 병참에도 약점을 갖고 있다. 외부의 지원이 없다해도 많은 기대를 할수도 없다.
반도 비핵화 원칙에 합의했 다. 양측은 핵무기를 시험,제 조, 생산, 반입, 보유, 저장, 배치, 사용하지 않는다는 약속 을 했다. 또 핵재처리나 우라 늄 농축시설도 갖지 않기로 합의했다.
그러나 北韓이 寧邊에 플 루토늄 생산, 재처리 시설이 있다는 것을 신고하지 않았 으나 南韓에 대한 군사적 위협은 줄어들지 않았을 뿐만 아니라 인정도 하지 않아 어느정도 접어들게 되었다.

고 있다는것을 감안하면 그들의 의도를 의심할 근거가 있다.
더욱이 검증절차도 아직 확정되지 않았다. 南北한 협정의 실효성 여부는 北韓의 군사적으로 어떤 사찰규정을 수락하느냐에 달려있다.
北韓의 핵개발 능력확보가 매우 임박한 것으로 믿고있다. 北韓이 핵무기를 갖게되면 동북아의 안정이 저해될것이 우려되고 있으며 뿐만아니라 北韓이 핵물질과 관련기술을

전통적인 우방의 對北韓 지원감소와 경제문제로 인해 北韓의 對南 군사적 우위는 90년대말까지 점차 잠식당할 것으로 예상되고 있다. 北韓의 군수산업은 60년대 기술에 의존하고 있으며 질적인 문제에 직면하고 있다. 89년 이래 주요무기가 반 CIS로부터 蘇聯이나 中國을

국제시장에 관매할 것이라는데 우려하지 않을수 없다.
◇北韓에 불리한 추세
北韓은 경제난과 다가오는 지도체제 변화로 美國과의 대결전략을 수정하지 않을수 니라 美國·日本·유엔등과의 관계를 권유할 가능성이있다.

더욱 검증절차도 아직 확 ... 어떤도 있는지 모른다.
... 北韓의 군사전략가들은 ... 으로 병력과 무기에서 수적으로 우위를 유지하고 있는 北 ... 동안, 南韓에 공격을 개시할 것을 권유할 가능성이있다.

92.3.28 〈중 앙〉   0091

長官報告事項

報告畢

1992. 4. 1.
美 洲 局
北 美 1 課 (32)

題目 : Solomon 次官補 上院 聽聞會 證言

> 92.3.31. Richard Solomon 國務部 東亞.太 次官補는 上院 ~~東亞.太.小委 外交~~ 委 外交
> 聽聞會에 參席, 同 次官補의 금번 아시아巡訪 結果에 대해 證言을 한바,
> 同 主要內容 下記 報告드립니다.

1. 韓國 關係

(總 選)

o 3.24. 한국 국회의원선거는 한국내 민주주의가 확고히 정착되고 있음을
  입증한 것으로 평가함.

(北韓 核/南.北 關係)

o IAEA 핵사찰 및 남북 상호사찰 문제가 협의되고 있으나, 북한은 상금
  핵무기 개발계획을 포기하지 않고 있음.
  - IAEA와 남북 상호사찰의 확실한 이행만이 국제사회의 우려 불식

o 남북 합의서 및 비핵 공동선언 채택이후 각 분과위 및 핵통제 공동위원회가
  개최되고 있는 등 일부 희망적 조짐도 보임.
  - 남.북한 핵사찰 추진일정 합의
  - 북한, 6월중 IAEA 사찰실시 언급

o 북한이 성실하게 약속을 이행한다면, IAEA 및 남북 상호사찰은 오는 6월
  까지 실시가 가능함.
  - 북한도 현재 화해.개혁 및 경제발전이라는 국제조류에 합류할 수 있는
    황금기회를 맞고 있음.
  - 여사한 사태진전은 한반도 비핵화, 통일을 위한 남북대화에 역사적 계기

o 미국은 북한이 핵문제 해결을 골자로 한 새로운 안보정책을 취하고, 지금
  까지 발표한 시간계획을 준수하는지를 예의주시하고 있음.
  - 북한의 핵문제 해결시에는 미.북한 관계의 괄목할 만한(significant)
    진전 가능

0092

(北韓의 對中東 미사일輸出)

ㅇ 대중동 미사일수출등 북한의 대량살상무기 확산에 대해 우려하고 있음.
  - 북한의 국제적 신뢰도 저해 및 국제사회의 대북 외교.경제 관계개선
    가능성 약화

2. 日本 關係

ㅇ 미국은 일본과의 전세계적 협력관계 일부로서 동아시아지역에서의 협력관계
  강화를 추진하고 있음.
  - 대인도지나 정책관련, 일본의 협조 평가
  - 북한 핵관련 미.일정책 협조

ㅇ 중국 무기수출 및 인권문제, 버마 인권문제 및 대몽고 지원등에 있어 향후
  미.일간의 협력이 필요함.

ㅇ 부쉬 대통령 방일이후 양국 경제.통상문제가 원만히 해결되고 있는데
  만족함.

3. 인도지나 關係

ㅇ 인도지나 3국 방문은 전반적으로 성공을 거두었으며, 합의사항 이행시
  인도지나 3국은 아.태 협력관계에 동참할 수 있을 것으로 전망함.
  - 월남전 POW/MIA 문제에 대해 진전

ㅇ 인도지나에 대한 인도주의적 원조 확대등 미국은 제반지원 노력을 경주
  하고 있음.
  - 캄보디아 UNTAC 활동지원 필요 강조

4. 評 價

ㅇ Solomon 차관보는 금번 아시아 순방의 주목적인 인도지나 3국 방문에 대해

ㅇ 북한 핵관련, Solomon 차관보는 IAEA 사찰뿐만 아니라 남북 상호사찰도
  6월중까지는 실시되어야 한다는 점을 강조
  대북한 제재 가능성 언급등 압력 행사보다는 핵사찰 수락에 따를
  중점을 두어 북한의 6월중 핵사찰을 촉구. 끝.

0093

長 官 報 告 事 項

報 告 畢

1992. 4. 1.
美 洲 局
北 美 1 課 (32)

題 目 : Solomon 次官補 上院 聽聞會 證言

92.3.31. Richard Solomon 國務部 東亞.太 次官補는 上院 東亞.太 小委
聽聞會에 參席, 同 次官補의 금번 아시아巡訪 結果에 대해 證言을 한바,
同 主要內容 下記 報告드립니다.

---

1. 韓國 關係

(總 選)

ㅇ 3.24. 한국 국회의원선거는 한국내 민주주의가 확고히 정착되고 있음을
입증한 것으로 평가함.

(北韓 核/南.北 關係)

ㅇ IAEA 핵사찰 및 남북 상호사찰 문제가 협의되고 있으나, 북한은 상금
핵무기 개발계획을 포기하지 않고 있음.
- IAEA와 남북 상호사찰의 확실한 이행만이 국제사회의 우려 불식
ㅇ 남북 합의서 및 비핵 공동선언 채택이후 각 분과위 및 핵통제 공동위원회가
개최되고 있는 등 일부 희망적 조짐도 보임.
- 남.북한 핵사찰 추진일정 합의
- 북한, 6월중 IAEA 사찰실시 언급
ㅇ 북한이 성실하게 약속을 이행한다면, IAEA 및 남북 상호사찰은 오는 6월
까지 실시가 가능함.
- 북한도 현재 화해.개혁 및 경제발전이라는 국제조류에 합류할 수 있는
황금기회를 맞고 있음.
- 여사한 사태진전은 한반도 비핵화, 통일을 위한 남북대화에 역사적 계기
ㅇ 미국은 북한이 핵문제 해결을 골자로 한 새로운 안보정책을 취하고, 지금
까지 발표한 시간계획을 준수하는지를 예의주시하고 있음.
- 북한의 핵문제 해결시에는 미.북한 관계의 괄목할 만한(significant)
진전 가능

0094

(北韓의 對中東 미사일輸出)

o 대중동 미사일수출등 북한의 대량살상무기 확산에 대해 우려하고 있음.
  - 북한의 국제적 신뢰도 저해 및 국제사회의 대북 외교.경제 관계개선
    가능성 약화

2. 日本 關係

o 미국은 일본과의 전세계적 협력관계 일부로서 동아시아지역에서의 협력관계
  강화를 추진하고 있음.
  - 대인도지나 정책관련, 일본의 협조 평가
  - 북한 핵관련 미.일정책 협조

o 중국 무기수출 및 인권문제, 버마 인권문제 및 대몽고 지원등에 있어 향후
  미.일간의 협력이 필요함.

o 부쉬 대통령 방일이후 양국 경제.통상문제가 원만히 해결되고 있는데
  만족함.

3. 인도지나 關係

o 인도지나 3국 방문은 전반적으로 성공을 거두었으며, 합의사항 이행시
  인도지나 3국은 아.태 협력관계에 동참할 수 있을 것으로 전망함.
  - 월남전 POW/MIA 문제에 대해 진전

o 인도지나에 대한 인도주의적 원조 확대등 미국은 제반지원 노력을 경주
  하고 있음.
  - 캄보디아 UNTAC 활동지원 필요 강조

4. 評 價

o Solomon 차관보는 금번 아시아 순방의 주목적인 인도지나 3국 방문을 주로
  설명하면서 캄보디아등 인도지나 상황을 긍정적으로 평가함.

o 북한 핵관련, Solomon 차관보는 IAEA 사찰뿐만 아니라 남북 상호사찰도
  6월중까지는 실시되어야 한다는 점을 강조하면서, 대북한 제재 가능성
  언급등 압력 행사보다는 핵사찰 수락에 따를 반대급부에 중점을 두어
  언급함. 끝.

0095

외 무 부

종 별 : 지 급

번 호 : USW-1665

일 시 : 92 0402 2004

수 신 : 장 관 (미이,미일,정특,기정,국방부)

발 신 : 주 미 대사

제 목 : 하원 군사위 청문회

연: USW-1105

1. 하원 군사위 국방정책 연구반(반장: LES ASPIN 의원, 민주-위스콘신)은 금 4.2(목) ROBERT RISCASSI 주한 미군사령관을 증인으로 출석시켜 "태평양 안보문제" 제하 남북한간 군사력 비교, 남북한간 분쟁 가능성및 주한 미군의 역할에 대해 청문회를 개최하였음.(당관 김형진 서기관 참석)

2. 동 청문회는 RISCASSI 사령관의 모두 증언 부분은 공개로, 이후 질의.응답은 비공개로 진행되었는바, 모두 증언에서 RISCASSI 사령관은 연호 3.4(수) 청문회의시의 증언문과 거의 같은 증언문(USW(F)-1999 로 기송부)을 제출하고 이를간략히 요약, 설명하였으며, 북한에 대한 IAEA 의 핵사찰이 이루어지더라도 엄밀한 사찰은 기대하기 어려우며, 이에따라 한국측은 보다 엄밀한 상호 사찰을 추진하고 있으나 구체적 진전이 없음을 강조하였음.

3. 비공개 협의 내용은 파악 가능한 대로 추보 예정임.끝.

(대사 현홍주-국장)

예고: '92.12.31. 까지

일반문서로 재분류(1992.12.31.)

검토필 (1992. 6. 20.)

미주국 안기부	장관 국방부	차관	1차보	2차보	미주국	외정실	분석관	청와대

PAGE 1

92.04.03   10:33

외신 2과   통제관 BX

0096

공   란

공　　　란

관리
번호 _____

외 무 부

종   별 :

번   호 : USW-1755   일   시 : 92 0407 1928

수   신 : 장 관 (미일,봉이,미이,정특)

발   신 : 주 미 대사

제   목 : 의회 보좌관 오찬 간담회

　　당지 KEI 는 금 4.7(화) DONALD P. GREGG 주한 미대사와 당관 구본영 공사를 연사로 초청, 한. 미 봉상관계를 주제로 표제 간담회를 개최한바(의회 보좌관20 여명 참석) 동 간담회 요지 아래 보고함.(당관 장원삼, 김형진 서기관 참석)

　1. 주제 발표 내용

　- 한. 미간 봉상관계는 지난 4 년간 미국의 대한 수출이 2 배이상 증가하는등 바람직한 방향으로 나아가고 있으나 문제는 아직도 한국내 미국 기업의 영업활동에 장애가 있다는 점으로 일본은 기업과 정부가 협력하여 외국기업의 진출을배척하고 있는 반면 한국의 경우에는 기업은 외국기업의 진출을 환영하고 있으나 정부가 외국기업 진출을 규제하고 있다는데 차이가 있음.

　- 한국정부가 추구하여야 할 것은 각종 법제도 및 절차의 공개성및 명료성으로서 부쉬 대통령 방한시 합의사항에 따라 작성되고 있는 금융시장 개방의 청사진도 이러한 방향으로 추진되어야 할것임. 본인으로서는 조순 신임 한국은행 총재의 역할에 기대를 걸고 있음.

　- 북한이 IAEA 사찰및 남. 북한 상호사찰에 원칙적으로 동의했다는 것은 기대 이상의 성과이나 사찰의 실제 수용을 지연하고 있음. 북한 핵개발등 북한에 대한 미국내 관심 제고는 환영하나 지나친 점이 있는바 북한이 핵무기를 개발 못하게 되기를 바라지만 개발하더라도 북한의 미약한 경제력및 미국의 억제력을 고려할때 큰 위협이 되지는 못할 것이라고 봄. 북한에 대해서도 일방적인 압력을 가하기 보다는 소련에서 성공을 거둔 것과 같은 CARROT 는 확대.균형화되고 있으며, 특히 92 년 1 월부터 미국의 대한 무역수지가 흑자로 반전되었음에도 불구하고 미국은 상당액의 대한적자를 기록하던 수년전과 같이 개별현안 발생시마다 이를 해결해 나가는 접근방식을 취하고 있는바, 이는 양자 관계를 너무 좁은 시각에서 보는데 기인하며 또한 미국의 많은

미주국	장관	차관	1차보	2차보	미주국	통상국	외정실	분석관
정와대	안기부							

기관이 적자심리(DEFICIT MENTALITY)를 가지고 불공정무역 행태를 찾아내려 하는데에도 기인한다고 봄.

- 통상분야에서 한.미 양국이 협력할수 있는 여지가 많이 있는바, 예를들어 대일 무역수지 적자문제는 여타국에게도 영향을 미칠수 있으므로 이에대해 미국이 양자간 감정문제로 다루기 보다는 동 문제를 다자화 하는 것이 해결 방편이 될수 있음.

또한 러시아나 중국에 대한 경제협력에 양국이 협조할 수 있다고 봄.

2. 질의.응답 요지

가. 부시 대통령은 재외공관이 기업활동의 첨병(POINTMEN)이라고 언급한바, 주한 미대사관의 기업을 위한 활동 정도는 ?

- 과거 한국에 근무할 당시만 해도 통상은 대사관의 큰 관심이 되지 않았으나 지금은 통상업무가 매우 많으며 직접 문제를 다루고 있음(WRESTLE PROBLEMS ON THE MAT).

나. 일본시장 개방을 위한 한.미 양국의 협력방안은 ?

- 한 예로 APEC 등을 이용할수 있을 것임. 대일 통상마찰을 미국이 양자문제로 다루기 보다 APEC 를 이용, 일본의 통상관행등을 연구하고 공동의 해결책을구할수 있을 것임.(구공자)

- 동북아시아의 큰 문제는 한.일 양국 관계인바, 한.미, 미.일 우호관계에도 불구하고 한.일 관계에는 긴장이 있는바 이는 무역마찰뿐 아니라 역사왜곡시비, 정신대 문제등에 기인함. 실제로 한국은 북한의 위협뿐만 아니라 일본의위협을 우려하고 있는바, 미국이 한.일 양국관계의 중재자 역할을 하여야 할 것임.(GREGG 대사). 끝.

(대사 현홍주-국장)

예고: 92.12.31. 까지

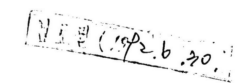

PAGE 2

0100

448 북한 핵문제 미국 동향

美國 의회조사국이 제출한 「北 核개발계획보고서」요지

"北 核개발은 駐韓美軍철수 협상용"

▲核무기개발계획실태＝北韓방 약96㎞지점의 寧邊에는 지난 80〜87년 사이 건설된 30메가와트級 원자로(원자폭탄 1개제조가능)한 플루토늄추출 가능)와 84년부터 건설중인 50〜1백 메가와트級 원자로(연간 2〜5개의 원자폭탄제조가능)한 플루토늄급 230을 추출할 수 있는 재처리시설, 분화구처럼 구획된 폭발실험장등이 존재한다.

인공위성촬영등에 따르면 이들 원자로에는 발전소用 전력線은 없고 원자폭탄 제조를 위한 많은 무장병사와 對비행포로 삼엄한 경비가 펼쳐지고 있다.

50〜1백메가와트級 원자로와 재처리시설은 빠르면 92년 중반에 완성, 그후 1년내에 원자폭탄발사장치가 제조될 것으로 추정된다.

▲외부지원＝北韓과학자들은 蘇聯·中國·파키스탄등지에서 硏修한 여가 많다. 蘇聯은 寧邊시설에 대한 직접지원은 하지않았지만 北韓은 核무기를 제조하면 美軍에 대항할 수 있는 抑止력을 갖기 위해서는 核무장이 불가피하다고 판단한 듯 ...

中國은 北韓의 재처리시설 건설에 기술을 제공했다는 정보가 있으나 아직은 추측단계다.

▲北韓의 의도＝〈核무장 의도 부정〉北韓은 寧邊시설이 「硏究시설」에 불과하다 ...

【東京＝李錫九특파원】

0101

외 무 부

종 별 :

번 호 : USW-1811

일 시 : 92 0409 1916

수 신 : 장 관 (미일, 미이, 정특, 기정)

발 신 : 주 미 대사

제 목 : 하원 군사위 청문회

1. 하원 군사위원회 국방정책 연구반(반장: LES ASPIN 의원, 민주-위스콘신)은 '지역위협 및 1990 년대 국방대책' 제하의 청문회를 속개, 금 4.9(목) CHARLES LARSON 태평양 사령관을 증인으로 출석시켜 아시아. 태평양지역 안보위협및이에대한 미국의 대책에 관한 청문회를 개최하였음. (당관 김형진 서기관 참석)

2. LARSON 사령관은 사전 준비한 증언문(증언문은 USW(F)-2160 으로 FAX 송부)을 제출하고 이를 중심으로 증언하였는바, 구소련연방으로 부터의 위협감소에 따라 중요성이 더욱 부각되고 있는 태평양지역에서 가장 큰 불안정의 요소는 세계에서 고립되어 핵무기 개발을 추진하고 있는 북한이며 두번째는 지난 45 년간 3차례 전쟁을 일으킨 인도-파키스탄으로 이러한 위협의 봉쇄가 중요하다고 언급하였음.

3. LARSON 사령관은 또한 아시아. 태평양 지역의 5 대 힘의 중심(POWER CENTER)인 러시아, 일본, 한반도, 중국, 인도중 어느 한나라가 헤게모니를 갖지 못하도록 균형을 유지하는 것이 미국의 역할이라고 언급하고, 한국, 일본의 방위분담 증에 따라 92 년말까지 18,000 명, 95 년말까지는 32,000 명의 아시아. 태평양 지역 주둔 미군을 철수할 예정이나 과거 미국이 고립주의를 채택하고 방위력을 충분히 유지하지 않음으로써 2 차 세계대전이라는 혼란을 야기한 경험을 되풀이 하여서는 안된다고 언급하였음.

4. 동맹국의 방위비 분담 정도에 대한 BILL DICKINSON 의원(공화-알라바마)및 ASPIN 의원의 질의에 대해 LARSON 사령관은 일본은 91 년 미군주둔 비용의 61퍼센트에 해당하는 22 억 8 천만불, 95 년 주둔비용의 73 퍼센트에 해당하는 38억불을 부담할 것인바, 같은 규모의 병력을 미국에 유지하는데 3 배의 비용이 소요되므로 미군 주둔은 경제적으로도 필요하다고 언급하고 한국은 88 년 방위비분담을 개시한 이래 92 년 주한 미군주둔 비용의 21 퍼센트에 해당하는 1 억 8 천만불, 95 년에는 주둔

미주국 안기부	장관 안기부	차관	1차보	2차보	미주국	외정실	분석관	청와대

PAGE 1

92.04.10   09:45

외신 2과 통제관 BX

0102

비용의 1/3 을 부담할 것이라고 답변하였음.

5. 주한 미지상군 유지 필요성에 대한 NORMAN SISISKY 의원(민주-버지니아)의 질의에 대하여 LARSON 사령관은 한국군이 한. 미 군사협력에서 주도적 역할을담당하는 방향으로 나아가고 있는바, 북한의 핵무기 개발 계획을 고려하여 주한 미군 철수계획의 2 단계를 연기한 것은 올바른 결정으로 생각한다고 언급하고한국이 기습공격을 받게 되는 경우 증원군을 파견하는 것은 페르시아만 지역에서 보다는 어려울 것이나 한국이 미국의 지원군이 도착할때까지 침략을 억제할 수 있을 것이라고 답변하였음. 끝.

(대사 현홍주-국장)

외 무 부

종   별 :

번   호 : AVW-0583   일   시 : 92 0410 2000

수   신 : 장 관(국기) 사본:주미대사(직송필)

발   신 : 주 오스트리아 대사

제   목 : 북한 핵관계 자료

　　　대:WAV-0463

　　　대호 첨부 4.9 중앙일보에 요지가 보도된 미국의회 조사국이 제출한 북한의 핵
개발계획에 대한 보고서를 FAX 송부하여 주시기 바람. 끝.

　　　(대사 이시영-국장)

국기국   중계

발 신 전 보

<table>
<tr><td>분류번호</td><td>보존기간</td></tr>
<tr><td></td><td></td></tr>
</table>

번 호 :　WAV-0503　920413 1927　FO　　종별 : 암호송신

수 신 :　주 ~~따~~ 오스트리아　대사. 총영사

발 신 :　장 관 （국기）

제 목 :　북한 핵관계 자료(CRS 보고서)

　　　　대 : AVW-0583

　　　　대호 미의회 조사국의 북한 핵개발계획에 대한 보고서를 별첨 fax 송부함.

　　첨부 : 상기 fax 　매.　끝.

　　　　　AVF-62

　　　　　　　　　　　　　　　　　（국제기구국장　김 재 섭）

<table>
<tr><td rowspan="2">보안통제</td><td>B</td></tr>
</table>

<table>
<tr><td rowspan="3">앙고재</td><td>82년 4월 13일</td><td>국제기구과</td><td>기안자 성명</td><td></td><td>과 장</td><td>심의관</td><td>국 장</td><td></td><td>차 관</td><td>장 관</td><td rowspan="3">외신과통제</td></tr>
<tr><td></td><td></td><td></td><td></td><td></td><td></td><td></td><td></td><td></td><td></td></tr>
<tr><td></td><td>신종영</td><td></td><td></td><td></td><td></td><td></td><td></td><td></td><td></td></tr>
</table>

0105

Order Code IB91141

CRS Issue Brief

North Korea's
Nuclear Weapons Program

Updated April 8, 1992

by
Larry A. Niksch
Foreign Affairs and National Defense Division

Congressional Research Service • The Library of Congress

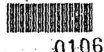

0106

CONTENTS

0107

North Korea's Nuclear Weapons Program

SUMMARY

North Korea is constructing nuclear reactors and a plutonium reprocessing plant at a site called Yongbyon. According to some U.S. officials and other knowledgeable people, this will give North Korea the ability to manufacture atomic weapons, possibly as early as mid-1992. North Korea also is upgrading potential delivery systems, including SCUD missiles.

Pyongyang has used concern over the Yongbyon facility to pressure the United States to remove U.S. nuclear weapons alleged to be stationed in South Korea and probably the withdrawal of all U.S. forces in South Korea. North Korea, too, may view nuclear weapons as giving it greater deterrence against military attack and/or retaliation by the United States and South Korea. The regime may believe that nuclear arms would strengthen it internationally and at home, as currently it faces diplomatic isolation and the collapse of supportive communist regimes in the Soviet Union and Eastern Europe.

Apparently responding to the U.S. withdrawal of nuclear weapons from South Korea and other U.S. and South Korean policy inducements, North Korea signed agreements with South Korea and the International Atomic Energy Agency (IAEA) providing for inspections of North Korean facilities; but it is uncertain whether North Korea will permit these to be implemented in the near future.

A potential North Korean nuclear weapons program has major implications for U.S. policy in a number of areas. It could add to military instability in Korea, where the United States has about 40,000 troops stationed. South Korean reactions could threaten U.S.-South Korean policy coordination and political instability in the South. The issue has become a major factor in U.S.-Japan diplomatic cooperation and could become important in military cooperation. U.S. relations with Russia and with China increasingly would be affected by this issue. North Korean production of nuclear arms would damage U.S. nuclear nonproliferation policy.

The Bush Administration has set as an objective of U.S. policy the dismantling of the reprocessing plant at Yongbyon. It views the securing of international inspection of Yongbyon as a useful interim goal but not totally adequate, since North Korea could complete the reprocessing plant under an inspection regime. The Bush Administration has gained assistance from numerous governments in pressuring North Korea to allow inspection, and it has offered to improve relations with North Korea if Pyongyang complies.

If North Korea completes the Yongbyon complex, the U.S. and South Korean governments might consider more coercive options. A request for U.N. Security Council action likely would be the first step. An air strike or a naval blockade are possible measures, but either would risk the outbreak of a war. A military buildup in and around Korea would aim at containing a North Korean nuclear threat, but would represent an abandonment of the dismantling objective. Military options would raise the issue of Japanese and other allied support.

IB91141   04-08-92

ISSUE DEFINITION

According to numerous press and journal articles (see **For Additional Reading**), U.S. intelligence estimates reportedly have concluded that a North Korean nuclear reactor and reprocessing facility presently under construction will give North Korea the ability to manufacture atomic weapons. This issue could have serious implications for the U.S. military/security role in Korea and Northeast Asia, and could threaten peace and stability there. It also could affect U.S. policy regarding the proliferation of nuclear weapons. A U.S. response could involve both diplomatic and military measures, involving not only North and South Korea, but also Japan, Russia, and China. Depending on how far the issue develops, Congress might be involved in at least four ways: (1) review of the findings of U.S. intelligence agencies; (2) oversight of the annual reports to Congress by the Bush Administration on the status of U.S. troops in South Korea; and (3) participation through hearings, floor debate, and legislation in consideration of U.S. policy responses.

BACKGROUND AND ANALYSIS

North Korea's apparent nuclear program is set against a security situation in the Korean peninsula that contains long-standing ideological and military tensions and dangers alongside significant political, diplomatic, and economic changes since 1987. The major elements include:

-- A high level of confrontation between North Korea and South Korea (Republic of Korea-R.O.K.): 1.1 million North Korean troops face 650,000 South Korean troops across the armistice line of 1953. North-South negotiators reached an agreement on reconciliation and cooperation in December 1991, but detailed accords still must be negotiated.

-- A deep ideological gap between a democratizing South Korea and a rigid, closed communist system in North Korea under Kim Il-sung, North Korea's President.

-- A "diplomatic revolution" in which North Korea's allies -- the Soviet Union and East European countries -- have established relations with South Korea, are building economic and other ties with it, and are reducing support for North Korea. China is moving in that direction, although more slowly. North Korea increasingly is isolated diplomatically and ideologically, and its economy is weakening. However, it continues to uphold its communist system.

-- North Korean initiative since 1990 aimed at normalizing relations with Japan, apparently to secure Japanese financial assistance. Negotiations between Japan and North Korea are ongoing.

-- Minimal contacts between the United States and North Korea: government-to-government discourse has been confined largely to sub-ambassadorial meetings between U.S. and North Korean officials in Beijing, China.

- A U.S. military presence of over 40,000 troops in South Korea, scheduled to be cut to about 35,000 by the end of 1992 in the first stage of a plan to reduce the size of U.S. forces. Under its "neither confirm nor deny" policy, the U.S. Defense Department never has stated whether the United States has nuclear weapons in South Korea. However, numerous reports indicate that the United States withdrew nuclear weapons from South Korea in October-December 1991.

North Korea's Nuclear Program

Several U.S. and Japanese journals have published articles on the North Korean nuclear weapons program. The following description is based largely on the Japanese journal, *Seiron*, February 1991, and by Janes Intelligence Review, September 1991. U.S. and French reconnaissance satellites reportedly have taken numerous photographs of a North Korean nuclear facility located at Yongbyon, which is about 60 miles north of the North Korean capital of Pyongyang. The photographs have shown several structures that have led U.S. intelligence agencies and other experts to conclude that North Korea is developing a plant and equipment that could produce atomic bombs:

- A relatively small -- no more than 30 megawatt -- atomic reactor, constructed between 1980 and 1987: it reportedly is capable of expending enough uranium fuel to produce about 7 kilograms of plutonium annually -- enough for the manufacture of a single atomic bomb every one or two years.

- A larger (50-200 megawatts) atomic reactor under construction since 1984: when operational, it reportedly would be capable of producing enough spent fuel for 18 to 50 kilograms of plutonium annually -- enough for 2 to 5 atomic bombs.

- A building with the size and shape of a plutonium reprocessing plant: such a reprocessing plant would allow the North Koreans to separate nuclear weapons-grade Plutonium-239 from the reactors' spent uranium fuel rods. This separation process is crucial to the ability to produce atomic bombs.

Satellite photographs reportedly also show that the atomic reactors have no attached power lines, which they would have if used for electric power generation. There are no electric power generation plants in the vicinity of Yongbyon. Large numbers of military guards are at the site, and the area is ringed with anti-aircraft weapons. Professor Toshibumi Sakata of Japan's Tokai University's Information and Technology Center has studied Yongbyon since 1984. He has stated that the evidence is substantial that North Korea is constructing an atomic weapons facility.

Some experts and reports point to possibilities that North Korea also may have other, hidden nuclear weapons facilities, similar to the recently discovered Iraqi facilities. Bakchon, 60 miles north of Pyongyang, has been cited by Professor Sakata and others as one such site.

Persons interviewed for this study believe that North Korea has been constructing the two reactors and the apparent reprocessing plant with its own resources and technology. North Korea reportedly has about 3,000 scientists and research personnel devoted to the Yongbyon program. Many have studied nuclear technology (though not necessarily nuclear weapons production) in the Soviet Union and China and reportedly Pakistan. The training of nuclear scientists at North Korean universities reportedly is intense. North Korea has uranium deposits, estimated at 26 million tons. North Korea is believed to have one uranium producing mine. The North Korean reactors appear to be based on design and technology of the 1940s and early 1950s -- a type often found in developing countries.

In March 1992, the Russian newspaper *Arguments and Facts* quoted from a classified Soviet KGB report of Feb. 22, 1990, that the KGB had received information from "a reliable source" that "the first North Korean atomic explosive device has been completed. . . in the city of Yongbyon." The KGB undoubtedly had an extensive intelligence gathering operation in North Korea in the 1980s when military cooperation between the Soviet Union and North Korea was extensive. If the KGB report is accurate, North Korea has produced the basic components of an atomic bomb, especially the detonator which triggers a nuclear explosion; thus, it would need only reprocessed plutonium for a complete atomic bomb. U.S. officials stated in early 1992 that North Korea's plutonium reprocessing plant at Yongbyon was close to being operational and possibly could begin to produce fissionable material in the summer of 1992. These officials believe that, once operational, the reprocessing plant could produce enough weapons-grade plutonium for a bomb within a few months. Thus, if such a timetable proves correct, North Korea could have an atomic weapon by the end of 1992 or early in 1993.

International Assistance

Knowledgeable individuals believe that the Soviet Union has not assisted directly in the development of Yongbyon in the 1980s. The U.S.S.R. provided North Korea with a small research reactor in the 1960s, which also is at Yongbyon. However, North Korean nuclear scientists continued to receive training in the U.S.S.R. up to the demise of the Soviet Union in December 1991.

Several analysts interviewed said that there is no direct evidence that China is assisting North Korea in its nuclear weapons program. Non-government experts, however, have noted the reports that China was helping North Korea in the development of missiles. The publication *Nucleonics* (June 21, 1990) asserted that "Some sources believe the country [North Korea] is being assisted by China...." Another publication *Nuclear Fuel* (Oct. 2, 1989) cited U.S. officials as saying that the subject of China's nuclear cooperation with North Korea "has been raised" with the Chinese government and that there was "speculation" that China had provided technology for the North Korean reprocessing plant.

North Korea's Delivery Systems

The international concern over the Yongbyon facility has been exacerbated by North Korea's reported progress in developing and acquiring weapons systems capable of transporting nuclear warheads to targets in South Korea and Japan. North Korea presently produces a variation of the SCUD-B missile with an estimated range of nearly 200 miles. This would cover about two thirds of South Korean territory. According to an analysis of North Korea's missile program by Joseph Bermudez and Seth Carus in *Janes Soviet Intelligence Review*, April 1989, and subsequent U.S., British, and South

Korean press reports, North Korea also is developing a more advanced SCUD missile with a range of over 400 miles. Experts believe this missile will be deployed in 1992. This SCUD is thought to be more suited to carry a nuclear warhead than the SCUD-B; it would include all of South Korea in its range and could reach Japanese territory. In addition to the SCUDs, several aircraft in the North Korean arsenal probably could carry atomic bombs.

North Korean Objectives

North Korean Denials of Atomic Weapons Intentions

North Korea has denied in all of its statements that it intends to produce atomic weapons. North Korean spokesmen have described Yongbyon as a research facility. However, North Korea has left open the possibility it could begin nuclear weapons production. The Soviet newspaper *Komsomolskaya Pravda*, the official newspaper of the Soviet Communist Party youth organization, reported on Nov. 29, 1990, from Pyongyang that: "During his September talks with Eduard Shevardnadze, the D.P.R.K. foreign minister said that, in the event of diplomatic relations being established between Moscow and Seoul, the D.P.R.K. would consider itself not bound by the pledges not to create its own nuclear weapons." According to Japanese press reports based on Soviet sources, Foreign Minister Kim Yong-nam also handed Shevardnadze a memorandum, one clause of which stated that if Moscow established relations with South Korea, the North Korean-Soviet military alliance would lose validity and that "we will have no option but to take measures to produce ourselves those weapons that we have heretofore relied on from our alliance."

Focus on U.S. Alleged Nuclear Weapons

One North Korean objective in constructing an apparent nuclear-capable facility at Yongbyon appears to have been to create a bargaining chip to force the withdrawal of U.S. nuclear weapons from South Korea. The North Korean Vice Minister of Foreign Affairs stated in April 1991 that North Korea's decision to sign the Nuclear Non-Proliferation Treaty (NPT) in 1985 "was aimed at creating a condition for the withdrawal of U.S. nuclear arms in the South." Since North Korea signed the NPT, it has not fulfilled the treaty obligation to place its nuclear installations under inspection by the International Atomic Energy Agency (IAEA). The North Korean government has asserted that it will not allow IAEA inspection until the United States removes nuclear weapons from South Korea and ends the "nuclear threat" to North Korea.

Pyongyang has laid out these conditions in the form of a number of proposals for negotiations with the United States: bilateral talks with the United States; tripartite talks involving North Korea, South Korea, and the United States; and an international conference involving North Korea, South Korea, the United States, China, and the Soviet Union aimed at creating a nuclear-free zone for Korea. The North Korean government also has stated that the United States must provide a "legal written document" or "legal assurances" that it will not use nuclear weapons against North Korea or pose a "nuclear threat" to North Korea. North Korean proposals also have called for inspection of U.S. military bases in South Korea by a joint North Korean-South Korean team.

A Possible U.S. Troop Withdrawal

The pronouncements and policies of the Kim Il-sung regime suggest that it seeks broader objectives than the removal of U.S. nuclear weapons from South Korea. One is to turn any negotiation over nuclear weapons into a broader negotiation for the withdrawal of all U.S. troops from South Korea; or, as a step in this direction, expand a negotiation to discuss restrictions on U.S. military exercises and various types of U.S. weapons systems in South Korea.

North Korea's demand that the United States end the "nuclear threat" is aimed at a broad array of U.S. military activities in South Korea. North Korea applies the term "nuclear threat" to U.S.-South Korean military exercises, which it usually describes as "nuclear war exercises." North Korea has been vehement in denouncing as a nuclear war exercise the big U.S.-South Korean Team Spirit exercise held annually, and North Korea has used Team Spirit several times as a pretext for breaking off negotiations with South Korea. North Korea also has described U.S. combat aircraft stationed in South Korea as posing a nuclear threat.

North Korea has called for an end of the U.S. "nuclear umbrella" protection of South Korea, an end to U.S. military overflights and port calls of South Korea, termination of U.S. military exercises in which nuclear "equipment" is used, and a total U.S. troop withdrawal.

Stronger Deterrence Against the United States and South Korea

North Korea also may have other objectives related to military deterrence. The North Korean government has displayed a detailed awareness of the capabilities of U.S. military forces in and around Korea. U.S. and British press reports from Pyongyang and Beijing have asserted that the North Korean government was shocked at the effectiveness of the United States and the allies in crushing Iraq during the Persian Gulf war, and that it was reassessing its own military strategy. Such a reassessment could strengthen the arguments in Pyongyang for a nuclear weapons capability to strengthen deterrence against any U.S. and/or South Korean decision to take military measures against North Korea.

In the North Korean context, deterrence has meant dissuading Seoul and Washington from retaliating against North Korea for the repeated aggressive and terrorist acts committed by the North Korean government, especially in the 1980s: the blowing up of 17 cabinet and top advisory officials of the R.O.K. government in Rangoon, Burma (1983), a commando attack on a South Korean nuclear power plant (1983), and the blowing up of a South Korean airliner (1987). The R.O.K. government reportedly came close to ordering retaliation for the airliner bombing. High-ranking North Korean officials, who advocate and plan such acts, could argue that possession of an atomic deterrence would give North Korea the flexibility to continue such a confrontational strategy in the future.

Prevention of Diplomatic and Political Erosion

North Korea's recent diplomatic setbacks and its growing political isolation could be used by proponents of an atomic weapons capability to argue that this would compel other governments to give more attention to North Korea and its interests. North

Korean statements to Soviet Foreign Minister Shevardnadze in September 1990, as described above, were an attempt to use the threat of nuclear weapons to influence the Soviet government on key policy issues affecting North Korea.

A nuclear weapons capability also could serve North Korea's policy of building relations with radical regimes like Iran, Syria, Libya, Cuba, (and possibly Iraq), including stepped-up sales of missiles and other arms to these states. Nuclear weapons technology could be a valuable commodity which Pyongyang could offer to these regimes (or other friendly countries) in exchange for economic and political support. A number of these governments reportedly are attempting to acquire nuclear weapons technology.

Dictatorial regimes often view advanced weapons systems as serving domestic political needs. North Korean leaders may believe that the status of a nuclear weapons power would provide the Kim Il-sung regime another pillar of strength and security at home, add to the mythology of Kim's invincibility, and help him ward off any domestic political challenges. The regime has demonstrated apprehension that the collapse of Eastern European and Soviet communist governments, political liberalization in the Soviet Union, and the 1989 pro-democracy movement in China could stimulate domestic opposition to Kim Il-sung and to Kim's plan to have his son, Kim Chong-il, succeed him. Government statements and other reports indicate that opposition exists.

Agreements with South Korea and the IAEA

On Jan. 31, 1992, North Korea signed an agreement with the International Atomic Energy Agency (IAEA) providing for IAEA inspection of nuclear facilities in North Korea. North Korea apparently decided to sign the accord in response to U.S. and South Korean moves since September 1991, including the withdrawal of U.S. nuclear weapons from South Korea and declarations by R.O.K. President Roh Tae-woo that there are no nuclear weapons on South Korean soil, that South Korea would not manufacture or possess nuclear weapons and would not build nuclear reprocessing plants, and that South Korea would agree to a system of mutual North-South inspections. Pressures from a worsening economy and China also may have been factors in the North Korean decision.

North Korea first signed an agreement with South Korea on Dec. 13, 1991, on reconciliation and cooperation, which contains a pledge of non-aggression and establishes committees to negotiate an opening of contacts, cooperation, and arms reduction. Then, on Dec. 31, 1991, it signed a Joint Declaration for a Nuclear-Free Korean Peninsula. North Korea and South Korea pledge not to possess, manufacture, or use nuclear weapons and not to possess reprocessing and uranium enrichment facilities. They agree to negotiate the establishment of a mutual nuclear inspection system.

Because of the reported U.S. intelligence estimates that Pyongyang's plutonium reprocessing plant will begin operating as early as mid-1992, key questions arising from these agreements are: (1) how quickly will North Korea ratify the IAEA agreement and submit to the IAEA a list of facilities for inspection; (2) how extensive the list will be and whether it will include all structures at Yongbyon and facilities at Bakchon; and (3) whether North Korea will negotiate seriously over a North-South inspection system and accept intrusive South Korean inspection of its facilities.

0114

In signing the IAEA agreement, North Korean officials said that ratification by North Korea's parliament could take up to 12 months. One official said later that ratification was possible in April 1992. This raises a strong possibility that North Korea hopes to delay any IAEA inspection, since the parliament has no record of independence from President Kim Il-sung. In meetings with South Korean officials, the North Koreans have rejected South Korea's proposal for "pilot inspections" of facilities in April 1992 and have counterproposed negotiations over the specifics of implementation of the December 31 denuclearization agreement and joint action to secure an international guarantee for a non-nuclear Korea. North Korea also has begun to charge that Japan is plotting to produce nuclear weapons, using Japanese plutonium reprocessing plants — thus suggesting a possible new North Korean condition or demand. Kim Il-sung raised the Japanese reprocessing issue during the Feb. 18-21, 1992, North-South Prime Ministers' meetings. He also issued new demands for a total U.S. military withdrawal from South Korea.

It now seems that there will be no inspection until June 1992 at the earliest. Since the signing of the December 31 Joint Declaration, there has been no sign of activity at Yongbyon to indicate that a dismantling of the reprocessing plant has begun.

Implications for U.S. Policy

The apparent North Korean nuclear weapons program has numerous foreign policy and security implications for the United States. These unquestionably would grow even more complex if North Korea completes the Yongbyon facility over the next 2 years.

Military Implications

North Korea's possession of nuclear weapons would increase the danger that any new Korean war would turn into a nuclear conflict. It likely would affect the perceptions of North Korean and U.S. and South Korean military strategists regarding the status and composition of deterrence and military strategy options in various contingencies. A more unstable situation would develop if North Korean leaders concluded that nuclear weapons gave them more military options toward South Korea, or if South Korean leaders decided on drastic military countermeasures. Moreover, many experts believe that the situation in North Korea and between North Korea and South Korea will be especially unstable during the period of succession following Kim Il-sung's death (he will be 80 years old in April) and that North Korea's possession of nuclear weapons would increase the danger of conflict even further.

South Korean Reactions

South Korea's reactions to a North Korean atomic weapons capability could become a serious problem for the United States. Both governments see this as a security threat; but South Korea views the issue within the confines of North Korea-South Korea relations, whereas, the U.S. Government also perceives it as a threat to its global non-proliferation policy. The U.S. Administration in Washington would perceive U.S. interests to lie in influencing South Korea to coordinate policy with the United States and refrain from adopting diverse or unilateral policies. So far, Seoul

CRS-7

and Washington have coordinated closely. However, several possible courses of action by South Korea could confront the United States with undesired situations.

Bush Administration officials and several executive branch specialists on Korea presently are concerned that the R.O.K. government may lower the priority it gives to the nuclear weapons issue in coming months, after reaching the agreement with North Korea on reconciliation and cooperation on Dec. 13, 1991. President Roh Tae-woo may wish to avoid a confrontation with North Korea over nuclear weapons in 1992 while he seeks to negotiate follow-up accords with Pyongyang (as provided for in the December 13 agreement) — even if North Korea nears completion of the Yongbyon facility. Presidential and National Assembly elections in 1992 may add political incentives for Roh to avoid a confrontation.

Nevertheless, there is sentiment within the R.O.K. government, particularly within the army and the intelligence organs, for a tougher policy. Such a policy could include consideration of a preemptive military response. On Apr. 12, 1991, South Korea's Defense Minister, Lee Jong-koo, stated that South Korea might launch a commando attack on Yongbyon if North Korea continued with its construction there. The influential South Korean magazine, *Wolgan Choson*, reported in the March 1991 issue that South Korean defense planners were studying the option of an aerial strike at Yongbyon. South Korean government officials reportedly told U.S. Defense Secretary Cheney in November 1991 that they did not favor the direct use of force against North Korea, but such sentiment no doubt exists.

A growth of nuclear tensions on the Korean peninsula thus could also endanger political stability in South Korea and the more democratic political system that has emerged since the end of military-dominated government in 1987. The potential exists for discord between the government and army over the proper response to the North Korean nuclear program, especially if military measures are considered. The army dominated the South Korean government from 1961-1987.

Some observers and commentators have expressed concern that the R.O.K. government would consider its own nuclear weapons program in response to North Korea. South Korea currently has nine nuclear reactors for the production of nuclear power. South Korea stores spent uranium fuel from these reactors. It has no reprocessing plant, but is believed to be technically capable of constructing one. During the late 1970s, President Park Chung-hee had government agencies examine a nuclear weapons option in response to U.S. proposals for the withdrawal of American troops from Korea.

U.S.-Japan Relations

The Japanese government's policy towards the North Korean nuclear weapons program became a central issue in U.S.-Japan security relations when Japan and North Korea agreed in September 1990 to negotiate the normalization of relations. The Bush Administration urged the Japanese government to press the North Koreans on the nuclear arms question in the talks.

The Japanese government has set as a condition for normalization that North Korea allow IAEA inspection of the Yongbyon facility. At the end of 1991, Japanese officials began to assert that North Korea must dismantle the reprocessing plant. Some observers believe that Japanese pressure may be the most effective kind of outside influence because of North Korea's worsening economic conditions and its apparent desire to secure Japanese financial assistance. Thus, the United States will have a continuing interest in Japanese diplomacy remaining in parallel with U.S. strategy.

Moreover, if the North Korean nuclear program should lead to a deteriorating security situation on the Korean peninsula, U.S. views regarding Japan's security role in Korea could change. The Persian Gulf crisis demonstrated the willingness of the U.S. Government to press Japan to make a major financial commitment and take a military role in an emerging international security crisis. (See CRS Report 91-444 F, Japan's Response to the Persian Gulf Crisis: Implications for U.S.-Japan Relations). Such sentiment among U.S. policymakers and resultant pressure could be stronger in the case of Korea, given the general trend in American attitudes and the U.S. awareness of Japan's own interests in Korea.

If the United States were to pressure for Japanese military involvement in Korea, acute tensions would arise inside Japan and South Korea, whose peoples share animosities toward one another based on the history of Japanese invasions and occupations of Korea, including the harsh occupation from 1905 to 1945. It also would place severe strains on the Japanese government's adherence to the pacifist provisions of Japan's constitution.

U.S. Relations with the Russia and China

A continued North Korean nuclear weapons program would become more central to U.S. bilateral relations with Russia and China. The United States would seek greater Russian and Chinese support in the forms of direct bilateral pressures on North Korea through denials of aid, cooperation with the United States in the United Nations, and backing for U.S. initiatives. The collapse of the Soviet Union enhances the prospects of Russian support for the U.S. policy. China, however, could face increasingly difficult choices between backing a more assertive U.S. policy and retaining supportive ties to its long-standing ally, North Korea. Russia and China could be expected to react negatively toward any Japanese military involvement in Korea, which historically has been the focus of Russian-Japanese-Chinese rivalries in Northeast Asia.

Impact on U.S. Nonproliferation Policy

The U.S. Government would view the North Korean manufacture of an atomic weapon as a serious breach of the U.S.-led international effort to prevent the further proliferation of nuclear weapons. Because North Korea is a signatory of the NPT, its production of nuclear weapons could undermine international support for the treaty. This could be especially damaging since the treaty is due for an extension in 1995. South Korean and Japanese abilities to produce nuclear weapons could present a danger of escalating proliferation in response to the North Korean manufacture of an atomic bomb. U.S. officials and other American experts fear that North Korea might provide nuclear weapons technology to other radical states, thus further undermining the NPT and the nonproliferation policy.

Current U.S. Policy

The Bush Administration policy has two objectives: 1) inspection of the Yongbyon and other suspected facilities by the IAEA and South Korea and 2) a dismantling of the apparent North Korean reprocessing plant. Several U.S. officials, interviewed for this study, portrayed IAEA and South Korean inspection as useful interim measures that could limit (but not necessarily stop) production of nuclear weapons. The ultimate U.S. goal is a dismantling of the reprocessing plant, according to several statements by Pentagon officials.

U.S. officials and other experts outlined in interviews the weaknesses of the IAEA regime and inspection system, and the NPT regime with regard to a state like North Korea. Under IAEA, governments can limit the number and types of facilities to be inspected. Governments are permitted to construct nuclear reprocessing plants and produce atomic weapons-grade plutonium; IAEA inspectors only monitor the stored plutonium. Nevertheless, weapons-grade plutonium can be hidden, and some experts fear that North Korea might try to hide some portion of reprocessed plutonium from inspectors. North Korea has allowed IAEA inspection of the small Soviet-supplied reactor at Yongbyon but has severely restricted the inspectors, recently limiting them to nighttime inspections. Signatories of the NPT cannot use such plutonium to produce an actual atomic bomb, but the treaty has a provision allowing any signatory to withdraw 90 days after giving notice. In the past, North Korea has threatened to withdraw.

The Bush Administration's strategy so far contains two elements, which it seeks to integrate into a program of pressure on North Korea. The first is to offer North Korea inducements to give up its nuclear weapons program. These are intended to meet North Korea's most often stated condition for allowing IAEA inspection and take away Pyongyang's justification for its nuclear weapons policy. The United States and South Korea have announced and affected several key inducements since September 1991. The United States withdrew nuclear weapons from South Korea by December 1991, after President Bush decided to do so in October. President Roh, as stated previously, declared South Korea free of nuclear weapons, disavowed nuclear weapons and reprocessing facilities, and offered North Korea mutual inspections -- including inspection of U.S. military bases in South Korea. The United States and South Korea also suspended the Team Spirit military exercise scheduled for February 1992. The United States initiated a diplomatic meeting with North Korea at the United Nations in January 1992, the highest level of diplomatic contact yet between them. Earlier, the Bush Administration issued a "negative security guarantee" to North Korea: a general statement of U.S. policy that the United States would not use nuclear weapons against a non-nuclear power unless that country staged an armed attack against the United States or a U.S. ally and received support from a nuclear weapons state.

The Bush Administration intends these inducements to reinforce the second element of its strategy: a strong diplomatic campaign to encourage other governments to pressure North Korea to agree to IAEA and South Korean inspections and abandon its nuclear weapons program. The State Department has urged Japan, Russia, China, the Western European bloc, Australia, and other countries to pressure North Korea through bilateral talks and in international fora. U.S.-R.O.K. inducements are intended to gain greater Chinese and Russian cooperation by satisfying their desires that the United States make concessions and overtures to North Korea on this and other issues.

CRS-10

The Bush Administration no doubt hopes that these inducements will show governments and publics in allied countries that the United States is making significant efforts to resolve the issue peacefully.

U.S. Policy Prior to North Korean Completion of the Reprocessing Plant

In coming months, the United States will face three complicating factors if North Korea continues with its policy to develop a nuclear weapons capability. This will be the case despite and to a degree because of North Korea's agreements with South Korea and the IAEA. One is the need to produce results within the time period prior to North Korea's completion of the reprocessing plant – possibly as early as mid-1992. A second factor is the possibility that U.S. goals may diverge from those of other governments if North Korea allowed an IAEA inspection in June 1992. It is not certain whether Japan, Russia, China, and other countries would press North Korea to dismantle the reprocessing plant if Pyongyang allowed inspection. A third factor will be the emergence of clearer South Korean priorities on the nuclear weapons issue as North-South negotiations proceed.

Consequently, Bush Administration policy in the first half of 1992 likely will turn more towards pressure on North Korea if Pyongyang does not respond to U.S.-R.O.K. inducements by allowing comprehensive IAEA and South Korean inspections of Yongbyon (and possibly Bakchon). U.S. strategy probably contains or will contain some or all of the following elements:

(1) The Bush Administration is pressing North Korea to ratify immediately the IAEA agreement and agree to full-scale IAEA inspection of all facilities at Yongbyon. According to press reports, the Administration is pressing for inspections no later than June 1992.

(2) The Administration has urged Japan and other allies not to make concessions to North Korea (i.e., Japanese financial aid) even if North Korea allows inspections but, instead, to demand a dismantling of the Yongbyon reprocessing plant.

(3) If North Korea continues with the construction of the reprocessing plant, the Administration can be expected to publicize this and accuse North Korea of violating the provisions banning reprocessing facilities contained in the North Korea-South Korea Joint Declaration for a Nuclear-Free Korean Peninsula. The Administration likely will seek from inspectors verification of a reprocessing plant.

(4) The Administration no doubt will press South Korea to insist on an intrusive inspection system in the North-South negotiations over a mutual inspection agreement; and it undoubtedly will offer South Korea advanced U.S. equipment to conduct inspections. At the Prime Ministers' meeting, Feb. 18-21, 1992, South Korea pressed North Korea unsuccessfully to begin "pilot" inspections by April.

(5) The Administration has urged South Korea to make future negotiations with North Korea on aspects of the Dec. 13, 1991, agreement on reconciliation and cooperation dependent on North Korean agreement to comprehensive inspections.

Options Beyond Diplomacy

The context and agenda of U.S. policy will change if North Korea completes a nuclear reprocessing plant and begins to produce atomic weapons grade plutonium. The United States would face a setback to both its security policy in the Northwest Pacific and its nonproliferation policy. The U.S. Administration would face the choice of adopting stronger measures or modifying the goal of securing North Korean abandonment of the program.

Consideration of Coercive Measures. If diplomacy fails, the U.S. Government might consider stronger measures. Statements by R.O.K. and U.S. officials and recent collective moves against Iraq's nuclear weapons program indicate that at least 4 options likely could be considered:

-- U.N. Security Council action: There are indications that the Bush Administration and South Korea may take the issue to the Security Council in 1992. U.S. proposals could be in stages, calling initially for a Security Council directive to North Korea to allow IAEA inspection of any suspected nuclear weapons facilities. If North Korea refused, the United States could propose economic sanctions or a total economic embargo. China's position could be the main obstacle to Security Council approval of sanctions. Chinese and Russian adherence to an embargo would be crucial to its successful implementation. An economic embargo would signal to North Korea a nearly total isolation on the nuclear weapons issue. It would hurt further the already weakening North Korean economy. Thus, it might contribute to the reported unhappiness over economic policy among some members of the North Korean elite. There is no guarantee, however, that the North Korean government would comply with Security Council conditions. Pyongyang might look to exploit leaks in an embargo, possibly through continued dealings with fellow radical states. North Korea could blunt a U.S.-R.O.K. initiative in the U.N. by allowing a single IAEA inspection in June 1992.

-- A United Nations-authorized air and naval blockade to enforce a U.N.-directed economic embargo against North Korea: this would be similar to the measures against Iraq after the invasion of Kuwait. It could be imposed in reaction to significant leaks in an economic embargo. A blockade would put extreme pressure on North Korea. If China participated, it would prevent Pyongyang from exporting nuclear weapons materials to other radical states. It possibly would have to be a protracted effort over many months. A blockade also would carry the risk of North Korean military action. However, the involvement of the United Nations and support of other governments, especially China and Russia, might deter North Korea from retaliating militarily. The United States and South Korea would require support and/or involvement from Japan, other allies, China, and Russia to obtain U.N. Security Council approval and the full implementation of an air and naval blockade. Securing Chinese consent could be especially difficult.

-- G-7 Action: If securing Security Council action proved impossible or had to be postponed, the United States and South Korea could move through the G-7 group to secure U.S., Western European, and Japanese economic sanctions on North Korea. The G-7 countries also could seek the cooperation of Russia and

CRS-12

92- 4-10 ; 18:14 ;

other potentially sympathetic governments. G-7 economic sanctions, backed by Russia, would penalize North Korea economically almost as much as a U.N.-imposed embargo. Japan would be the key to the effectiveness. The most effective sanctions (G-7 or U.N.) would require Japan to cut off the flow of money and capital from the pro-North Korean segment of the ethnic Korean community in Japan. This has been for years North Korea's chief source of foreign exchange. However, the Japanese government could face domestic turmoil instigated by ethnic Koreans. Imposing an embargo would be a politically difficult decision.

— A surgical air strike aimed at destroying the Yongbyon facility and any other discovered in the future: South Korean and U.S. officials have spoken of this option. Air operations in the Persian Gulf war indicate that this likely would be effective in eliminating the reprocessing facility and the nuclear reactors at Yongbyon. However, it would not eliminate North Korea's nuclear weapons program if Pyongyang has other, more concealed facilities in other locations for producing nuclear weapons materials. An air strike would carry a high risk that North Korea would retaliate militarily against a selected target or targets in South Korea or, worse, that North Korea might launch an invasion of South Korea. If North Korea did not retaliate militarily, its record suggests that it might launch future terrorists acts against South Korea and the United States.

— A buildup of U.S. conventional and nuclear forces in and around Korea but no direct military action against North Korea: this would represent a modification of the basic U.S. objective of preventing North Korea from fulfilling its nuclear weapons program. A new primary goal would be to contain and deter an expected nuclear armed North Korea. A force buildup also would be intended to reassure South Korea of U.S. resolve if the United States decided against direct military action against North Korea. In November 1991, Secretary Cheney announced that the United States would not withdraw troops from South Korea during the 1993-95 stage of a planned Western Pacific force reduction. (The United States is withdrawing about 13,000 troops from Korea and Japan in the 1991-1992 period.) A military buildup would add several billion dollars annually to the cost of U.S. military forces in the Western Pacific (about $16.4 million annually, including forces in Alaska, Hawaii, and Guam, according to an August 1991 General Accounting Office report).

FOR ADDITIONAL READING

Bermudez, Joseph A. North Korea's nuclear programme. Jane's intelligence review, September 1991: 404-411.

Mack, Andrew. North Korea and the bomb. Foreign policy, summer 1991: 87-104.

Spector, Leonard S. and Jacqueline R. Smith. North Korea: The next nuclear nightmare? Arms control today, March 1991: 8-13.

CRS-13

9

관리	
번호	

외 무 부

종 별 :

번 호 : USW-1839   일 시 : 92 0410 1858

수 신 : 장관(미일)동구일,정총)

발 신 : 주 미 대사

제 목 : 미의회 북한 핵관계 보고서 발간

대: WUS-1182

연: USW-1334(3.16)

1. 당관 박인국 서기관은 금 4.10 LARRY NIKSCH CRD(CONRESSIONAL RESEARCHSERVICE) 아주담당관을 면담하고 자신이 집필한 북한 핵무기 개발에 관한 CRS 보고서 4.8 자 개정판을 입수하였는 바 금번 개정판은 북한의 핵개발 현황, 북한의 핵개발 목적, 북한 핵문제를 위요한 미국의 정책 그리고 북한 핵개발 저지가 실패하였을 때의 제제 대안들에 관해 언급하고 있음.(사본 팩스편 송부)

2. NIKSCH 담당관은 금번 개정판 내용은 3.11 자 판과 동일하며 대호 KGB 극비문서 관련 내용만 추가 되었다고 언급하면서 CRS 내 러시아 전문가들은 "논거와 사실"지의 편집 관행상 오보를 했을 가능성이 없다는 결론을 내리고 동지 보도내용을 매우 심각하게 받아들이고 있다고 하면서 80 년대에 쏘-북한 관계의 특수성을 고려할 때 KGB 가 북한 권력층 내부 침투대가로 쏘련 핵기술 지원을 주도했을 가능성이 농후하다는 견해를 표명하면서 동지 보도 내용에 관한 추가 정보가 있는지를 문의하였음.

3. 상기 KGB 문서 보도관련 당관 보고와 추가 정보가 있으면 봉보 바람.

첨부:USWF-2231

(대사 현홍주-국장)

예고:일반 92.12.31.

미주국	차관	1차보	구주국	외정실	분석관	청와대	안기부

주 미 대 사 관

USW(F) : 2231   년월일 : 92.4.10 시간 : 18:58

수 신 : 장 관 (미일, 동구일, 경흥)

발 신 : 주 미 대 사

제 목 : 첨부   (출처 :   )

보 안 통 제	乙

(-   -   )

외신 1과 똥 제	

0123

공 란

공 란

분류번호	보존기간

발 신 전 보

번 호 : WUS-1975   920427 1904 FO   종별 : _____

수 신 : 주 미 대사. 총영사

발 신 : 장 관 (미이)

제 목 : 미 회계감사국 보고서

4. 26(일)자 국내 언론들은 귀지발 연합통신을 인용, 미 회계감사국(GAO)이

4. 23. 상하 양원 군사위에 제출한 보고서("Perspectives on Worldwide

Threats and Implications for U.S. Forces" 제하) 내용과 함께 동 보고서

에 게재된 미전략연구소 테일러 부소장의 한국전 가상 논문 내용에 관해

상세 보도하고 있는바 동 GAO 보고서 전문 입수 송부바라며 아울러 동

보고서 내용에 대한 귀관의 1차적 평가도 함께 보고 바람. 끝.

(미주국장 정태익)

예고 : 92. 12. 31. 일반

검토필(1992. 6. 30)

예고문에 의거 재분류(19)
직위   성명

보 안 통 제	

앙 고 재		기안자 성명		과 장	심의관	국 장		차 관	장 관		외신과통제

0126

"북한의 한국공격 가능성 20%"

미 회계감사국 보고·테일러 논문 요지

미국 의회의 예산심의와 법안 형성에 근거를 제시하는 일을 맡고 있는 회계감사국(GAO)은 최근 한 보고서에서 동아시아와 태평양지역의 위협과 관련해 여러 선택 가운데 북한이 남한을 공격할 가능성을 배제할 수 없으며 이 경우 전쟁양상은 1백20여일 지속되는 비교적 장기전이 될 것이라고 주장했다.

23일 상하 양원 군사위원회에 제출된 '세계의 위협과 미군에 대한 그 의미'란 제목의 이 보고서는 냉전 이후의 새로운 세계에서 미국에 대한 군사위협 발생 가능성과 그 의미, 필요한 대응 등에 관해 지난해 10월 회계감사국 주최로 정부관리들과 민간 안보전문가들이 모여 토의한 결과를 간추린 것이다.

이 보고서에 실린 윌리엄 테일러 미국 전략국제연구소 부소장의 논문 '동아시아와 태평양─북한의 군사위협과 미국의 대응'도 미국의 한반도 군사전략과 관련히 주목된다.

다음은 회계감사국의 보고서와 테일러의 논문 요지이다.
〈편집자〉
◇미국 회계감사국 보고서
미국은 중국을 위협으로 인식하고 있지 않지만 중국은 지역

분쟁 해결을 위해 한정된 지역에서 단기간에 집중적으로 무력을 쓰는 전략을 채택한 듯하며 지역패권의 확립을 꾀하는 조짐이 강하다. 중앙에서 관리하는 중국의 핵구기는 옛 소련의 핵무기보다도 우려를 불러일으키고 있다.

특히 남중국해에 관한 중국의 주장이 관철되면 해상수송로를

미군 첨단정밀무기로 우위지켜
한국 분담 증대 압력…중, 지역패권 조짐

통제할 수 있어 남한, 일본, 대만의 석유수송에 위협을 주게 된다.

불안정하고 예측불가능한 북한은 남북 병합에 전력투구하는 등 위험이 증대되고 있다. 또 동중국해와 동해에서 미 해군 활동을 위협하기에 충분한 미사일공격 가능 고속정을 보유하고 있어 미 해군의 계속적인 주둔이 필요하다.
◇테일러의 논문
북한이 앞으로 2년 동안 남한을 침공할 가능성은 객관적이라고 생각되는 요인들을 바탕으로 분석하면 20%쯤이다.

한반도에서 전쟁이 일어나면

한국과 미국은 지역국가와 세계의 많은 나라들이 가담한 걸프전과 같은 강력한 유대를 이루지는 못할 것이다. 그리고 한국에는 석유가 없다. 북한의 남침은 일본에도 위협이 되겠지만 일본 헌법은 군사적 모험을 금지하고 있다. 일본이 가담한다면 그 형태는 잠수함 수색활동, 공중정찰, 기뢰제거 등 중요하지만 소극적인 것이 될 것이다.

북한은 대규모의 특수부대를 갖고 있고 이라크보다 소련식 전략에 더 충실하며 해군은 20척의 공격용 잠수함과 몇십척의 미사일 탑재 군함을 보유하고 있어 전쟁 초기에 이들이 파괴되지 않을 경우 미국과 연합국의 군함을 격침할 능력을 보유할 것이다.

한반도의 전쟁은 걸프전 때보다는 훨씬 힘들 것이다. 한반도의 분쟁이 1백20여일은 지속된다고 평가한 91년 합참 보고서는 정확한 것 같다.

한반도에서도 걸프전 때처럼 첨단 정밀무기를 이용하는 집중적인 공군력 사용이 미국의 중요한 군사적 우위를 지켜줄 것이다.

걸프전에서 그 가치를 빛낸, 여러 각도에서 정밀무기를 발사할 수 있는 무장헬리콥터의 기동성과 유연성은 한반도에서도 유용할 것이다. 미국은 유사시 증원군을 바다와 하늘을 통해 한반도에 투입해야 하며 이 병력 배치작전이 한반도에서의 작전 승패를 좌우할 것이다. 지상군 수송과 장비 이동을 위해 전략적 기동성을 강화하는 방안이 요구된다.

전쟁이 일어나면 3개 사단을 30일 안에 배치한다는 미국의 새로운 전략은 성공이 의문시된다. 한미연합사 사령관은 공중공격으로 시간을 벌어야 하며 그 속도는 하루에 2천5백회 출격한 걸프전 때보다 더 빨라야 하고 B-52 중폭격기에 의한 폭격도 강화돼야 할 것이다.

한반도에서의 비상사태를 고려해 공군을 전진배치하고 일본, 알류샨 열도 등지에 전쟁물자를 비축하는 전략이 채택될 경우 한국 정부가 여기에 필요한 경비 분담을 더 요구받을 것이다.

주한미군은 1만명선으로 감축될 수 있다. 제2사단을 어떻게 감축하느냐에 따라 상당한 경비를 절감할 수 있으며 북한의 전사력 감축을 유도할 수 있다.

한국 정부는 현역 2개 여단을 보강함으로써 그 공백을 메울 수도 있다. 또한 한국으로부터 미군의 완전 철수를 요구하는 미국 여론도 무마할 수 있을 것이다.
〈워싱턴=연합〉

한겨레 (92. 4. 26)

0127

가상韓国戰 北남침 격퇴 百20일 걸린다

테일러 美전략연구소 부소장 분석

개전初 남한 항구·공항 집중공습 당해

「多国籍軍」난망… 美 무장헬機 위력 발휘

[워싱턴=윌리엄테일러] 美전략국제문제 연구소의 부소장은 23일 美의회 계감사원(GAO)이 상하 원 군사위에 제출한 보고서에 수록된 연구논문을 통해 북한의 군사력을 객관적이라고 생각되는 요 인대로 걸프戰과 한반도의 가상 전쟁을 집중 비교했다.

다음은「동아시아와 태평 양:북한의 군사위협과 미 국의 대응」이란 그의 논문 요지이다.

앞으로 2년간 北韓이 한반도에서 전쟁이 일어 나면 한국과 미국이 북한 에 대항하여 각국의 유대 를 결집할수도 있겠지만지 금은 강력한 유대를 만들지 는 못할것이다. 그러나 英 국방장관이나 韓美 연합사 令관의 입장에서는 담장오 적으로 중요한 국가로만든 흡밥 전쟁이 일어날 가능 석유가 한국에는 없다. 일 석이 50%로 높아질 것이 본도 딜레마에 빠질 것이 다.

북한이 남침한다면 日 本에도 위협이 되겠지만고 고 병참기지 활용문제를 놓 본의 헌법은 군사적모험을 금지하고 있다. 아마 일본 이 가담할수있는 형태는저 그리고 쿠웨이트를 세계 량상을 제시하고 있다.

한반도에서 전쟁이 일어 날 경우 미국과 연합국의 군비보다 훨씬 능력을 보유할 것이다.

한반도 전쟁은 걸프전 때 보다는 훨씬 힘들고 걸 프전때의 1백시간보다 91년의 한국군보고서는 한반도 의 북한이 약 1백20은 지속된다고 평가했으며 어 느모로보나 그 평가는 정 확하다고 같다.

걸프戰에서 공군력의 중 요성이 가장 분명히 확인 되었으며 한반도에서도 첨 도에서도 유용할 것이다.

◇윌리엄 테일러

는 달리 분쟁 그 순간부터 개입할 것으로 생각할수있 다. 또 아라비아 사막과는 달리 한반도가 구릉투성한 산과 깊은 계곡 등 세계에 서 가장 어려운 전투 지형 을 갖고 있다는 점도 다른

북한은 남에 침투할 대규모의 특수부대를 갖고 있고, 이라크 보다는 소련 식전략에 보다 충실하며 해군은 20척의 공격용 잠

단 정밀 무기를 이용하는 집중적인 공군력 사용이 미국의 중요한 군사적 우위를 지켜 줄 것이다.

그러나 일부 무기들은 산악지대라는 지형상의 제 약 때문에 걸프전에서 같은 위력을 휘두르지못할수도있다. 걸프전은 현대전에서 헬 리콥터의 가치를 일깨워주 었으며 여러 각도에서 정 밀무기를 발사할 수 있는 무장헬리콥터의 능력은 지 상군에게 귀중한 자산이 되 고 있는데 근무장헬리콥터 의 기동성과 유연성이 한반 도에서도 유용할 것이다.

전 (92.4.26)

0128

476 북한 핵문제 미국 동향

"韓半島 분쟁再發땐 100일이상 持久戰"

―테일러 美전략연구소 副所長의 가상시나리오

"2년이내 南侵가능성은 20%線 美증원군 空海신속배치가 관건"

北韓의 金日成주석(오른쪽)이 24일 平壤에서 열린 人民軍창설 60주년기념행사에 참석차, 金正日(왼쪽)과 캄보디아의 시아누크公(가운데)이 박수를 치고있다. 〈平壤 AP연합〉

서울
(92. 4. 26)

Kim Il-sung may attack S. Korea to stay in power: GAO report

WASHINGTON (Yonhap) — One of North Korean President Kim Il-sung's three choices if he is to rescue his country from its desperate economic situation is attacking South Korea to stay in power, according to a report submitted to the U.S. Senate and the House by the U.S. Government Accounting Office (GAO).

In an April 16 report, titled "Perspectives on Worldwide Threats and Implications for U.S. Forces," that summarized the views presented at the Oct. 31 conference, the GAO report said Kim had three choices.

"First, he could keep the society isolated from outside help, but this would probably lead to a coup or a revolution. Second, he could open the country gradually, and if he held onto power during the transition of the regime to his son, Kim Jong-il, he might buy time. Third, he could attack South Korea to stay in power," it said.

With 60 percent of North Korean forces deployed close to the Demilitarized Zone and well protected, 30 percent of the South Korean army would be decimated in the first half hour.

"One participant said that North
(Continued on Page 12)

AP-Yonhap

North Korea's leader, Kim Il-sung (far right), acknowledges cheers from his men during a gathering Friday in Pyongyang to celebrate the 60th anniversary of the founding of the (North) Korean People's Army. Clapping at far left is Kim Jong-il, son of the North Korean leader. At center is Cambodian Prince Norodom Sihanouk. Others are unidentified.

K. H (92. 4. 26)

0130

GAO report

From Page 1

Korea might attack South Korea at any time, resulting in a war that would probably last about 120 days....

"In such a war, the United States would need to hold some part of the peninsula and reinforce rapidly. If the United States reinforced quickly, South Korean and U.S. forces would stop the North Korean troops, and North Korea would lose the war. The United States does not currently have the aircraft or sealift to do this. The United States would have to maintain staging areas and capabilities in Japan to be able to counter a North Korean attack.

Most participants, according to the report, agreed that the United States needs a military presence in East Asia to protect U.S. interests.

"The United States will need to retain a presence to deter China, enhance Japanese confidence in U.S. security, and allay Southeast Asian concerns. U.S. forces will assure Japan that it does not need to build an offensive capability, which would concern other countries, especially in Southeast Asia and China, that were victims of Japanese aggression in World War II," the report said.

China, which sees North Korea as its only close ideological ally, would not permit U.N. Security Council resolutions against the North or boycott council meetings, the report said.

The GAO-sponsored conference was held to offer insight into potential military threats to U.S. security interests and necessary modifications to current and planned U.S.

■forces to meet those threats.

South Korea should be able to defend itself by 1995 or 1996, a participants said.

"The United States should draw down to one reinforced brigade or reinforced battalion task force under the 2nd Infantry — about 10,000 ground troops. There may be a U.S. promise to South Korea not to go below 30,000, but Congress will not keep that many troops there...The United States also needs to have ready-deployment sealift capabilities for heavy forces that may be required in a Korean conflict...

"The United States is shifting military responsibility slowly. It plans to withdraw 7,000 forces between now and 1993, with follow-on withdrawals that are anticipated to result in a level of 10,000 troops. South Korea is prepared to pick up the slack from these reductions-....South Korea should be able to defend itself by 1995 or 1996. Hopefully, by that time, North Korea will no longer pose a threat."

As for U.S. forces in Japan, the report said the United States might be able to withdraw its forces from Japan in four to five years, "but it should not do anything precipitous because that might encourage a North Korean attack, given Kim Il-sung's desperate situation."

Once the North Korean threat goes away, Japan could dissolve the U.S.-Japanese security treaty.

The report quoted the book "The Japan That Can Say No" as saying: "Only the nuclear situation in North Korea makes the treaty necessary, and once that threat is gone, it is Japan's business to expand militarily in Asia if it wishes. This is a minority position, however, that is regarded as extreme even within the conservative wing of the ruling Liberal Democratic Party."

외 무 부

종 별 :

번 호 : USW-2124   일 시 : 92 0427 2105

수 신 : 장 관 (미일, 미이, 정특, 국기, 기정)

발 신 : 주 미 대사

제 목 : 미 안보관계 회계감사원 보고서

대: WUS-1975

1. 주재국 회계감사원(GAO)은 미국 안보에 대한 잠재적인 군사적 위협에 대처하기 위한 미 군사력 조정 필요성에 관한 협의를 위해 91.10.31. "미국의 국가안보에 대한 전세계에서의 위협" 주제하의 세미나를 개최하였으며 동 세미나의 결과 보고서를 지난 4.23. 상. 하원 군사위원회에 제출하였음.(동 보고서는 본문및 회의 참석자들의 발표문을 수록한 부록으로 구성되어 있는바, 보고서의 아국관계 부분및 TAYLOR CSIS 부소장의 발표문은 USW(F)-2628 로 FAX 송부하며 동 보고서는 명 4.28. 파편 송부 예정임)

2. 상기 보고서의 4 항 "동아시아와 태평양" 부분중 "북한의 위협"이라는 소제목하에 요약된 세미나 토의 내용에 따르면 한 참석자는 북한이 세계 제 4 위의 군사력을 보유하고 있으며, GNP 의 25 % 를 군사비에 지출하고 있고, 북한은 동지나해와 동해에서 미국의 해상작전에 위협을 주기에 충분한 정도의 미사일 탑재 공격선을 보유하고 있다고 하면서 미국은 동 위협에 대처하기 위한 상주 해군력이 필요하다고 주장하였음. 검토필 (1'2. 6. 3이 인 l3

3. 다른 참석자들은 북한이 어느때라도 남침을 감행, 전쟁이 야기될 수 있는바, 동 전쟁은 약 120 일간 지속될 것이며, 전쟁개시 30 분만에 한국군의 30 %가 손실되고 서울이 함락될 것이라고 언급하였으며, 또 다른 참석자들은 한국의 군사력을 감안할때 서울은 함락되지 않을 것으로 본다는 견해를 피력하였음.

4. 세미나 참석자중 한사람인 WILLIAM TAYLOR CSIS 부소장은 상기 세미나에서 "동아시아와 태평양: 북한의 위협및 미국의 대응" 이라는 제목하에 발표문을 제출하였는바, TAYLOR 부장은 유럽과는 달리 동아시아, 특히 한반도의 상황에는 실질적 변화가 없으며 북한이 장래 2 년내 한국에 대해 무력을 사용할 가능성이 약 20

미주국 안기부	장관	차관	1차보	미주국	국기국	외정실	분석관	청와대

0132

PAGE 1   92.04.28   11:15

외신 2과 통제관 BX

% 정도 된다고 평가하였음.

또한 TAYLOR 부소장은 미국이 한반도에서의 위협에 대처하기 위한 방안은 신속한 병력 이용이 가능하도록 전함과 항공기에 대한 군사비를 증대하거나 장비와 병력의 전진배치를 늘리는 것인바, 장비와 병력의 전진배치가 보다 합리적인 방안이라고 언급하였음.

5. 상기 세미나는 작년 10 월 냉전종식 이후 미국의 적정 군사력 유지 수준에 관한 각계의 의견 수렴을 위해 개최된 것이며 북한의 위협 부분은 북한 핵무기 개발문제가 본격적으로 거론되기 이전에 이루어진 것으로 일반적인 대한반도 안보문제를 다룬 것임.

첨부: USW(F)-2628(10 매). 끝.

(대사 현홍주-국장)

예고: 92.12.31. 까지

주 미 대 사 관

USW(F) : 2628　　　년월일 : 92.4.27. 시간 : 2105

수　신 : 장　관 (미안, 미이, 정통, 국기, 기정)

발　신 : 주 미 대 사

제　목 : 첨부물

보등 안제 838

(출처 :　　　　)

(2628 - 10 -1)

외신 1과 통 제

0134

GAO

United States
General Accounting Office
Washington, D.C. 20548

National Security and
International Affairs Division

B-247586

April 16, 1992

The Honorable Sam Nunn
Chairman, Committee on Armed Services
United States Senate

The Honorable Les Aspin
Chairman, Committee on Armed Services
House of Representatives

This report summarizes the views presented on October 31, 1991, at a
GAO-sponsored conference on worldwide threats to U.S. national security.[1]
The conference was designed to provide insight into potential military
threats to U.S. security interests and necessary modifications to current
and planned U.S. forces to meet those threats.

Conference participants, including defense analysts and retired military
officers, discussed and analyzed the possibility of U.S. and allied
involvement in various regional contingencies in Europe and the Soviet
Union, East Asia and the Pacific, and the Near East and South Asia. Topics
ranged from the possibility of nuclear war to a general discussion of
low-intensity conflict. To serve as a starting point for discussion, we asked
several of the participants to provide papers representing a wide range of
views.

The participants agreed that for many years the Soviet/Warsaw Pact threat
to Europe shaped U.S. force planning but that the Soviet Union[2] no longer
posed a conventional threat. Nuclear weapons held by the former Soviet
republics and other nations, however, remain a concern. There was no
agreement on the methodology for sizing U.S. forces. Some argued for
sizing based on specific threats; others argued for flexibility to meet any
and all contingencies and cited the Gulf War as an example.

The participants suggested several options for responding to the changing
security environment, including assisting the former Soviet republics with
denuclearization, reducing forward deployed U.S. forces in Europe and the
Pacific, increasing U.S. efforts at missile nonproliferation in the Near East,

---

[1] In April 1988, GAO co-sponsored a congressionally mandated conference on the NATO-Warsaw Pact
balance of conventional forces (GAO/NSIAD-89-23).

[2] In October 1991, the breakup of the Soviet Union was in process.

0135

and reforming the organization and control of low-intensity conflict operations.

Details of the conference are in appendixes I through V. Following the conference, we gave participants an opportunity to revise their discussion papers and comment on the abstracts prepared by our staff. The papers are included in a supplement to this report. Abstracts of the papers are in appendix VI. A list of conference participants and their biographies are in appendix VII. This report and the supplement reflect the participants' views and opinions, which are not necessarily those of GAO.

We are sending copies of this report and its supplement to the Secretary of Defense, the Secretary of State, and appropriate congressional members. Copies will also be made available to others on request.

This report was prepared under the direction of Joseph E. Kelley, Director, Security and International Relations Issues, who may be reached on (202) 275-4128 if you or your staff have any questions. Other major contributors are listed in appendix VIII.

Frank C. Conahan
Assistant Comptroller General

0136

The North Korean Threat

According to one participant, North Korea is unstable and unpredictable and the threat there is growing. Before Iraq attacked Kuwait, Defense Secretary Cheney said that his main area of concern was the Korean peninsula. With Iraq's military reduced, North Korea has the fourth largest military in the world. It devotes about 25 percent of its gross national product to the military, which directs all its energies to reunification with South Korea. It uses Soviet equipment, doctrine, strategy, and tactics. It has large, forward-deployed forces and rapid deployment and airlift capabilities that threaten South Korea. Its navy has enough missile-capable, fast attack craft to threaten U.S. naval operations in the East China Sea and the Sea of Japan. The United States needs a naval presence to deal with this threat.

North Korea is in serious economic trouble. Most analysts estimate its annual economic growth rate as -2 percent; more likely, it is -8 percent. The country has a shortage of basic items, including rice, meat, milk, and winter clothing. It has defaulted on international loans and cannot get further credits, and the United Kingdom, France, Australia, and New Zealand have frozen its assets. The Soviet Union and China are unable to help, and China does not want a military crisis in Korea to detract from China's own priorities. Earlier this year, the United States and South Korea persuaded the Japanese not to make reparation payments to North Korea. Kim Il Sung has three choices. First, he could keep the society isolated from outside help, but this would probably lead to a coup or a revolution. Second, he could open the country gradually, and if he held onto power during the transition of the regime to his son, Kim Il Jong, he might buy time. Third, he could attack South Korea to stay in power.

One participant noted that North Korea is so desperate economically that the regime could collapse, as happened in Eastern Europe. The United States should pursue 4 to 5 years of holding action and not run any risks. Another said that, with South Korea, Japan, and the Soviet Union, the United States has the funds, technology, and managerial expertise to exert leverage with North Korea. A third noted that North Korea wants a meaningful relationship with the United States and Japan.

A New Korean War

One participant said that North Korea might attack South Korea at any time, resulting in a war that would probably last about 120 days. The North Koreans have 60 percent of their forces deployed close to the demilitarized zone and well protected. Forty thousand U.S. troops and the South Korean army could not stop them. In the first half-hour, 30 percent of the South

Korean army would be decimated. Seoul would fall quickly; it is only 25 miles from the demilitarized zone. Some participants agreed that Seoul would fall, but others stated that South Korean's military capability and training are impressive, and Seoul would not be lost.

In such a war, the United States would need to hold some part of the peninsula and reinforce rapidly. If the United States reinforced quickly, South Korean and U.S. forces would stop the North Korean troops, and North Korea would lose the war. The United States does not currently have the airlift or sealift to do this. The United States would have to maintain staging areas and capabilities in Japan to be able to counter a North Korean attack. That is the main expense caused by the North Korean threat, not the U.S. forces in Korea. It is not clear how the United States would react if North Korea used chemical weapons in a conflict. U.S. troops in Korea have the same chemical defense equipment that U.S. troops had in the Gulf War. The United States does not know if that would be enough because it was not used in the Gulf War.

The Gulf War and a New Korean War

The United States should be very careful in applying to North Korea lessons learned from the Gulf War. Unlike the Iraqis, the North Koreans would fight. The Gulf War involved a broad coalition based on common vital interests, staging from a neighboring allied country with an unimpeded buildup of forces over months, and climate and terrain that were well suited to air and tank operations.

A participant asked what the Europeans would do as signatories to the U.N. treaty in a new Korean war. Another replied that the United States would not get the Europeans to help in a Korean war. They have an interest in principle but no hard interest. The United States was able to build a military coalition based on oil, but it would not be able to build one based on vital interests in Korea. Moreover, China would not permit U.N. Security Council resolutions against North Korea or boycott its meetings, as the Soviets did in 1950. The Chinese do not want war in Korea, but North Korea is their only close ideological ally, and they would not vote for U.N. action against it. Another observed that 230,000 allied forces (other than U.S.) were in the Gulf War but only about 38,700 U.N. troops (other than Korean and U.S.) have been in Korea at any one time. Although we think of a large U.N. command in the Korean War, the United Nations contributed only a few battalions. Another observed that this force level would be appropriate coalition warfare.

0138

based at Kunsan. These would be supported by Japan-based forces of one to two tactical fighter wings, one carrier battle group, one amphibious readiness group, and one Marine expeditionary force. In a crisis, these forces could be augmented by a reinforced division, a tactical air wing based in Hawaii or Alaska, and five U.S.-based carrier battle groups. This is the right force level, but it is probably more than Congress will approve.

U.S. Forces in Korea

Participants said that U.S. forces are in Korea to maintain deterrence and reassure Japan. Deterrence requires a U.S. presence on the ground and offshore air and naval capabilities, but it does not require 43,700 troops. The United States should draw down to one reinforced brigade or reinforced battalion task force under the 2d Infantry Division—about 10,000 ground troops. There may be a U.S. promise to South Korea not to go below 30,000, but Congress will not keep that many troops there. The United States does not need enough troops to deter North Korea, only enough in a forward position at Tanduchan or Unchon to engage the United States in a conflict. The United States also needs to have ready-deployment sealift capabilities for heavy forces that may be required in a Korean conflict. The South Koreans want the U.S. forces there, and Japan wants the Korean peninsula to be stable and not under North Korean or Soviet control.

South Korean Forces

A participant asked why South Korea is still dependent on the United States, given its growth in gross national product, population, sophistication, and technology. South Korea could substitute for U.S. forces there without a major effect on its economy, but it has been unable since 1954 to build up its forces sufficiently to deter North Korea. One responded that there would be no problem if it were only a question of troops in Korea. The United States needs offshore capabilities because if North Korea attacked, it would reach Seoul immediately. The U.S. forces in South Korea are a trip wire.

Another said that after the Korean War, U.S. policy was to keep South Korea impotent lest it attack North Korea and to retain U.S. forces on the peninsula to maintain stability. The United States opposed greater South Korean military spending and promoted economic development. Because of this focus, South Korea could not be expected to build up the capabilities that North Korea did. South Korea devotes far less of the gross national product to the military than does North Korea. The gross national product in South Korea is $5,000 to $6,000 per capita and in North Korea

0139

is $450 per capita. South Korea's economic improvement is astounding, but high inflation and massive modernization are causing problems.

Another stated that South Korea is less dependent on the United States than it has been in the past. The United States is shifting military responsibility slowly. It plans to withdraw 7,000 forces between now and 1993, with follow-on withdrawals that are anticipated to result in a level of 10,000 troops. South Korea is prepared to pick up the slack from these reductions. The United States has shifted much to the South Korean army. The Ground Component Commander of U.N. forces, a Korean, is directly under the U.S. Commander. South Korea has picked up much of the burden sharing, and they are doing more. South Korea should be able to defend itself by 1995 or 1996. Hopefully, by that time, North Korea will no longer pose a threat.

Nuclear Weapons in Korea

Participants said that the President's September 27, 1991, announcement on withdrawing nuclear weapons from South Korea was a U.S. coup. U.S. nuclear weapons there are a political liability and are redundant because the United States has many other systems for delivering nuclear weapons. They are also old, expensive to maintain, dangerous to handle, and subject to terrorist seizures. They should have been withdrawn long ago. They are an obstacle to North-South Korean arms control and confidence-building measures toward reunification. South Korea does not want a linkage between U.S. nuclear weapons and North Korea's policy of refusing International Atomic Energy Agency inspections of its nuclear facilities, saying that, as a matter of principle, North Korea should permit such inspections. The North Koreans, however, have always held that withdrawal of U.S. nuclear weapons is essential if North Korea is to limit its nuclear development. Thus, the United States satisfied one of the main demands that North Korea made for permitting inspections.

U.S. Forces in Japan

The United States maintains forces in Japan to provide (1) staging areas and support facilities for a Korean conflict and (2) stability in the area. A participant asked whether the United States would need forward bases in Japan and Okinawa to support a Korean war if South Korea could defend itself militarily or the North Korean regime collapsed in the near future. This implies a significant drawdown of U.S. forces from Northeast Asia in 4 to 5 years. One replied that the United States might be able to withdraw its forces from Japan in 4 to 5 years, but it should not do anything precipitous because that might encourage a North Korean attack, given

East Asia and the Pacific: the North Korean Threat and U.S. Responses

by William J. Taylor, Jr.

While there has been great political change in the world, especially in Europe, the situation in East Asia, specifically on the Korean peninsula, has not been substantially altered. The peace, stability, and nonhostile orientation of East Asia are critical to U.S. security and economic interests.

The only way to maintain these conditions will be to maintain a continued military, political, and economic U.S. presence in the region.

While there has been a recent rapprochement between the North and South Koreans towards some form of reunification, the threat of possible military action by the North Koreans remains. In large part this stems from the fact that the North and South have very different views on how and under what system of government Korea would be reunified. Each is pursuing a unique strategy for reunification, but the South's is the most successful. However, North Korea enjoys a quantitative edge over the South in military capability. There is probably about a 20-percent chance that the North will use military force against the South at some point in the future.

Because of the real and substantial threat that North Korea poses, previous U.S./South Korean war plans must be reviewed in light of lessons learned from the Gulf War. The Gulf War provides six lessons for U.S. planners: (1) the Gulf War was a unique experience; (2) the ability to deploy over a 6-month period was crucial; (3) high technology weapons have revolutionized warfare; (4) the quality of people, not technology alone, wins conflicts; (5) the United States lacks sufficient power projection capabilities; and (6) air defense capabilities are critical.

On the Korean peninsula, the United States will have to tailor its Pacific forces for deterrence, a forward presence (tripwire forces), a crisis response, and a capability for reconstitution from forces based in the continental United States. Deterrence against North Korean aggression will have to hinge on the existence of credible resources for rapid power projection.

To meet the threat on the Korean peninsula, the United States will require either capital investment in ships and aircraft designed for rapid, strategic lift or, more reasonably, increased reliance on forward maritime prepositioning of equipment and supplies. Options for prepositioning include offshore bases and equipment stored in South Korea. Ultimately, the United States will have to have greater power projection assets to support land-based tripwire forces to offset planned and future force reductions.

Biographical Sketches

Gordon Adams	Dr. Adams, a member of the Council on Foreign Relations, is founder and director of the Defense Budget Project, a nonpartisan research organization. He has written extensively on the defense budget and national security, has testified before congressional committees, and has appeared on television and radio programs.
Barry M. Blechman	Dr. Blechman is chairman of the Henry L. Stimson Center, a nonprofit research organization, and is the founder and president of Defense Forecasts, Inc. Previously, he worked for the U.S. Army, the Center for Naval Analyses, and the Brookings Institution and served as the deputy director of the U.S. Arms Control and Disarmament Agency.
Louis J. Cantori	Dr. Cantori is a professor of political science at the University of Maryland and an adjunct professor at the Center for Contemporary Arab Studies, Georgetown University. A former Marine, he has been a visiting professor at the U.S. Military Academy and a lecturer at the U.S. Air Force Academy. He has published extensively.
Stanley S. Fine	Admiral Fine, who serves on the Comptroller General's Consultant Panel, retired from the Navy in 1979. His last assignment was as the Department of the Navy's budget director. Since retirement, he has served as an officer and director in various businesses and has written and lectured on national security issues.
Randall Forsberg	Dr. Forsberg is the founder and director of the Institute for Defense and Disarmament Studies, a nonprofit research center in Cambridge, Massachusetts. Previously, Dr. Forsberg founded the national freeze clearinghouse, chaired the National Freeze Advisory Board, and was president of Freeze Voter '84. She also worked at the Stockholm International Peace Research Institute.
Rose Gottemoeller	Ms. Gottemoeller is a social scientist at the RAND Corporation. She specializes in Soviet national security decision-making and strategic force doctrine. Previously, she worked at the International Institute for Strategic Studies in London, the National Oceanic and Atmospheric Administration, the Battelle Memorial Institute, and the Washington-Moscow Direct Communications Link ("Hotline").
A. James Gregor	Dr. Gregor is a professor of political science at the University of California, Berkeley. He is the author of 16 books, 10 monographs, and about 100 articles in professional journals. He is a Guggenheim fellow and a fellow of the Institute for Advanced Study in the Social Sciences at Hebrew University. He also serves on several editorial boards.
Alan M. Jones	Dr. Jones is a principal with the Systems Research and Applications Corporation. In this capacity, he has conducted studies on NATO's conventional-nuclear force mix and arms control issues. Previously, he analyzed strategic and theater nuclear and space weapons issues at the U.S. Arms Control and Disarmament Agency. He served as our conference rapporteur.
Robert C. Kingston	General Kingston (USA, ret.) was commissioned from the Officers' Candidate School in December 1949. He served in special operations units in both Korea and Vietnam and commanded combat units in all 10 officer grades. He was the first commander-in-chief, U.S. Central Command. He has a master's degree in foreign relations.
Frederick J. Kroesen	General Kroesen (USA, ret.) served as commander-in-chief, U.S. Army, Europe, from 1979 to 1983 and vice chief, U.S. Army, from 1978 to 1979. He is currently a senior fellow at the Institute of Land Warfare and a self-employed consultant specializing in national and international defense matters.
Edward C. Meyer	General Meyer (USA, ret.) served as a field officer in Korea and in the Vietnam War. After duty with the 82nd Airborne Division as assistant division commander and deputy commandant of the Army War College, he commanded the 3rd Infantry Division in Germany; was deputy for operations and plans on the Army General Staff; and was chief of staff, U.S. Army, and a member of the Joint Chiefs of Staff. He is currently a managing partner of Cilluffo Associates, L.P., and an international consultant.

(continued)

Appendix VII
Biographical Sketches

Janne E. Nolan	Dr. Nolan is a senior fellow at the Brookings Institution and an adjunct professor at Georgetown University. She was a senior designee to the Senate Armed Services Committee while working at the U.S. Arms Control and Disarmament Agency during the Carter administration and has served as an advisor to several congressional and presidential campaigns. She is the author of several books and numerous articles.
Raymond E. Peet	Admiral Peet (USN, ret.) serves on the Comptroller General's Consultant Panel and, since retirement, has served as consultant or director to numerous U.S. firms. He has served in field commands and held several policy positions, including commanding officer of the first U.S. nuclear-powered cruiser; commander, First Fleet in the Pacific; acting assistant secretary of defense for international security affairs; and director, Defense Security Assistance Agency.
Jeffrey Record	Dr. Record is a senior fellow at the BDM International Center for Technology and Public Policy Research. The author of many books and articles on military affairs, Dr. Record was formerly a legislative assistant for national security affairs to Senator Sam Nunn. For the past 6 years, he has served as a military commentator for the Baltimore Sun.
Eugene N. Russell	Colonel Russell (USA, ret.) works as a defense consultant. He was commissioned from the ROTC program at the Ohio State University and had a variety of assignments in infantry and special operations units, including the 5th Special Forces Group (Airborne) and the 1st Cavalry Division (Airmobile) in Vietnam. He commanded the 3rd Battalion, 7th Special Forces Group (ABN), 1st SF. He is a graduate of the National War College.
Edwin H. Simmons	General Simmons (USMC, ret.) serves on the Comptroller General's Consultant Panel and is the director of Marine Corps History and Museums. His uniformed service spanned 36 years, from 1942 to 1978. He is widely published on military affairs and history.
Harry G. Summers, Jr.	Colonel Summers (USA, ret.) is a distinguished fellow of the Army War College and a syndicated columnist for the Los Angeles Times. His sequel to his award-winning analysis of the Vietnam War, On Strategy II: A Critical Analysis of the Gulf War, is forthcoming from Dell Publishing in February 1992.
William J. Taylor, Jr.	Dr. Taylor, a retired U.S. Army colonel, is vice president of the International Security Programs and director of Political-Military Studies at the Center for Strategic and International Studies. He has been director of National Security Studies, West Point, and a visiting professor at the U.S. National War College. He has published extensively.
R. James Woolsey	Mr. Woolsey was the U.S. representative to the Talks on Conventional Forces in Europe and, from 1977 to 1979, the under secretary of the Navy. Among other positions, he was general counsel to the Senate Armed Services Committee, an advisor to the U.S. Delegation to Strategic Arms Limitation Talks (SALT I), and a member of the President's Blue Ribbon Commission on Defense Management. He is currently a partner at the law firm of Shea & Gardner, Washington, D.C. He served as our conference moderator.

0143

정 리 보 존 문 서 목 록

기록물종류	일반공문서철	등록번호	2021010098	등록일자	2021-01-15
분류번호	726.64	국가코드	US	보존기간	준영구
명 칭	북한 핵문제 : 미국 의회 동향, 1992. 전3권				
생 산 과	북미1과/북미2과	생산년도	1992~1992	담당그룹	
권 차 명	V.3 5-12월				
내용목차	* 7.8 하원 외무위원회 아태소위원회, 아시아지역 정세발전에 관한 청문회 개최 7.22 하원 외무위원회, 북한 핵문제 공개설명회 개최(Blix ,IAEA 사무총장 참석)				

0001

9

외 무 부

관리
번호 P2-524

종 별 :

번 호 : USW-2313   일 시 : 92 0506 1910

수 신 : 장관(미일,미이,재일,정총,정특,기정)

발 신 : 주 미 대사

제 목 : 솔라즈 하원 외무위 아태소위원장 만찬

1. 본직은 작 5.5(화) 저녁 미하원 외무위 아태소위 STEPHEN SOLARZ 위원장부처를 관저로 초청, 만찬을 가졌는 바, 동 요지 다음과 같음.

가. LA 흑인 폭동 사태

SOLARZ 의원은 최근 LA 흑인 폭동 사태에 대해 위로의 말을 전하면서 이번 사건이 미국의 고질적 문제인 흑백문제에서 발단되었음에도 불구하고 한인 사회가 크게 피해를 입게 되어 유감스러우며, 앞으로 흑인등 소수민족 사회와의 관계가 개선되도록 양측이 노력하는 것이 필요하나 여기에는 어디까지나 한계가 있을것으로 전망하면서 한인사회가 이번 일을 계기로 하여 미국 정부 또는 언론등을 대상으로 영향력을 발휘할 수 있도록 교민들의 세력을 조직화 하는 노력을 착수하는 것이 중요하다고 말함. 또한 동 의원은 의회 차원에서 자신이 도울수 있는 일이 있다면 언제든지 연락해 줄 것을 요망하였음.

나. 북한 핵 개발 문제

검토필 (1) P2. 6. 3 이인

. SOLARZ 의원은 북한이 핵 물질에 대한 최초보고서 관련 시설목록을 IAEA 에 신속히 제출한 것은 다행스러운 일이나 첫째, 핵 재처리 시설이 과연 포함되어 있는지의 여부, 또 북한이 실제 사찰에 어느정도 성의있게 임할 것인지가 관건이고, 앞으로 IAEA 가 특별사찰을 해야될 상황에 처할 경우 북한의 태도가 어떤 것이냐에 대하여 주시하지 않을 수 없다고 말하고

. 남북한 합의에 의한 상호사찰이 반드시 이루어져야 IAEA 사찰의 약점이 보강되리라 보는데 이에관한 남북 대화에 진전이 없다는데 대해 실망하고 있으며, 한국정부의 일부에서 IAEA 사찰만 실시되면 남북 상호사찰은 실시하지 않아도되지 않겠느냐는 시각이 있다는 말을 듣고 매우 걱정스럽게 여기고 있다고 언급함.

. 또한 SOLARZ 의원은 북한을 다루는데 있어서 강온양면 정책(STICK AND CARROT)

미주국 장관 차관 1차보 미주국 영교국 외정실 외정실 분석관
청와대 안기부   0002

PAGE 1   92.05.07 10:08
외신 2과 통제관 BX

이 필요하다는 점은 인정하나 북한 정권의 <u>지금까지의 전력에 비추어 볼때</u> CARROT 은
<u>되도록 유보하고 STICK 의 위협을 더 강조하는 것이 현시점에서의 정책의 기조가</u>
되어야 한다고 말하고

. IAEA 의 사찰이 만족스럽게 이루어 진다면 이것은 한미 양국이 그간 협조해온
정책이 성공하고 있음을 증명하는 것이긴 하지만 이 정도의 성과로 만족하지 말고 계속
상호사찰을 추구함으로써 북한의 핵 위협을 완전히 제거할때 까지 계속 압력을 넣어야
할 것이라고 언급함.

다. 북한의 최근 동향

. SOLARZ 의원은 최근 북한이 보여주고 있는 일련의 유화 제스쳐는 경제적, 외교적
곤경에서 벗어나려는 임시 방편일뿐 진정한 변화의 시작이라고 보기에는 아직
이르다고 믿는다고 말하고

. 자신이 1980 년과 작년 두차례에 걸쳐 북한을 방문하고 김일성을 만나본
소감으로서는 현재와 같은 체제가 계속되는 한 진정한 변화는 있을수 없으며 북한이
국제사회와의 관계를 개선하려면 그 체제가 가진 근본 문제에 변화가 있어야 한다고
언급함.

. 또한 동 의원은 일체의 인간적 기본권이 무시되고 있고 수용소 군도가 도처에
산재해 있으며 인권이라는 문제를 거론키도 어려울 정도로 외부에 폐쇄되어있는
북한이기 때문에 현 단계에 큰 변화를 기대하기 어렵다고 말하면서

. 핵 사찰 문제의 진전에 따라 미행정부로서는 부분적으로 이에 상응하는 조치를
취하게 되겠지만 아직은 조심스럽게 다루어야될 단계라고 본다고 말하고, 다만 남북
상호사찰 까지가 완전하게 실시되는 단계에 이르면 미국정부로서는 북한을 고립된
채로 내버려 두는것 보다는 정상적인 접촉 창구의 운영이라는 면에서 외교관계등을
열어야 한다는 압력에 당면하게 될것으로 예상한다고 언급함.

2. 본직은 이에 대하여

가. LA 사태 수습을 위하여 특히 영세 상인들의 생업 복귀를 위해 의회로 부터
물질적, 정신적 지원이 이루어 진다면 한국교민들이 크게 감사할 것이고 한미
관계에도 도움이 될것이므로 동 의원은 성원을 기대한다고 말하고

나. 북한은 핵 문제를 다루는데 있어서 4 단계 D 전략을 채택해 왔는바, 최초에는
모든것은 부인(DENY) 하다가, 국제적 압력이 점증되자 되도록 시간끌기(DELAY) 하려고
시도하면서, 한편으로는 그들의 핵 개발 계획을 은폐(DEISGUISE) 하려고 노력중이며,

마지막으로 도저히 탈출구가 없을 때에만 핵개발을 포기(DISCARD) 한다는 전략을 구사해 왔고 현재는 2 단계에서 3 단계로 넘어가는 단계로판단되며

　　다. 우리 정부의 정책은 어디까지나 IAEA 사찰과 동시에 남북 상호사찰을 관철코자 하는 것이며 현재까지 한미 양국의 정책이 성과를 거두고 있다는 평가에 대해서는 동 의원과 같은 견해라고 언급하고

　　라. 북한의 변화가 비록 일시적 미봉책에 불과하더라도 일단 변화가 시작되면 정책 입안자의 희망과는 관계없이 빠른 속도록 진전될수 있는 가능성도 없지 않으므로 지금까지 취해온 강온 양면 정책의 적절한 구사가 계속 되어야 할 것이라는 견해를 표명함.

　　(대사 현홍주-국장)

　　예고:일반 92.12.31.

관리번호 82 -802

외 무 부

종 별 :

번 호 : USW-3112　　　　　　　　　　일 시 : 92 0618 1853

수 신 : 장관(미이, 미일, 정총, 정안, 국기), 사본:주오지리대사, 청와대외교안보

발 신 : 주미대사

제 목 : 하원 아태소위 수석전문위원 면담

1. 당관 조일환 참사관은 6.17 하원 외무위 아태소위(위원장 STEPHEN SOLARZ)의 STANLEY ROTH 수석전문위원을 면담하고 북한 핵문제에 대해 상호 의견을 교환한바. 요지 다음 보고함(안총기 서기관 배석).

2. 조참사관은 최근 BLIX IAEA 사무총장의방북, IAEA 임시 사찰결과 및 남북핵통제 공동위원회의 상호사찰 협의 진행상황을 상세히 설명한후 BLIX 사무총장의 방북 및 임시 사찰을 통해 북한이 핵재처리 시설을 건설중에 있다는 점과 플루토늄을 생산했다는 점이 밝혀짐으로서 북한이 그동안 국제 사회에 거짓말을 해오고 있었다는 사실이 명백이 드러났으며 북한은 현재 IAEA 사찰을 최대한 활용, 남북 상호사찰의 필요성 및 핵개발 포기에 대한 국제적 압력을 희석시키기위해 노력하는 한편 경수로 원자료 기술을 제공받는 조건으로 핵 재처리 시설을 포기 할뜻을 비치면서 남북비핵화 공동선언의 기본적 의무를 회피하려 하고 있다고설명하고 기 생산된 플루토늄의 은식 가능성 및 별도의 재처리시설 존재 여부 확인등 핵의혹 해소를 위하여 상호 사찰의 실시가 무엇보다도 긴요하며 이를 위한지속적인 국제 압력이 요구되고있다고 언급함.

3. 이에대해 ROTH 전문위원은 상기 설명에 동감을 표하고 다음요지로 언급함

가. 91.12 월 솔라즈 의원 방북시 김염남 북한외교부장은 북한이 단 1 개의원자로를 보유하고 있을 뿐이라고 언급하였으나 지난번 북한이 공개한 비디오 테잎은 전혀 다른 내용이였는바 솔라즈의원은 북한이 거짓말을 하고있다는 사실을 오래전부터 알고 있었음.

나. IAEA 사찰은 북한이 재처리 시설 및 플루토늄생산 사실을 확인 시켜 줌으로서 북한핵개발에 대한 국제사회의 새로운 의심을 불러 일으키는 한편 일본등주변국을 긴장시키고있는바 북한이 IAEA 사찰 허용을 통해 남북상호 사찰을 회피하고 핵개발 에 대한 국제 압력 및 제재를 모면하고자 하는 전략은 성공하지 못하고 있음.

미주국 안기부	장관 중계	1차보	미주국	국기국	외정실		문석관	청와대

0005

(다) 향후 IAEA 의 북한 핵사찰 문제와 관련 아래 3 단계의 시나리오를 가상할 수 있다고봄.

〈첫째〉 우선 단기적으로 IAEA 로 하여금 보다 철저한 사찰을 실시하도록 하는것임. 북한이 플루토늄을 생산한 사실이 알려진 이상 IAEA 는 북한이 재처리 연료를 얼마나 사용했는지, 어떠한 사설로 플루토늄을 생산했는지등 플루토륨생산의 OPERATING RECORD 을 요구하게 될 것이며 이러한 과정을 통해 북한이 생산한 플루토늄의 양, 별도 재처리 시설문제 여부등 북한이 밝히지 않고있는 내용을파악할수 있게 되는 경우임.

〈둘째〉 IAEA 가 사찰을 종료하게 될때까지도 북한의 핵무기 개발에 대한 특별한 내용이 밝혀지지 않을경우 미.일.유럽등 한국의 우방국들은 한반도 비핵화 공동선언에 의거 IAEA 사찰시 북한에 존재하고있는 것으로 이미 밝혀진 핵재처리시설을 폐기(DISMANTLE) 하도록 요구할수 있을것임. 한반도 비핵화 공동 선언은남북한이 상호 핵재처리 시설을 보유하지 못하게 하고 있다는 점에서 매우 유용하고 중요하며 따라서 상호 사찰 실시를 위한 협상에 진전이 없더라도 동 선언을 절대 파기해서는 안된다고봄.〈셋째〉 가능성이 매우 희박한것으로 보지만 북한이 핵재처리 시설을 폐기하는경우 미.일로서도 북한과의 관계를 적절한 방법으로 다소 발전시키게 될 것으로 봄.

(4) 조참사관은 IAEA 사찰을 통해 북한 핵개발에 관한 모든 의혹이 완전히 해소된다면 다행이겠으나 이락의 경우에서 보았듯이 IAEA 사찰이 완벽하지 않으므로 남북한 상호사찰이 반드시 이루어져야 할 것이라고 설명하고 이를 위해 우방국들에 의한 대북한 압력을 계속 가중시켜 나가는것이 중요하다고 강조함.

(5) 이에대해 ROTH 전문위원은 남북한 상호사찰의 중요성에는 자신도 전적으로 동감하며 솔라즈의원도 상호사찰 실시 문제에 진전이 있기를 기대하고 있다고말하고 다만 IAEA 는 이락에 대한 핵사찰에서 실패한 경험이이 있기때문에 북한에 대한 사찰은 보다 철저한(TOUGH) 방법으로 실시해 나갈 것으로 보며 또한이락에 대한 사찰때와 달리 현재는 IAEA 이사국간에 긴밀한 상호 정보교환을하고있기 때문에 IAEA 사찰이 이락의 경우와는 다를것이며 현재까지는 당초 예상 보다는 긍정적인 결과를 낳고있는것으로 본다고 언급함.

(6) 조참사관이 북한 핵문제에 관한 청문회 개최 계획에 진전이 있느냐고 문의한데 대해 ROTH 전문위원은 솔라즈 의원이 BLIX IAEA 사무총장으로 하여금 아태 소위

청문회에 증언토록 할목적으로 BLIX 사무총장의 방미를 동총장 북한 방문 직전에
구두초청 하였으나 BLIX 사무총장은 IAEA 사찰팀이 북한을 다녀온후 검토 하자고
응답한바 있다고 말하고 조만간 BLIX 사무총장 에게 다시한번 방미를 초청할
예정이라고 언급함. ROTH 전문위원은 또한 GATES CIA 국장을 공개 청문회에서
증언토록 하는것을 검토하고 있다고 언급함. 끝

(대사 현홍주- 국장)

예고: 92.12..31.일반 고문에
의거 일반문서   됨

솔라즈, 北韓핵해결의 최종수 〓 군사공격

韓, 美에 군사조치 선택 배제말라 권고

(워싱턴 AP=聯合) 美외교정책에 관한 의회의 한 지도자인 스티븐 솔라즈 하원 아시아 太平洋 소위원회 위원장은 20일 韓美양국이 핵폭탄을 개발하는 것이 아닌가 의심이 가는 北韓의 계획을 제거하기 위한 최종 수단으로서 군사공격을 선택할 자유를 간직해야 한다고 말했다.

솔라즈 亞太위원장은 보수적 정책연구 집단인 헤리티지 재단이 주관한 한국에 관한 세미나에서 "군사조치 선택 등 어떤 조치의 선택도 배제되어서는 안된다"고 강조했다.

솔라즈 위원장은 북한에 대한 공격을 자신이 주창하고 있는 것은 아니라면서 "그러나 북한의 군사지도자들에게 무력사용에 관해서는 염려할 필요가 없다"는 생각을 준다면 그것은 큰 잘못일것"이라고 말했다.

그는 세계의 가장 심각한 안보상의 한 도전이라고 많은 지도자들이 말한 북한의 핵문제를 해결하려는 장기간에 걸친 서방측 노력에 있어 이제 "우리는 진실의 순간에 접근하고 있다"고 말하고 유엔전문기관인 국제원자력기구(IAEA)가 이라크의 핵무기 개발계획을 탐지하지 못한 "씁쓸한 前例에 비추어" 앞으로 있을 IAEA의 북한 핵사찰을 완전히 신뢰한다면 그것은 잘못일 것이라고 지적했다.

솔라즈 위원장은 이어 IAEA는 금지된 핵시설이 아닌가 의심이 가는 北韓의 어느 지점도 不時에 사찰할 권리가 있음을 주장해야 한다고 말하고 신뢰를 실제로 창출하기 위해선 이 권리가 南北韓의 상호 상대방 시설물 사찰로 보완되어야 하다고 덧붙였다.

솔라즈 의원은 북한이 핵무기 제조를 모색하고 있지 않다는 보장은 북한이 오래동안 남을 속여왔기때문에 신뢰도가 낮다고 평가하고 북한이 지하에 무기공장을 세우고 터널을 파는데 전문지식을 갖추고 있다는데 주목했다.

그는 미국이 北韓과는 레이건 前대통령이 소련에 대해 취한 "신뢰하지만 檢證한다"는 접근방식에서 "불신하고 검증하는" 접근방식으로 확대해야 한다면서 핵문제가 일단 해결되면 무역개발 및 관계중신을 위해 "회유와 위협" 정책을 써서 북한에 대해 미사일 수출에 반대하는 미사일 기술 통제규칙을 수락하는 것과 같은 조건과 인권기준을 충족시키도록 요구할것을 주장했다.

지난 80년과 91년 북한을 방문한 솔라즈 위원장은 북한이 "오늘날 세계에서 최악의 인권 침해국은 아니라 하더라도 인권 침해국속에 든다"고 말했다.(끝)

0008

외 무 부

종 별 : 긴 급

번 호 : USW-3466　　　　　　　　　일 시 : 92 0709 0057

수 신 : 장 관(미일,미이,아이,아동)

발 신 : 주 미국 대사

제 목 : 하원 외무위 아.태소위 청문회

1. 하원 외무위 아.태소위 (위원장 : STEPHEN SOLARZ)는 금 7.8 RICHARD SOLOMON 국무부 동아.태 담당 차관보 (주 필리핀 대사 내정)를 증인으로 출석시킨 가운데 최근 아시아 지역 정세발전에 관한 청문회를 개최함.(당관 조일환참사관 및 안총기서기관 참석)

2. SOLOMON 차관보는 증언문 없이 한국 및 필리핀, 캄보디아, 중국, 버마등에 대해 간단히 언급한후 질의 응답에 들어 갔으며, 주요 질의 응답 요지는 아래와 같음.

　가. 북한 핵문제

(SOLARZ 의원)

질문 : 북한에 대한 IAEA 사찰을 통해 얻은 결론은 무엇인가 ?

답변 : IAEA 사찰 협상 이전에는 우리의 외교적 노력이 얼마나 효과가 있을것 인가에 대한 서로 다른 견해가 있었으나 우리는 현재까지 북한이 보여준 협조에 대해 다소 의외라고 생각하면서 긍정적으로 보고 있음.

(SURPRISED AND PLEASED)

그러나 아직도 한반도에 위험요소는 상존 하고 있으며, 해결해야 할 많은 문제가 남아 있음.

IAEA 사찰을 통해 북한은 재처리 실험을 하고 있다는 것을 시인하였으며, BLIX IAEA 사무총장의 사찰결과 발표 내용으로 미루어 볼때 북한이 많은 사람들이 우려 했던 것 만큼의 재처리 능력이 있는 것은 아니라고 보여지나 북한이 재처리 시설 개발을 위해 노력하고 있다는 것이 일단 확인됨.

질문 : BLIX 사무총장은 북한이 언제쯤 재처리 능력을 갖게 될 것으로 판단하고 있는가 ?

답변 : BLIX 총장이 발표한 바는 없으나 본인이 느끼기로는 북한이 재처리 능력을

미주국	장관	차관	1차보	아주국	아주국	미주국	외정실	분석관
청와대	안기부							

보유하는 단계에 이르기 위해서는 수년이 있어야 할 것으로 봄. 또한 재처리 시설이 과연 가동할 수 있을지에 대해서도 의문이 있음.

질문 : IAEA 는 북한에 대해 특별 또는 강제 사찰(SPECIAL OR CHALLENGEINSPECTION)을 할 수 있는 권리를 요구 하였는가 ?

답변: IAEA 는 동 사찰을 요구 했고, 북한은 IAEA 가 북한내의 어떤시설도 방문을 허용하겠다고 한바 있으며, 우리는 이것을 사찰을 허용하는 것으로 보고 있음. 그러나 IAEA 사찰 절차는 통상(NORMALLY) 신고된 시설을 다루도록 계획 (DESIGN)되어 있고, 군사시설에 대한 사찰을 다루지 않기 때문에 미국 정부는 남북 상호 사찰에 특별한 비중을 두고 있음.

질문 : IAEA 를 통해 특별 강제 사찰 합의가 이행되는 경우 남. 북 상호사찰의 중요성은 무엇인가 ?

답변 : 미국의 대 한국정책은 남. 북 대화를 통해 한반도에서의 긴장 완화, 무기통제등을 촉진 시키는 것임. 북한은 남한과의 협의를 중지하고 미국 또는 국제기구와의 협의만 계속하려할 우려도 있는바, 이것은 미국이 지지할 수 없음.

질문 : 현재 상호사찰에 대한 남. 북한간 대화의 진전은 ?

답변 : 금년 3 월 양측은 JNCC 를 구성한 바 있으나 그이후 사찰제도 수립 노력에는 진전이 없음. 미국은 남. 북 상호 사찰에 진전이 없는한 북한과의관계 개선을 추진하지 않을 것임을 북한측에 이야기 하고 있음.

질문 : IAEA 가 비밀 (CLANDESTINE)시설에 대한 사찰을 시도할 준비가 되어있다고 보는가 ?

답변 : IAEA 는 진지하게 노력하고 있다고 봄. 그러나 본인으로서는 남한 또는 북한이 대화를 진전시키고자 하는 동기 (INCENTIVE)가 약화되지 않는 것이 중요하다고 봄. 왜냐하면 이러한 남. 북한 대화의 진전이 궁극적인한반도 안정의 기초이기 때문임.

질문 : 남. 북한 비핵화 공동 선언에 따르면 북한은 현재 건설중인 재처리 시설을 폐기 (DISMANTLE)해야 하는가 ? 또한 남한은 북한에 대해 동 시설 폐기를 요구하고 있는가 ?

답변 : 동 시설은 아직 완성되지 않았기 때문에 재처리 시설이 아니며 따라서 북한의 폐기의무가 없다고 말할 수도 있을 것임. 한국 정부는 동 시설의폐기 요구는 하고 있지 않으며 현재 사찰제도를 수립하기 위해 보다 주력하고 있음. 한가지

PAGE 2

0010

덧불이자면 북한은 핵 폐기물을 이미 재처리하여 지하에 보관하고 있을 가능성도 있으며, 우리는 북한이 은밀한 핵 개발계획을 갖지 못하도록 하는 사찰제도를 원하고 있음.

질문 : 미.북한 관계 진전상황 및 대북한 관계 개선 조건은 ?

답변 : 88 년 북경에 참사관급 접촉 경로가 마련되었는바, 현재로서는 이것이 유일한 대화 채널임. 지난 1 월 뉴욕에서 KANTER 차관이 김용순 국제부장을 접촉한 바 있으며, 동 접촉시 북한에서 IAEA 및 상호사찰이 모두 이행되면 대화 채널을 격상시킬 것이라고 이야기한 바 있는바 미국은 이경우 뉴욕에서 대화채널을 가질수 있을 것임.

북한과의 대화채널 격상을 위해서는 핵문제 뿐만 아니라 미사일 판매, 유해송환, 테러 활동등과 관련한 문제가 모두 해결되어야함.

질문 : 남.북한 상호 사찰이 합의되더라도 다른 모든 조건들이 충족될때 까지 북한과의 관계 개선은 보류할 것인가 ?

답변 ; 미국의 기본정책은 남. 북한 대결이 종식되도록 하는것이며, 미국의 우방인 한국의 입장을 저해(UNDERCUT)하지 않고앞서 나가지는 않을 것임.

(LAGOMARSINO 의원)

질문 :북한과 러시아, 중국관계는 ?

답변 : 북한의 대 러시아 관계는 예전과 같이 우호적이지는 않다고 보며, 중국과의 관계는 다소 증진되었다고 봄.

질문 : 최근 일본신문에는 북한 외교관이 주한 미군의 철수가 더이상 북한의 우선적인 목표(TOP OBJECTIVE)가 아니라고 말한 것으로 보도 되었는바, 주한 미군에 대한 북한의 입장은 무엇인가 ?

답변 ; 북한 지도층에서는 내부적으로 많은 논란이 있겠지만 북한의 외교정책도 흥미로운 방향으로 변화하고 (EVOLVE) 있다고 봄. 북한이 IAEA 핵 사찰을 허용하기 까지에도 북한 지도층에서 많은 토의와 견해차이가 있었을 것으로봄. 또한 1988 년이래 비공식 자격으로 방문하는 북한관리에게 비자를 발급해 오고 있는바, 미국을 방문한 북한 인사가 미군의 한국 주둔이 지역정세 안정을 위해 기여하고 있는 것으로 생각하고 있다는 인상을 받은 바 있음.

나. 캄보디아 문제

- 솔라즈의원은 캄보디아 정세와 관련 태국 및 중국의 대 크메르루즈 지원 여부등에 대해 문의 하였는바, SOLOMON 차관보는 현재 크메르루즈가 상황을 매우

PAGE 3

0011

어렵게 만들고 있으나 국제적 평화 노력에 따르게될 것으로 본다고 말하고, 태국 및 중국이 크메르루즈를 지원하고 있다는 직접적 증거는 없으나, 미국은 두나라에게 크메르루즈를 지원하지 말도록 요청 했다고 답변함.

　　다. 중국 관계

　- SOLARZ 의원은 대중국 MFN 관련 조건부과에 대한 행정부의 견해를 문의하였는바, SOLOMON 차관보는 미국은 다른 어면 나라보다도 많은 대 중국제재 (SANCTIONS)를 유지하고 있으며 무역은 변화를 유도 하기 위한수단(VEHICLE)이므로 재한을 두어 서는 안될 것이라고 답변함.

　- LAGOMARSINO 의원은 중국이 북한으로부터 미군 POW 를 이송 받아 고문했다는 보도에 대해 문의하였는바, SOLOMON 차관보는 중국으로 이송되었을 가능성이 있는 전쟁포로 명단을 최근 러시아로부터 접수한 바있으며, 중국에 대해 관련정보 제공을 요청했다고 답변함.

　　라. 베트남 관계

　- LAGOMARSINO 의원은 베트남으로 부터의 POW/MIA 송환에 대한 진전상황을 문의하였는바, SOLOMON 차관보는 현재 약 100 여 건의 생존자 목격 보고가 있다고 언급하고, 미.베트남 관계는 인도적, 경제적 분야에서 진전을 보이고 있다고 답변함.

　　바. 필리핀 관계

　- SOLARZ 의원은 필리핀 기지로 부터 미군이 철수한 후에도 미.필리핀 방위조약의 유지가 정당화 될 수 있는지를 질문하였는바, SOLOMON 차관보는미군은 필리핀과 역사적으로 특별한 관계를 유지하고 있으며, 지역적 안정을 확보하기 위하여 필리핀과의 협조가 필요하다고 본다고 답변함.끝.

　　(대사 현홍주 - 국장)
　　예고:92.12.31. 까지　　일반문서로 재분류(1992.12.31.)

검 토 필 (1992. 6. 30.)

주 미 대 사 관 "긴급"

USE(T) : 45444   년월일 : 92.7.8   시간 : 2240

수 신 : 장 관 (미일)

발 신 : 주미대사

제 목 : 하원외무위 아태소위
질의응답.

보 안 통 제	

(출처 :   )

조

(45444 - 11 - 1)

외신 1과 통 제	

0013

HEARING OF THE HOUSE FOREIGN AFFAIRS COMMITTEE ASIA-PACIFIC SUBCOMMITTEE;
SUBJECT: REVIEW OF DEVELOPMENTS IN ASIA; CHAIRED BY: REP. STEPHEN J.
SOLARZ (D-NY); WITNESSES: RICHARD SOLOMAN, ASSISTANT SECRETARY OF STATE
FOR EAST ASIA   WEDNESDAY, JULY 8, 1992
K-3-5 page# 1

    dest=hill,hsforaff,asia,philip,fns21447,fns13688,fns11182,fns13821,skor
    dest+=camb,armfor,defense,forpolus,nkor,nucweapon,
    dest+=un,thail,viet,
    data

    reached in early March did really set a framework that we thought
was important, and we wanted to make a response to that move.

    REP. SOLARZ: Well, if I recall correctly, the embargo can be
lifted in Phase Two?

    MR. SOLOMON: Well, it is a process that is already begun and
proceeds step by step. I mean, in a sense, it began when last year
we permitted the repatriation of funds from Vietnamese in this
country to their families. Then we allowed group travel. Now we
have telecommunications. Now we have lifted the controls over NGO
humanitarian programs, and we permit trade in humanitarian or basic
human needs products. So, it is a process that will continue to
unfold.

    REP. SOLARZ: Let me ask you about North Korea and the nuclear
program there. The IAEA has conducted its initial inspection. What
can you tell us about what they found, what conclusions they reached
and we reached as a result of their inspection, and what issues, if
any, remain outstanding in terms of the IAEA's negotiations with the
North?

    MR. SOLOMON: Let me say the following about the Korean
nuclear issue: As you know, there were deep divisions of opinion
about how far we would get with this diplomatic effort to try to
deal with a military challenge, and I think we've been surprised and
thus far pleased with the amount of cooperation that has been shown
by the North Koreans with the one proviso that there's still deep
distrust and many of the basic issues that make Korea still such a
dangerous place -- the very heavily-armed confrontation across the
DMZ, uncertainties about the North Korean nuclear activities which
remain -- indicate that there's still a great deal of work to be
done.

    Having said that, I would say that, following the President's
September 27th initiative on nuclear policy last year, we were, as I
say, surprised and pleased to see first the two very important
agreements reached between North and South Korea on national
reconciliation and a non-nuclear peninsula in the end of the year
last year, the signing of the full-scope safeguards agreement, and
then a level of inspection by the IAEA when Mr. Blix (sp) went over
there, even getting into the tunnels and into the buildings that
were of such concern in a way that was very helpful.

    Having said that, then you've got to look at what, in fact,
was found. The North Koreans did fess up that they had been
conducting experiments in reprocessing, and while my understanding

                4544 —11—2

HEARING OF THE HOUSE FOREIGN AFFAIRS COMMITTEE ASIA-PACIFIC SUBCOMMITTEE;
SUBJECT: REVIEW OF DEVELOPMENTS IN ASIA; CHAIRED BY: REP. STEPHEN J.
SOLARZ (D-NY); WITNESSES: RICHARD SOLOMAN, ASSISTANT SECRETARY OF STATE
FOR EAST ASIA   WEDNESDAY, JULY 8, 1992
K-3-5 page: 2
     is that the results that Mr. Blix and his people interpreted from
their visit indicate that the North Koreans were not as close to a
reprocessing capability as some people had feared looking in from
the outside. The fact is they were headed in that direction.

     REP. SOLARZ: When -- on the basis of what Mr. Blix found,
when did he think they would have achieved the reprocessing capacity
if an agreement had not been reached?

     MR. SOLOMON: Mr. Blix has not made public all of his
information, but my sense is, and I think you should go to the IAEA,
is that the North Koreans were -- it was a matter of years, not
months, before they got to that stage. And, frankly, there have
even been some questions or rumors raised about whether the
facilities would ever function. But I'm not a specialist. I
haven't had a direct readout, and I'm not sufficient to give more
data.

     REP. SOLARZ: But I gather that what we had thought was a
reprocessing facility was, in fact, designed to be a reprocessing
facility?

     MR. SOLOMON: I think that's correct.

     REP. SOLARZ: Right. But Mr. Blix found it wasn't yet
operational?

     MR. SOLOMON: Correct.

     REP. SOLARZ: Now, has the IAEA asked for the right to make
special or challenge inspections?

     MR. SOLOMON: Yes, it has.

     REP. SOLARZ: And what has the North said?

     MR. SOLOMON: They said they are agreeable to those kinds of
inspections.

     REP. SOLARZ: They are?

     MR. SOLOMON: Yes.

     REP. SOLARZ: That is, I should think, extraordinarily
significant.

     MR. SOLOMON: Well, they made a number of comments indicating
receptivity even to our inspections. However, let me just emphasize
one fundamental element in our policy, and that is we put particular
weight on the North-South dialogue and the North-South agreement on
inspections, because the IAEA inspection process is limited to
declared facilities. It does not deal with military bases or other
kinds of facilities.

                    444 —11-3

REP. SOLARZ: Well, then I -- maybe I didn't communicate
clearly. But when I asked you if the North had agreed to permit
challenge inspections, what I had in mind was an arrangement in
which the IAEA would be able to select literally any place in the
country and they would then be permitted to inspect it. Given the
extent to which we know from history that they have a tendency to
dig down and tunnel deep, one can't preclude the possibility of
underground facilities.

MR. SOLOMON: Correct.

REP. SOLARZ: And, therefore, an ability on the part of the
IAEA to go wherever they want to go, I should think, is essential in
giving the rest of the world some confidence that they don't have
secret facilities somewhere. Now, you're telling me that the only
inspection arrangement -- challenge inspection arrangements the
North has agreed to is challenge inspections of declared facilities?

MR. SOLOMON: My colleague has reminded that the North
Koreans, the DPRK, has told the International Atomic Energy Agency
that it may visit, and we presume this means inspect, any facility
in North Korea, not just at the declared facilities.

REP. SOLARZ: Well, that is very important. Does the IAEA
have such arrangements in other countries?

MR. SOLOMON: I'm not a specialist on this, and I really don't
want to give you an answer. But I think normally the inspections
are designed to take care of declared facilities.

REP. SOLARZ: Right. So, if we -- for example, if someone
gave information to the IAEA which suggested the existence of a
clandestine facility at such and such a location, as you understand
it, the IAEA would be able to send a team to that site?

MR. SOLOMON: That's my understanding according to --

REP. SOLARZ: Well, if that agreement is actually implemented,
then what is the significance of the North-South arrangement on
bilateral inspection?

MR. SOLOMON: It provides another layer of confidence on the
inspections on the nuclear issue. But more than that, Mr. Chairman,
I -- this is the point I was trying to get to -- a constant element
in our Korea policy has been to make the North-South dialogue the
primary component of tension reduction, hopefully arms control, and
reconciliation on the peninsula. And one of the things that worries
me is that the North will, in effect, stop at where they are, try to
work with us, the international community, work around direct
dealings with that South. And that is something we will not
support.

REP. SOLARZ: Well, what is the status of the North-South
dialogue in general, but with respect to the nuclear question in

4444-11-4

0016

HEARING OF THE HOUSE FOREIGN AFFAIRS COMMITTEE ASIA-PACIFIC SUBCOMMITTEE;
SUBJECT: REVIEW OF DEVELOPMENTS IN ASIA; CHAIRED BY: REP. STEPHEN J.
SOLARZ (D-NY); WITNESSES: RICHARD SOLOMAN, ASSISTANT SECRETARY OF STATE
FOR EAST ASIA   WEDNESDAY, JULY 8, 1992
K-3-5 page 4
    particular?

        MR. SOLOMON: I think it was on March 16th the two sides did
form this joint nuclear control commission. Since that time, they
have had not-very-fruitful negotiations on an inspection regime.
And, as you know, we have told the North that, until there are
inspections carried out under the North-South regime, we will not
advance our relations with the North.

        REP. SOLARZ: If the North is willing to permit IAEA
inspectors to traipse all over the country and to go where they
want, why would they not be willing to reach an agreement with the
South?

        MR. SOLOMON: You can speculate as well as I. I think the
process of reconciliation between North and South, just as the
process of reconciling the differences between the various Cambodian
parties, is a very difficult, long-term process.

        REP. SOLARZ: Is it our impression that the IAEA is prepared
to exercise the right to challenge inspections and that, if they
have any reason to believe that there may be clandestine facilities,
that they will send inspectors to the locations where those
facilities are believed to be present?

        MR. SOLOMON: I believe so, yes.

        REP. SOLARZ: So, you're not concerned that the IAEA may be
lackadaisical or indifferent, that it was only interested in getting
a paper right? Your view is that it is fully prepared to exercise
that right?

        MR. SOLOMON: Everything I've heard about Mr. Blix and his
effort -- his people is that they are serious-minded. What I am
concerned about is anything that would weaken the incentives on the
part of the North and the South to advance the dialogue.

        REP. SOLARZ: Now, is that --

        MR. SOLOMON: I think that's the basis for eventual stability
on the peninsula.

        REP. SOLARZ: Well, I expect the basis for eventual stability
on the peninsula is a change of government in the North in which
they become more democratic. But, in any case, as I understand it,
in the North-South nuclear agreement establishing a nuclear-free
Korean Peninsula, they agreed to preclude or prohibit the
establishment of reprocessing facilities.

        MR. SOLOMON: That's correct.

        REP. SOLARZ: Does that mean that the North is now obligated
to dismantle this radio-chemical laboratory which now -- which turns
out, in fact, to be a reprocessing facility in construction.

0017

HEARING OF THE HOUSE FOREIGN AFFAIRS COMMITTEE ASIA-PACIFIC SUBCOMMITTEE;
SUBJECT: REVIEW OF DEVELOPMENTS IN ASIA; CHAIRED BY: REP. STEPHEN J.
SOLARZ (D-NY); WITNESSES: RICHARD SOLOMAN, ASSISTANT SECRETARY OF STATE
FOR EAST ASIA   WEDNESDAY, JULY 8, 1992
K-3-5 page# 5

CONTINUED

4744 - 11 - 6

HEARING OF THE HOUSE FOREIGN AFFAIRS COMMITTEE ASIA-PACIFIC SUBCOMMITTEE;
SUBJECT: REVIEW OF DEVELOPMENTS IN ASIA; CHAIRED BY: REP. STEPHEN J.
SOLARZ (D-NY); WITNESSES: RICHARD SOLOMAN, ASSISTANT SECRETARY OF STATE
FOR EAST ASIA   WEDNESDAY, JULY 8, 1992
K-3-6 page# 1

        dest=hill,hsforaff,asia,philip,fns21447,fns13688,fns11182,fns13821,skor
        dest+=camb,armfor,defense,forpolus,nkor,nucweapon,
        dest+=un,viet,pak,mia,pov,russia,prc,
        data

        MR. SOLOMON: Nomkay (ph), right. You can get off into a word
game about whether something that is not functioning and is unlikely
to function for a long period of time as a reprocessing facility is
or is not a reprocessing facility. You know, it may only look like
part of a duck, but you suspect it might in time become a duck. Do
you expect dismantlement or not? I mean, there's a certain
Krasnoyarsk radar quality to this issue.

        REP. SOLARZ: We had this in Pakistan, too, my friend from
California will recall. When is a nuclear device a nuclear device?

        MR. SOLOMON: When it goes bang, right?

        REP. SOLARZ: Well, is the South -- (laughter) -- is the South
insisting that it be dismantled or does it -- or not?

        MR. SOLOMON: My understanding is they have not gotten to that
point and they're still at a point of trying to establish the
parameters of an inspection process. But let me just say again we
are determined, as others, to ensure that reprocessing is not
promoted on the peninsula.

        REP. SOLARZ: Well, I recall Mr. Blix saying once that, if, in
fact, the North had a reprocessing facility even if they declared
it, it would have to be dismantled because the only conceivable
purpose for a reprocessing facility would to be make fissile
material for nuclear weapons. And so, I'd like to know, is Mr. Blix
asking that this facility be dismantled or not?

        MR. SOLOMON: This issue has not been defined in the kind of
concrete, brick-by-brick terms that you're talking about now, but
it's clearly an issue that's lying there on the table to be looked
at.

        REP. SOLARZ: But, in any case, you're saying that the
completion of that reprocessing facility was years away or the
making of nuclear weapons was years away?

        MR. SOLOMON: Reprocessing facility itself. But I should say
that there still remains concern, as you've expressed yourself, that
the reprocessing of spent fuel could already or -- be -- have been
carried out elsewhere in hot cells in small facilities in these
tunnels that we're aware are dug everywhere else and that, again,
we're determined to see an inspection regime and other developments
which will preclude a secret nuclear program from developing.

        REP. SOLARZ: And what is the status of our relationship with

HEARING OF THE HOUSE FOREIGN AFFAIRS COMMITTEE ASIA-PACIFIC SUBCOMMITTEE;
SUBJECT: REVIEW OF DEVELOPMENTS IN ASIA; CHAIRED BY: REP. STEPHEN J.
SOLARZ (D-NY); WITNESSES: RICHARD SOLOMAN, ASSISTANT SECRETARY OF STATE
FOR EAST ASIA   WEDNESDAY, JULY 8, 1992
K-3-6 page# 2

North Korea at the present time? And what have we said to them we
are willing to do with respect to normalizing our diplomatic and
economic relationship and what they would have to do beyond what
they've already done to make it possible for us to move in that
direction?

MR. SOLOMON: As you recall, in the fall of 1988, we
established a channel to the North Koreans in Beijing at the
political counsel level. That channel persists, and it is our
primary channel -- really our only channel -- of communication at
this point.

Back last January, we did have a one-time meeting at a
political level. Undersecretary Kanter led our declaration in New
York. We met with Mr. Kim Young-sun, who's the head of the foreign
affairs committee in the party in their Supreme Peoples Assembly, a
man who does, apparently, have close ties to the leadership. And we
had a full, thorough exchange of views. We said at that time that,
if the two agreements that had been reached a few weeks earlier with
the South and the IAEA arrangements were implemented and you had
implemented inspections under both regimes, then we would upgrade
our dialogue to a political level and we would be glad to hold it in
New York if that was the most convenient place.

Upgrading that dialogue still left some very serious issues to
be discussed. We have been concerned for some time about North
Korean proliferation activity through missile sales. And we want
the repatriation of Korean War remains. There's been some progress
there. Thirty sets of remains were returned not too long ago
through the MAC. We were very pleased about that development.
Propaganda has been toned down. But we've concerned in the -- about
past Korean support for terrorist activities. They made a public
statement disavowing state-sponsored terrorism. But we do have
other issues that we would want to sort out as we try to move to
improve our relations.

But the fundamental step forward is sort of one step of a two-
step process that has been made -- that is, the IAEA inspections.
We still await the joint North-South inspection.

REP. SOLARZ: Well, if the North-South inspections were agreed
upon, then what would be the justification for not establishing some
kind of diplomatic relationship with an interest section or an
embassy? I mean, the Russians and the Chinese, I gather, now have
diplomatic facilities in the South. I assume you don't -- we don't
take the position that literally every issue has to be resolved
before we can have some form of diplomatic relations. I mean, we
have differences with many countries.

I mean, this -- solving this nuclear question was of paramount
importance if, in fact, it is satisfactorily resolved and they're in
a dialogue with the South, it seems to me that our larger interest
in trying to sort of open up the North to introduce, hopefully, a
greater measure of realism on their part in order to diminish the   0020

4444-11-8

HEARING OF THE HOUSE FOREIGN AFFAIRS COMMITTEE ASIA-PACIFIC SUBCOMMITTEE;
SUBJECT: REVIEW OF DEVELOPMENTS IN ASIA; CHAIRED BY: REP. STEPHEN J.
SOLARZ (D-NY); WITNESSES: RICHARD SOLOMAN, ASSISTANT SECRETARY OF STATE
FOR EAST ASIA   WEDNESDAY, JULY 8, 1992
K-3-6 page# 3
   prospects for reckless moves in the future constitutes a fairly
   compelling justification for some fairly dramatic steps on our part
   in comparison to what our policy has been for the last 30 years.
   And I'm a little bit surprised to hear that, even if the nuclear
   question is satisfactorily resolved, we're still -- you know, the
   relationship creeps forward in its petty pace until the last
   syllable of recorded time.

       To close --

       MR. SOLOMON: Mr. Chairman, again, I think you would have to
   say that, looked at even in the fullness of the past 50 years, in
   the last nine months we've made extremely rapid progress in moving
   away from what has been one of the most dangerous military
   confrontations left from the Cold War era. So, I don't believe this
   is in any sense a petty pace. You're raising appropriate questions.
   You're right on the cutting edge of policy, and I'm sure my
   successor will have the pleasure of working out a game plan or a
   road map or something else that might include the sort of thing that
   you're talking about.

       However, let me again come back to what has been a fundamental
   point in our policy for many decades, since the division of the
   peninsula, that we want to see the North-South confrontation ended.
   We don't want to undercut the position of our ally in South Korea.
   And we want the North-South dialogue to be which we -- we will keep
   up with it rather than lead it, I would think --

       REP. SOLARZ: Does the South want us to establish or refrain
   from establishing diplomatic relations at this point with the North
   and to --

       MR. SOLOMON: We haven't really addressed the issue in those
   terms yet.

       REP. SOLARZ: Mr. Lagomarsino?

       REP. ROBERT LAGOMARSINO (R-CA): Thank you, Mr. Chairman.

       You mentioned the return of what was it? Thirty remains from
   North Korea?

       MR. SOLOMON: Correct.

       REP. LAGOMARSINO: From the Korean War?

       MR. SOLOMON: Right.

       REP. LAGOMARSINO: Do you think the North Koreans are aware of
   the -- that cooperation on this issue will benefit them just as the
   beginning with the nuclear question? In other words, I guess a good
   way to put it -- are they aware of how big an issue that is starting
   to become here? It hasn't been before, but it -- my sense is that
   it's starting to become nearly as big an issue as the Vietnam MIA-

HEARING OF THE HOUSE FOREIGN AFFAIRS COMMITTEE ASIA-PACIFIC SUBCOMMITTEE;
SUBJECT: REVIEW OF DEVELOPMENTS IN ASIA; CHAIRED BY: REP. STEPHEN J.
SOLARZ (D-NY); WITNESSES: RICHARD SOLOMAN, ASSISTANT SECRETARY OF STATE
FOR EAST ASIA   WEDNESDAY, JULY 8, 1992
K-3-6 page# 4
     POW issue.

     MR. SOLOMON: For the very fact that I think they read the
world's press and they know how much of an issue it's been in terms
of our dealings with Vietnam, I sense they understand that this is a
matter that the American people care deeply about.

     REP. LAGOMARSINO: How would you assess the relationship of
North Korea at this point with Russia and with China? Closer
together? Further apart?

     MR. SOLOMON: My sense is that North Korea's relations
certainly with the former Soviet Union in its last days, perhaps
with the case of Russia today, has not been all that friendly and
forthcoming, whereas I think their relations with China have
improved somewhat. But as the Chairman pointed out, here you have
both China and Russia having diplomatic facilities in the South,
supporting South Korea's entry into the UN, and I think this
indicates that they are pursuing a balanced foreign policy that
can't make people in the North all that happy.

     REP. LAGOMARSINO: How -- and how would you assess the clout

                    CONTINUED

der.chill,hsforaff,asia,philip,fns21447,fns13688,fns11182,fns13821,skor
dest=camb,armfor,defense,forpolus,nkor,nucweapon,prc,philip,elecfor
dest=un,viet,prc,prepdns,
data

of Kim Jong Ill (ph), is that how you pronounce his name, with
China?

MR. SOLOMON: You got it right. It

REP. LAGOMANSINO: It's interesting. China, I think, is the
only foreign country, at least that I know of, that he's ever
visited and again, we really don't have much insight, much
information on this kind of an issue other than the sense there is
something of a relationship there. The Chinese, I think, have tried
to supplant the influence that the former Soviet Union in North
Korea to a limited degree.

REP. LAGOMANSINO: Could you tell us, for the record, what
the DPRC position on the U.S. treaty commitment to South Korea and
the presence of U.S. military forces on the Korean peninsula is?

I might just say, the reason I ask that is there was a
Japanese newspaper report not long ago that quoted a diplomat, a
North Korean diplomat, as saying or implying that insofar as North
Korea is concerned the immediate withdrawal of U.S. troops from
South Korea is no longer a top objective of North Korea.

MR. SOLOMON: Let me say two things on that point. First, I
think North Korean foreign policy is evolving in some interesting
ways, but with some real debate and perhaps some serious divisions
within the leadership. I mean, I find it difficult to believe that
the opening up of the nuclear facilities to inspection could have
occurred without some very vigorous debate and again, maybe some
serious differences within the leadership, but it has occurred.

We sense a similar evolution in policy, which we get wisps of
in our contacts with North Korean officials, and as part of the
initiative of 1988, we have been somewhat more forthcoming in giving
visas to North Korean officials in unofficial capacities. That is,
a member of their Institute for Peace and Disarmament or one or
another quasi-academic think tank kind of organization.

These individuals come to the United States. We've had
discussions with them and we do get the impression that they see our
presence now as contributing, in some measure, to regional
stability. And exactly what that means, what operational form it
would take regarding their attitude towards the treaty that we have
and will maintain with our ally in the South regarding our true
presence there is an interesting question and hopefully, if the
dialogue does advance, that will be one of the issues.

4544—11—11

외 무 부

종 별 : 지 급

번 호 : USW-3470

일 시 : 92 0709 1656

수 신 : 장 관 (미이,미일)

발 신 : 주 미 대사

제 목 : SOLOMON 차관보 증언

대: WUS-3221

연: USW-3465

1. 당관 임성준 참사관은 금 7.9(목) 오후 국무부 KARTMAN 한국과장과 면담, 작일 SOLOMON 차관보의 하원 아태소위 증언에 대한 ~~대하~~ 아측 입장을 상세히 설명하고 북한 핵문제 특히 남북 상호사찰 문제와 관련 미행정부 입장이 유연하게 변경된 것인지 여부등에 관하여 문의하였던바, 동 과장은 아래 요지로 답변하였음.(비공식 증언기록 제공)

- 작일 청문회시 SOLOMON 차관보가 몇군데 잘못 발언한 부분 (MISSTATEMENT)이 있어 사실확인과 의회기록 (CONGRESSIONAL RECORD)을 위하여 수정(CORRECTION)할 예정이며 언론에 대하여도 문의가 있는 경우 바로 잡아줄 예정임.

- 작일 혼선은 SOLARZ 아태소위원장의 독특한 청문회 진행 스타일 때문에 발생한 것으로 보임.(동 위원장은 청문회 참석 증인에 대하여 쉴새없이 질문을 퍼붓는 스타일로 청문회를 진행시켜오고 있으며, 질문 자체가 잘못된 내용과 논리를 담고 있을 경우에는 이에대한 답변도 동일한 오류에 빠져들기 쉬움)

- (임참사관이 특히 수정을 요하는 부분이 어느곳인지를 문의한데 대하여) 북한의 핵재처리 시설에 관한 언급중 우리측이 동 시설의 폐기를 요구하지 않았다는 부분은 명백하게 오류이므로 동 시설의 건설중단(HALT)을 요구하였다는 내용으로 수정할 예정이며, 핵재처리 문제와 관련 IAEA BLIX 총장이 언급한 것으로인용된 부분도 사실과 다른 내용이 많으므로 수정되어야 할 것으로 보며, 금후미.북한 관계개선 문제와 관련 한.미간에 사전 협의가 아직 이루어지지 않은 것으로 오해될 만한 부분이 있어 동 부분도 수정할 예정이라고 설명하였음.

- 하원 아태소위로 부터 SOLOMON 차관보에 대한 출석 요청이 있었을때, 동아태국

미주국	장관	차관	1차보	미주국	외정실	분석관	청와대	안기부

92.07.10   07:28

외신 2과 통제관 EC

0024

특히 한국과에서는 북한 핵문제등에 관하여 기존 정책의 변화가 없고 특별히 덧붙여 발언할 내용도 없기 때문에 SOLOMON 차관보의 출석이 바람직하지 않은 것으로 건의하였으나, 동 차관보의 재직기간을 통하여 SOLARZ 위원장의 개인적인 지원을 많이 받은데 대한 일종의 의무감을 느껴 거절하기 어려웠다는 배경을 설명하였음.

2. 상기 면담기회에 임참사관은 현재 북한 핵문제 해결이 교착상태에 빠져 있으나, 현재 미행정부가 핵문제 해결이후 대북한 정책방향에 관하여 구체적으로 검토하는 바가 있는지 문의하였던바, KARTMAN 과장은 이미 북한측에 밝힌바와 같이 핵문제가 해결된 이후의 단계는 북한측과 대화를 정례화 한다는 방향외에는 결정된 사항이 아무것도 없으며 향후 몇개월간은 철저한 남. 북한 상호사찰이 실현되는데에 역량을 쏟아갈 것임을 재다짐하였음. 끝.

(대사 현홍주-차관)

예고: 92.12.31. 일반

〔핵문서로 재분류(1992.12.31.)〕

〔검토필(1992.6.30.)〕

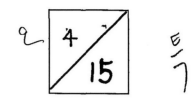

솔로몬 次官補 議會 聽聞會 發言

1992.7.10.

外 務 部

솔로몬 國務部 東亞·太 次官補는 7.9. 開催된 下院 外務委 亞·太 小委 聽聞會 質疑 應答時 北韓 核問題 等에 대해 言及한 바, 同 要旨를 아래 報告 드립니다.

1. 솔로몬 次官補 言及 要旨

(北韓 核問題)

o 블릭스 IAEA 事務總長 訪北 및 1차 IAEA 臨時査察 結果, 北側의 核再處理施設 能力 保有 意圖는 明白하나, 完全한 核再處理 能力을 갖추는 데는 수년이 걸릴것으로 보여짐.

   - 美側의 韓半島內 核再處理施設 許容 不可 立場은 不變

o 北韓은 신고된 施設외에도 IAEA 側이 원하는 施設에 대한 開放을 約束한 바 있어, 特別査察을 受容한 것으로 看做할 수 있다고 봄.

0026

o 南·北 相互查察은 軍事施設도 對象으로 하고 있기 때문에
北韓 核問題에 대해 確信을 갖게 해주며, 특히 南·北間의
緊張緩和, 軍備 統制 및 和解까지도 發展될 수 있다는
점에서 매우 重要함.

 - 美側은 北韓이 南·北間의 直接 對話를 回避하려는
   어떠한 試圖도 排擊

 - 相互查察 實施 以前 北韓과의 關係 改善은 不可

(美·北韓 關係)

o 今年 1.22. 美·北韓 高位接觸時 美側은 IAEA 및 相互查察
實施될 境遇, 뉴욕 等地에서 美·北韓間 定例的인 政策級
接觸 許容 立場을 傳達함.

 - 現在 IAEA 査察 條件은 充足된 바, 相互查察 實施가
   關鍵

o 美·北韓 政策級 接觸이 이루어지더라도 美·北 關係 改善
에는 北韓의 諸般問題 解決이 必要함.

 - 北側이 韓國戰 失踪者 遺骸 送還, 對美誹謗 自制,
   테러리즘 非難 聲明 등 一部 宥和적 措置를 취하고
   있는 점에 留意

   · 미사일 輸出등 기타 問題 解決 必要

0027

(駐韓 美軍의 役割)

o 最近 訪美 北韓人士와 接觸時, 北側이 駐韓美軍의 存在가
  地域安定에 寄與하는 役割을 하고 있다는 점을 認定하고
  있다는 印象을 받은 바 있음.
  - 核査察 關聯 北韓指導部內 異見과 論難이 있는 것으로
    觀察되며, 駐韓美軍에 대해서도 類似한 內部 狀況 感知
  - 향후 北側의 明確한 意圖 및 立場 把握 可能

2. 分析 및 對策

o 솔로몬 次官補가 北韓이 IAEA 의 特別査察을 受容한 것으로
  看做하는 입장을 表明한 것은 블릭스 IAEA 事務總長 訪北時
  北側 言及 內容을 旣定事實化시켜 北韓이 이를 回避할 수
  없도록 하려는 意圖로 觀察되나, 이로인해 國際 社會內
  相互査察 實施 必要性에 대한 認識을 희석시킬 憂慮가 있는
  것으로 보임.
  - 上記 我側 憂慮를 美側에 傳達
  - IAEA 特別査察보다 相互査察 制度下의 强制査察이
    査察의 卽刻性 및 實效性 側面에서 한층 優越함을
    强調토록 美側에 協調를 要請

o 따라서 相互査察의 특수한 役割 및 重要性을 들어 北韓
  開放化를 위해서는 旣存 立場의 維持가 보다 有效한 점을
  美國은 물론 餘他 關係國과의 協議時 계속 强調 豫定

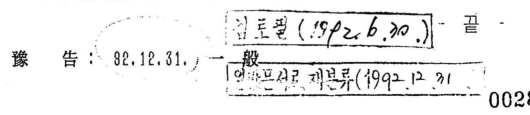

검토필 (1992. 6. 30.)   - 끝 -

豫 告 : 92.12.31.   一 般

일반문서로 재분류(1992. 12. 31

0028

관리 번호	92-642

외 무 부

종   별 :

번   호 : USW-3568   일   시 : 92 0715 1857

수   신 : 장 관 (미이,미이,정총,정안,국기) 사본:주오지리대사

발   신 : 주 미 대사

제   목 : 북한 핵문제 관련 BLIX 사무총장 공개 설명회

보통문서로 ~~재분류(1992.12.31)~~

연: USW-3112

1. 하원 외무위 아. 태소위 (위원장: STEPHEN SOLARZ)의 STANLEY ROTH 수석전문위원은 금 7.15. 당관 조일환 참사관에게 HANS BLIX IAEA 사무총장이 연호 SOLARZ 의원의 초청을 수락하여 워싱턴을 방문, 하원 외무위의 아. 태소위, 군축.국제안보.과학소위(위원장: DANTE FASCELL), 국제경제정책. 통상소위(위원장: SAM GEJDENSON)등 3 개 소위가 공동으로 7.22(수) 개최할 예정인 북한 핵문제 관련 공개 설명회에 참석하여 IAEA 의 북한 핵 사찰 결과등에 대한 설명을 하게 될예정이라고 알려왔음.

2. 조참사관은 이에대해 BLIX 총장이 미 의회의 청문회에서 증언하는 것인지와 방미기간, 수행원등에 관해 문의한바, 동 전문위원은 아래와같이 답변함.

가. BLIX 사무총장이 SOLARZ 위원장의 아. 태소위 청문회 참석 구두 초청에대해 긍정적 의사를 표명해 옴에 따라 지난주 상기 3 개 소위원장 공동명의로 공개 설명회에 참석해 줄것을 요청하는 초청장이 발송된바 있음.

나. BLIX 총장은 7.20-23 간 방미하는 것으로 알고 있으며, 수행원 2 명중 1명은 IAEA 의 북한 핵사찰에 참가했던 직원이 될 것임.

다. 금번 북한 핵문제 설명회는 IAEA 측에서 청문회 (HEARING)라고 부르는 것을 원치 않음에 따라 공개설명회 (PUBLIC BRIEFING)라고 부르게 되었으나, 금번 설명회에서 BLIX 총장의 모두 발언과 질의.응답이 있을 예정이므로 사실상 일반 청문회와 같은 것으로 볼수 있으며, 만약 민감한 질문이 제기되어 BLIX 총장이 비공개로 답변하기를 원하는 경우에는 공개설명회 이후 별도로 비공개 설명회를 개최하게 될 가능성도 있음.

3. 동 설명회 개최 관련 동향 추보 예정임.끝.

미주국 정와대	장관 안기부	차관 중계	1차보	미주국	국기국	외정실	외정실	분석관

0029

PAGE 1

(대사 현홍주-국장)
예고: 92.12.31. 일반

외 무 부

관리 번호 92-1972

종   별 :

번   호 : USW-3668   일   시 : 92 0722 2248

수   신 : 장관 (미이,미일,정총,정안,국기,기정)사본:주오지리,유엔대사(중계필)

발   신 : 주 미 대사

제   목 : 하원 외무위 북한 핵문제 공개 설명회

     연: USW-3568

     1.   하원   외무위   아태소위(위원장: STEPHEN   SOLARZ),
군축.국제안보.과학소위(위원장: DANTE FASCELL), 국제경제 정책.무역소위(위원장:
SAM GEJDENSEN)는 금 7.22. BLIX IAEA 사무총장을 참석시킨 가운데 연호 북한
핵문제에 관한 공개 설명회를 개최함.(당관 조일환 참사관및 안총기 서기관 참석)

     2. BLIX 사무총장은 모두 발언을 통해 북한 핵문제와 관련 아래 요지로 언급함.

     - 북한과 같이 장기간 동안 핵시설을 보유한 나라의 경우 신고된 시설의 목록이
완벽한지의 여부를 입증하기는 쉽지 않음.

     - 북한은 1990 년 실험실을 통해 소량의 플루토늄을 추출했다고 시인하였으며,
IAEA 가 더이상의 플루토늄 보유 가능성을 문의한데 대해 이를 부인함.

     - 북한은 플루토늄을 추출한 이후 중간단계의 PILOT PLANT 를 거치지 않고 길이
190 M, 높이 9 층의 거대한 시설을 건설하고 있는바, 이것은 일반적인 산업국가에서는
있을수 없는 일임.

     - 북한의 5MW 원자로의 연료(CORE)가 원래의 연료인지 여부는 앞으로 1 년 이내에
있게될 것으로 예상되는 연료 교체시 확실히 알수 있을 것임.

     3. 이어 계속된 질의.응답의 주요 내용은 아래와 같음.

     (IAEA 의 불시사찰 권한 여부)

     - SOLARZ 의원은 북한이 IAEA 에 의한 불시(CHALLENGE) 사찰 또는 특별(SPECIAL)
사찰에 동의하였는지와 이러한 사찰을 IAEA 가 북한에 대해 요구하였는지를 문의함.

     - 이에대해 BLIX 사무총장은 IAEA 는 신고되어야할 핵물질 또는 시설이 신고되지
않고 있다고 믿을만한 이유가 있을 경우 해당 국가에게 먼저 해명(EXPLANATION)을
요구할수 있으며, 해당국가의 해명이 만족스럽지 않을 경우 그지역에 대한

미주국 정와대	장관 안기부	차관 중계	1차보	미주국	국기국	외정실	외정실	분석관

0031

PAGE 1   92.07.23   13:36

외신 2과 통제관 BX

특별(SPECIAL)사찰을 요구할수 있다고 말하고, 이것은 군축협상에 있어서 <u>의심이 없는</u> 경우에도 일정 장소를 사찰할수 있는 <u>불시사찰의 개념</u>과는 다른 것이며, IAEA 는 특별사찰을 협정 가입국에 아직 요구한 적이 없다고 답변함.

BLIX 총장은 그러나 자신이 북한을 방문했을때 북한 관리들에게 IAEA 가 북한내 어떤 장소를 언제든지 방문할수 있도록 허용하는 것을 공표하는 것이 바람직하다고 조언한바 있으며, 자신의 보도자료에 이러한 내용을 삽입하는 것을 북한측이 받아들인바 있다고 부언함.

(북한의 핵물질 은닉 가능성)

- SOLARZ 의원은 만일 북한이 핵물질을 생산하여 은닉하고 있다는 정보가 있는 경우 어떠한 사찰 절차가 이루어질 것인가를 질문함.

- BLIX 사무총장은 그러한 경우 특별 사찰이 요구되어야 할 것이며, 숨겨놓은 핵물질이 발견되는 경우 협정 위반이 될 것이므로 IAEA 이사회및 안보리에 보고되어 차후의 조치가 취해지게 된다고 설명하고, 특별사찰이 거부될 경우도 같은 절차가 취해질 것이라고 답변함.

(북한이 건설중인 핵재처리 시설의 용도) → 新聞보다는 nuance 가 있다가 다름.

- SOLARZ 의원은 북한이 건설중인 핵재처리 <u>시설이 평화적 목적으로 이용될수도 있는지를</u> 문의함.

- 이에대해 BLIX 사무총장은 자신이 북한측에게 동 시설의 용도를 문의했을때 북한관리들은 MIXED OXIDE 연료생산 목적, 증식로에 사용하는 목적, 폐기물 처리(WASTE DISPOSAL) 목적등을 들었으나, 북한의 경우 MIXED OXIDE 연료를 이용할수 있는 경수로 원자로도 없고, 증식로 개발은 더욱 가능성이 없음. 본인의 판단으로는 이러한 목적을 위해 플루토늄이 반드시 필요하지도 않음.

(핵재처리 시설 폐기 요구 여부)

- SOLARZ 의원은 북한이 건설중인 핵재처리 시설을 폐기하도록 요구할 계획은 없는지를 문의하였는바, BLIX 총장은 IAEA 가 동시설의 폐기를 요구할수는 없으며, 안전조치 협정상의 회원국 의무는 모든 것을 신고하는 것이라고 답변하고,실제로 북한관리들은 플루토늄을 생산하더라도 모두 신고하면 되지 않느냐고 주장한바 있다고 부언함.

(IAEA 안전조치 협정 해석문제)

- LEACH 의원은 IAEA 가 안전조치 협정상 광범위한 권리를 보유하고 있음에도

PAGE 2

0032

불구하고 불시사찰의 권리가 없는 것으로 축소해석하고 있는 것이 아니냐고 질문하고, 북한은 IAEA 사찰을 보다 철저한 사찰인 남. 북한 상호 사찰을 회피하는 구실로서 이용하고 있으므로 IAEA 가 권한을 보다 광범하게 해석하는 것이 바람직할 것이라고 언급함.

   - 이에대해 BLIX 총장은 자신에게 각 회원국의 어디든지 사찰할수 있는 권리는 없는 것으로 안다고 말하고 LEACH 의원의 견해와 같이 북한에 대해서는 불시사찰이 바람직할수도 있으나 이러한 권한은 회원국 모두에게 적용될 수 있어야만 한다는 점도 유의해야 할 것이라고 답변함.

   4. 관찰및 평가

   - 금일 설명회는 국제기구 소속 직원이 미 의회를 상대로 설명하는 것이었으나 일반 청문회와 같은 형식으로 진행되었으며, BLIX 총장이 서두에 핵 비확산문제 일반에 대해 언급하였음에도 불구하고 의원들의 질의는 북한 핵문제에 거의 집중됨.

   - 설명회 참석 의원들은 IAEA 의 불시사찰 권한 보유여부에 대해 특별히 집중적인 관심을 표명하였는바, 이것은 IAEA 사찰제도의 한계성에 대한 의원들의 의심을 반영한 것으로 보이며, BLIX 사무총장에 대한 특별사찰및 불시사찰의 구분 설명과 IAEA 의 불시사찰 권한 불보유 설명은 남. 북한 상호사찰의 중요성을 간접적으로 부각시킨 것으로 평가됨. 끝.

   (대사 현홍주-국장)

   예고: 92.12.31. 까지

7/23 신
7.24 즉오 시본
비꼬 신청했

주 미 대 사 관

USW(F) : 4836   년월일 : 92. 7. 22 시간 : 20:00

수 신 : 장 관 (미이)

발 신 : 주미대사

제 목 : BLIX. IAEA 사무총장 설명회 (출처 :   )

	보 안
	통 제

배부처	장관실	차관실	일차보	이차보	외경정실	분석관	아주국	미주국	구주국	중아국	국기국	경제국	통상국	문협국	의연원	청와대	안기부	공보처	경기원	상공부	재무부	농수부	동자부	환경처	과기처
								O																	

(4836 - 33 - 1)

외신 1과	
통 제	

0034

HOUSE FOREIGN AFFAIRS COMMITTEE / SUBCMTE ON ASIAN AND PACIFIC AFFAIRS
SUBCMTE, ON ARMS CONTROL, INT'L SECURITY & SCIENCE
SUBCMTE ON INT'L ECONOMIC POLICY & TRADE
CHAIRMAN: REP. STEPHEN SOLARZ, D-NY TOPIC: NORTH KOREA NUCLEAR PROGRAM
WITNESS: DR. HANS BLIX, DIRECTOR, IAEA WEDNESDAY, JULY 22, 1992
H-3-1 page# 1

        dest=hill,hsforaff,nkor,skor,fns21447,fns14094,nucweapon,asia,pacific
        dest+=iran,libya,india,pak,israel,alg,arg,braz,safr,latamer
        data

        REP. SOLARZ: The Subcommittees will come to order. The
Subcommittee on Asian and Pacific Affairs, as well as the
Subcommittee on Arms Control, International Security, and Science,
and the Subcommittee on International Economic Policy and Trade is
pleased to welcome Dr. Hans Blix to today's briefing on the North
Korean Nuclear Program. I particularly appreciate the willingness
of Dr. Blix and his colleagues to travel all the way from Vienna to
appear before us today.

        There have been many significant developments since I last had
the opportunity, in 1991, to discuss the North Korean Nuclear
Program with Dr. Blix. North Korea has, of course, both signed and
ratified an inspection agreement with the IAEA since that time.

        Dr. Blix then visited North Korea in May of this year, and two
adhoc IAEA inspections have been conducted, one in June and one in
July. I gather that negotiations are nearing completion with the
North for a facility's attachment, which will regularize inspection
procedures.

        Despite all of these developments, however, I must say that I
still have some very serious concerns about the North Korean Nuclear
Program. First, North Korea has publicly admitted that it has
already reprocessed small amounts of plutonium. If the North has,
at least, a limited operational reprocessing capability, how can the
international community be assured that the North does not already
possess significantly greater amounts of plutonium than it now
claims.

        Second, North Korea claims that it has no spent fuel from the
(5-MWE?) reactor. It has been, at least, intermittently operational
since 1986. At today's briefing, we hope to find out if it is
technically possible to determine through the inspection process
whether or not the original reactor core is still in this reactor,
as the North claims.

        Third, after his trip to Pyongyang in May of this year, Dr.
Blix publicly stated his conclusion that the facility which the
North calls a radio chemical laboratory would, in fact, be a
reprocessing facility once it is completed. Given the fact that
there appears to be no legitimate use for such a facility in North
Korea, will the IAEA insist that the North decommission this
facility.

                                                              · 0035
        Finally, it is unclear to me precisely what the North's
position is with respect to special inspections. We hope to learn
from Dr. Blix today whether the North has explicitly indicated to
the IAEA if it will accept the IAEA's right to conduct special or

HOUSE FOREIGN AFFAIRS COMMITTEE / SUBCMTE ON ASIAN AND PACIFIC AFFAIRS
SUBCMTE, ON ARMS CONTROL, INT'L SECURITY & SCIENCE
SUBCMTE ON INT'L ECONOMIC POLICY & TRADE
CHAIRMAN: REP. STEPHEN SOLARZ, D-NY TOPIC: NORTH KOREA NUCLEAR PROGRAM
WITNESS: DR. HANS BLIX, DIRECTOR, IAEA WEDNESDAY, JULY 22, 1992
H-3-1 page# 2
         challenge inspections at any facility in the North, including, if
         necessary, North Korean military facilities. We hope that today's
         briefing by Dr. Blix will shed some light on these and many other
         issues.

         Once again, I'd like to thank Dr. Blix and his colleagues, Dr.
         Perricos and Mr. Villaros, for their willingness to brief us on this
         very important issue. Dr. Blix, before I ask you to give the
         Subcommittees the benefit of your wisdom, experience and
         information, I would like to yield to my very good friend from the
         state of Iowa, the distinguished Ranking Member of the Subcommittee
         on Asian and Pacific Affairs, Mr. Leach.

         REP. JIM LEACH (R-IA): I thank the distinguished, Hispanic
         Chair, for yielding. Let me just mention, by way of introduction,
         that this is one of the most burrowed and burrowing societies in the
         world. And that, as we all understand, you have been allowed to
         inspect what the North Koreans have allowed you to inspect. And
         it's certainly my view, and I'm sure the Chairman shares this, that
         the principle to challenge inspections are very important in this
         type of circumstance. And one of the issues the international
         community is going to have to deal with is how those take place and
         what rights and discretions are given the IAEA.

         My own view is, personally, to give extraordinary discretion
         to the IAEA itself, without the need for super approvals form,
         whether it be the UN Security Council, or whatever.

         I would also stress that from an American perspective, we
         place a great deal of emphasis on the signed agreement between North
         and South Korea bilateral agreement, in which the North has agreed
         to inspections by the South, and that there should be no implication
         that one agreed to inspection by North Korea for the IAEA should, in
         any way, undercut their obligations under their North-South
         agreement. And I would certainly hope that the IAEA would be as
         cooperative as possible in advancing this particular bilateral
         agreement, and ensuring data with South Korea, as well as relevant
         reciprocal data with the North.

         Finally, I would just say that it is my understanding that
         North Korea has some sort of misleading belief that they've got a
         bargaining tool with the United States based upon their control of
         several remains from the Korean War. And certainly, our society
         places a great deal of emphasis on POW-MIA issues, including those
         of remains. But I think everybody should understand that remains
         aren't bargained for, and particularly in policy terms of this
         nature. And that, we in America,, if there's going to be any hope
         of being cooperative with bringing North Korea into the new world of
         the 21st Century, are going to have to insist on a very tough NPT
         type of circumstance inspections, and what I would assume would be
         the dismantling of facilities that are in the process of being made.

         Thank you very much, Mr. Chairman.   0036

HOUSE FOREIGN AFFAIRS COMMITTEE / SUBCMTE ON ASIAN AND PACIFIC AFFAIRS
SUBCMTE, ON ARMS CONTROL, INT'L SECURITY & SCIENCE
SUBCMTE ON INT'L ECONOMIC POLICY & TRADE
CHAIRMAN: REP. STEPHEN SOLARZ, D-NY TOPIC: NORTH KOREA NUCLEAR PROGRAM
WITNESS: DR. HANS BLIX, DIRECTOR, IAEA WEDNESDAY, JULY 22, 1992
H-3-1 page# 3
          REP. SOLARZ: Thank you, Mr. Leach. Dr. Blix, please proceed.

          HANS BLIX: Thank you very much, Mr. Chairman. I am very
pleased to have the opportunity to brief your Committee on a subject
that is central on the International Atomic Energy Agency's work,
namely nuclear non-proliferation and the safeguards verification.
And I understand very well that you are focussing upon the question
North Korea, and I will be glad to answer questions and also my
introductory remarks, if you will allow me to make them -- to make
some specific points about the,, what we term, the (EPRK?), North
Korea. But I think some preliminary comments are in place.

          There has been much concern about -- among governments --
about various countries, some of them nonproliferation adherence,
and others not. Among those, that have appeared to have a
nonproliferation treaty, there have been concerns expressed by
governments about North Korea, about Iran, about Libya, and also
concerns about some states that are not parties to the
nonproliferation treaty -- evidently they are India, Pakistan,
Israel, and also Algeria.

          I'll be very glad to answer questions on these matters and I
have, as you know, to collaborators with me. Mr. Villaros on my
right side -- (inaudible) -- special assistance, who was with me in
the North Korea. He also went with me to Libya, and he has also
been on an IEA mission to a number of sites in Iran. And I have on
my left side Mr. Perricos, who is a senior member of our Safeguards
Department, and who has been the chief inspector in most of the IEA
missions to Iraq. All together, we have had 13 missions. And I
think he has headed seven of these missions.

          The first introductory point I should like to make is that we
had reason, not only to register concern, but also some satisfaction
in the nonproliferation field in the past year. Argentina and
Brazil have now concluded an agreement, creating a joint --
(inaudible) -- control system. And they have made a safeguards
agreement with the IEA opening up all their installations for IEA
inspections.   A

          South Africa, which for a long time refrained from adhering to
nonproliferation treaty, has done so, and concluding a safeguards
agreement with us. And we are now verifying the completeness of
that declaration. North Korea is another case where the country,
for many years, did not sign a safeguards agreement with the agency,
but has done so in the year and ratified it. And thereafter,
submitted a list, what we term an original inventory. And we are
now verifying that.

          And as you said, Mr. Chairman, we have sent two adhoc
inspection missions to it, in order to verify these lists. It is a
rather long list. We have made it public. The question is, then,
whether it is complete or not. That's the outlook for
nonproliferation, in my view, in the world. It's not altogether 0037
gloomy, even if there are a number of sources of concern.

HOUSE FOREIGN AFFAIRS COMMITTEE / SUBCMTE ON ASIAN AND PACIFIC AFFAIRS
SUBCMTE, ON ARMS CONTROL, INT'L SECURITY & SCIENCE
SUBCMTE ON INT'L ECONOMIC POLICY & TRADE
CHAIRMAN: REP. STEPHEN SOLARZ, D-NY TOPIC: NORTH KOREA NUCLEAR PROGRAM
WITNESS: DR. HANS BLIX, DIRECTOR, IAEA WEDNESDAY, JULY 22, 1992
H-3-1 page# 4

Indeed, there are good hopes that the Tlatelolco Treaty, for a
nuclear weapon free Latin America, may come into force next year --
Cuba having signalled that they would not stand in the way, but
would also join the Treaty, if all others did.

There are also some optimistic signals in view of discussions
on the peace conference in the Middle East, and hopes that
discussions about a nuclear weapon free zone for that area might
move forward.

The second introductory point, apart form this optimistic one,
I would like to make is that nonproliferation efforts consist of
many elements. And if anyone looks to the IAEA inspections as the
(bull work?) against nonproliferation, they are bound to be
disappointed. We are not claiming to be the (bull work?) against
nonproliferation.

The verification and the inspectors of the IEA is not a
nuclear police, but they are observers and they are reporters. They
cannot stop anything from taking place, but they can report to the
world about it. The risk of detection may serve some measure of
deterrent from a diversion, but it is not a executive power that can
stop it.

REP. SOLARZ: Dr. Blix, on that note, let me say that we have
here a problem of proliferation with votes. And the bells you've
just heard were the second bells on a 15 minute vote, which means we
only have a few minutes left. So, with your permission, the
Subcommittees will stand temporarily in recess while Mr. Leach and I
go to cast our votes. And then we will be back in about 10 minutes
and you can proceed with your statement.

MR. BLIX: Thank you.

(Committees recess)

REP. SOLARZ: The subcommittee will resume its deliberations.
Dr. Blix, please proceed.

(MORE)

0038

1A26-23-6

HOUSE FOREIGN AFFAIRS COMMITTEE / SUBCMTE ON ASIAN AND PACIFIC AFFAIRS
SUBCMTE, ON ARMS CONTROL, INT'L SECURITY & SCIENCE
SUBCMTE ON INT'L ECONOMIC POLICY & TRADE
CHAIRMAN: REP. STEPHEN SOLARZ, D-NY TOPIC: NORTH KOREA NUCLEAR PROGRAM
WITNESS: DR. HANS BLIX, DIRECTOR, IAEA WEDNESDAY, JULY 22, 1992
H-3-2 page# 1

dest=hill,hsforaff,nkor,skor,fns21447,fns14094,nucweapon,asia,pacific
dest+=armscont,russia,iraq,un,cyprus,safr
data

      MR. BLIX: Thank you Mr. Chairman. I was making some
introductory remarks about the situation on the non-proliferation
stage, and saying that anyone who would look to the IEA safeguards
as the bulwark against non-proliferation would have to be
disappointed because we're not shaming any such overall role.

      In reality, the efforts to prevent further spread of nuclear
weapons to further countries is countered by several different
barriers, the first of which certainly is the political one.
Detente in an area is likely to help to maintain non-proliferation
military alliances offering umbrellas to allied states also likely
to obviate their incentives to go for nuclear weapons.

      Nuclear disarmament is another area which is important to
induce countries to commit themselves to non-proliferation, and the
recent very important agreements that are being reached in this
regard I see as encouragement for complete adherence to non-
proliferation in the world.

      There are also rewards for commitments to non-proliferation
like a transfer of technology to developing countries. Many
developing countries are very eager to have that reward. On the
whole, the agency is not engaged in dealing with the political
incentives and disincentives to commit to non-proliferation. We
are, however, dealing as an instrument of member states with the
transfer of technology to developing countries, chiefly in non-power
sectors, in nuclear sectors dealing with, say, industry, agriculture
or medicine.

      A second barrier against non-proliferation in which we are
not involved are the export controls which help to retard and make
it more difficult to a state that would be bent on proliferation.
These excellent controls are agreed upon between supplier states and
we do not have any part in those negotiations. They have recently
taken place at a meeting in Warsaw where they have agreed upon
restrictions on the export of dual-use equipment and sensitive
equipment.

      The IEA safeguards inspections were developed a little over 20
years ago at a time when the concern about non-proliferation was
chiefly directed to industrialized states and they are zeroed in on
the fissionable material, on plutonium and enriched uranium. It is
the world's first on-site inspection system. We have about 200
inspectors who travel to countries and inspect the installations and
the materials, and the cost of the system annually is about $70
million.

0039

      We have suffered from the zero gross that has been inflicted

HOUSE FOREIGN AFFAIRS COMMITTEE / SUBCMTE ON ASIAN AND PACIFIC AFFAIRS
SUBCMTE, ON ARMS CONTROL, INT'L SECURITY & SCIENCE
SUBCMTE ON INT'L ECONOMIC POLICY & TRADE
CHAIRMAN: REP. STEPHEN SOLARZ, D-NY TOPIC: NORTH KOREA NUCLEAR PROGRAM
WITNESS: DR. HANS BLIX, DIRECTOR, IAEA WEDNESDAY, JULY 22, 1992
H-3-2 page# 2

upon all-international organizations. We have been living at zero
gross for eight years. In addition to that, we have been, last year
and this year, had the problem that Russia has not been paying at
all which gave us a deficit of $25 million last year and a deficit
of $25 million this year. And unless the United States succeeds in
paying its share for 1992 early in October, we will be broke in
October.

Now, the safeguards we perform in North Korea and in other
places are in the first place, based upon the state's declaration of
the fissionable material that they have and on the installations
which they have.. And we have verified these.

We make no assumption that these declarations are correct and
truthful, and as we verify them and as we verify the use and the
movements of nuclear materials, we find, in fact, many
inconsistencies and many anomalies, and they are pursued and they
are cleared up so far.

It is, in fact, our duty not to have faith in any of the
declarations that are given to us. There are certainly in the
industrialized states difficulties and limitations in this system,
the risk of non-detection is not zero, but to have a system that
would have much finer meshes than the one we have now would cost
quite a lot and we would also probably have a great many more false
alarms.

Compared to those problems relating to industrial countries,
the problem that we have seen in the wake of the Iraqi revelations
are much greater, namely the problem that a country might have non-
declared material in non-declared installations. And that goes then
to the original inventory which they submit tb us.

In open societies it is harder to conceal any installation.
In very closed societies, and Iraq certainly was one of them, and
still is, North Korea is another closed society, it is more
difficult. The lessons learned from Iraq to reduce the risk of non-
detection are very important and I think we have drawn them in the
past here, and I would summarize them as three.

First, for the inspection to be successful, we must have
access to information about possibly secret installations, those
that have not been declared. And we try to get that through
information about exports from individual countries, we try to scan
media for any clues. We also have asked member states to give us
information on the basis of their national systems;. WE must also
have access to the sites to visit, not only routine inspections in
the sites declared, but also have the right to go to a site where we
think that there are reasons to believe that some nuclear material
or installations which have not been declared, which should have
been declared, are located. And we have had a discussion of this in
the Board of Governors of the IEA and a conclusion by the chairman
that we do have the right to perform what you term rightly, special
inspections. And I'd be glad to elaborate on that theme in a   0040

N P2 l - 22 - 1

HOUSE FOREIGN AFFAIRS COMMITTEE / SUBCMTE ON ASIAN AND PACIFIC AFFAIRS
SUBCMTE, ON ARMS CONTROL, INT'L SECURITY & SCIENCE
SUBCMTE ON INT'L ECONOMIC POLICY & TRADE
CHAIRMAN: REP. STEPHEN SOLARZ, D-NY TOPIC: NORTH KOREA NUCLEAR PROGRAM
WITNESS: DR. HANS BLIX, DIRECTOR, IAEA WEDNESDAY, JULY 22, 1992
H-3-2 page# 3
     moment.

     The third access we need to have is access to the Security
Council. We need to be able to go to the Security Council and ask
for its backing and support in case we are not given the right to
inspection which we can claim. Unless per chance specifically we
wanted to go to North Korea. As you rightly said, they delayed
their acceptance of the safeguards agreement but have signed that
and ratified it in the past year. And they submitted, in accordance
with the rules, the original inventory. In fact, they submitted it
somewhat earlier than they really were obliged to do, and thereafter
they invited me to pay an official visit during which they had the
opportunity to explain their nuclear program to me.

     My visit was not an inspection. The inspection took place
late in May and early in June. That was the first ad hoc
inspection, and a second inspection has now taken place that's just
come back to Vienna. The question you were asking, of course, is
the inventory of installations and material which they submitted to
us, is it complete? There is an inherent difficulty in assessing
that question when you are confronted with a large nuclear program
which has been in place for several years.

     If a country like Cyprus opens up and submits an inventory, it
will be very limited, and we can gradually follow their development
of a nuclear industry, research reactors, and so forth. It is much
more difficult when a country like South Africa, or North Korea
which had been in the nuclear field for quite some time with
extensive installations, extensive deals, come in to verify that
this is full and complete.

     It is not possible for any inspector to -- whether in the
nuclear field or in other fields -- to search every square kilometer
of whole countries. In Iraq, in fact, we have had the most
extensive rights to move around anywhere, to go into any house
practically, to go into -- stop trains or trucks -- and even after a
year of this effort, we cannot say a hundred percent sure that there
is nothing hidden yet. In North Korea, we do not have such
extensive rights or movements as in Iraq.

     What we can do is look for coherence in the program that they
have declared, and examine the installations, take samples, and
watch if there are any inconsistencies. And we do do that in the
case of North Korea. We do not want to issue any false alarms, nor
do we want to issue any undeserved clean bill of health.

     In North Korea, they declared what they term a radio chemical
laboratory. They explained to me that they termed it a laboratory
because it is not yet ready. They have performed some tests. They
declared to us that they had actually reprocessed a gram quantity of
plutonium in this laboratory in 1990.

                                                              0041
     I have stated in, coming out of North Korea, that if this
installation were to be completed and to function, we would not have

HOUSE FOREIGN AFFAIRS COMMITTEE / SUBCMTE ON ASIAN AND PACIFIC AFFAIRS
SUBCMTE, ON ARMS CONTROL, INT'L SECURITY & SCIENCE
SUBCMTE ON INT'L ECONOMIC POLICY & TRADE
CHAIRMAN: REP. STEPHEN SOLARZ, D-NY   TOPIC: NORTH KOREA NUCLEAR PROGRAM
WITNESS: DR. HANS BLIX, DIRECTOR, IAEA WEDNESDAY, JULY 22, 1992
H-3-2   page# 4
any hesitation in terming it a reprocessing plant in the terminology
of the industrialized world. A question that we have asked
ourselves, and we did indeed ask the North Korean nuclear
authorities, was there never a -- (inaudible) -- plant before they
built this installation. What they term a laboratory is about 190
meters long, six stories high, is therefore a very sizable
construction. It was explained to us that they have made
experiments quite a number of years ago in which they identified
plutonium and that between that' and the construction of this plant,
there was no -- (inaudible) -- plant, it was emphatically denied and
they took great pains to explain to us how it was possible to go
from a laboratory small scale experiment to this large plant.

Our experts deem it possible that it could be done, but it
still is certainly procedure that would not have been followed in an
industrialized country. And questions are therefore bound to arise
about this point.

You raised the question whether there was more plutonium than
the amount that they have declared and I have stated that these are
gram quantities. We asked of course also the question whether there
was more and this was emphatically negated.

Whether these answers are correct is subject to analysis in
the International Atomic Energy Agency. You asked me also in your
introduction whether the -- we can verify whether it's the original
core that is still in the five megawatt plant and I understand from
our experts that, at least when they changed the core, which we
expect to be within a year's time, they will be able to establish
that question. Whether it was feasible to do so earlier I'm not
quite sure and on that particular question I would like to turn it
over to Mr. Perricos to say what he can about it. And I'd be glad
to take many of the other questions and focus upon those that you
have put.

MR. PERRICOS: Well, Mr. Chairman, there is always a question
when you go to a reactor to find out how much that reactor has been
really been used. And of course the present situation in the North
Korean five megawatt electrical reactor is I think much more
important.

The way that you can try to find out is basically by, first of
all, looking at the records, trying to find out the records are
consistent, and, of course, that is not enough. The records will
show you when fuel was in and out of the reactor, when the reactor
was up and when the reactor was down, and then you try to get
through all this information and integrate the power across the
core.

This creates a certain burn of the fuel, the fuel is being
burned. Uranium is being burned, producing plutonium and other
fission products. You can measure through the fission products what
was the burn-up of that fuel. This has been done in some of the
fuel which were damaged and has been found in the reactor. The   0042

//ADL-32_9

HOUSE FOREIGN AFFAIRS COMMITTEE / SUBCMTE ON ASIAN AND PACIFIC AFFAIRS
SUBCMTE, ON ARMS CONTROL, INT'L SECURITY & SCIENCE
SUBCMTE ON INT'L ECONOMIC POLICY & TRADE
CHAIRMAN: REP. STEPHEN SOLARZ, D-NY TOPIC: NORTH KOREA NUCLEAR PROGRAM
WITNESS: DR. HANS BLIX, DIRECTOR, IAEA WEDNESDAY, JULY 22, 1992
H-3-2 page# 5
results cannot just be expanded to cover the whole core. So, the
way that the procedures now are being followed is that the whole
core is in a way being kept intact by applying surveillance methods
and by different counters around the core that would permit us to
know if any fuel is getting out of the reactor or getting in.

When that reactor will be refueled, and that will have to
happen within a few months, that will be the time when we are going
to be able to measure all the fuel, knowing from exactly which
position it has come, and therefore verify according to the
statements in the operation records, this particular fuel is really
new fuel that came out after or just before the agency started
implementing

(MORE)

0043

4836-33-10

HOUSE FOREIGN AFFAIRS COMMITTEE / SUBCMTE ON ASIAN AND PACIFIC AFFAIRS
SUBCMTE, ON ARMS CONTROL, INT'L SECURITY & SCIENCE
SUBCMTE ON INT'L ECONOMIC POLICY & TRADE
CHAIRMAN: REP. STEPHEN SOLARZ, D-NY TOPIC: NORTH KOREA NUCLEAR PROGRAM
WITNESS: DR. HANS BLIX, DIRECTOR, IAEA WEDNESDAY, JULY 22, 1992
H-3-3 page# 1

    dest=hill,hsforaff,nkor,skor,fns21447,fns14094,nucweapon,asia,pacific
    dest+=armscont,japan,iraq,un
    data

        the safeguards, or in reality it is sure that was there since 1986
        when that reactor started operating.

            So, we have done all the preliminary work in order to freeze
        the situation. And with the first opportunity when the reactor is
        going to shut down, we will continue with the actual -- (inaudible)
        -- issue.

            REP. SOLARZ: Thank you very much for your testimony, Dr.
        Blix, and for your comments. We have been joined by the very
        distinguished chairman of the Foreign Affairs Committee, Mr.
        Fascell. And if you would like to begin with any questions --

            REP. FASCELL: No, go ahead, I'll follow up.

            REP. SOLARZ: Well, if not, then why don't I begin with some
        questions.

            Let me say at the outset, Dr. Blix, that the North Korean
        nuclear program potentially constitutes a threat to the entire
        international non-proliferation regime, if it should turn out,
        despite of their presumptive cooperation with the IAEA, they are in
        fact continuing an effort to produce on a clandestine basis
        materials with which to make nuclear weapons. If that were to
        happen, it would produce a chain of consequences, almost too dire to
        contemplate. Not only would it increase the possibility of a
        nuclear war on the Korean Peninsula; it would generate tremendous
        pressures on South Korea and Japan to become nuclear powers as well;
        it could very easily lead to widespread nuclear proliferation to the
        sale by North Korea to rogue regimes of either the fissile material
        or off-the-rack weapons. So, clearly, we have a major interest in
        preventing a rogue regime, like the one in Pyongyang, from becoming
        a nuclear weapon state.

            Now, given the extent to which we know from history that North
        Korea is engaged in clandestine activities, particularly
        underground. During the Korean War, for example, they had major
        munitions factories underground and in caves in mountains. We know
        they've dug tunnels beneath the 38th Parallel from the North to the
        South. And it seems to many of us, therefore, that the key to our
        ability to have any confidence that your inspection regime will be
        designed to have a high possibility of detecting any efforts by the
        North to violate its pledges and promises is in their willingness to
        permit the IAEA to conduct special or challenge inspections.

            So it would be helpful if you could let us know, first,
        whether the North has agreed to permit you to conduct such challenge
        or special inspections; and, if so, under what circumstances and

                                                                      0044

HOUSE FOREIGN AFFAIRS COMMITTEE / SUBCMTE ON ASIAN AND PACIFIC AFFAIRS
SUBCMTE, ON ARMS CONTROL, INT'L SECURITY & SCIENCE
SUBCMTE ON INT'L ECONOMIC POLICY & TRADE
CHAIRMAN: REP. STEPHEN SOLARZ, D-NY TOPIC: NORTH KOREA NUCLEAR PROGRAM
WITNESS: DR. HANS BLIX, DIRECTOR, IAEA WEDNESDAY, JULY 22, 1992
H-3-3 page# 2

conditions. Are you free to go wherever you want to go without
advance notice? Or must you first get their permission? And, if
so, how long a period of time would have to elapse between the
moment when you tell them you want to go to a particular site and
the moment when your inspectors are acctually permitted to go there?

MR. BLIX: Each safeguard agreement concluded under the Non-
Proliferation Treaty contains provisions about so-called special
inspections. We have extensive discussion about the nature of those
inspections in the Board of Goverors of the IAEA which concluded, by
a statement of the chairman of the Board, reaffirming the right of
the Agency to perform special inspections in order to have access to
additional information and locations in accordance with our statutes
and all comprehensive safeguards agreement.

I interpret that as meaning that where we have reasons to
believe that there are either installations or nuclear materials
which should have been declared but have not been declared. I can
first ask for explanations. And, if the explanations are
unsatisfactory, demand that a special inspection go to this site.

REP. SOLARZ: Have you gotten an agreement from North Korea in
principle to permit you to conduct such inspection?

MR. BLIX: We have not asked any member states for specific
consent to this procedure. I would assume that anything that is
laid down in a safeguard agreement with a member state, and which is
reaffirmed by the Board of Goverors, will be respected. And I do
not propose to ask any advance specific information from anyone. We
will meet that point when we get to it.

I have, however, when I was there, in response to their
question what can they do in order to give reassurance to the world
that there is nothing undeclared, suggested to them that they might
declare in advance that the Agency would be invited to go to
anyplace at anytime in North Korea, regardless of whether these
sites, this installation, was listed by them in the original
inventory. And in the press release that I issued before I left
North Korea, this particular point was included in the sentence that
stated that with a view to creating transparence(?) and confidence,
officials of the Agency are invited to visit any site and
installation they wish to see, irrespective of whether it was found
on the initial list submitted to the IAEA. This partiuclar point
was approved and accepted by them. We have not tested that. We
have not had reason yet to ask to go see any such site.

REP. SOLARZ: So, if I understand you correctly, you're saying
in effect that the North has now said that your people are invited
to go wherever they want whenever they want to?

MR. BLIX: That is correct.

REP. SOLARZ: But you have not put that offer to the test yet?

0045

HOUSE FOREIGN AFFAIRS COMMITTEE / SUBCMTE ON ASIAN AND PACIFIC AFFAIRS
SUBCMTE, ON ARMS CONTROL, INT'L SECURITY & SCIENCE
SUBCMTE ON INT'L ECONOMIC POLICY & TRADE
CHAIRMAN: REP. STEPHEN SOLARZ, D-NY TOPIC: NORTH KOREA NUCLEAR PROGRAM
WITNESS: DR. HANS BLIX, DIRECTOR, IAEA WEDNESDAY, JULY 22, 1992
H-3-3 page# 3

MR. BLIX: For the time being we are busy examining the plants
they have opened up and analyzing the results from other sites.
They are somewhat different from the challenged inspections I think.
that you are referring to. By challenged inspections, one usually
means in arms control context, the right of another state' or
organization to go to a site, regardless of whether there are any
suspicions. Such a right does not exist in our safeguards agreement
with them. The safeguards agreement lays down the right to special
inspections; and there we must have, as I've said, some reasons to
believe that something may exist. In terms of the invitation to
visit, we do not need to have any such specific grounds.

REP. SOLARZ: If you are given a reason to believe that they
may be conducting prohibited activities or that they may have
possession of prohibited materials at a particular site, are you
obligated to share that information with the North Koreans, or is it
sufficient for you to be persuaded that it may be accurate and
therefore you are going to ask to inspect a particular location?

MR. BLIX: I think our duty would be first to ask for an
explanation to be given in a very short time. And, secondly, if the
explanation was not satisfactory, we could demand a special
inspection. I could also take them up on the offer to go to any
installation.

Now, you ask -- there is one element that is important, and
you referred to it, and that's the element of time: How much time
would be needed? There have been discussions in the public
suggesting that you would need what are called "surprise"
inspections or "snap" inspections. And two such inspections are
very important in the case of Iraq, when our inspectors discovered
on trucks equipment that came from the nuclear installations. And
in the second instance, where they were looking after documents and
did indeed find documents which perhaps the Iraqis thought had been
taken out. Here speed was of the essence.

But I would say that when you are looking for secret nuclear
installations or materials, speed generally, or great speed
generally, is not of the essence. We are looking for research(?)
reactors, reprocessing plants, enrichment plants. And these things
are not very mobile.

REP. SOLARZ: But what if you're looking for the fissile
material itself? Supposing they have already produced, or in the
process of producing fissile material at a clandestine facility, and
you receive information that they may have that fissile material at
such-and-such a place, if you tell them that we have information you
may have fissile material at such-and-such a place, it stands to
reason that by the time they let you show up the material will have
been removed.

MR. BLIX: That is true. Fissile material is more mobile.
But they must have been produced somewhere, and those installations
are not so mobile.

4836-33-13   0046

HOUSE FOREIGN AFFAIRS COMMITTEE / SUBCMTE ON ASIAN AND PACIFIC AFFAIRS
SUBCMTE, ON ARMS CONTROL, INT'L SECURITY & SCIENCE
SUBCMTE ON INT'L ECONOMIC POLICY & TRADE
CHAIRMAN: REP. STEPHEN SOLARZ, D-NY   TOPIC: NORTH KOREA NUCLEAR PROGRAM
WITNESS: DR. HANS BLIX, DIRECTOR, IAEA   WEDNESDAY, JULY 22, 1992
H-3-3   page# 4

REP. SOLARZ: So -- but how would you deal with the question
of trying to follow up on a report of the existence of fissile
material as distinguished from much larger and complex
installations?

MR. BLIX: Well, in -- I think we would probably have an
indication that the fissile material was produced somewhere. If you
only have the information that the fissile material, a kilogram or
several kilograms of plutonium is hidden in such-and-such a place,
then I think the chances are not very great that we would get there
so fast that we would be able to see it. A special inspection would
have to be requested. We would have to use inspectors that are
designated.

REP. SOLARZ: Right.

MR. BLIX: They would have to travel there. They might even
require simple visa requirements -- so it could not be that fast.

REP. SOLARZ: And in the event that you detected clandestine
fissile material, do you have the authority to take possession of
it?

MR. BLIX: Yes. In that case that would be a violation of the
safeguards agreement. So if we discovered fissile material that had
not been declared, we would immediately report to the Board of
Goverors, and the Board of Goverors would be obliged to report on to
the Security Council.

REP. SOLARZ: Then it would be up to the Security Council --

MR. BLIX: That's right.

REP. SOLARZ: -- to decide what to do?

MR. BLIX: That's right. Also in the case that they denied us
access. If we want to go for a special inspection, and it is turned
down or -- and the state is dragging their feet, we would also
report to the Board, and the Board would regard it, I expect, as a
violation of the safeguards agreement, and it would be immediately
submitted to the Security Council.

REP. SOLARZ: You indicated that the reprocessing facility was
not yet completed. How long do you think it would take them to
complete it if they made a decision to finish the job?

MR. BLIX: We were told that they had ordered certain
equipment from North Korean industries, and they had not been

(MORE)

0047

4836-33-1CC

HOUSE FOREIGN AFFAIRS COMMITTEE / SUBCMTE ON ASIAN AND PACIFIC AFFAIRS
SUBCMTE, ON ARMS CONTROL, INT'L SECURITY & SCIENCE
SUBCMTE ON INT'L ECONOMIC POLICY & TRADE
CHAIRMAN: REP. STEPHEN SOLARZ, D-NY TOPIC: NORTH KOREA NUCLEAR PROGRAM
WITNESS: DR. HANS BLIX, DIRECTOR, IAEA WEDNESDAY, JULY 22, 1992
H-3-4 page# 1

    dest=hill,hsforaff,nkor,skor,fns21447,fns14094,nucweapon,asia,pacific
    dest+=armscont,
    data

        delivered yet. Hence the implication was that they are still
    building on the construction of this plant. There was no sign of
    such construction going on when we were there. But there was no
    indication of termination either. I cannot tell you how long a time
    it would be. It depends upon the delivery capacity of these
    industries. But it's important to note that right now there was no
    production going on.

        REP. SOLARZ: If I recall correctly, under your regime a
    member state that signs an agreement with you submits a list of
    nuclear installations and facilities that are designed purely for
    peaceful purposes. Is that correct?

        MR. BLIX: Under the Non-Proliferation Treaty they are obliged
    to use nuclear energy only for peaceful purposes. However, the
    safeguards agreements specify what they have to submit for our
    inspection.

        REP. SOLARZ: So North Korea is a signatory of the NPT.

        MR. BLIX: Right.

        REP. SOLARZ: Okay. Is there any peaceful purpose for this
    yet to be completed reprocessing facility that you can think of,
    given the state of their nuclear energy program?

        MR. BLIX: Well, of course in our discussions I asked them why
    did they want to build a reprocessing installation. And the answer
    was, first, that they might wish to have plutonium for making (mixed
    oxide ?) fuels. And I remarked that they do not have any (light
    water ?) reactors in which they could use such fuels, and none is
    under construction.

        Secondly, they replied that they might wish to use it for
    breed reactors in the future. And a breed reactor of course is an
    even more remote possibility for them.

        The third explanation would be that it would enter into the
    waste disposal concept, their so-called closed-fuel cycle. In the
    Western world this is a fairly common concept; however, it is by no
    means a necessary one. And, also we have in fact in our discussions
    I think admitted that the reprocessing plant was not a very
    essential part of their nuclear program and they explained, as
    you've probably seen in media, that they were interested in
    switching to a more economic line of reactor.   0048

        REP. SOLARZ: Would you agree then with those who have said

HOUSE FOREIGN AFFAIRS COMMITTEE / SUBCMTE ON ASIAN AND PACIFIC AFFAIRS
SUBCMTE, ON ARMS CONTROL, INT'L SECURITY & SCIENCE
SUBCMTE ON INT'L ECONOMIC POLICY & TRADE
CHAIRMAN: REP. STEPHEN SOLARZ, D-NY. TOPIC: NORTH KOREA NUCLEAR PROGRAM
WITNESS: DR. HANS BLIX, DIRECTOR, IAEA WEDNESDAY, JULY 22, 1992
H-3-4 page# 2

that the primary -- that's the sole purpose of this reprocessing
facility, was in fact to enable them to produce fissile materials
for nuclear weapons?

MR. BLIX: Well, I cannot say. I don't want to draw the
conclusion that, yes, positively it was. I can say that we do not
see any good, solid reason why they would need the plutonium for the
two purposes that were mentioned.

REP. SOLARZ: If that is the case, do you think that they
should decommission or demobilize or destroy this facility?

MR. BLIX: I don't think that would hurt their peaceful
nuclear program.

REP. SOLARZ: Right. Is the IAEA going to make such a request
of them?

MR. BLIX: No. I don't think that we can do it. I cannot
predict what the Board would do. But under the safeguards agreement
the strict obligation is to declare everything. In fact, the North
Koreans, when we discussed this, said, "Look, why is all this
concern about the plutonium? If we produce plutonium it will be
declared and under safeguards. And there are other countries in the
world that are reprocessing same(?) fuels." I pointed out that this
is right, but they have much vaster nuclear programs in which they
can make immediate use, or at least a future use of the plutonium
for mixed (oxile ?) fuel or for breed reactors.

REP. SOLARZ: Mr. Leach?

REP. LEACH: I'd like to pursue several of the issues that
have just been talked about. One of the concerns in some parts --
(inaudible) -- is that the IAEA inspection of a declared facility
has been used as an excuse for the North not to comply with their
agreement with the South which involves more intrusive inspections
of potentially undeclared facilities. And, also, the agreement with
the South does involve, as I understand it, a dismantlement
implicitly of any reprocessing facilities. And there are a couple
of things that I think ought to be raised.

One, I mean just by clarification, you have indicated that it
would certainly be your assumption that the IAEA would report to the
Security Council if it were denied access to any facility. But
that, as I understand it, does not imply that you have to go to the
Security Council to get permission to seek access to an undeclared
facility. Is that correct?

MR. BLIX: That's correct.

REP. LEACH: So your assumption is that you, as the 'IAEA,' have
the right for the so-called challenged snap inspection without   0049
seeking permission from the Security Council or any other outside
organization. Is that correct?

HOUSE FOREIGN AFFAIRS COMMITTEE / SUBCMTE ON ASIAN AND PACIFIC AFFAIRS
SUBCMTE, ON ARMS CONTROL, INT'L SECURITY & SCIENCE
SUBCMTE ON INT'L ECONOMIC POLICY & TRADE
CHAIRMAN: REP. STEPHEN SOLARZ, D-NY TOPIC: NORTH KOREA NUCLEAR PROGRAM
WITNESS: DR. HANS BLIX, DIRECTOR, IAEA WEDNESDAY, JULY 22, 1992
H-3-4 page# 3

MR. BLIX: I don't term them either snap or challenged
inspections -- special inspections, yes, without any authorization
from the Security Council.

REP. LEACH: Are you making a distinction between --

MR. BLIX: Well, snap inspections are usually referred to as
something that can sort of parachute in quickly.

REP. LEACH: Yeah.

MR. BLIX: And that is not characteristic with what we are
doing.

REP. LEACH: So there is a difference. I want to be careful
here. I don't care about what's a characteristic. I'm talking
about right and authority.

MR. BLIX: Right.

REP. LEACH: Is it the position of yourself, as director of
the IAEA, that you have the right to a challenged or snap
inspection?

MR. BLIX: (Inaudible) -- inspections. I speak to the --

REP. LEACH: Okay, I know you do, and that is why I want to
get -- You say you have a right to a special inspection, but you do
not say you have a right to a challenged or snap inspection?

MR. BLIX: Because I define them as somewhat different from
the special inspections.

REP. LEACH: Why do you not have a right? I mean, it is my
understanding of your charter that there is nothing that bars you
from a challenged or snap inspection. What, in your judgment,
precludes you from having that right?

MR. BLIX: A challenged inspection I would take to be one that
you can demand to go to anyplace, whether you suspect that place, or
have a reason to believe that there is something in it or not.

REP. LEACH: I realize there is a distinction between the two.
I accept the distinction. What I am asking you is whether you
believe you don't have that right. Now, let me give you an example.
If we take the North and South Korean situation, let us assume that
the South Koreans believe that there is a suspicious something going
on, and it is very likely to be on a military base. Would you take
the position that you do not have the right to do a challenged
inspection on that military base, or would you take the position
that you do have the legal right to do it, although it's a
judgmental call on whether you would do it?

0050

HOUSE FOREIGN AFFAIRS COMMITTEE / SUBCMTE ON ASIAN AND PACIFIC AFFAIRS
SUBCMTE. ON ARMS. CONTROL, INT'L SECURITY & SCIENCE
SUBCMTE ON INT'L ECONOMIC POLICY & TRADE
CHAIRMAN: REP. STEPHEN SOLARZ, D-NY TOPIC: NORTH KOREA NUCLEAR PROGRAM
WITNESS: DR. HANS BLIX, DIRECTOR, IAEA WEDNESDAY, JULY 22, 1992
H-3-4 page# 4
        MR. BLIX: I would --

    REP. LEACH: So my first question is: Do you have the right?
And my second question is: Do you not want to do it? I mean, there
are two issues.

    MR. BLIX: I would --

    REP. LEACH: Do you have the right to such an --

    MR. BLIX: I would take the view that if we had reason to
believe that there is something nuclear at the military installation
which should have been declared, then I can requset a special
inspection at that military installation. There is no restriction
mentioned in the Board of Goverors' conclusion about our rights to
special inspections.

    REP. LEACH: But one of the problems here, and again coming
back to the distinction between challenged and special, as you've
drawn them out, is that under the challenged circumstance there
might be a generalized belief that a country may be doing something,
but you just might not know where they are doing it. And if you
draw this distinction between challenged and special, adn say you
cannot do a challenged, you're depriving yourself of the right to
doing something that it might take seven different locations, each
of which would have a one-in-seven or one-in-twenty chance that
something might be going wrong. So all I'm trying to nail down is
how aggressive is the IAEA, and therefore how much confidence should
a government that wants to be supportive of the IAEA will it be.
And I must tell you if you deny the right to challenge inspections,
the confidence level deteriorates. And whether it deteriorates
significantly or slightly is a matter of judgment. And so I do want
-- I think it's fair to ask: First, legally, do you have the right
to a challenged inspection? Yes or no?

    MR. BLIX: Could I hear your definition of a challenged
inspection?

    REP. LEACH: You -- well, I -- Let me give my definition. I
mean, my definition is a challenged inspection would be on the
territory of a country that -- where there's a belief that
suspicious activity may be carried on, although you may not know for
sure if that is the exact location. Can you do a challenged
inspection in that circumstance?

    MR. BLIX: The definition of special inspections that I would
have is that we would have reasons to believe at a specific point
there is something which should have been declared and which had not
been declared. I do not think that concept allows us to vaguely say
that we would like to go to anyplace in that country. That was the
reason why I asked North Koreans

    (MORE)

0051

4836-33-18

HOUSE FOREIGN AFFAIRS COMMITTEE / SUBCMTE ON ASIAN AND PACIFIC AFFAIRS
SUBCMTE, ON ARMS CONTROL, INT'L SECURITY & SCIENCE
SUBCMTE ON INT'L ECONOMIC POLICY & TRADE
CHAIRMAN: REP. STEPHEN SOLARZ, D-NY TOPIC: NORTH KOREA NUCLEAR PROGRAM
WITNESS: DR. HANS BLIX, DIRECTOR, IAEA WEDNESDAY, JULY 22, 1992
H-3-5 page# 1

dest=hill,hsforaff,nkor,skor,fns21447,fns14094,nucweapon,asia,pacific
dest+=armscont,un,iraq
data

also to issue a standing invitation for us to go to places where we
would not have such suspicions and where we (got it?).

REP. LEACH: Well, Mr. Blix, we're talking about an
evidentiary threshold here, and one of the problems in--in a world
in which clandestine activity takes place, and in some societies in
which it's more clandestine than others by historical record,
whether we're talking Iraq or--or North Korea is the difficulty of
establishing this evidentiary threshold.

Now, let me give some examples. Let's say photo evidence from
satellites indicates an un-understood reason for a facility or that
there is a particularly high level of security around a particular
military site in a country in which this type of activity is--may
well be going on. Is that not large enough for the IAEA to become
involved in, or is it large enough?

MR. BLIX: Well, I agree with you that there can often be
questions of how high is the evidentiary threshold. If I were in
doubt, I would also have the possibility to go to the board of
governors, under which--to which I am subordinated, of course--and
ask them to instruct me to undertake an inspection.

The Security Council is evidently also free in the face of
evidence--

REP. LEACH: To direct you?

MR. BLIX: --to--to demand or request of the agency that we
perform an inspection, and you might also realize that the rules
that the safeguard agreements under NTTE (ph) are drawn up with a
view not only to the North Korea, but to all other countries in the
world.

REP. LEACH: That is understood. And then--and then let me--I
mean, you live this, and so no one is closer to it than yourself,
but in a general political science way, sometimes governments like
to give decentralized authority to bureaucracies so that you can
avoid some delicate political kinds of questions.

MR. BLIX: Mm-hmm (acknowledgement).

REP. LEACH: And it would be my personal opinion that the IAEA
ought to have far more power than an OSHA inspector. And OSHA
inspectors in the United States of America--and OSHA implies
Occupational Safety and Health--have very capricious authority to go
where they want to look for violations of safety and health. And it
would strike me that the authority of the IAEA should be perceived

0052

11月26-23-19

HOUSE FOREIGN AFFAIRS COMMITTEE / SUBCMTE ON ASIAN AND PACIFIC AFFAIRS
SUBCMTE, ON ARMS CONTROL, INT'L SECURITY & SCIENCE
SUBCMTE ON INT'L ECONOMIC POLICY & TRADE
CHAIRMAN: REP. STEPHEN SOLARZ, D-NY TOPIC: NORTH KOREA NUCLEAR PROGRAM
WITNESS: DR. HANS BLIX, DIRECTOR, IAEA WEDNESDAY, JULY 22, 1992
H-3-5 page# 2
to be quite gigantic and that the goal should be that the IAEA
should be insulated from having to seek political approval, whether
it be from the Security Council, where--

MR. BLIX: Mm-hmm (acknowledgement).

REP. LEACH: --at given points in time, a veto authority may
exist, where a country that has the veto authority might be
protecting a client or itself. 'And so I am personally disappointed,
and I--and I stress this--that--that you're making this distinction
as large as you're making it, and it would be my hope that that
distinction would weaken.

And now it also underscores in the position of North Korea
that there is this bilateral arrangement, and that North Korea might
be using your inspection capacities as an excuse not to abide by an
agreement with the South which appears to be more intrusive than
you've allocated your own rights and authorities.

Now, I realize in international affairs, there's a lot of
discussion on how broad these authorities of the IAEA should be, but
I--I would hope that the agency would pushing to--be pushing to
expand, rather than retract, your own perceived authority and let
people complain that you have too much authority, rather than too
little. I mean, that that--that that's where the burden of proof
should be.

Now, does that--would you care to comment on that?

MR. BLIX: Well, let me just tell you that I have no objection
to more authority being conferred upon me--latitude to go anywhere
in the member states, but I cannot read the discussions in the board
of governors in the agency as conferring upon me an authority to go
to places where I do not have any suspicion at all that there is
anything--something--that should have been declared.

You have mentioned the North-South agreement, and we, of
course, have studied that agreement, and I am on record publicly as
saying that we think it is desirable that this agreement enter into
force and be implemented, and I have explained to the North Korean
authorities that safeguards if a (specific form? formal) of
transparency regulates it, formal transparencies they are obliged to
undertake vis-a-vis us. There is nothing to stop them from going
beyond that transparency which the safeguards agreement implies and
open up to South Korea or to other concerned states.

In fact, if their intention or wish is to create confidence
about what they are doing, then it is advisable for them to open
up--(inaudible)--and I think they haven't (have?) quite understood,
well understood that point.   . 0053

Another matter is whether they actually are implementing this
agreement. I understand that the talks between North and South are
not going so well so far.

HOUSE FOREIGN AFFAIRS COMMITTEE / SUBCMTE ON ASIAN AND PACIFIC AFFAIRS
SUBCMTE, ON ARMS CONTROL, INT'L SECURITY & SCIENCE
SUBCMTE ON INT'L ECONOMIC POLICY & TRADE
CHAIRMAN: REP. STEPHEN SOLARZ, D-NY TOPIC: NORTH KOREA NUCLEAR PROGRAM
WITNESS: DR. HANS BLIX, DIRECTOR, IAEA WEDNESDAY, JULY 22, 1992
H-3-5 page# 3

REP. LEACH: I appreciate that. As you know, our former
ambassador to the United Nations, Tom Pickering, as well as others,
have suggested that the Security Council ought to be considering
ways of sharing information and taking more seriously the
proliferation issue, including cooperation on such things as
challenge inspections. And so this discourse is something that is
not new to the agency, and so I--I would only stress from my
perspective that I--I would hope you would go back to your board and
say that there appears to be a--a willingness in more quarters than
has hitherto been perhaps the case for the board taking on greater
authority than apparently the board to date has--has suggested it's
willing to.

But I--I think it is absolutely intolerable, and I use this
carefully, intolerable that in certain circumstances such as North
Korea, [the] International Atomic Energy Agency does not feel it has
the power to make what could be described as challenge or snap
inspections of undeclared facilities. And for the world community
to have great confidence in the proliferation inspection regime, I
think that circumstance has to be addressed, and--and I would say
that the evidence--I mean, when the world community was taken aback
by how far Iraq had gone, when it looked like we were preparing for
possible engagement that Iraq's preparation had been exaggerated by
so-called knowledgeable sources and after the engagement it was
discovered that instead of exaggerating, it had been underestimated,
that we should be very concerned. And it highlights and should
highlight to your agency the import of this particular issue.

REP. SOLARZ: If the gentleman will yield--

REP. LEACH: Yes.

REP. SOLARZ: --there--there is one ambiguity here that
perhaps you can clear up. Dr. Blix, you've made it clear that you
feel that unless you have some reason to believe that a prohibited
activity is going on, you don't have the right to conduct a special
inspection. But supposing you are given reason to believe that they
do have clandestine fissile material which is mobile and can be
moved rapidly at a particular site?

Under those circumstances, as you interpret your charter, are
you obligated to let the North know in advance that you want to go
to that particular site to determine if they have fissile material,
or are you in a position that you understand your right to simply
dispatch your inspectors to such a site to determine whether the
information you've received is accurate?

MR. BLIX: I think the present rules require that you request
an explanation first. I am simply reporting to you what the rules
say. Now, that does not mean that the explanation, that you have to
wait very long for that, but you must realize that sending   0054
inspectors into North Korea or to any other country is not just to
parachute them into the country.

HOUSE FOREIGN AFFAIRS COMMITTEE / SUBCMTE ON ASIAN AND PACIFIC AFFAIRS
SUBCMTE, ON ARMS CONTROL, INT'L SECURITY & SCIENCE
SUBCMTE ON INT'L ECONOMIC POLICY & TRADE
CHAIRMAN: REP. STEPHEN SOLARZ, D-NY TOPIC: NORTH KOREA NUCLEAR PROGRAM
WITNESS: DR. HANS BLIX, DIRECTOR, IAEA WEDNESDAY, JULY 22, 1992
H-3-5 page# 4

REP. LEACH: Will the gentleman yield? There's a--there's
another legal distinction here that's very crucial. I mean, the
chairman asked your interpretation of your charter. I think there's
a major distinction between charter interpretation and board
president or board uneasiness. In my view of your charter, there's
a very broad authority, but you have carefully laid out this morning
that you--

MR. BLIX: (Are you talking about?) the UN charter or--

REP. LEACH: No, I mean IAEA.

MR. BLIX: The safeguards agreement.

REP. LEACH: Yeah, the safeguards agreement. But you say your
board is very reluctant to authorize, and I think those are two
different circumstances, are they not? Or am I--am I misreading
that situation?

MR. BLIX: Well, what I am saying is that when the board
discussed the institutional special inspections, that so far has
never been used to an additional location. I could not read from
that discussion of the board, to which I am subordinated, a--an
authorization for me to request a special inspection to go in any--

REP. LEACH: I--I appreciate that, but I think it's important
for us to understand that if the board shifted their view, they are
not under a legal restraint not to--to do that, are they? Is that
not fair to--to--to assess?

MR. BLIX: The board is free to--even to modify the
agreements, of course.

May I take it that your view is that in the--in the case of
North Koreans, it would be highly desirable for the agency and for
the director general to be able to say that I now send this team in,
and it is to be (inspected? expected?). And by the same token, I
take it that you must conclude that this age--this power should
exist in relation to all other countries, as well, who have (NT-
type?) safeguards?

REP. LEACH: Who have potential, yes. And I--and I think
there may be distinctions you want to make between the likelihood of
countries and circumstances, but certainly I agree with exactly that
assessment.

REP. SOLARZ: Well, I am told that Dr. Blix will have to leave
by 3:00, so I want to--let me first before yielding to Mr.
Lagomarsino--(inaudible)--say when he leaves, I would hope the
members could remain for us to proceed with the markup of the Hong
Kong Policy Act, with respect to which I believe consensus has
already been established and which we can take up expeditiously. 0055

4836-33-22

HOUSE FOREIGN AFFAIRS COMMITTEE / SUBCMTE ON ASIAN AND PACIFIC AFFAIRS
SUBCMTE, ON ARMS CONTROL, INT'L SECURITY & SCIENCE
SUBCMTE ON INT'L ECONOMIC POLICY & TRADE
CHAIRMAN: REP. STEPHEN SOLARZ, D-NY TOPIC: NORTH KOREA NUCLEAR PROGRAM
WITNESS: DR. HANS BLIX, DIRECTOR, IAEA WEDNESDAY, JULY 22, 1992
H-3-6 page# 1

dest=hill,hsforaff,nkor,skor,fns21447,fns14094,nucweapon,asia,pacific
dest+=armscont,un,iraq,iran,india,ussr,alg,india,cuba,pak,israel
data

Dr. Blix, I would also hope that you would be prepared to
accept some written questions from us, covering areas that we
weren't able to get into before you leave, and which hopefully you
could submit written responses to for the record.

MR. BLIX: I'd be very glad to. I've seen some of the written
questions in advance. We'd be glad to respond to those. But let me
reaffirm that I have--would be delighted to have more power than I
interpret the agreement and the board giving me now, but I think
there would be hesitation and reluctance in the (state?) community
to confer upon an international official the right to send
inspectors, inspections at very short notice to any--any site
anywhere in the country, whether suspicions exist or not. It may
well be desirable that such an authority exist, but I have to be
honest with you and say that so far there is not.

It might also be difficult for the Security Council to do such
a thing in a very quick, very short moment.

REP. SOLARZ: Mr. Lagomarsino.

REP. ROBERT LAGOMARSINO (R-CA): Thank you, Mr. Chairman.

First of all, let me ask you, to--to what extent do you rely
on intelligence sources from--from whatever country in determining
where you want to make inspections--without--without, obviously,
without going into detail about how you get the intelligence and so
on.

MR. BLIX: To a limit--very limited extent. In fact, it's
only the last few years that we have been asking member states to
give us intelligence. The basic information we act upon are the
declarations of member states, and of course if we suspect that a
country is deliberately hiding something, then you cannot at all
rely upon that and, in fact, well, we don't rely upon it. We don't
have faith in--in anybody.

But we look--(inaudible)--upon media reports and we will be
getting information about exports to countries. This could very
well have been helpful in the case of Iraq to see that suspicious
activities were going on.

REP. LAGOMARSINO: Now, with respect to Iraq, obviously that's
a--that is a different situation because of the UN resolution?

MR. BLIX: Yes, the US resolution--UN resolution and the
agreement between Iraq and the secretary-general gives us freedom to
go anywhere in that country--(inaudible)--much wider than what we   0056

HOUSE FOREIGN AFFAIRS COMMITTEE / SUBCMTE ON ASIAN AND PACIFIC AFFAIRS
SUBCMTE, ON ARMS CONTROL, INT'L SECURITY & SCIENCE
SUBCMTE ON INT'L ECONOMIC POLICY & TRADE
CHAIRMAN: REP. STEPHEN SOLARZ, D-NY   TOPIC: NORTH KOREA NUCLEAR PROGRAM
WITNESS: DR. HANS BLIX, DIRECTOR, IAEA   WEDNESDAY, JULY 22, 1992
H-3-6   page# 2
have under the Nonproliferation Treaty generally.

REP. LAGOMARSINO: So there you don't have to tell the Iraqis,
at least theoretically, that you're going to come there tomorrow at
3:00?

MR. BLIX: No.

REP. LAGOMARSINO: You can just go.

MR. BLIX: No, there are no visa requirements, nothing of that
sort. We do not need to have any designation of inspectors. The
freedom is much greater. We have much worse--more strong--stronger
restrictions in the normal procedures.

REP. LAGOMARSINO: You know, in one way of putting it, I
guess, the discussion of the production of fissile material by North
Korea has focused on the back end of the nuclear fuel cycle
production of plutonium. What about the--have you analyzed the
front end, the--for example, the enrichment of uranium?

MR. BLIX: There is no sign that they've been devoting
themselves to enriched uranium.

REP. LAGOMARSINO: There--there is no sign of that?

MR. BLIX: No, there is no such sign. That we have--I mean, I
cannot exclude it--

REP. LAGOMARSINO: Because that's something you would be
looking for and looking at.

MR. BLIX: We would everywhere, but there is no sign of that.

REP. LAGOMARSINO: Is there any evidence of the North Koreans
colluding with others on their nuclear program or on the other
states' nuclear program--for example, Iraq or Iran or India?

MR. BLIX: We have not seen any evidence of that. We--their
links have been mainly to the Soviet Union in the past. Most of
their nuclear scientists were trained in Dubno.

REP. LAGOMARSINO: Did you--did you inspect Iran?

MR. BLIX: Yes--(inaudible)--

REP. LAGOMARSINO: How about Algeria?

MR. BLIX: Algeria is not a partner to the Nonproliferation
Treaty, but they have some nuclear installations which they have
purchased on the condition that they be submitted to safeguards.
Included among them is a research reactor, which they've bought from
China and which we've sent inspectors to, yes.   0057

                    11836 33-24

HOUSE FOREIGN AFFAIRS COMMITTEE / SUBCMTE ON ASIAN AND PACIFIC AFFAIRS
SUBCMTE, ON ARMS CONTROL, INT'L SECURITY & SCIENCE
SUBCMTE ON INT'L ECONOMIC POLICY & TRADE
CHAIRMAN: REP. STEPHEN SOLARZ, D-NY TOPIC: NORTH KOREA NUCLEAR PROGRAM
WITNESS: DR. HANS BLIX, DIRECTOR, IAEA WEDNESDAY, JULY 22, 1992
H-3-6 page# 3

REP. LAGOMARSINO: So you do inspect that?

MR. BLIX: Yes.

REP. LAGOMARSINO: How about--

MR. BLIX: (I can thus?) say nothing about what the Algerians
are doing outside the sites which we are--which are submitted to
safeguards, but those which are submitted, yes. Of course we
inspect them.

REP. LAGOMARSINO: Well, do you have any suspicions about what
Algeria might be doing in non-covered--

MR. BLIX: No, we have--I cannot tell you that we have any--
any suspicions or question marks regarding those reactors which
are--which we are visiting, but we are not giving any clean bill of
health in general terms.

REP. LAGOMARSINO: All right. And what about India? Do you
inspect any facilities in India?

MR. BLIX: Yes. India is also not a partner to the
Nonproliferation Treaty, and it's well known that they have both the
capacity to enrich uranium and to reprocess. We are inspecting some
plants, and we do not have any particular problems with that
inspection, but, of course, that doesn't mean that India--India
could not do whatever they like in other areas.

REP. LAGOMARSINO: Then you have no access to those?

MR. BLIX: No. The same applies tof Pakistan.

REP. LAGOMARSINO: Well, what about Cuba?

MR. BLIX: The same applies to Israel. In Cuba, they are
building nuclear power plants which will be subject to safeguards
and they have not yet the obligation to submit all their nuclear
installations. If they ratify the Tlatelolco treaty, then they will
have to enter into a full-scale safeguards agreement with us.

REP. LAGOMARSINO: Do you know where North Korea is getting
its reactor fuel from?

MR. BLIX: Yes, they declare that they are acquiring it from
their own territory. It's natural uranium and, in fact, I went to
two uranium mines and facilities where they are producing the fuel--
(inaudible; off-mike question)--uranium metal for the reactors.
They do not need enrichment for that. This is natural uranium.

REP. LAGOMARSINO: You may have testified about this before,
but let me ask you again--how great have been--if at all--were the
discrepancies between the inventories and the information they 0058
actually provided to you in the first place?

HOUSE FOREIGN AFFAIRS COMMITTEE / SUBCMTE ON ASIAN AND PACIFIC AFFAIRS
SUBCMTE, ON ARMS CONTROL, INT'L SECURITY & SCIENCE
SUBCMTE ON INT'L ECONOMIC POLICY & TRADE
CHAIRMAN: REP. STEPHEN SOLARZ, D-NY   TOPIC: NORTH KOREA NUCLEAR PROGRAM
WITNESS: DR. HANS BLIX, DIRECTOR, IAEA   WEDNESDAY, JULY 22, 1992
H-3-6   page# 4

MR. BLIX: We have not established any--any differences between or discrepancies between the inventory and what we have seen and verified so far--(inaudible; crosstalk)--exclude that it will come in the future.

REP. LAGOMARSINO: So in other words, what they told you they had checked out?

MR. BLIX: For the time being, yes.

REP. LAGOMARSINO: For the time being.

MR. BLIX: Of course, this is subject to analysis, and I am not drawing any conclusions.

REP. LAGOMARSINO: I'm still, I guess, confused about the difference between a special inspection and a challenge inspection. Let me see if--maybe I do understand it. In your terminology, anyway, a special inspection is one where you--you call up the Iraq--well, not the Iraqis, you just do it there--but the North Koreans and you say, "We have information that fissile material is being stored in such-and-such a place and we want an explanation of that." That would be--and then they give you the explanation or they don't, and then you would do the inspection.

A challenge inspection, I guess, under your terminology, would be where you just go there and say, "Here we are, folks. We want to look at this."

MR. BLIX: No, we would just say that we want to see this particular place. We don't have to explain whether there are any reasons to believe that they have been cheating--(inaudible)--

REP. LAGOMARSINO: Right. Now--now, do you, in the case of a special inspection, have to tell them what your information is?

MR. BLIX: We have never done it, so--

REP. LAGOMARSINO: Oh.

MR. BLIX: --it will have to be tailor-made, and there is no--there are no procedures accepted by the board so far. I think that we would have to say that we have reason to believe that there is something not declared in this particular place. I don't think that we will have to specify what our sources are.

REP. LAGOMARSINO: Okay. Thank you.

REP. SOLARZ: Mr. Goss.

(MORE)

0059

HOUSE FOREIGN AFFAIRS COMMITTEE / SUBCMTE ON ASIAN AND PACIFIC AFFAIRS
SUBCMTE, ON ARMS CONTROL, INT'L SECURITY & SCIENCE
SUBCMTE ON INT'L ECONOMIC POLICY & TRADE
CHAIRMAN: REP. STEPHEN SOLARZ, D-NY TOPIC: NORTH KOREA NUCLEAR PROGRAM
WITNESS: DR. HANS BLIX, DIRECTOR, IAEA WEDNESDAY, JULY 22, 1992
H-3-6 page# 5

0060

4836-33-27

HOUSE FOREIGN AFFAIRS COMMITTEE / SUBCMTE ON ASIAN AND PACIFIC AFFAIRS
SUBCMTE, ON ARMS CONTROL, INT'L SECURITY & SCIENCE
SUBCMTE ON INT'L ECONOMIC POLICY & TRADE
CHAIRMAN: REP. STEPHEN SOLARZ, D-NY   TOPIC: NORTH KOREA NUCLEAR PROGRAM
WITNESS: DR. HANS BLIX, DIRECTOR, IAEA   WEDNESDAY, JULY 22, 1992
H-3-7   page# 1

```
dest=hill,hsforaff,nkor,skor,fns21447,fns14094,nucweapon,asia,pacific
dest+=armscont,un,iraq
data
```

REP. PETER GOSS (R-FL): Thank you, Mr. Chairman. I apologize
for coming in late and for the interruption, but there are--I think
most of this has been covered, but I just would like to try and get
to a bottom line, if I might and--and let me oversimplify. On a
scale of, say, one to 10, how much of the information that you need
to know to do your job can you get? Forty percent? Sixty percent?

MR. BLIX: From where do you mean?

REP. GOSS: Sorry?

MR. BLIX: From where?

REP. GOSS: From the North Koreans.

MR. BLIX: --(inaudible)--well, they have declared
installations and nuclear material to us.

REP. GOSS: I understand that, but that wasn't the question.

MR. BLIX: We verify that. I mean, I cannot make assumptions
on how much hypothetically could they be cheating about.

REP. GOSS: All right. That was the question.

(Laughter)

MR. BLIX: If I knew, we would try to go there.

REP. GOSS: Well, that really does get to the heart of the
question. Let me ask it another way--do you have serious worries
that we are missing something beyond what is declared that we should
be taking steps to do something about?

MR. BLIX: We have a professional duty to be seriously worried
everywhere. In the case of North Korea, at the beginning of the
hearing, I explained that we find it usual--I would even say
exceptional--that a country can build a fairly large installation
for reprocessing without having gone through the--(audio break)--at
length with the North Korean authorities. This is a specific matter
relating to North Korea.

REP. GOSS: I guess, then, my question is on a scale of one to
10, what is your degree of satisfaction after your discussions?
                                                                    0061
MR. BLIX: Well, they took great pains to try to explain how
in Korean culture they do take big jumps from a very small scale to

HOUSE FOREIGN AFFAIRS COMMITTEE / SUBCMTE ON ASIAN AND PACIFIC AFFAIRS
SUBCMTE, ON ARMS CONTROL, INT'L SECURITY & SCIENCE
SUBCMTE ON INT'L ECONOMIC POLICY & TRADE
CHAIRMAN: REP. STEPHEN SOLARZ, D-NY   TOPIC: NORTH KOREA NUCLEAR PROGRAM
WITNESS: DR. HANS BLIX, DIRECTOR, IAEA   WEDNESDAY, JULY 22, 1992
H-3-7 /page# 2

something very big, but this is a question of judgment whether one
regards this as plausible. The way to that--(inaudible)--and which
the chairman was probing about, was can we see from the Fimedelar
(ph) plant how much fuel could there have been available for
reprocessing? This is another way of verifying it. We are neither
giving a clean bill of health nor sounding--want to sound an alarm.
We want to analyze this before we come up with any assessment.

          REP. GOSS: I yield to the chairman.

          REP. SOLARZ: Thank the gentleman for yielding. Let me put it
somewhat differently. Have the North Koreans turned down any
requests by you or your associates to inspect any facilities in the
country or any requests for information regarding its nuclear
program?

          MR. BLIX: Not so far.

          REP. SOLARZ: So, so far, they've let you go everywhere you
want to go and they've given you all the information that you've
asked for--so far as you know?

          MR. BLIX: We have gone to the installations which they have
declared in the original inventory. They have shown us the material
that was there. I was taken some places which was also not in the
original inventory.

          REP. SOLARZ: And what, if anything, is the IAEA doing
differently in North Korea as compared to your practice in Iraq
before the war to help ensure that no undeclared activities go
undetected?

          MR. BLIX: In Iraq, we are going to sites which are designated
for inspection by the special commission attached--

          REP. SOLARZ: I know what you're doing in Iraq. My question
is, are you doing anything in North Korea that you didn't do in Iraq
before the Gulf War to help make sure that the North Koreans, unlike
the Iraqis, don't have undeclared programs or facilities?

          MR. BLIX: Well, we welcome intelligence information if anyone
is willing to give it to us.

          REP. SOLARZ: Mr. Goss?

          REP. GOSS: I'm reclaiming my time for one final follow-up,
and I appreciate the chairman's assistance in going the direction
you did.

               (MORE)

                                                      0062

                              4836-73-29

HOUSE FOREIGN AFFAIRS COMMITTEE / SUBCMTE ON ASIAN AND PACIFIC AFFAIRS
SUBCMTE, ON ARMS CONTROL, INT'L SECURITY & SCIENCE
SUBCMTE ON INT'L ECONOMIC POLICY & TRADE
CHAIRMAN: REP. STEPHEN SOLARZ, D-NY TOPIC: NORTH KOREA NUCLEAR PROGRAM
WITNESS: DR. HANS BLIX, DIRECTOR, IAEA WEDNESDAY, JULY 22, 1992
H-3-8-E page# 1

     dest=hill,hsforaff,nkor,skor,fns21447,fns14094,nucweapon,asia,pacific
     dest+=armscont,un,iraq
     data

          MR. BLIX: Excuse me, if I may please. Mr. Perricos reminds me
     there is something else to say on this and that is that in the case
     of Iraq we were not aware of any reprocessing activities nor indeed
     have found any subsequently.

          In the case of North Korea, where the country declared an
     installation devoted to reprocess, of course, that higher detail
     requires much more analysis.

          REP. GOSS: I guess I wanted to get back to my satisfaction
     question again in terms of your mission, world peace and so forth,
     and containing nuclear proliferation.

          Do you feel that there is an unusual threat emanating from
     North Korea with regard to nuclear production of any type, either in
     terms of proliferation or in terms of potential unilateral action or
     use for regional geopolitical gains? Do you see anything
     extraordinary on your radar scope there? Any blip or any spike in
     the chart that means that you're going to go back there and spend
     some more time and more energy there than, say, in other areas where
     declarations are made also?

          MR. BLIX: Well, you're using precisely the term I would like
     to you when you mentioned radar. The safeguards inspections are
     like a radar scanning the horizon and saying here and now you have
     this and that. We cannot radar scan the minds of people. We cannot
     give any clean bill of health.

          REP. GOSS: We understand.

          MR. BLIX: Therefore, we report what we are seeing and we
     also want to be precise of what we have not been able to see or
     cannot see at the moment.

          I do not -- it's not my job to tell you whether you should be
     concerned or not about the activities in North Korea. I have
     advised the North Korean authorities that if they do wish to have
     detente in that area, than maximum transparency, not only vis-a-vis
     the agency but also vis-a-vis South Korea and other interested
     states is important. And I fully realize the very great potential
     for a conflict in this area if there were indeed to be a building in
     nuclear weapons capacity is evident in relation to South Korea,
     Japan, et cetera. I have no difficulty understanding that.   0063

          REP. GOSS: I don't think any of us do. I think that's why we
     asked the question. We are concerned that the monitoring as it is
     does in fact do the job satisfactory to detect that and prevent that
     from happening. And I guess I'm going to leave from this particular

HOUSE FOREIGN AFFAIRS COMMITTEE / SUBCMTE ON ASIAN AND PACIFIC AFFAIRS
SUBCMTE. ON ARMS. CONTROL, INT'L SECURITY & SCIENCE
SUBCMTE ON INT'L ECONOMIC POLICY & TRADE
CHAIRMAN: REP. STEPHEN SOLARZ, D-NY TOPIC: NORTH KOREA NUCLEAR PROGRAM
WITNESS: DR. HANS BLIX, DIRECTOR, IAEA WEDNESDAY, JULY 22, 1992
H-3-8-E page# 2

meeting with the unknown of knowing how satisfied how satisfied you
are that the monitoring is complete enough, unless you'd like to
suggest that you are more satisfied or less satisfied.

MR. BLIX: From the point of view of the monitoring, you would
like to have maximum freedom of movement and maximum right. And I
would be welcome to have the kind of capacity there which is
suggested. However, I'm not entirely hopeful that the governments of
the world whether at the IEA or in the UN would like to confer upon
one single authority that power.

The agreement between South and North Korea has a clause which
says that the South and the North, in order to verify the nuclear
station shall conduct inspections of the object selected by the
other side and agreed upon between the two sides in accordance with
procedures, et cetera.

I don't know whether this is interpreted as the right to
challenge inspections but the words "and agreed upon," seem to me at
least to open the possibility for some restrictions.

REP. GOSS: Thank you very much.

Mr. Chairman, you've been very generous. Thank you.

REP. SOLARZ: Thank you.

Mr. Leach, you had a final question?

REP. LEACH: Yes. Well, Mr. Blix, many of us believe you're
the most important inspection agency in the world. And ironically in
terms of American politics some of us thing our bureaucracies have
gotten too much power. But at least with regard to yours, I think
you have too little.

And one of the things that I don't know if you've ever really
dealt with is the whole area of enforcement and dismantlement. I
mean, if this reprocessing facility should be dismantled, do you
have the capacity to dismantle it?

And secondly, do you need an air force or is that something
your Board would have some doubts about providing you?

MR. BLIX: Well, you are raising such a broad prospective now.
We have the ambition to survive October, which we will not, unless
the United States gives us contribution for this year. There have
been questions of whether we should have a satellite capacity. And
that, too, I think, is rather dreamy at the time when we are at zero
growth.

The specific question about dismantlement --

REP. LEACH: Well, let me say --

0064

HOUSE FOREIGN AFFAIRS COMMITTEE / SUBCMTE ON ASIAN AND PACIFIC AFFAIRS
SUBCMTE, ON ARMS CONTROL, INT'L SECURITY & SCIENCE
SUBCMTE ON INT'L ECONOMIC POLICY & TRADE
CHAIRMAN: REP. STEPHEN SOLARZ, D-NY   TOPIC: NORTH KOREA NUCLEAR PROGRAM
WITNESS: DR. HANS BLIX, DIRECTOR, IAEA   WEDNESDAY, JULY 22, 1992
H-3-8-E   page# 3

MR. BLIX: -- I could answer in the following manner. In Iraq we have been given the task by the Security Council either to destroy or to remove or render harmless the weapons capacity and weapons material production capacity of Iraq and we are giving the Iraqis instructions what they should destroy.

And Mr. Perricos here on my side has personally supervised how they were blowing up building worth a couple of hundred million dollars. So yes, we can have role in the field of dismantlement if we are given that task by the Security Council. It is not a task I think that exists under the Safeguards Agreement, though.

REP. LEACH: I appreciate that. Let me just say from my perspective, you're working in an extraordinary area of difficulty with a great deal of commitment and facility and it's an embarrassment that the United States has not been more forthcoming in our procedures on funding. It's an agency certainly that we have an obligation, despite whatever problems we have here at home, to give a higher and not lower priority. We will do the best we can to support you.

Thank you.

REP. SOLARZ: Yes. I wouldn't want you to feel your presence here had not produced some benefits, Dr. Blix, because I think you've made such a powerful case for the kind of work you do. I'm sure each of us will do everything we can to encourage the Administration and Congress to make sure that the necessary U.S. contribution to your agency is forthcoming so that you can continue your work.

Two final very brief questions. I understand that when you were there you were permitted to briefly see some underground tunnels in the Yong B'ong (ph) area. And in the two subsequent inspections that took place, were these tunnels look at in any greater detail? Do you know what the purpose of the tunnels is?

MR. BLIX: No. I think our host wanted to show these tunnels because there had been media reports about them. They were empty with the exception of some arrangement for air-conditioning and they were not declared in their original inventory. We did not see any reason why they should have been.

REP. SOLARZ: And has the North indicated to you the precise number of damaged fuel rods that were removed?

MR. BLIX: Yes.

REP. SOLARZ: How many?

MR. BLIX: Well, I'm afraid that figure is one that belongs to the quantity of things that fall under Safeguard confidential. I doubt the figure is in itself terribly interesting.

0065

4836 -33 -32

HOUSE FOREIGN AFFAIRS COMMITTEE / SUBCMTE ON ASIAN AND PACIFIC AFFAIRS
SUBCMTE, ON ARMS CONTROL, INT'L SECURITY & SCIENCE
SUBCMTE ON INT'L ECONOMIC POLICY & TRADE
CHAIRMAN: REP. STEPHEN SOLARZ, D-NY   TOPIC: NORTH KOREA NUCLEAR PROGRAM
WITNESS: DR. HANS BLIX, DIRECTOR, IAEA   WEDNESDAY, JULY 22, 1992
H-3-8-E page# 4
        REP. SOLARZ: Well, let me thank you very much. We will have
some follow-up questions for you which hopefully you can give us
written answers to for the record.

        I want to thank you for coming. This has been very.
illuminating. It certainly helps us to discharge our
responsibilities and I don't have to tell you how important your
mission is and encourage you to continue pursuing it with great
diligence.

        Thank you very much. .

                        END

                                                              0066.

                          ㅛ아36-33-33

공　　　　란

공 란

외 무 부

종 별 :

번 호 : USW-3679   일 시 : 92 0723 1736

수 신 : 장관(미이,미일,정총,국기) 사본:주오지리대사-본부중계필

발 신 : 주 미 대사

제 목 : BLIX 사무총장 NPC 조찬 간담회

연: USW-3568

워싱턴을 방문중인 HANS BLIX IAEA사무총장은 금 7.23 당지 NATIONAL PRESS CLUB 에서 핵 확산 방지에 대한 조찬 간담회를 가졌는바, 동 요지 아래 보고함.(당관 안총기 서기관참석)

1. BLIX 사무총장은 자신의 금번 워싱톤 방문목적은 핵융합 원자로 건설합의, 미하원에서의 설명회, 국무부 및 국방부등 미행정부 관리들과의 핵 안전조치 및 검증문제협의등을 위한 것이었다고 말함.

2. BLIX 총장은 최근 아르헨티나, 브라질, 쿠바,남아공등에 있어서 핵 확산방지및 안전조치에 대한 많은 진전이 있었다고 평가하고 최근 우크라이나, 벨라루스, 카작스탄등 구소련공화국들의 핵물질 보유가 새로운 문제로 대두 되었으나, 이들이 곧 NPT 제도에 동참하게 되면 효과적인 조처가 이루어질 것이라고 설명함.

3. 북한 핵 문제와 관련 BLIX 총장은 북한의 안전조치 협정 비준, 신고목록 제출등 에의한 사찰이 실시됨으로서 그동안 많은 진전이 있었으나, 아직도 의문점은 남아 있 다고설명하고, 북한이 IAEA 사찰시 원자로 접근등에있어 다소 거부적인(RELUCTANT) 태도를 보였는지 여부를 묻는 질문에 대해 북한은 사찰과정에서 아직까지는 협조적이 었다고 답변함.(NO LACK OF COOPERATION)

4. BLIX 총장은 이락의 경우는 폐쇄된 사회에서 외부에 의해 발견되지 않은 채 핵 시설을 건설할 수 있다는 것을 보여주는 좋은 사례라고 지적하고, 이락에 대한 사찰과 관련하여 IAEA 에대한 비난이 있으나, 이것은 IAEA 가 보다 큰 권한을 가지고 있는 것으로 오해하고 있는데서 비롯된 것이며, IAEA 는 핵 확산방지 문제에 대한 경찰(POLICE) 이 아니고 관찰자(OBSERVER)일 뿐이라고 언급함. 또한 BLIX 총장은 이락의 경우처럼 신고하지 않은 시설에 대한 특별사찰이 가능하기 위해서는 별도의 정보가

미주국   미주국   국기국   외정실   중계

IAEA 에 제공되어야 한다고 말하고, 현재 IAEA 는 회원국으로 부터 정보를 제공받고 있다고 부언함.

5. 한편 BLIX 총장은 미국, 소련등 큰 몫의 IAEA 분담금을 맡고 있는 나라들의 분담금지불이 지연되고 있어서 IAEA 의 재정 형편이 매우 어려우며, 현재대로 라면 금년 10월부터 IAEA의 재원은 고갈될 상황에 있다고 설명하면서 IAEA 재원 유지를 위한 협조를 당부함.

(대사 현홍주-국장)

美下院 外務委 北韓 核問題 公開說明會

1992. 7. 23.

外 務 部

美下院 外務委는 7. 22. 「한스 블릭스」 IAEA 事務總長을 參席시킨 가운데 北韓 核問題에 관한 公開說明會를 가진 바, 同 要旨 아래 報告드립니다.

1. 「블릭스」 事務總長 冒頭發言 要旨

o 北韓과 같이 장기간 核施設을 보유한 나라의 경우, 申告된 施設의 目錄이 완벽한지 與否를 立證하는 것은 容易치 않음.

o 北韓은 90년 實驗室을 통한 그램 단위의 플루토늄 抽出을 是認하였으나 그이상의 플루토늄 抽出은 否認함.

o 大型 再處理施設(길이 190m, 높이 6층)을 건설중인 北韓은 중간 단계의 試驗施設(pilot plant) 存在를 否認하나, 이는 일반적인 産業國家에서는 있을 수 없는 일임.

o 北韓의 核開發 疑惑 관련, 지나치게 놀랄 일은 아니나 섣부른 安心을 할 상황은 아님.

2. 質疑. 應答 要旨

o IAEA의 대북한 强制査察 또는 特別査察 權限 與否
  - 「솔라즈」 의원은 北韓이 IAEA에 의한 强制査察 또는 特別 査察에 同意 하였는지 問議함.

- 「블릭스」 總長은 다음과 같이 답변함.

　. IAEA는 未申告 疑心이 있을 경우 該當國家에게 먼저 解明을
　　요구하고 동 解明이 不滿足스러울 경우 特別查察을 要求할
　　수 있음.

　. 동 IAEA 核安全措置協定上의 特別查察은, 未申告 疑心 여부에
　　관계없이 일정 장소를 查察할 수 있는 軍縮條約上의 强制查察
　　과 같이 강력한 것이 아님.

　. 北韓이 IAEA가 원할 경우 北韓内 어느 장소든지 訪問을 許容
　　한다고 한것은, IAEA 特別查察制度의 한계를 다소 補完해 줄
　　수 있음.

o IAEA 查察의 效率性 및 南北相互查察의 必要性
- 「리치」 의원은 北韓이 IAEA 查察을 徹底하고 效果的인 南北
　相互查察을 回避하는 구실로 이용하고 있다고 말하고 IAEA 特別
　查察의 效率性을 問議함.
- 「블릭스」 사무총장은 IAEA 特別查察의 限界性을 認定하면서,
　北韓이 南北相互查察을 통해 核에 관한 透明性을 더욱 提高시키는
　것이 바람직하다고 답변

o 北韓의 核物質 隱匿 可能性
- 「솔라즈」 의원은 만일 北韓이 核物質을 生産하여 隱匿하고
　있다는 情報가 있을 경우의 查察 節次를 問議함.

- 2 -

0072

- 「블릭스」 사무총장은, 그러한 경우 特別査察이 要求되며
  또한 隱匿된 核物質이 발견되는 경우에는 IAEA 理事會 및
  安保理에 報告되어 必要한 措置가 취해질 것이라고 答辯

o 北韓의 再處理施設 現況
- 「블릭스」 총장은 再處理施設의 建設이 현재는 一時 中斷된
  것으로 보이나 必要 部品을 주문중이라는 北韓의 답변으로
  보아 建設을 繼續할 것으로 본다고 答辯

3. 分析 및 評價

o 금번 「블릭스」 총장의 證言은 美議會內 北韓 核問題를 다루는
  주요 의원들에 대해 北韓의 核再處理施設이 아무런 經濟的
  妥當性이 없는 것임을 再確認시킴으로써, 北韓의 核武器 開發
  推進 事實을 다시한번 周知시키는 契機가 됨.

o 특히 IAEA 特別査察制度가 일반 軍縮條約上의 강력한 不時强制
  査察과 다른 脆弱한 制度임이 분명히 確認됨으로써, 北韓의
  核武器 開發을 철저히 檢證. 遮斷하기 위해서는 徹底하고 强制的인
  南北相互査察이 必須的이라는 사실을 美國內 朝. 野에 충분히
  認識시킴.

- 끝 -

- 3 -

長官報告事項

報告畢

1992. 7. 24.
國際機構局
國際機構課(38)

題 目 : IAEA 사무총장의 미하원 소위 설명회

92.7.23 '블럭스' IAEA 사무총장의 미하원 외무위 공개 설명회에서 발언한
내용중 IAEA의 특별사찰 실시 권한과 대북한 사찰관련 특기사항을 아래
보고 드립니다.

1. IAEA의 특별사찰 실시문제

o IAEA는 협정당사국내에 신고되지 않은 핵시설 또는 물질 이 있다고 믿을 근거가
  있을때 이에 대한 특별사찰 (special inspection) 을 실시 할 수 있는 권한이
  있음

  * 92.2월이사회는 미신고 핵시설 및 물질관련 추가정보(additional information)
    를 입수하여 관련 장소(locations)를 사찰하기 위한 IAEA의 특별사찰 실시
    권한을 재확인함

o 그러나 IAEA의 특별사찰은 군축 검증 차원에서 의심이 있건 없건 아무장소나
  사찰할 수 있는 강제사찰(challenge inspection)과는 의미가 다름

  * IAEA는 미신고 의심이 있을 경우 당사국에 먼저 해명을 요구하고, 동 해명이
    불충분한 경우 당사국과 협의를 거쳐 특별사찰 실시 (안전조치협정 제77조)

  * 당사국이 특별사찰 실시를 계속 거부하거나 특별사찰 실시 결과 협정의무
    위반사실(미신고 핵물질등) 이 발견되는 경우 동내용을 안보리에 보고 (IAEA
    헌장 제12조C)

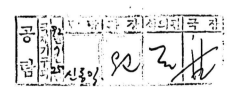

0074

o 시간적 요소가 중요하기 때문에 기습사찰(surprise inspection)이 필요하다는
주장도 있지만 비밀 핵시설이나 물질을 찾고 있을 경우 사찰실시 속도가 그렇게
중요한 것은 아님

  - 원자로, 재처리공장, 농축공장등의 시설은 그렇게 쉽게 옮길수 있는 것이
    아니며, 핵물질도 이동은 가능하지만 ~~어딘가 시설에서 생산됐을 것이~~므로 생산된 시설을 찾는것이 중요함
    시간은 다투는 사항은 아님
    ~~찾아낼 수 있을 것임~~
  - 또 IAEA는 ~~상세쌍령의~~ 기습사찰 권한이 없음

o 신고되지 않은 군사시설에 어떤 핵 물질이 있다고 믿을만한 근거가 있을때
  IAEA는 동 군사시설에 대해서도 특별사찰은 요구할수 있을것임
  - 이는
  ~~*~~ NPT상 핵무기 비보유국가들중 전면 안전조치협정 체결 당사국에 한해 적용
  가능함 ~~특별사찰은 ~~ 한 선례는 없음.

o 이라크의 경우에는 안보리 결의(제687호)에 의거 이라크내 모든 시설을 자유 IAEA사찰단이
  롭게 사찰할 수 있는 광범위한 권한을 부여 받았으나, 북한의 ~~경우에~~는 이같은 대하여 IAEA
  사찰권한을 갖고 있지 못함
  - 단, 북한은 언제, 어느장소(신고하지 않은 시설 포함)라도 IAEA 관리의 방문
    을 허용할 것이라고 약속한 바 있음

2. 북한이 신고한 핵시설 및 물질관련 특기사항

가. 방사화학 실험실
  o 소규모의 실험시설(pilot plant)의 단계 를 거치지 않고 바로 대규모 재
    처리공장의 건설이 가능할 수 있었는지에 대해 북한측은 명확히 설명하고
    있지 못함
    - 전문가들 견해에 의하면 일반 산업국가에서는 있을 수 없는 일이지만
      (안전도 문제를 전혀 고려하지 않는다면) 가능은 할것 이라함
    - 동시설의 건설은 현재 중단된 상태이며, 어떠한 것도 생산치 못하고 있음
  o 북한의 핵 재처리시설 건설 목적이 핵무기 제조를 위한것이라고 결론을
    내릴수는 없지만, 재처리시설이 없다 하더라도 북한의 평화적 핵개발
    계획이 손상되지 않을 것임
    - 그러나 IAEA는 북한에 대해 동 재처리 시설의 해체(dismantle)를 요구
      할수 있는 권한이 없음

0075

나. 사용후 핵연료의 양과 플루토늄 추출양

    ㅇ 5MW 원자로 노심(core)에 있는 핵연료가 87년 최초로 장입된 핵연료인지 여부는 앞으로 1년이내 에 예상되는 핵연료 교체시 확인 가능

       - 앞으로 장입될 새로운 핵연료는 감시장치 설치등을 통해 전용 여부를 철저히 확인할 수 있을 것임

       - 북한은 동 원자로에서 수거한 손상된 핵연료봉(damaged fuel rod)의 숫자를 보고했으나, 안전조치 비밀 규정에 따라 밝힐수는 없음

    ㅇ 북한은 90.3월 방사화학실험실에서 그램단위 플루토늄 추출을 시인했으나 그 이상의 플루토늄 추출은 강력히 부인함

다. 농축 우라늄 시설

    ㅇ 북한이 핵연료 주기연구를 하고 있으나 우라늄농축을 시도하고 있다는 흔적은 없음

       - 북한은 원자로 연료로 자국내에서 생산된 천연우라늄을 사용하고 있기 때문에 아직까지 농축우라늄의 필요성은 없는것으로 판단

라. 북한 최초보고서의 성실성

    ㅇ 현재까지는 북한이 신고한 내용과 IAEA가 실제 검증한 결과간에 차이가 없는 것으로 보임

    ㅇ 그러나 북한의 핵능력에 대한 평가와 관련 확실한 보증을 주거나 경종을 울릴 단계 는 아님

3. 기타

  ㅇ IAEA가 강제사찰을 실시할 수 있는 보다 강력한 권한을 갖게 되기를 바라는 바 이나, 회원국 모두 가 그러한 강력한 사찰권한의 부여를 인정하려고 하지는 않음

  ㅇ IAEA는 지난 수년전부터 당사국이 신고한 내용이외에 극히 제한된 범위(very limited extent)의 외부 정보를 받고는 있으나, 이를 전적으로 신뢰할 수는 없음

    - IAEA는 사찰강화를 위해 외부로부터의 지속적인 첩보 정보제공을 환영함. 끝

0076

長 官 報 告 事 項

報 告 畢

1992. 7. 24.
國際機構局
國際機構課(38)

題 目 : IAEA 사무총장의 미하원 소위 설명회

> 92.7.23 '블릭스' IAEA 사무총장의 미하원 외무위 공개 설명회에서 발언한
> 내용중 IAEA의 특별사찰 실시 권한과 대북한 사찰관련 특기사항을 아래
> 보고 드립니다.

---

① IAEA의 특별사찰 실시문제

○ IAEA는 협정당사국내에 신고되지 않은 핵시설 또는 물질 이 있다고 믿을 근거가
  있을때 이에 대한 특별사찰 (special inspection) 을 실시 할 수 있는 권한이
  있음

  * 92.2월이사회는 미신고 핵시설 및 물질관련 추가정보(additional information)
    를 입수하여 관련 장소(locations)를 사찰하기 위한 IAEA의 특별사찰 실시
    권한을 재확인함

○ 그러나 IAEA의 특별사찰은 군축 검증 차원에서 의심이 있건 없건 아무장소나
  사찰할 수 있는 강제사찰(challenge inspection)라는 의미가 다름

  * IAEA는 미신고 의심이 있을 경우 당사국에 먼저 해명을 요구하고, 동 해명이
    불충분한 경우 당사국과 협의를 거쳐 특별사찰 실시 (안전조치협정 제77조)

  * 당사국이 특별사찰 실시를 계속 거부하거나 특별사찰 실시 결과 협정의무
    위반사실(미신고 핵물질등) 이 발견되는 경우 동내용을 안보리에 보고 (IAEA
    헌장 제12조C)

0077

o 시간적 요소가 중요하기 때문에 기습사찰(surprise inspection)이 필요하다는
  주장도 있지만 비밀 핵시설이나 물질을 찾고 있을 경우 사찰실시 속도가 그렇게
  중요한 것은 아님

  - 원자로, 재처리공장, 농축공장등의 시설은 그렇게 쉽게 옮길수 있는 것이
    아니며, 핵물질도 이동은 가능하지만 생산된 시설을 찾는것이 중요하므로
    시간을 다투는 사항은 아님

  - 또한 IAEA는 강제적 성격의 기습사찰 권한이 없음

o 신고되지 않은 군사시설에 어떤 핵 물질이 있다고 믿을만한 근거가 있을때
  IAEA는 동 군사시설에 대해서도 특별사찰은 요구할수 있을것임

  - 이는 NPT상 핵무기 비보유국가들중 전면 안전조치협정 체결 당사국에 한해
    적용 가능함

o 이라크의 경우에는 안보리 결의(제687호)에 의거 IAEA 사찰단이 이라크내 모든
  시설을 자유롭게 사찰할 수 있는 광범위한 권한을 부여 받았으나, 북한에 대하
  여 IAEA는 이같은 사찰권한을 갖고 있지 못함

  - 단, 북한은 언제, 어느장소(신고하지 않은 시설 포함)라도 IAEA 관리의 방문
    을 허용할 것이라고 약속한 바 있음

② 북한이 신고한 핵시설 및 물질관련 특기사항

가. 방사화학 실험실

  o 소규모의 실험시설(pilot plant)의 단계를 거치지 않고 바로 대규모 재
    처리공장의 건설이 가능할 수 있었는지에 대해 북한측은 명확히 설명하고
    있지 못함

    - 전문가들 견해에 의하면 일반 산업국가에서는 있을 수 없는 일이지만
      (안전도 문제를 전혀 고려하지 않는다면) 가능은 할것 이라함

    - 동시설의 건설은 현재 중단된 상태이며, 어떠한 것도 생산치 못하고 있음

  o 북한의 핵 재처리시설 건설 목적이 핵무기 제조를 위한것이라고 결론을
    내릴수는 없지만, 재처리시설이 없다 하더라도 북한의 평화적 핵개발
    계획이 손상되지 않을 것임

    - 그러나 IAEA는 북한에 대해 동 재처리 시설의 해체(dismantle)를 요구
      할수 있는 권한이 없음

0078

나. 사용후 핵연료의 양과 플루토늄 추출양

　　○ 5MW 원자로 노심(core)에 있는 핵연료가 87년 최초로 장입된 핵연료인지
　　여부는 앞으로 1년이내에 예상되는 핵연료 교체시 확인 가능

　　　- 앞으로 장입될 새로운 핵연료는 감시장치 설치등을 통해 전용 여부를
　　　철저히 확인할 수 있을 것임

　　　- 북한은 동 원자로에서 수거한 손상된 핵연료봉(damaged fuel rod)의
　　　숫자를 보고했으나, 안전조치 비밀 규정에 따라 밝힐수는 없음

　　○ 북한은 90.3월 방사화학실험실에서 그램단위 플루토늄 추출을 시인했으나
　　그 이상의 플루토늄 추출은 강력히 부인함

다. 농축 우라늄 시설

　　○ 북한이 핵연료 주기연구를 하고 있으나 우라늄농축을 시도하고 있다는
　　흔적은 없음

　　　- 북한은 원자로 연료로 자국내에서 생산된 천연우라늄을 사용하고 있기
　　　때문에 아직까지 농축우라늄의 필요성은 없는것으로 판단

라. 북한 최초보고서의 성실성

　　○ 현재까지는 북한이 신고한 내용과 IAEA가 실제 검증한 결과간에 차이가
　　없는 것으로 보임

　　○ 그러나 북한의 핵능력에 대한 평가와 관련 확실한 보증을 주거나 경종을
　　울릴 단계는 아님

3. 기타

○ IAEA가 강제사찰을 실시할 수 있는 보다 강력한 권한을 갖게 되기를 바라는 바
이나, 회원국 모두가 그러한 강력한 사찰권한의 부여를 인정하려고 하지는 않음

○ IAEA는 지난 수년전부터 당사국이 신고한 내용이외에 극히 제한된 범위(very
limited extent)의 외부 정보를 받고는 있으나, 이를 전적으로 신뢰할 수는
없음

　　- IAEA는 사찰강화를 위해 외부로부터의 지속적인 첩보 정보제공을 환영함　끝

0079

「블릭스」 IAEA 事務總長 訪美活動 報告

1992. 7. 24.

外 務 部

> 「한스 블릭스」 IAEA 事務總長의 7. 19~23간 訪美中 主要 發言 內容 및 特記
> 事項을 아래 報告합니다.

1. 美下院 外務委 公開說明會(7. 22)

　가. 「블릭스」 事務總長 冒頭發言 要旨

　　ㅇ 北韓과 같이 장기간 核施設을 보유한 나라의 경우, 申告된 施設의 目錄이
　　　완벽한지 與否를 立證하는 것은 容易치 않음.

　　ㅇ 北韓은 90년 實驗室을 통한 그램 단위의 플루토늄 抽出을 是認하였으나
　　　그 이상의 플루토늄 抽出은 否認함.

　　ㅇ 大型 再處理施設(길이 190m, 높이 6층)을 건설중인 北韓은 중간 단계의
　　　試驗施設(pilot plant) 存在를 否認하나, 이는 일반적인 産業國家에서는
　　　있을 수 없는 일임.

　　ㅇ 北韓의 核開發 疑惑 관련, 지나치게 놀랄 일은 아니나 섣부르게 安心을
　　　할 상황도 아님.

　나. 質疑.應答時 「블릭스」 總長 答辯 要旨

　　ㅇ IAEA의 대북한 强制査察 또는 特別査察 權限 與否
　　　- IAEA는 未申告 疑心이 있을 경우 該當國家에게 먼저 解明을 요구하고
　　　　동 解明이 不滿足스러울 경우 特別査察을 要求할 수 있음.

- 1 -

0080

- 동 IAEA 核安全措置協定上의 特別査察은, 未申告 疑心 여부에 관계
  없이 일정 장소를 査察할 수 있는 軍縮條約上의 强制査察과 같이
  강력한 것이 아님.
- 北韓이 IAEA가 원할 경우 北韓內 어느 장소든지 訪問을 許容한다고
  한 것은, IAEA 特別査察制度의 한게를 다소 補完해 줄 수 있음.
o IAEA 査察의 效率性 및 南北相互査察의 必要性
  - IAEA 特別査察은 限界性이 있으므로, 北韓이 南北相互査察을 통해
    核에 관한 透明性을 더욱 提高시키는 것이 바람직함.
o 北韓의 核物質 隱匿 可能性
  - 核物質 隱匿 情報가 있을 경우 特別査察이 要求되며 또한 隱匿된
    核物質이 발견되는 경우에는 IAEA 理事會 및 安保理에 報告되어
    必要한 措置가 취해질 것임.
o 北韓의 再處理施設 現況
  - 再處理施設의 建設이 현재는 一時 中斷된 것으로 보이나 必要部品을
    주문중이라는 北韓의 답변으로 보아 建設을 繼續할 것으로 보임.

2. 美 主要人士 面談 結果(7. 20~23)

  가. 面談 人士

    o 캔터 國務部次官, 월포비츠 國防部次官, 케네디 核非擴散大使等

  나. 面談 內容

    o 미측 인사들은 「블릭스」 事務總長이 그간 南北相互査察을 支持해온
      입장을 評價하면서, 이러한 입장의 繼續的 堅持를 要請함.

- 2 -

ㅇ 「블릭스」總長은
  - 北韓에 대한 査察과 관련, IAEA는 示範再處理施設(pilot plant)
    存在等 再處理 關聯 施設 및 지금까지 生産된 使用後 核燃料의
    處理 現況 等에 비중을 두고 있으며,
  - 北韓이 硬水爐 技術 移轉等 다른 목표를 위한 흥정용으로 再處理
    施設을 維持하고 있다는 인상을 받고 있다고 言及함.

3. 評 價

ㅇ 금번 「블릭스」 총장의 訪美 活動은 美行政府 및 議會內 北韓 核問題를
  다루는 主要人士들에 대해 北韓의 核再處理施設이 아무런 經濟的 妥當性이
  없는 것임을 再確認시킴으로써, 北韓의 核武器 開發 推進 事實을 다시한번
  周知시키는 契機가 됨.

ㅇ 특히 下院 外務委 公開說明會를 통해 IAEA 特別査察制度가 일반 軍縮
  條約上의 강력한 不時强制査察과는 다른 脆弱한 制度임이 분명히 確認
  됨으로써, 北韓의 核武器 開發을 철저히 檢證.遮斷하기 위해서는 徹底하고
  强制的인 南北相互査察이 必須的이라는 사실을 美國內 朝.野에 충분히
  認識시킴.

- 끝 -

블릭스 IAEA 사무총장 미 청문회 증언

북한 어느곳이든 사찰가능 밝혀

재처리시설 핵개발용 주장에 동의안해

《편집자》

다음은 한스 블릭스 국제원자력기구(IAEA) 사무총장의 미국 하원 외교위 아시아·태평양 소위 청문회에서 가진 문답내용이다.

솔라즈 의원 = 국제원자력기구의 사찰반의 성공을 거두려면 신고되지 않은 핵시설 또는 핵물질이 있다고 믿을 이유가 있을 때, 그러한 곳에 대한 사찰을 할 수 있어야 한다. 국제원자력기구의 사찰반은 그러한 특별사찰을 할 수 있는 권한이 국제원자력기구 규약에 따라서 있다고 보는가?

블릭스 = 그러한 권한이 있다. 국제원자력기구 사무총장이 미국 외교위 아시아·태평양 소위의 청문회에서 답변한 문답내용이다.

...

솔라즈 = 그렇다.

...

외 무 부

```
관리
번호  92-2694
```

종 별 :

번 호 : USW-6040

일 시 : 92 1209 1943

수 신 : 장 관 (미일,통이,정총)

발 신 : 주 미 대사

제 목 : 하원 정보위원장 면담

1. 본직은 금 12.9(수) DLC 부회장으로서 CLINTON 정권 인수팀과 밀접한 관계에 있는 DAVE MCCURDY(민주-오클라호마) 하원 정보위원장을 면담하고 상호 의견을 교환하였는바, 동 요지 아래 보고함. (조일환 참사관 배석)

2. 본직은 북한은 미국의 정권 교체와 관련 신행정부가 들어서면 미국의 대북한 정책이 보다 북한에 유리한 방향으로 변화되지 않을까를 기대하고 있는 것으로 보이며 지난해 12 월 남. 북한 불가침 협정체결 및 한반도 비핵화 선언 서명이래 대화를 계속하고 있다는 인상을 대외적으로 주기위하여 대화의 단절까지는 이르지 않고 있으나 실질적 대화는 이루어지지 못하고 있는 상황이고, 핵사찰제도 마련을 위한 협의에 전혀 진전을 보지 못하고 있다고 설명함.

3. 본직은 IAEA 가 핵 안전협정에 따라 4 차례의 사찰을 실시, 북한의 플루토늄 생산 가능성을 확인하였으나, 북한이 원자로 사용 연료에 대한 사찰을 회피하고 있어 이미 WEAPON-GRADE 의 플루토늄을 생산했을 가능성에 대한 의혹이 커지고 있으며 IAEA 사찰이 진행중인 과정에서도 영변 핵시설에 대한 은폐기도를하는등 속임수를 쓰고 있음이 드러나고 있고, 따라서 남. 북한간 상호 사찰의 필요성이 더욱 강조되고 있으나 북한은 핵 사찰 규정 마련을 계속 거부하고 있다고 설명하고 남. 북한 JNCC 회의가 열리고 있으나 진전을 보지 못하고 있음을 설명함.

4. 본직은 북한이 미국과의 정치적 관계 개선및 일본과의 경제적 관계 개선을 도모하기 위해서 IAEA 사찰은 받아 들이면서도 남. 북한 상호 사찰은 거부하고 있는바, 북한 핵 개발에 대한 정확한 정보수집이 무엇 보다도 중요하다고 언급 하고, 그간 한. 미간 긴밀한 정보 협조를 고맙게 생각하고 있으며 신 행정부와도 정보 분야에서의 지속적이고 긴밀한 협조가 유지되기를 희망한다고 피력함.본직은 또한 핵문제를 떠나서도 북한의 모험주의 시도 가능성과 북한내 정권 이양 과정에서 발생할

미주국	장관	차관	1차보	통상국	외정실	분석관	청와대	안기부

PAGE 1

92.12.10   10:27

수 있는 돌발사태등 제반 문제에 대비하기 위해서도 북한에 대한 정보 활동 강화가 매우 중요하다고 언급함.

5. MCCURDY 의원은 자신이 신행정부 인사들과 긴밀한 협조관계를 유지하고 있으며, 선거운동 기간중에도 외교정책 분야에 대해 많은 조언을 해 왔다고 전제한후, CLINTON 당선자는 남. 북한 협상의 성공 및 북한의 위협이 사라질때 까지 미국의 대 한반도 정책에 변화가 있어서는 안된다고 믿고 있다고 말하고, 현재 양국이 매우 긴밀한 관계를 유지하고 있는데 대해 만족하며 현재로서는 미국의 기본정책을 바꾸어야 할 아무런 이유가 없는 것으로 본다는 견해를 표명하고, 북한이 이에 대하여 헛된 기대를 갖지 말기 바란다고 언급함. 또한 동의원은 금년중 의회내에서 해외주둔 미군을 감축해야 한다는 논의가 있었으나 주로 구라파 주둔 미군을 대상으로 한 것이었으며 이문제는 앞으로 행정부와 긴밀한 협의를 해 나가게 될 것이라고 언급함. 동의원은 지난 수년간 노대통령이 이룩한 외교적성과는 경탄할 만한 것이라고 말하고 궁지에 몰린 북한을 다루기 위한 현명한 대처가 필요함을 강조함.

6. MCCURDY 의원은 최근 미국내에서는 경제. 통상문제와 관련한 압력이 표출되고 있는바, 자신은 자유, 개방무역을 신봉하고 있다고 말하고, 한국등이 이러한 압력으로 부터 벗어나는 방법중의 하나는 미국의 신행정부가 해결해야할 민족주의 대두, 경제질서의 혼란, 기아등 여러가지 문제의 해결과 관련하여 예를 들자면 SOMALIA 사태 수습 노력등에 한국이 적극참여하는 것도 의회내의 대한 인식을 좋게 만드는데 중요한 SIGNAL 이 될 수 있을 것이라는 견해를 표명함.

7. 이에 대해 본직은 한국은 유엔 회원국의 하나로서 가능한 최대의 역할과책임을 다 할 것이라고 말하고, SOMALIA 사태관련 지원문제는 현재 한국에서 선거가 진행되고 있는 상황이어서 이에 관해 논의 되기는 어려운 상황이나 선거후에는 적절한 지원 방안이 검토될 것으로 본다고 언급해 두었음. 또한 본직은 공정 무역 문제와 관련 현재 한. 미 양국간 영업환경 개선을 위해 매우 긴밀한 협의가 이루어지고 있고 한국으로서는 최대한 노력하고 있다고 설명함.

8. 본직은 4 년전 민주당 정강에는 한반도 문제가 언급되지 않았으나 금번에 주한 미군의 계속 주둔 필요성등 민주당의 한반도 안보공약 내용이 정강에 포함된 것은 북한을 포함한 아시아 각국에게 매우 중요하고도 강력한 메세지를 준 것으로 평가된다고 언급하고 민주당 정강에 한반도 문제를 포함시킨데 대해 사의를 표명함.

9. MCCURDY 의원은 금번 민주당 정강 작성에는 자신이 부회장직을 맡고 있는 DLC

PAGE 2

가 많이 관여 했다고 말하고, 현재 자신의 보좌관중의 하나가 국무부 정권 인수반에 포함되어 정책 수립에 참여하고 있으며, 향후에도 돈독한 한. 미 관계가 지속적으로 유지되어야 한다는 자신의 입장이 국무부의 정책수립 과정에도 계속 반영될 것이라고 말함.

10. 본직은 신행정부의 정책수립에 DLC 의 역할이 보다 커질 것으로 기대한다고 말하고 앞으로 DLC 회원들과 보다 긴밀한 관계를 유지하기를 바란다고 표명하였던바, MCCURDY 의원은 자신이 소련의 민주화, 핵 비확산, 유고 및 구소연방 공화국에서의 긴장상태와 아울러 한반도 문제에 대해 큰 관심을 가지고 있다고 말하고 한. 미간의 긴밀한 협조관계 및 미국의 대한 안보 공약 유지 필요성을 다시 한번 강조함.

11. 본직은 동의원이 편리한 시기에 방한할 기회를 갖도록 초청하였는바, MCCURDY 의원은 그간 국내 문제에 몰두하여 한동안 해외여행을 못하였으며 적절한 시기에 해외 방문기회가 있으면 한국도 포함시키도록 노력하겠다고 언급함. 끝.

(대사 현홍주-국장)
예고 : 93.6.30. 일반

외교문서 비밀해제: 북한 핵 문제 13

북한 핵 문제 미국 동향

초판인쇄 2024년 03월 15일
초판발행 2024년 03월 15일

지은이 한국학술정보(주)
펴낸이 채종준
펴낸곳 한국학술정보(주)
주 소 경기도 파주시 회동길 230(문발동)
전 화 031-908-3181(대표)
팩 스 031-908-3189
홈페이지 http://ebook.kstudy.com
E-mail 출판사업부 publish@kstudy.com
등 록 제일산-115호(2000. 6. 19)

ISBN 979-11-7217-086-8 94340
     979-11-7217-073-8 94340 (set)